This Is a Sociology Reader

Edited by ANGELA LASK, *Pima College*
RICHARD L. ROE and STUDENTS

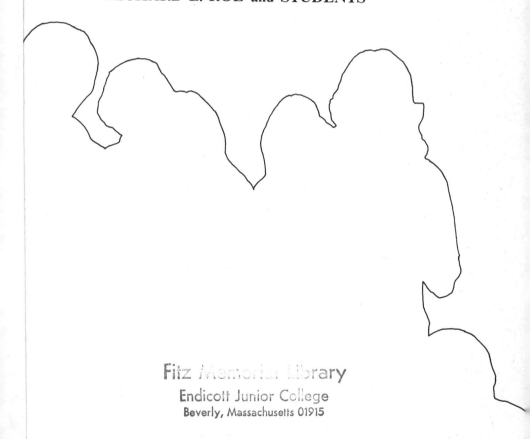

Rinehart Press
San Francisco

Student advisors:

Dana Dunn
John Giardenelli
Scott Glover
Fred Gomez
Molly Hunt
Rich Jones
Pat Pace
Dema Staley
Dimitri Zerdavis

Student co-ordinator:

Rich Jones

Design and photography:

Louis Neiheisel

© 1973 by Rinehart Press
5643 Paradise Drive
Corte Madera, Calif. 94925

A division of Holt, Rinehart and Winston, Inc.

Library of Congress Catalog Card Number: 72-90208

ISBN: 0-03-005991-7

PRINTED IN THE UNITED STATES OF AMERICA

3 4 5 6   090   9 8 7 6 5 4 3 2 1

Δια Θεία Χαρικλια
ἡ Θείο Κυριάκος

For Aunt Kay and Uncle Charlie

Preface

Commenting upon the novelty of the field of sociology more than half a century ago, Georg Simmel noted that the "indefiniteness and indefensibility of boundaries afford right of asylum to everybody." To some readers this remark may well seem applicable to this collection of readings: many of the selections in this reader, and the organizational format in which they are presented, would seem to have little to do with the more formal preoccupations of sociology.

This has been intentional. This reader has been designed to be a reader, not a textbook. It does not attempt to deal with the more traditional domain material of sociology, but rather to stir the imaginations, and specifically, the sociological imaginations, of students attending introductory sociology courses. This reader does not intend to teach. It intends to incite people to think.

The framework for this reader has been succinctly put by Zbigniew Brzezinski: "The paradox of our time is that humanity is becoming simultaneously more unified and more fragmented." We have tried to actualize this statement with diverse selections which we feel illustrate the dynamics of contemporary change. In the attempt to vitalize both the selections and their presentation, we invited several students to engage in dialogues and conversations concerning the format and material of the book. After hearing their complaints about the composition of other sociology readers, we asked their aid in the construction of this one. The conversations and arguments that ensued were so refreshing in their directness that we have included portions of them as introductory statements to the major sections of the book. The involved and often agitated discussions that went into the composition of this reader have, we feel, produced both a vital and novel way of introducing any student to the sociological imagination.

Angela Lask
Richard L. Roe

Acknowledgments

The diversity of this sociology reader reflects the heterogeneous influences that I have encountered as an instructor and as a sociologist. I would like to thank therefore those persons who have contributed to enriching my perspective.

To my colleagues at Mt. San Antonio College: Ann Krueger, Myron Erickson, Bob Amick, Stan Honer, Ken Irvine, Jack Y. Brennecke; my colleagues at El Camino College: Art Ellish, Stephen Jama, Logan Fox, Don Fridley, Mike Pelsinger, Connie McCord, Aviva James, Bob Lee, Wally Cohen; and to Herman Loether at California State College, Dominguez Hills, and Franz Adler, California State University at Los Angeles, many thanks.

I owe thanks to those persons I have met as students who have profoundly affected me: Maxine Feldman, Richard Hamilton, Bill Mangiali, Roger Hastings, Trent Cornell, Craig Roberts, Jon O'Day, Wilbur Hightower, Tim Richards, Johanna Gulick, Mike Dunn, Mike Gualano, William Lee Felts, Sue Banales, Barbie Woods, Holly Laird, Joe Carter, John Tyndall, Elisse Golombek, Barbara Wasko, Diona Lee Wright, Pat Regan and all my sisters at the El Camino Women's Center.

I would also like to thank the students who served as advisors to this book: Dana Dunn, John Giardinelli, Scott Glover, Fred Gomez, Molly Hunt, Rich Jones, Pat Pace, Dema Staley and Dimitri Zerdavis. Special thanks to Rich Jones for his coordination of the dialogues.

A final note of appreciation to Emmett Dingley, Editor, and Richard Raihall, Publisher, Rinehart Press, for their encouragement.

To Emanuel Lask, for so much. To Tony and Tina.

And to the 11:00 class, for ecstasy. . . .

Angela Lask

Contents

PART III—BEGINNINGS

Who Reads a Sociology Reader?

CAST OF CHARACTERS
PARTICIPATING IN DIALOGS

ANGELA	A Sociology instructor
DICK	A publisher's editor
SCOTT	
DANA	
DEMA	
JOHN	Students
RICH	
PAT	
MOLLY	

The first dialog takes place in Angela's classroom; the remaining dialogs at Angela's California home, minutes away from campus.

SCOTT: Sociology students—and that's about all.

DICK: And who are you?

DANA: I have a couple of reactions to that.

DICK: I'd like to hear them.

DANA: Well, I don't think that the average age of students today is nineteen.

DEMA: In the state college I transferred to, the average age is twenty-seven.

ANGELA: I wanted to talk to you about this, Dick; more and more of my students are thirty, forty, even in their fifties.

DICK: Why do you think that is? Are they returning veterans?

SCOTT: Oh, a *lot* are.

ANGELA: And a lot are housewives, women getting out of the house.

DANA: And a lot are unemployed engineers.

DICK: I think maybe you have a freak example in your class, Angela. I've been to colleges all over California and the nation and the average age of the students who are going to read this book is a lot younger, around nineteen. How old were you when you went back to school, Dana?

DANA: Twenty-five.

DICK: What did you do between eighteen and twenty-five?

RICH: Between eighteen and twenty, I just dropped out.

DICK: I may be wrong. Maybe there are a lot of people like Dana in introductory Sociology classes. What about the other classes you have? Is it the same?

PAT: My Psychology and English classes this semester were full of young people, you know, a younger class, but the students in every Sociology class I've had are much older.

DICK: I wonder why that is?

JOHN: Maybe in Sociology you feel like you get more of an overall thing. It seems that Introduction to Sociology covers more ground than Introduction to Psychology. I mean, it seems to have something for everybody.

RICH: I think John's right—Sociology means more to more people. Police Science students and Business students take an Introduction to Sociology class at El Camino, and a lot of nursing students do, too. Sociology has something to say to these people about their lives. Subjects like English you only take to fill an elective, or if you're an English major.

DANA: Well, in a way the whole thing about how old the average student is, is really a question about what's happening to education. That there are older people coming back to school doesn't mean anything by itself. But it points back to a kind of redefinition of education. It's becoming more experimental.

DICK: Experimental . . . what do you mean?

DANA: I mean that a job is something that you *experience;* you're involved with it. Education should help you choose a job objective or, if necessary, choose another career ten years after you've begun work. That's why the older people are back in school.

DICK: There's a trend in this direction, but a majority of students still go directly from high school to college. Enrollment is increasing in two-year colleges and community colleges.

DANA: Colleges which emphasize career objectives! The boom in community colleges is the result of having to have some college experience in the job market, in the labor force. If you're talking about what's happening now, about contemporary education, the people who are going to read this book are *not* all nineteen years old. And, more important, they will want different things out of Sociology.

DICK: Okay. Let's say we've got a new breed of student in two-year colleges, but we still have the 19-year-olds, too. What does the field of Sociology offer these younger students?

DANA: Tools they can use in the real world, for one thing; ideas that will help them understand their experience in society. Education seems to be going in two directions. Part of the time you study in a college

BASICS: PEOPLE

environment. But other times you leave the classroom to become involved in community service, or to find a job, and that's education, too. It's as if you had two teachers, one in the classroom, and the other, the community itself.

MOLLY: Wait a minute. A lot of younger students who are in junior college don't know what they're doing there. That includes me. I don't have any special interest or career objective.

SCOTT: Is that why you're taking Introduction to Sociology? Because you didn't know what else to do with yourself? What are you getting out of it?

MOLLY: I signed up because I thought it might be a little more interesting than some of the other courses. And I did get something out of it because it wasn't abstract. It was about things that happen to me.

ANGELA: That's why I've tried to make this selection of readings something that can handle a lot of different interests and outlooks. The main thing is to deal with things that people can see happening right around them, and suggest, or lead up to, a more abstract way of dealing with those things. This is why most of the sociology readers I could use for an introductory course are out of touch; they assume a consensus of interest that I just don't find in the classroom anymore.

RICH: Teachers seem to write books for other teachers. As far as actually helping the students, most of them are really out of touch.

ANGELA: Now we've got a chance to put together a Reader that *does* touch people where they live. You and Dick and I can pick from anything that's available.

Part 1
Basics: People

Bodies: The Social Context of Health

Bodies: The Social Context of Sexuality

Words: The Social Context of Language

Interactions

Bodies: The Social Context of Health

In man . . . and particularly in higher societies, social causes substitute themselves for organic causes. The organism is spiritualized.

EMILE DURKHEIM

DICK: I'm wondering, are sociologists going to wonder about the validity of our subject for this section?

ANGELA: They certainly will!

DICK: I mean, isn't this a new area for a sociology reader?

ANGELA: Of course it's new. The relationship between ourselves and our environment is extremely important, and, although it *is* sociological, most Introduction to Sociology courses don't deal with it.

RICH: But they should. Too often we discuss society as if we were standing outside looking at it. But the way society can affect your health brings it home that you're not free of society. It's all one unit; you're part of what you're looking at.

ANGELA: You mean, you see society and yourself at the same time?

RICH: I mean, my health, or who I think I am, is influenced by what goes on outside my skin.

SCOTT: Will it make you mentally ill to be born in this society? I mean, if you're born into an environment that is unstable, are you going to end up unstable or mentally ill yourself?

DEMA: Physical illness goes along with that, too.

SCOTT: It's the same thing, just manifested in bodily form.

RICH: But it's not just that; the society determines what to consider sick. I mean, you can be rotting from pollution, and your lungs are turning into baggies full of ashes, and society doesn't think that's sick . . . that's normal behavior. Society determines what it wants to consider sick.

SCOTT: People have a hard time relating to mental illness, or to the concept of a "sick" society, but they can relate a little better when someone tells them that they're dying from pollution or smog. Concrete physical subjects like health are more acceptable; they fit into sociology books under headings like "Urban Ecology."

1. O Rotten Gotham—Sliding Down into the Behavioral Sink

TOM WOLFE

I just spent two days with Edward T. Hall, an anthropologist, watching thousands of my fellow New Yorkers short-circuiting themselves into hot little twitching death balls with jolts of their own adrenalin. Dr. Hall says it is overcrowding that does it. Overcrowding gets the adrenalin going, and the adrenalin gets them hyped up. And here they are, hyped up, turning bilious, nephritic, queer, autistic, sadistic, barren, batty, sloppy, hot-in-the-pants, chancred-on-the-flankers, leering, puling, numb—the usual in New York, in other words, and God knows what else. Dr. Hall has the theory that over-crowding has already thrown New York into a state of behavioral sink. Behavioral sink is a term from ethology, which is the study of how animals relate to their environment. Among animals, the sink winds up with a "population collapse" or "massive die-off." O rotten Gotham.

It got to be easy to look at New Yorkers as animals, especially looking down from some place like a balcony at Grand Central at the rush hour Friday afternoon. The floor was filled with the poor white humans, running around, dodging, blinking their eyes, making a sound like a pen full of starlings or rats or something.

"Listen to them skid," says Dr. Hall.

He was right. The poor old etiolate animals were out there skidding on their rubber soles. You could hear it once he pointed it out. They stop short to keep from hitting somebody or because they are disoriented and they suddenly stop and look around, and they skid on their rubbersole shoes, and a screech goes up. They pour out onto the floor down the escalators from the Pan-Am Building, from 42nd Street, from Lexington Avenue, up out of subways, down into subways, railroad trains, up into helicopters—

"You can also hear the helicopters all the way down here," says Dr. Hall. The sound of the helicopters using the roof of the Pan-Am Building nearly fifty stories up beats right through. "If it weren't for this ceiling"—he is referring to the very high ceiling in Grand Central—"this place would be unbearable with this kind of crowding. And yet they'll probably never 'waste' space like this again."

Bodies: The Social Context of Health 9

They screech! And the adrenal glands in all those poor white animals enlarge, micrometer by micrometer, to the size of cantaloupes. Dr. Hall pulls a Minox camera out of a holster he has on his belt and starts shooting away at the human scurry. The Sink!

Dr. Hall has the Minox up to his eye—he is a slender man, calm, 52 years old, young-looking, an anthropologist who has worked with Navajos, Hopis, Spanish-Americans, Negroes, Trukese. He was the most important anthropologist in the government during the crucial years of the foreign aid program, the 1950's. He directed both the Point Four training program and the Human Relations Area Files. He wrote *The Silent Language* and *The Hidden Dimension,* two books that are picking up the kind of "underground" following his friend Marshall McLuhan started picking up about five years ago. He teaches at the Illinois Institute of Technology, lives with his wife, Mildred, in a high-ceilinged town house on one of the last great residential streets in downtown Chicago, Astor Street; has a grown son and daughter, loves good food, good wine, the relaxed, civilized life—but comes to New York with a Minox at his eye to record—perfect!—The Sink.

We really got down in there by walking down into the Lexington Avenue line subway stop under Grand Central. We inhaled those nice big fluffy fumes of human sweat, urine, effluvia, and sebaceous secretions. One old female human was already stroked out on the upper level, on a stretcher, with two policemen standing by. The other humans barely looked at her. They rushed into line. They bellied each other, haunch to paunch, down the stairs. Human heads shone through the gratings. The species North European tried to create bubbles of space around themselves, about a foot and a half in diameter—

"See, he's reacting against the line," says Dr. Hall.

—but the species Mediterranean presses on in. The hell with bubbles of space. The species North European resents that, this male human behind him presses forward toward the booth . . . *breathing* on him, he's disgusted, he pulls out of the line entirely, the species Mediterranean resents him for resenting it, and neither of them realizes what the hell they are getting irritable about exactly. And in all of them the old adrenals grow another micrometer.

Dr. Hall whips out the Minox. Too perfect! The bottom of The Sink.

It is the sheer overcrowding, such as occurs in the business sections of Manhattan five days a week and in Harlem, Bedford-Stuyvesant, southeast Bronx every day—sheer overcrowding is converting New Yorkers into animals in a sink pen. Dr. Hall's argument runs as follows: all animals, including birds, seem to have a built-in, inherited requirement to have a certain amount of territory, space, to lead their lives in. Even if they have all the food they need, and there are no predatory animals threatening them, they cannot tolerate crowding beyond a certain point. No more than two hundred wild Norway rats can survive on a quarter acre of ground, for example, even when they are given all the food they can eat. They just die off.

But why? To find out, ethologists have run experiments on all sorts of animals, from stickleback crabs to Sika deer. In one major experiment, an ethologist named John Calhoun put some domesticated white Norway rats in a pen with four sections to it, connected by ramps. Calhoun knew from previous experiments that the rats tend to split up into groups of ten to twelve and that the pen, therefore, would hold forty to forty-eight rats comfortably, assuming they formed four equal groups. He allowed them to reproduce until there were eighty rats, balanced between male and female, but did not let it get any more crowded. He kept them supplied with plenty of food, water, and nesting materials. In other words, all their more obvious needs were taken care of. A less obvious need—space—was not. To the human eye, the pen did not even look especially crowded. But to the rats, it was crowded beyond endurance.

The entire colony was soon plunged into a profound behavioral sink. "The sink," said Calhoun, "is the outcome of any behavioral process that collects animals together in unusually great numbers. The unhealthy connotations of the term are not accidental: a behavioral sink does act to aggravate all forms of pathology that can be found within a group."

For a start, long before the rat population reached eighty, a status hierarchy had developed in the pen. Two dominant male rats took over the two end sections, acquired harems of eight to ten females each, and forced the rest of the rats into the two middle pens. All the overcrowding took place in the middle pens. That was where the "sink" hit. The aristocrat rats at the ends grew bigger, sleeker, healthier, and more secure the whole time.

In The Sink, meanwhile, nest building, courting, sex behavior, reproduction, social organization, health—all of it went to pieces. Normally, Norway rats have a mating ritual in which the male chases the female, the female ducks down into a burrow and sticks her head up to watch the male. He performs a little dance outside the burrow, then she comes out, and he mounts her, usually for a few seconds. When The Sink set in, however, no more than three males—the dominant males in the middle sections—kept up the old customs. The rest tried everything from satyrism to homosexuality or else gave up on sex altogether. Some of the subordinate males spent all their time chasing females. Three or four might chase one female at the same time, and instead of stopping at the burrow entrance for the ritual, they would charge right in. Once mounted, they would hold on for minutes instead of the usual seconds.

Homosexuality rose sharply. So did bisexuality. Some males would mount anything—males, females, babies, senescent rats, anything. Still other males dropped sexual activity altogether, wouldn't fight and, in fact, would hardly move except when the other rats slept. Occasionally a female from the aristocrat rats' harems would come over the ramps and into the middle sections to sample life in The Sink. When she had had enough, she would run back up the ramp. Sink males would give chase up to the top of the ramp, which is to say, to the very edge of the aristocratic preserve. But one glance from one of the king rats would stop them cold and they would return to The Sink.

The slumming females from the harems had their adventures and then returned to a placid, healthy life. Females in The Sink, however, were ravaged, physically and psychologically. Pregnant rats had trouble continuing pregnancy. The rate of miscarriages increased significantly, and females started dying from tumors and other disorders of the mammary glands, sex organs, uterus, ovaries, and Fallopian tubes. Typically, their kidneys, livers, and adrenals were also enlarged or diseased or showed other signs associated with stress.

Child-rearing became totally disorganized. The females lost the interest or the stamina to build nests and did not keep them up if they did build them. In the general filth and confusion, they would not put themselves out to save offspring they were momentarily separated from. Frantic, even sadistic competition among the males was going on all around them and rendering their lives chaotic. The males began unprovoked and senseless assaults upon one another, often in the form of tail-biting. Ordinarily, rats will suppress this kind of behavior when it crops up. In The Sink, male rats gave up all policing and just looked out for themselves. The "pecking order" among males in The Sink was never stable. Normally, male rats set up a three-class structure. Under the pressure of overcrowding, however, they broke up into all sorts of unstable subclasses, cliques, packs—and constantly pushed, probed, explored, tested one another's power. Anyone was fair game, except for the aristocrats in the end pens.

Calhoun kept the population down to eighty, so that the next stage, "population collapse" or "massive die-off," did not occur. But the autopsies showed that the pattern—as in the diseases among the female rats—was already there.

The classic study of die-off was John J. Christian's study of Sika deer on James Island in the Chesapeake Bay, west of Cambridge, Maryland. Four or five of the deer had been released on the island, which was 280 acres and uninhabited, in 1916. By 1955 they had bred freely into a herd of 280 to 300. The population density was only about one deer per acre at this point, but Christian knew that this was already too high for the Sikas' inborn space requirements, and something would give before long. For two years the number of deer remained 280 to 300. But suddenly, in 1958, over half the deer died; 161 carcasses were recovered. In 1959 more deer died and the population steadied at about 80.

In two years, two-thirds of the herd had died. Why? It was not starvation. In fact, all the deer collected were in excellent condition, with well-developed muscles, shining coats, and fat deposits between the muscles. In practically all the deer, however, the adrenal glands had enlarged by 50 percent. Christian concluded that the die-off was due to "shock following severe metabolic disturbance, probably as a result of prolonged adrenocortical hyperactivity. . . . There was no evidence of infection, starvation, or other obvious cause to explain the mass mortality." In other words, the constant stress of overpopulation, plus the normal stress of the cold of the winter, had kept the adrenalin flowing so constantly in the deer that their systems were depleted of blood sugar and they died of shock.

Well, the white humans are still skidding and darting across the floor of Grand Central. Dr. Hall listens a moment longer to the skidding and the darting noises, and then says, "You know, I've been on commuter trains here

BASICS: PEOPLE

after everyone has been through one of these rushes, and I'll tell you, there is enough acid flowing in the stomachs in every car to dissolve the rails underneath."

Just a little invisible acid bath for the linings to round off the day. The ulcers the acids cause, of course, are the one disease people have already been taught to associate with the stress of city life. But overcrowding, as Dr. Hall sees it, raises a lot more hell with the body than just ulcers. In everyday life in New York—just the usual, getting to work, working in massively congested areas like 42nd Street between Fifth Avenue and Lexington, especially now that the Pan-Am Building is set in there, working in cubicles such as those in the editorial offices at Time-Life, Inc., which Dr. Hall cites as typical of New York's poor handling of space, working in cubicles with low ceilings and, often, no access to a window, while construction crews all over Manhattan drive everybody up the Masonite wall with air-pressure generators with noises up to the boil-a-brain decibel levels, then rushing to get home, piling into subways and trains, fighting for time and for space, the usual day in New York —the whole now-normal thing keeps shooting jolts of adrenalin into the body, breaking down the body's defenses and winding up with the work-a-daddy human animal stroked out at the breakfast table with his head apoplexed like a cauliflower out of his $6.95 semispread Pima-cotton shirt, and nosed over into a plate of No-Kloresto egg substitute, signing off with the black thrombosis, cancer, kidney, liver, or stomach failure, and the adrenals ooze to a halt, the size of eggplants in July.

One of the people whose work Dr. Hall is interested in on this score is Rene Dubos at the Rockefeller Institute. Dubos's work indicates that specific organisms, such as the tuberculosis bacillus or a pneumonia virus, can seldom be considered "the cause" of a disease. The germ or virus, apparently, has to work in combination with other things that have already broken the body down in some way—such as the old adrenal hyperactivity. Dr. Hall would like to see some autopsy studies made to record the size of adrenal glands in New York, especially of people crowded into slums and people who go through the full rush-hour-work-rush-hour cycle every day. He is afraid that until there is some clinical, statistical data on how overcrowding actually ravages the human body, no one will be willing to do anything about it. Even in so obvious a thing as air pollution, the pattern is familiar. Until people can actually see the smoke or smell the sulphur or feel the sting in their eyes, politicians will not get excited about it, even though it is well known that many of the lethal substances polluting the air are invisible and odorless. For one thing, most politicians are like the aristocrat rats. They are insulated from The Sink by practically sultanic buffers—limousines, chauffeurs, secretaries, aides-de-camp, doormen, shuttered houses, high-floor apartments. They almost never ride subways, fight rush hours, much less live in the slums or work in the Pan-Am Building.

We took a cab from Grand Central to go up to Harlem, and by 48th Street we were already socked into one of those great, total traffic jams on First

Avenue on Friday afternoon. Dr. Hall motions for me to survey the scene, and there they all are, humans, male and female, behind the glass of their automobile windows, soundlessly going through the torture of their own adrenalin jolts. This male over here contracts his jaw muscles so hard that they bunch up into a great cheese Danish pattern. He twists his lips, he bleeds from the eyeballs, he shouts . . . soundlessly behind glass . . . the fat corrugates on the back of his neck, his whole body shakes as he pounds the heel of his hand into the steering wheel. The female human in the car ahead of him whips her head around, she bares her teeth, she screams . . . soundlessly behind glass . . . she throws her hands up in the air, Whaddya expect me—Yah, yuh stupid—and they all sit there, trapped in their own congestion, bleeding hate all over each other, shorting out the ganglia and—goddam it—

Dr. Hall sits back and watches it all. This is it! The Sink! And where is everybody's wandering boy?

Dr. Hall says, "We need a study in which drivers who go through these rush hours every day would wear GSR bands."

GSR?

"Galvanic skin response. It measures the electric potential of the skin, which is a function of sweating. If a person gets highly nervous, his palms begin to sweat. It is an index of tension. There are some other fairly simple devices that would record respiration and pulse. I think everybody who goes through this kind of experience all the time should take his own pulse—not literally—but just be aware of what's happening to him. You can usually tell when stress is beginning to get you physically."

In testing people crowded into New York's slums, Dr. Hall would like to take it one step further—gather information on the plasma hydrocortisone level in the blood or the corticosteroids in the urine. Both have been demonstrated to be reliable indicators of stress, and testing procedures are simple.

The slums—we finally made it up to East Harlem. We drove into 101st Street, and there was a new, avant-garde little church building, the Church of the Epiphany, which Dr. Hall liked—and, next to it, a pile of rubble where a row of buildings had been torn down, and from the back windows of the tenements beyond several people were busy "airmailing," throwing garbage out the window, into the rubble, beer cans, red shreds, the No-Money-Down Eames roller stand for a TV set, all flying through the air onto the scaggy sump. We drove around some more in Harlem, and a sequence was repeated, trash, buildings falling down, buildings torn down, rubble, scaggy sumps or, suddenly, a cluster of high-rise apartment projects, with fences around the grass.

"You know what this city looks like?" Dr. Hall said. "It looks bombed out. I used to live at Broadway and 124th Street back in 1946 when I was studying at Columbia. I can't tell you how much Harlem has changed in twenty years. It looks bombed out. It's broken down. People who live in New York get used to it and don't realize how filthy the city has become. The whole thing is typical of a behavioral sink. So is something like the Kitty Genovese case—a girl raped and murdered in the courtyard of an apartment complex and forty or fifty people look on from their apartments and nobody even calls the police. That kind of apathy and anomie is typical of the general psychological deterioration of The Sink."

He looked at the high-rise housing projects and found them mainly testimony to how little planners know about humans' basic animal requirements for space.

"Even on the simplest terms," he said, "it is pointless to build one of these blocks much over five stories high. Suppose a family lives on the fifteenth floor. The mother will be completely cut off from her children if they are playing down below, because the elevators are constantly broken in these projects, and it often takes half an hour, literally half an hour, to get the elevator if it is running. That's very common. A mother in that situation is just as much a victim of overcrowding as if she were back in the tenement block. Some Negro leaders have a bitter joke about how the white man is solving the slum problem by stacking Negroes up vertically, and there is a lot to that."

For one thing, says Dr. Hall, planners have no idea of the different space requirements of people from different cultures, such as Negroes and Puerto Ricans. They are all treated as if they were minute, compact middle-class whites. As with the Sika deer, who are overcrowded at one per acre, overcrowding is a relative thing for the human animal, as well. Each species has its own feeling for space. The feeling may be "subjective," but it is quite real.

Dr. Hall's theories on space and territory are based on the same information, gathered by biologists, ethologists, and anthropologists, chiefly, as Robert Ardrey's. Ardrey has written two well-publicized books, *African Genesis* and *The Territorial Imperative. Life* magazine ran big excerpts from *The Territorial Imperative,* all about how the drive to acquire territory and property and add to it and achieve status is built into all animals, including man, over thousands of centuries of genetic history, etc., and is a more powerful drive than sex. *Life's* big display prompted Marshall McLuhan to crack, "They see this as a great historic justification for free enterprise and Republicanism. If the birds do it and the stickleback crabs do it, then it's right for man." To people like Hall and McLuhan, and Ardrey, for that matter, the right or wrong of it is irrelevant. The only thing they find inexcusable is the kind of thinking, by influential people, that isn't even aware of all this. Such as the thinking of most city planners.

"The planners always show you a bird's-eye view of what they are doing," he said. "You've seen those scale models. Everyone stands around the table and looks down and says that's great. It never occurs to anyone that they are taking a bird's-eye view. In the end, these projects do turn out fine, when viewed from an airplane."

As an anthropologist, Dr. Hall has to shake his head every time he hears planners talking about fully integrated housing projects for the year 1980 or 1990, as if by then all cultural groups will have the same feeling for space and will live placidly side by side, happy as the happy burghers who plan all the good clean bird's-eye views. According to his findings, the very fact that every cultural group does have its own peculiar, unspoken feeling for space is what is responsible for much of the uneasiness one group feels around the other.

It is like the North European and the Mediterranean in the subway line. The North European, without ever realizing it, tries to keep a bubble of space around himself, and the moment a stranger invades that sphere, he feels threatened. Mediterranean peoples tend to come from cultures where everyone is much more involved physically, publicly, with one another on a day-to-day basis and feels no uneasiness about mixing it up in public, but may have very different ideas about space inside the home. Even Negroes brought up in America have a different vocabulary of space and gesture from the North European Americans who, historically, have been their models, according to Dr. Hall. The failure of Negroes and whites to communicate well often boils down to things like this: some white will be interviewing a Negro for a job; the Negro's culture has taught him to show somebody you are interested by looking right at him and listening intently to what he has to say. But the species North European requires something more. He expects his listener to nod from time to time, as if to say, "Yes, keep going." If he doesn't get this nodding, he feels anxious, for fear the listener doesn't agree with him or has switched off. The Negro may learn that the white expects this sort of thing, but he isn't used to the precise kind of nodding that is customary, and so he may start overresponding, nodding like mad, and at this point the North European is liable to think he has some kind of stupid Uncle Tom on his hands, and the guy still doesn't get the job.

The whole handling of space in New York is so chaotic, says Dr. Hall, that even middle-class housing now seems to be based on the bird's-eye models for slum projects. He took a look at the big Park West Village development, set up originally to provide housing in Manhattan for families in the middle-income range, and found its handling of space very much like a slum project with slightly larger balconies. He felt the time has come to start subsidizing the middle class in New York on its own terms—namely, the kind of truly "human" spaces that still remain in brownstones.

"I think New York City should seriously consider a program of encouraging the middle-class development of an area like Chelsea, which is already starting to come up. People are beginning to renovate houses there on their own, and I think if the city would subsidize that sort of thing with tax reliefs and so forth, you would be amazed at what would result. What New York needs is a string of minor successes in the housing field, just to show everyone that it can be done, and I think the middle class can still do that for you. The alternative is to keep on doing what you're doing now, trying to lift a very large lower class up by main force almost and finding it a very slow and discouraging process."

"But before deciding how to redesign space in New York," he said, "people must first simply realize how severe the problem already is. And the handwriting is already on the wall."

"A study published in 1962," he said, "surveyed a representative sample of people living in New York slums and found only 18 percent of them free from emotional symptoms. Thirty-eight percent were in need of psychiatric help, and 23 percent were seriously disturbed or incapacitated. Now, this study was published in 1962, which means the work probably went on from 1955 to 1960. There is no telling how bad it is now. In a behavioral sink, crises can develop rapidly."

Dr. Hall would like to see a large-scale study similar to that undertaken by two sociopsychologists, Chombart de Lauwe and his wife, in a French working-class town. They found a direct relationship between crowding and general breakdown. In families where people were crowded into the apartment so that there was less than 86 to 108 square feet per person, social and physical disorders doubled. That would mean that for four people the smallest floor space they could tolerate would be an apartment, say, 12 by 30 feet.

What would one find in Harlem? "It is fairly obvious," Dr. Hall wrote in *The Hidden Dimension,* "that the American Negroes and people of Spanish culture who are flocking to our cities are being very seriously stressed. Not only are they in a setting that does not fit them, but they have passed the limits of their own tolerance of stress. The United States is faced with the fact that two of its creative and sensitive peoples are in the process of being destroyed and like Samson could bring down the structure that houses us all."

Dr. Hall goes out to the airport, to go back to Chicago, and I am coming back in a cab, along the East River Drive. It is four in the afternoon, but already the damned drive is clogging up. There is a 1959 Oldsmobile just to the right of me. There are about eight people in there, a lot of popeyed silhouettes against a leopard-skin dashboard, leopard-skin seats—and the driver is classic. He has a mustache, sideburns down to his jaw socket, and a tattoo on his forearm like a Rossetti painting of Jane Burden Morris with her hair long. All right; it is even touching, like a postcard photo of the main drag in San Pedro, California. But suddenly Sideburns guns it and cuts in front of my cab so that my driver has to hit the brakes, and then hardly 100 feet ahead Sideburns hits a wall of traffic himself and has to hit his brakes, and then it happens. A stuffed white Angora animal, a dog, no, it's a Pekingese cat, is mounted in his rear window—as soon as he hits the brakes its *eyes* light up Nighttown pink. To keep from ramming him, my driver has to hit the brakes again, too, and so here I am, out in an insane, jammed-up expressway at four in the afternoon shuddering to a stop while a stuffed Pekingese grows bigger and bigger and brighter in the eyeballs directly in front of me. Jolt! Nighttown pink! Hey—that's me the adrenalin is hitting, *I* am this white human sitting in a projectile heading amid a mass of clotted humans toward a white Angora stuffed goddam leopard-dash Pekingese freaking cat—kill that damned Angora—Jolt!—got me—another micrometer on the old adrenals—

From *Family Circle,* May 1972 (adapted from "Social Readjustment Rating Scale," by T. H. Holmes and R. H. Rahe, *Journal of Psychosomatic Research,* 1967). Reprinted by permission.

2. Avoid Sickness—How Life Changes Affect Your Health

SUSAN WISE WOLFE

If (1) you suffer a year in which your husband dies, your daughter leaves home to marry a man you abhor and, because of straitened finances, you have to sell your house, move into an apartment and get a job—your chances of getting sick are eight out of 10.

If (2) you enjoy a year in which your husband recovers from a serious illness, makes such a financial success of his new business that you can move into your dream house and give your daughter a Christmas wedding to a man you adore, your chances of getting sick are—*eight out of 10.*

That disaster and sorrow often lead to illness will surprise few. The idea that achievement and happiness can also do so may amaze many. Yet those are the twin results of studies spanning more than two decades by Dr. Thomas H. Holmes, professor of psychiatry, and various of his associates at the University of Washington School of Medicine, Seattle.

It is simply *change* in sufficient amount that is the culprit. If enough things that require you to cope occur within a two-year period, you can expect to get sick. Types of change do not matter.

These findings were among those presented by Dr. Holmes and Dr. Minora Masuda to a symposium of the American Academy for the Advancement of Science in December, 1970. Sickness included not only disease and bodily malfunction but also emotional disorders and accidental injury.

In a recent interview, Dr. Holmes re-emphasized these points:

"It doesn't matter whether basically you are the sort of person who likes change or not," he stated firmly. "It still makes you sick. Nor does it matter whether you are happy or sad about a particular change, nor yet whether it is socially desirable or undesirable."

How to measure what changes? That effort began years ago with the "life chart" of famed psychiatrist Dr. Adolph Meyer, a device for organizing medical data as a dynamic biography. Other scientists, notably the late Dr. Harold G. Wolff of Cornell, added to the data. Strong evidence emerged that "stressful" life events were correlated to the history of many illnesses.

BASICS: PEOPLE

Dr. Holmes, who received his advanced medical training at Cornell, returned there, after a three-year World War II Army stint, to work with Dr. Wolff two more years. He has been at the University of Washington since 1949, deep into research regarding change and health.

Out of this has come, at long last, a table called the Social Readjustment Rating Scale, giving numerical value to various life events. It was first published by Dr. Holmes and his young colleague, Dr. Richard Rahe, in the *Journal of Psychosomatic Research.*

The scale lists 43 specific events, ranking them in order of descending importance. As might be expected, death of a spouse carried the most weight —100 Life Change Units (LCU). Minor violations of the law have the least —11 LCU. In between are changing aspects of a person's life, from birth to death, encompassing the private and vocational, the individual and the social, the "good" and the "bad." All have in common that they require coping and adaptation.

In evolving the rating scale, Dr. Rahe and Dr. Holmes asked 394 volunteers to rate the amount of adjustment they thought might be necessary for each change. Marriage was used as the basis for comparison, all others being classified as requiring either more or less coping than getting married. Results were incorporated into the scale.

In part of the double-checking, a study was carried out among college-age persons by Libby O. Ruch, and another, involving seventh-grade students, average age 13—the youngest group yet tested—by Suzanne Pasley. Both were consistent with the original results.

"I think what we do, actually, is tell the public what it already knows," Dr. Holmes said. "But what is important is the cultural state of mind that results from what you've forgotten. You know a whole lot of things you are never called on to articulate. Or, even if you are called on, you can't. But your brain knows. That is what our research points out. If you ask a good question, Mother Nature is ready to give an answer.

"So we ask people to tell us what everybody knows, and they do. They all agree that death of a spouse requires twice as much change and adjustment as marriage—and 10 times as much as a traffic ticket. People in Japan and San Salvador and Spain, France, Sweden and America all agree that this is so."

They do. Cross-cultural studies have been done in several nations and among certain minority groups within the United States. In each instance, despite certain variations (such as a mortgage carrying more import in one country than in another), the results have been essentially the same. The similarities are notable, not the differences.

Perhaps most remarkable is the extremely high consensus between the group in Japan and the one in America. The cultures seem to be so opposite in so many ways that it was wondered whether the rating scale could be employed accurately in Japan. It did not work out that way; the differences were minor. Why?

"I suppose I would say that there are similarities between all cultures, no matter how diverse," Dr. Holmes replied. "The wife—or spouse—means about the same in all cultures. Or the relationship with in-laws. All require about the same amount of change and adjustment. Or the economic area requires about as much coping in one culture as another."

The validity of the rating scale established, the next question was how many life-change units in the already ascertained two-year "risk period" were necessary to cause sickness?

In a pilot study, Dr. Rahe and Dr. Holmes investigated 88 resident physicians, whose listing of "major health changes" for the preceding 10 years were analyzed in relation to their life changes during that time period.

No significant health problems were noted in those with a lower than 150 LCU count in a two-year span. Those with 150–199 LCU were adjudged to have a "mild life crisis." Approximately one third of this group had been sick. "Moderate life crisis" occurred in the 200–299 LCU range and, of these, approximately half had developed illness.

"Major life crisis" was defined as a total of 300 or more LCU. Of this group, *sickness had hit no fewer than 80 percent.*

"The cut-off point is about 300," Dr. Holmes commented. "The curve seems to flatten at the top; beyond that point more change does not increase your risk. At 300, eight out of 10 get sick; but there is no way of predicting which eight —nor which two will not get sick."

Nevertheless, the scale has proved to be an excellent predictive tool. Dr. Steven Bramwell, while still a medical student, used it to predict which players were likely to be injured in an upcoming football season. Even though the three-month playing period was much less than the two-year risk period, half the high-risk group were injured before it was over. A fourth of the medium-risk and nine percent of the low-risk men were hurt. Of 10 injured more than once, seven were "high-risk."

"You see," Dr. Holmes amplified, "1971 and 1972 predicts illness in 1973 and 1974. Of course, each time you get sick you add more points, and this increases the likelihood you'll get sick again. Which explains why illnesses are not randomly distributed in a person's life, but tend to run in clusters."

Further verification is being obtained from Dr. Rahe's present work with the United States Navy Medical neuropsychiatric research unit in San Diego.

"What he has been doing," Dr. Holmes reported, " is to study personnel of cruisers and battleships and predicting illness onset. He's got something like six cruisers and three battleships, which is a lot of people."

And is it working out as in previous studies? The answer was a succinct "Yes."

All of which indicates that anyone who tallies a score of 300 LCU in any two-year period is a walking accident or illness waiting to happen. Dr. Holmes agreed. "I know I quit driving on the freeway when my total got to 300," he said. "And, at least, I didn't have an accident, which could have been fatal."

SOCIAL READJUSTMENT RATING SCALE

Rank	Life Event	Life Crisis Units
1	Death of spouse	100
2	Divorce	73
3	Marital separation	65
4	Jail term	63
5	Death of close family membwer	63
6	Personal injury or illness	53
7	Marriage	50
8	Fired at work	47
9	Marital reconciliation	45
10	Retirement	45
11	Change in health of family member	44
12	Pregnancy	40
13	Sex difficulties	39
14	Gain of new family member	39
15	Business readjustment	39
16	Change in financial state	38
17	Death of a close friend	37
18	Change to different line of work	36
19	Change in number of arguments with spouse	35
20	Mortgage over $10,000	31
21	Foreclosure of mortgage or loan	30
22	Change in responsibilities at work	29
23	Son or daughter leaving home	29
24	Trouble with in-laws	29
25	Outstanding personal achievement	28
26	Wife begins or stops work	26
27	Begin or end school	26
28	Change in living conditions	25
29	Revision of personal habits	24
30	Trouble with boss	23
31	Change in work hours or conditions	20
32	Change in residence	20
33	Change in school	20
34	Change in recreation	19
35	Change in church activities	19
36	Change in social activities	18
37	Mortgage or loan less than $10,000	17
38	Change in sleeping habits	16
39	Change in number of family get-togethers	15
40	Change in eating habits	15
41	Vacation	13
42	Christmas	12
43	Minor violations of the law	11

Adapted with permission from "Social Readjustment Rating Scale" by T. H. Holmes and R. H. Rahe, *Journal of Psychosomatic Research,* 1967.

HOW TO USE: Add up value of Life Crisis Units for Life Events experienced in two-year period.

0 to 150—No significant problems
150 to 199—Mild life crisis (33 percent chance of illness)
200 to 299—Moderate life crisis (50 percent chance of illness)
300 or over—Major life crisis (80 percent chance of illness)

Examples: Analysis of situations in paragraphs 1 and 2 (*above*). It is assumed in each case that "you" is a woman; therefore items such as "wife begins or stops work" do not apply. But such items as "retirement" and "change to a different line of work" (leaving home for an office) do.

Life Event	*Life Crisis Units*
1. Death of spouse	100
Son or daughter leaving home	29
Gain of a new family member	39
Trouble with in-laws (the new son-in-law abhors you, too)	29
Change in financial state (less money)	38
Change in residence	20
Change in social activities	18
Change in recreation (now alone)	19
Change to a different line of work (office, not house)	36
Change in living conditions (poorer)	25
Total	**353**
2. Change in health of family member (improved)	44
Change in financial state	38
Retirement	45
Mortgage over $10,000 (assumed)	31
Change in residence	20
Gain of new family member	39
Son or daughter leaving home	29
Christmas	12
Change in social activities (more)	18
Change in recreation (now husband can accompany you)	19
Change in living conditions (richer)	25
Total	**320**

BASICS: PEOPLE

Just what he did have he didn't say.

It might also seem that this information might be frightening to many people. Not so, said Dr. Holmes, who related: "We've had thousands of fan letters from our appearances on mid-morning television talks. And the interesting thing is that people don't react fearfully at all. They seem reassured.

"Why? Well, now—so they say—they understand why all these things have been happening. Why their husband got sick, or they've been feeling blue and so on. They seem to feel that they can do something about the situation now that they comprehend it. They don't blame the environment. Therefore, they think they now know what they can do. Exactly what, they don't tell me. I have my own opinions, though," he said.

What might they be? "Well, you know the old adage that to be forewarned is to be forearmed? If you know what your danger is, you are likely to be more careful. You are likely to pay attention to the danger signals. You are more likely to pace yourself.

"All of which is to say that, forewarned, people are likely to stabilize their life. Now, I don't mean anything like jumping into bed and pulling the covers over your head. To do that is to create a major change in your personal habits, which only runs your score up still more.

"But let's consider the average homemaker between the ages of 25 and 45. What are the things that are likely to require modification of her life-style? One big example is when her children start school, thus freeing some of her time. She has many choices of what to do with that time; perhaps too many. So what she can do is plan carefully—what she wants to go into, how much of her time she wants to devote to it, how big an effort she wants to make. Evaluate carefully all the pros and cons in advance. Anticipate every possible problem, including her relationship with women in general, and then with groups of women. The secret is to figure it all out in advance. Don't wait till you're in the midst and then try to cope, because you are likely to make the wrong decision then—it can't be very objective. The best thing during times of life crisis is to analyze and to avoid the impulsive at all costs."

Innate health weaknesses are most likely to come to the fore in a life crisis. "That is when people get diabetes, for example," Dr. Holmes noted. "They have a genetic endowment that gives them the potential for diabetes, but they don't get the disease until the life crisis comes. Persons who know they are potential diabetics can make their life as stable as possible."

"I hope you will notice," Dr. Holmes remarked, "that I have not used the word 'stress.' That's an interesting kind of paradox for me because I spent the first 20 years of my professional life trying to sell that word. But it has come to mean a thousand different things—so much so that now it is almost meaningless unless you stop to define it. What we are talking about is *change,* and the fascinating thing about the scale is that it includes all kinds, pleasant and unpleasant.

"In a sense," he added, "pleasant changes can require more coping, at least for Americans. That is because most Americans are very used to having to cope with undesirable things. They are not so accustomed to having things go just right."

But what of those two out of 10 persons who, despite high-risk LCU scores, don't get sick.

"I don't know," Dr. Holmes admitted candidly. "Nobody knows. Doctors, you see, know a lot about sickness; they know very little about health.

"That is our next field of investigation," he continued. "We are going to try to find out what personality and/or physiological traits distinguish the two who stay healthy from the eight who don't. I have some ideas—such characteristics as 'flexibility' or 'easy adaptability.' But I don't know yet.

"We are also doing research to see if we can prevent illness by using some of the little devices we've been talking about. This will be a long-term population study, where we use simple educational methods—make people aware of the scale and its implications. Make them aware of their risk in terms of the scale and suggest they do some of the things we have mentioned. Then we will follow them up and find out if it has any effect on the amount of illness they have. I can't *prove*—yet—that it is going to keep anyone well. But I'm betting it will. This is one of the major tenets of preventive medicine—that education is one way to accomplish primary prevention."

In the meantime, we can all try Dr. Holmes' suggestions in our own lives. We may be able to demonstrate for ourselves that analyzing and understanding our own life-change situation may help in avoiding some ailments.

There is yet another aspect of the matter that might prove encouraging to some, Dr. Holmes pointed out. "There *are* worse things than being sick, you know," he said smilingly. "If you have a high LCU and are then offered a fine new job, losing the career opportunity would surely be worse than having a bout of illness. . . . I'd take the job. Or marry the person I had chosen. Or go to college. Missing out on any of these things would be much worse than getting sick."

In the meantime, if you can plan in advance so that these joyful occasions do not push your LCU total too high, you probably can have both happiness and health. It's certainly worth a try.

Bodies:
The Social
Context of
Sexuality

I can't get no satisfaction.

MICK JAGGER

DICK: I can see that sexuality is influenced by society, but the selections you have here all sound like a plug for women's liberation.

ANGELA: If the women's movement has illustrated the social definition of sexuality before the sociologists have, that seems to reflect upon the failures of sociology, doesn't it?

MOLLY: I don't know about that, but I think readings like these should be available to kids when they come out of high school. Where else can they get correct information on human sexuality?

RICH: Try to find some articles that aren't full of academic jargon. I was twenty-one before I ever heard of a multiple orgasm. I looked it up in Masters and Johnson, and they were too clinical. They had nothing on its social implications.

DICK: But if it's all from women's liberation . . .

RICH: It's *not* all from women's liberation. It transcends that. I don't want to know what the neurological characteristics of a multiple orgasm are, I want to know how the ability of a woman to have multiple orgasms is going to affect my relationship with her. That's what's good about Brenton's article on male sexuality. It explains that society has a male role and tells how that role influences male sexuality.

DEMA: Sex roles, and the way they influence sexuality, are important to men *and* women.

ANGELA: Yes, sexuality is really basic.

MOLLY: Angela, when I read "The Myth of the Vaginal Orgasm" in your class I found it really exciting. And I learned a lot about the problems women had because men were telling them what sort of orgasms they were supposed to have.

PAT: Oh, I don't know. I don't remember anyone ever telling me that I had to have vaginal orgasms.

MOLLY: Aren't you glad they didn't?

3. The Myth of the Vaginal Orgasm

ANNE KOEDT*

Whenever female orgasm and frigidity are discussed, a false distinction is made between the vaginal and the clitoral orgasm. Frigidity has generally been defined by men as the failure of women to have vaginal orgasms. Actually the vagina is not a highly sensitive area and is not constructed to achieve orgasm. It is the clitoris which is the center of sexual sensitivity and which is the female equivalent of the penis.

I think this explains a great many things: First of all, the fact that the so-called frigidity rate among women is phenomenally high. Rather than tracing female frigidity to the false assumptions about female anatomy, our "experts" have declared frigidity a psychological problem of women. Those women who complained about it were recommended psychiatrists, so that they might discover their "problem"—diagnosed generally as a failure to adjust to their role as women.

The facts of female anatomy and sexual response tell a different story. Although there are many areas for sexual arousal, there is only one area for sexual climax; that area is the clitoris. All orgasms are extensions of sensation from this area. Since the clitoris is not necessarily stimulated sufficiently in the conventional sexual positions, we are left "frigid."

Aside from physical stimulation, which is the common cause of orgasm for most people, there is also stimulation through primarily mental processes. Some women, for example, may achieve orgasm through sexual fantasies, or through fetishes. However, while the stimulation may be psychological, the orgasm manifests itself physically. Thus, while the cause is psychological, the *effect* is still physical, and the orgasm necessarily takes place in the sexual organ equipped for sexual climax—the clitoris. The orgasm experience may also differ in degree of intensity—some more localized, and some more diffuse and sensitive. But they are all clitoral orgasms.

*Anne Koedt, a founder of the radical feminist movement in New York (New York Radical Women, The Feminists, and currently New York Radical Feminists), is an editor of *Notes* and is now at work on a book about female sexuality.

All this leads to some interesting questions about conventional sex and our role in it. Men have orgasms essentially by friction with the vagina, not the clitoral area, which is external and not able to cause friction the way penetration does. Women have thus been defined sexually in terms of what pleases men; our own biology has not been properly analyzed. Instead, we are fed the myth of the liberated woman and her vaginal orgasm—an orgasm which in fact does not exist.

What we must do is redefine our sexuality. We must discard the "normal" concepts of sex and create new guidelines which take into account mutual sexual enjoyment. While the idea of mutual enjoyment is liberally applauded in marriage manuals, it is not followed to its logical conclusion. We must begin to demand that if certain sexual positions now defined as "standard" are not mutually conducive to orgasm, they no longer be defined as standard. New techniques must be used or devised which transforms this particular aspect of our current sexual exploitation.

Freud—A Father of the Vaginal Orgasm

Freud contended that the clitoral orgasm was adolescent, and that upon puberty, when women began having intercourse with men, women should transfer the center of orgasm to the vagina. The vagina, it was assumed, was able to produce a parallel, but more mature, orgasm than the clitoris. Much work was done to elaborate on this theory, but little was done to challenge the basic assumptions.

To fully appreciate this incredible invention, perhaps Freud's general attitude about women should first be recalled. Mary Ellman, in *Thinking About Women,* summed it up this way:

> Everything in Freud's patronizing and fearful attitude toward women follows from their lack of a penis, but it is only in his essay *The Psychology of Women* that Freud makes explicit . . . the deprecations of women which are implicit in his work. He then prescribes for them the abandonment of the life of the mind, which will interfere with their sexual function. When the psychoanalyzed patient is male, the analyst sets himself the task of developing the man's capacities; but with women patients, the job is to resign them to the limits of their sexuality. As Mr. Rieff puts it: For Freud, "Analysis cannot encourage in women new energies for success and achievement, but only teach them the lesson of rational resignation."

It was Freud's feelings about women's secondary and inferior relationship to men that formed the basis for his theories on female sexuality.

Once having laid down the law about the nature of our sexuality, Freud not so strangely discovered a tremendous problem of frigidity in women. His recommended cure for a woman who was frigid was psychiatric care. She was suffering from failure to mentally adjust to her "natural" role as a woman.

BASICS: PEOPLE

Frank S. Caprio, a contemporary follower of these ideas, states:

> . . . whenever a woman is incapable of achieving an orgasm via coitus, provided her husband is an adequate partner, and prefers clitoral stimulation to any other form of sexual activity, she can be regarded as suffering from frigidity and requires psychiatric assistance. (*The Sexually Adequate Female,* p. 64.)

The explanation given was that women were envious of men—"renunciation of womanhood." Thus it was diagnosed as an anti-male phenomenon.

It is important to emphasize that Freud did not base his theory upon a study of woman's anatomy, but rather upon his assumptions of woman as an inferior appendage to man, and her consequent social and psychological role. In their attempts to deal with the ensuing problem of mass frigidity, Freudians created elaborate mental gymnastics. Marie Bonaparte, in *Female Sexuality,* goes so far as to suggest surgery to help women back on their rightful path. Having discovered a strange connection between the non-frigid woman and the location of the clitoris near the vagina,

> it then occurred to me that where, in certain women, this gap was excessive, and clitoridal fixation obdurate, a clitoridal-vaginal reconciliation might be effected by surgical means, which would then benefit the normal erotic function. Professor Halban, of Vienna, as much a biologist as surgeon, became interested in the problem and worked out a simple operative technique. In this, the suspensory ligament of the clitoris was severed and the clitoris secured to the underlying structures, thus fixing it in a lower position, with eventual reduction of the labia minora. (p. 148)

But the severest damage was not in the area of surgery, where Freudians ran around absurdly trying to change female anatomy to fit their basic assumptions. The worst damage was done to the mental health of women, who either suffered silently with self-blame, or flocked to psychiatrists looking desperately for the hidden and terrible repression that had kept from them their vaginal destiny.

Lack of Evidence?

One may perhaps at first claim that these are unknown and unexplored areas, but upon closer examination this is certainly not true today, nor was it true even in the past. For example, men have known that women suffered from frigidity often during intercourse. So the problem was there. Also, there is much specific evidence. Men knew that the clitoris was and is the essential organ for masturbation, whether in children or adult women. So obviously women made it clear where *they* thought their sexuality was located. Men also seem suspiciously aware of the clitoral powers during "foreplay," when they want to arouse women and produce the necessary lubrication for penetration. Foreplay is a concept created for male purposes, but works to the disadvantage of many women, since as soon as the woman is aroused the man changes to vaginal stimulation, leaving her both aroused and unsatisfied.

It has also been known that women need no anesthesia inside the vagina during surgery, thus pointing to the fact that the vagina is in fact not a highly sensitive area.

Today, with extensive knowledge of anatomy, with Kinsey, and Masters and Johnson, to mention just a few sources, there is no ignorance on the subject. There are, however, social reasons why this knowledge has not been popularized. We are living in a male society which has not sought change in women's role.

Anatomical Evidence

Rather than starting with what women *ought* to feel, it would seem logical to start out with the anatomical facts regarding the clitoris and vagina.

The Clitoris is a small equivalent of the penis, except for the fact that the urethra does not go through it as in the man's penis. Its erection is similar to the male erection, and the head of the clitoris has the same type of structure and function as the head of the penis. G. Lombard Kelly, in *Sexual Feeling in Married Men and Women,* says:

> The head of the clitoris is also composed of erectile tissue, and it possesses a very sensitive epithelium or surface covering, supplied with special nerve endings called genital corpuscles, which are peculiarly adapted for sensory stimulation that under proper mental conditions terminates in the sexual orgasm. No other part of the female generative tract has such corpuscles. (Pocketbooks; p. 35.)

The clitoris has no other function than that of sexual pleasure.

The Vagina—Its functions are related to the reproductive function. Principally, 1) menstruation, 2) receive penis, 3) hold semen, and 4) birth passage. The interior of the vagina, which according to the defenders of the vaginally caused orgasm is the center and producer of the orgasm, is:

> like nearly all other internal body structures, poorly supplied with end organs of touch. The internal entodermal origin of the lining of the vagina makes it similar in this respect to the rectum and other parts of the digestive tract. (Kinsey, *Sexual Behavior in the Human Female,* p. 580.)

The degree of insensitivity inside the vagina is so high that "Among the women who were tested in our gynecologic sample, less than 14% were at all conscious that they had been touched." (Kinsey, p. 580.)

Even the importance of the vagina as an *erotic* center (as opposed to an orgasmic center) has been found to be minor.

Other Areas—Labia minora and the vestibule of the vagina. These two sensitive areas may trigger off a clitoral orgasm. Because they can be effectively stimulated during "normal" coitus; though infrequent, this kind of stimulation is incorrectly thought to be vaginal orgasm. However, it is important to distinguish between areas which can stimulate the clitoris, incapable of producing the orgasm themselves, and the clitoris:

> Regardless of what means of excitation is used to bring the individual to the state of sexual climax, the sensation is perceived by the genital corpuscles and is localized where they are situated: in the head of the clitoris or penis. (Kelly, p. 49.)

Psychologically Stimulated Orgasm—Aside from the above mentioned direct and indirect stimulations of the clitoris, there is a third way an orgasm may be triggered. This is through mental (cortical) stimulation, where the imagination stimulates the brain, which in turn stimulates the genital corpuscles of the glands to set off an orgasm.

Women Who Say They Have Vaginal Orgasms

Confusion—Because of the lack of knowledge of their own anatomy, some women accept the idea that an orgasm *felt* during "normal" intercourse was vaginally caused. This confusion is caused by a combination of two factors. One, failing to locate the center of the orgasm, and two, by a desire to fit her experience to the male-defined idea of sexual normalcy. Considering that women know little about their anatomy, it is easy to be confused.

Deception—The vast majority of women who pretend vaginal orgasm to their men are faking it to "get the job." In a new best-selling Danish book, *I Accuse* Mette Ejlersen specifically deals with this common problem, which she calls the "sex comedy." This comedy has many causes. First of all, the man brings a great deal of pressure to bear on the woman, because he considers his ability as a lover at stake. So as not to offend his ego, the woman will comply with the prescribed role and go through simulated ecstasy. In some of the other Danish women mentioned, women who were left frigid were turned off to sex, and pretended vaginal orgasm to hurry up the sex act. Others admitted that they had faked vaginal orgasm to catch a man. In one case, the woman pretended vaginal orgasm to get him to leave his first wife, who admitted being vaginally frigid. Later she was forced to continue the deception, since obviously she couldn't tell him to stimulate her clitorally.

Many more women were simply afraid to establish their right to equal enjoyment, seeing the sexual act as being primarily for the man's benefit, and any pleasure that the woman got as an added extra.

Other women, with just enough ego to reject the man's idea that they needed psychiatric care, refused to admit their frigidity. They wouldn't accept self-blame, but they didn't know how to solve the problem, not knowing the physiological facts about themselves. So they were left in a peculiar limbo.

Again, perhaps one of the most infuriating and damaging results of this whole charade has been that women who were perfectly healthy sexually were

Bodies: The Social Context of Sexuality   **33**

taught that they were not. So in addition to being sexually deprived, these women were told to blame themselves when they deserved no blame. Looking for a cure to a problem that has none can lead a woman on an endless path of self-hatred and insecurity. For she is told by her analyst that not even in her one role allowed in a male society—the role of a woman—is she successful. She is put on the defensive, with phony data as evidence that she better try to be even more feminine, think more feminine, and reject her envy of men. That is, shuffle even harder, baby.

Why Men Maintain the Myth

1. *Sexual Penetration is Preferred*—The best stimulant for the penis is the woman's vagina. It supplies the necessary friction and lubrication. From a strictly technical point of view this position offers the best physical conditions, even though the man may try other positions for variation.

2. *The Invisible Woman*—One of the elements of male chauvinism is the refusal or inability to see women as total, separate human beings. Rather, men have chosen to define women only in terms of how they benefitted men's lives. Sexually, a woman was not seen as an individual wanting to share equally in the sexual act, any more than she was seen as a person with independent desires when she did anything else in society. Thus, it was easy to make up what was convenient about women; for on top of that, society has been a function of male interests, and women were not organized to form even a vocal opposition to the male experts.

3. *The Penis as Epitome of Masculinity*—Men define their lives primarily in terms of masculinity. It is a universal form of ego-boosting. That is, in every society, however homogeneous (i.e., with the absence of racial, ethnic, or major economic differences) there is always a group, women, to oppress.

The essence of male chauvinism is in the psychological superiority men exercise over women. This kind of superior-inferior definition of self, rather than positive definition based upon one's own achievements and development, has of course chained victim and oppressor both. But by far the most brutalized of the two is the victim.

An analogy is racism, where the white racist compensates for his feelings of unworthiness by creating an image of the black man (it is primarily a male struggle) as biologically inferior to him. Because of his power in a white male power structure, the white man can socially enforce this mythical division.

To the extent that men try to rationalize and justify male superiority through physical differentiation, masculinity may be symbolized by being the *most* muscular, the most hairy; having the deepest voice, and the biggest penis. Women, on the other hand, are approved of (i.e., called feminine) if they are weak, petite, shave their legs; have high soft voices, and no penis.

Since the clitoris is almost identical to the penis, one finds a great deal of evidence of men in various societies trying to either ignore the clitoris and emphasize the vagina (as did Freud), or, as in some places in the Mideast,

BASICS: PEOPLE

actually performing clitoridectomy. Freud saw this ancient and still practiced custom as a way of further "feminizing" the female by removing this cardinal vestige of her masculinity. It should be noted also that a big clitoris is considered ugly and masculine. Some cultures engage in the practice of pouring a chemical on the clitoris to make it shrivel up into proper size.

It seems clear to me that men in fact fear the clitoris as a threat to masculinity.

4. *Sexually Expendable Male*—Men fear that they will become sexually expendable if the clitoris is substituted for the vagina as the center of pleasure for women. Actually this has a great deal of validity if one considers *only* the anatomy. The position of the penis inside the vagina, while perfect for reproduction, does not necessarily stimulate an orgasm in women because the clitoris is located externally and higher up. Women must rely upon indirect stimulation in the "normal" position.

Lesbian sexuality could make an excellent case, based upon anatomical data, for the extinction of the male organ. Albert Ellis says something to the effect that a man without a penis can make a woman an excellent lover.

Considering that the vagina is very desirable from a man's point of view, purely on physical grounds, one begins to see the dilemma for men. And it forces us as well to discard many "physical" arguments explaining why women go to bed with men. What is left, it seems to me, are primarily psychological reasons why women select men at the exclusion of women as sexual partners.

5. *Control of Women*—One reason given to explain the Mideastern practice of clitoridectomy is that it will keep the women from straying. By removing the sexual organ capable of orgasm, it must be assumed that her sexual drive will diminish. Considering how men look upon their women as property, particularly in very backward nations, we should begin to consider a great deal more why it is not in the men's interest to have women totally free sexually. The double standard, as practiced for example in Latin America, is set up to keep the woman as total property of the husband, while he is free to have affairs as he wishes.

6. *Lesbianism and Bisexuality*—Aside from the strictly anatomical reasons why women might equally seek other women as lovers, there is a fear on men's part that women will seek the company of other women on a full, human basis. The establishment of clitoral orgasm as fact would threaten the heterosexual *institution*. For it would indicate that sexual pleasure was obtainable from either men *or* women, thus making heterosexuality not an absolute, but an option. It would thus open up the whole question of *human* sexual relationships beyond the confines of the present male-female role system.

Bodies: The Social Context of Sexuality   **35**

4. Sex

G E R M A I N E   G R E E R

Women's sexual organs are shrouded in mystery.

It is assumed that most of them are internal and hidden, but even the ones that are external are relatively shady. When little girls begin to ask questions their mothers provide them, if they are lucky, with crude diagrams of the sexual apparatus, in which the organs of pleasure feature much less prominently than the intricacies of tubes and ovaries. I myself did not realize that the tissues of my vagina were quite normal until I saw a meticulously engraved dissection in an eighteenth-century anatomy textbook. The little girl is not encouraged to explore her own genitals or to identify the tissues of which they are composed, or to understand the mechanism of lubrication and erection. The very idea is distasteful. Because of this strange modesty, which a young woman will find extends even into the doctor's office, where the doctor is loath to examine her, and loath to expatiate on what he finds, female orgasm has become more and more of a mystery, at the same time as it has been exalted as a duty. Its actual nature has become a matter for metaphysical speculation. All kinds of false ideas are still in circulation about women, although they were disproved years ago; many men refuse to relinquish the notion of female ejaculation, which although it has a long and prestigious history is utterly fanciful.

Part of the modesty about the female genitalia stems from actual distaste. The worst name anyone can be called is *cunt.* The best thing a cunt can be is small and unobtrusive: the anxiety about the bigness of the penis is only equaled by anxiety about the smallness of the cunt. No woman wants to find out that she has a twat like a horse-collar: she hopes she is not sloppy or smelly, and obligingly obliterates all signs of her menstruation in the cause of public decency. Women were not always so reticent: in ballad literature we can find lovely examples of women vaunting their genitals, like the lusty wench who admonished a timid tailor in round terms because he did not dare measure her fringed purse with his yard:

> You'l find the purse so deep,
> You'l hardly come to the treasure.

BASICS: PEOPLE

Another praised her shameful part in these terms:

> I have a gallant Pin-box,
>   the like you ne'er did see,
> It is where never was the Pox
>   something above my knee . . .
> O 'tis a gallant Pin-box
>   you never saw the peer;
> Then Ile not leave my Pin-box
>   for fifty pound a year.

Early gynecology was entirely in the hands of men, some of whom, like Samuel Collins, described the vagina so lovingly that any woman who read his words would have been greatly cheered. Of course such books were not meant to be seen by women at all. He speaks of the vagina as the Temple of Venus and the *mons veneris* as Venus's cushion, but he abandons euphemism to describe the wonders of the female erection:

> . . . the Nymphs . . . being extended do compress the Penis and speak a delight in the act of Coition. . . . The use of the blood-vessels is to impart Vital Liquor into the substance of the Clitoris, and of the Nerves to impregnate it with a choyce Juyce inspired with animal Spirits (full of Elastick Particles making it Vigorous and Tense). . . . The Glands of the Vagina . . . being heated in Coition, do throw off the rarified fermented serous Liquor, through many Meatus into the Cavity of the Vagina, and thereby rendereth its passage very moist and slippery, which is pleasant in Coition. . . . The Hypogastrick Arteries do sport themselves in numerous Ramulets about the sides and other parts of the Vagina, which are so many inlets of blood to make it warm and turgid in the Act of Coition.

Collins's description is an active one: the vagina *speaks, throws,* is *tense* and *vigorous.* He and his contemporaries assumed that young women were even more eager for intercourse than young men. Some of the terms they used to describe the tissues of the female genitalia in action are very informative and exact, although unscientific. The vagina is said to be lined "with tunicles like the petals of a full-blown rose," with "Wrinckle on wrinckle" which "do give delight in Copulations." The vagina was classified as "sensitive enough" which is an exact description. They were aware of the special role of the clitoris, in causing the "sweetness of love" and the "fury of venery."

The notion that healthy and well-adjusted women would have orgasms originating in the vagina was a metaphysical interpolation in the empirical observations of these pioneers. Collins took the clitoris for granted, as a dear part of a beloved organ; he did not underemphasize the role of the vagina in creating pleasure, as we have seen. Unhappily we have accepted, along with the reinstatement of the clitoris after its proscription by the Freudians, a notion of the utter passivity and even irrelevance of the vagina. Love-making has become another male skill, of which women are the judges. The skills that the Wife of Bath used to make her husbands swink, the athletic sphincters of the Tahitian girls who can keep their men inside them all night, are alike unknown

Bodies: The Social Context of Sexuality

to us. All the vulgar linguistic emphasis is placed upon the *poking* element; *fucking, screwing, rooting, shagging* are all acts performed upon the passive female: the names for the penis are all *tool* names. The only genuine intersexual words we have for sex are the obsolete *swive,* and the ambiguous *ball.* Propagandists like Theodore Faithfull (and me) are trying to alter the emphasis of the current imagery. To a man who had difficulty getting an erection Faithfull wrote:

> If you ignore any idea of erection and concentrate your attention on your girl-friend, ignore the clitoris and use your fingers to caress her internally and if you follow such activity by a close association of your sex organs you may soon find that she can draw your sex organ into her vagina without any need on your part for erection.

This sounds like therapeutic lying, nevertheless serious attempts have been made to increase women's participation in copulation. A. H. Kegel, teaching women how to overcome the bladder weakness that often afflicts women, showed them how to exercise the pubococcygeal muscles and found inadvertently that this increased their sexual enjoyment. What their mates thought of it is not on record. The incontinence resulted from the same suppression of activity that inhibited sexual pleasure; we might find that if we restored women's competence in managing their own musculature many of their pelvic disturbances would cease, and their sexual enjoyment might correspondingly grow. Of course we cannot do this until we find out how the pelvis ought to operate: as long as women cannot operate it, we cannot observe its action, and so the circle perpetuates itself. If the right chain reaction could happen, women might find that the clitoris was more directly involved in intercourse, and could be brought to climax by a less pompous and deliberate way than digital massage. In any case, women will have to accept part of the responsibility for their own and their partners' enjoyment, and this involves a measure of control and conscious cooperation. Part of the battle will be won if they can change their attitude towards sex, and embrace and stimulate the penis instead of *taking* it. Enlightened women have long sung the praises of the female superior position, because they are not weighted down by the heavier male body, and can respond more spontaneously. It is after all a question of communication, and communication is not advanced by the *he talk, me listen* formula.

The banishment of the fantasy of the vaginal orgasm is ultimately a service, but the substitution of the clitoral spasm for genuine gratification may turn out to be a disaster for sexuality. Masters and Johnson's conclusions have produced some unlooked for side-effects, like the veritable clitoromania which infects Mette Eiljersen's book, *I accuse!* While speaking of women's orgasms as resulting from the "right touches on the button," she condemns sexologists who

> recommend ... the stimulation of the clitoris as part of the prelude to intercourse, to that which most men consider to be the "real thing." What is in fact

the "real thing" for them is *completely devoid of sensation* for the woman.

This is the heart of the matter! Concealed for hundreds of years by humble, shy and subservient women.

Not all the women in history have been humble and subservient to such an extent. It is nonsense to say that a woman feels nothing when a man is moving his penis in her vagina: the orgasm is qualitatively different when the vagina can undulate around the penis instead of vacancy. The differentiation between the simple inevitable pleasure of men and the tricky responses of women is not altogether valid. If ejaculation meant release for all men, given the constant manufacture of sperm and the resultant pressure to have intercourse, men could copulate without transport or disappointment with anyone. The process described by the experts, in which man dutifully does the rounds of the erogenous zones, spends an equal amount of time on each nipple, turns his attention to the clitoris (usually too directly), leads through the stages of digital or lingual stimulation and then politely lets himself into the vagina, perhaps waiting until the retraction of the clitoris tells him that he is welcome, is laborious and inhumanly computerized. The implication that there is a statistically ideal fuck which will always result in satisfaction if the right procedures are followed is depressing and misleading. There is no substitute for excitement: not all the massage in the world will insure satisfaction, for it is a matter of psychosexual release. Real satisfaction is not enshrined in a tiny cluster of nerves but in the sexual involvement of the whole person. Women's continued high enjoyment of sex, which continues after orgasm, observed by men with wonder, is not based on the clitoris, which does not respond particularly well to continued stimulus, but in a general sensual response. If we localize female response in the clitoris we impose upon women the same limitation of sex which has stunted the male's response. The male sexual idea of virility without languor or amorousness is profoundly desolating: when the release is expressed in mechanical terms it is sought mechanically. Sex becomes masturbation in the vagina.

Many women who greeted the conclusions of Masters and Johnson with cries of "I told you so!" and "I am normal!" will feel that this criticism is a betrayal. They have discovered sexual pleasure after being denied it but the fact that they have only ever experienced gratification from clitoral stimulation is evidence for my case, because it is the index of the desexualization of the whole body, the substitution of genitality for sexuality. The ideal marriage as measured by the electronic equipment in the Reproductive Biology Research Foundation laboratories is enfeebled—dull sex for dull people. The sexual personality is basically antiauthoritarian. If the system wishes to enforce complete suggestibility in its subjects, it will have to tame sex. Masters and Johnson supplied the blueprint for standard, low-agitation, cool-out monogamy. If women are to avoid this last reduction of their humanity, they must hold out not just for orgasm but for ecstasy.

Bodies: The Social Context of Sexuality   **39**

The organization of sexuality reflects the basic features of the performance principle and its organization of society. Freud emphasizes the aspect of centralization. It is especially operative in the "unification" of the various objects of the partial instincts into one libidinous object of the opposite sex, and in the establishment of genital supremacy. In both cases, the unifying process is repressive—that is to say, the partial instincts do not develop freely into a "higher" stage of gratification which preserved their objectives, but are cut off and reduced to subservient functions. This process achieves the socially necessary desexualization of the body, leaving most of the rest free for use as the instrument of labor. The temporal reduction of the libido is thus supplemented by its spatial reduction.

If women find that the clitoris has become the only site of their pleasure instead of acting as a kind of sexual over-drive in a more general response, they will find themselves dominated by the performance ethic, which would not itself be a regression if the performance principle in our society included enterprise and creativity. But enterprise and creativity are connected with libido which does not survive the civilizing process. Women must struggle to keep alternative possibilities open, at the same time as they struggle to attain the kind of strength that can avail itself of them.

The permissive society has done much to neutralize sexual drives by containing them. Sex for many has become a sorry business, a mechanical release involving neither discovery nor triumph, stressing human isolation more disheartheningly than ever before. The orgies feared by the Puritans have not materialized on every street corner, although more girls permit more (joyless) liberties than they might have done before. Homosexuality in many forms, indeed any kind of sex which can escape the dead hand of the institution— group sex, criminal sex, child-violation, bondage and discipline—has flourished, while simple sexual energy seems to be steadily diffusing and dissipating. This is not because enlightenment is harmful, or because repression is a necessary goad to human impotence, but because sexual enlightenment happened under government subsidy, so that its discoveries were released in bad prose and clinical jargon upon the world. The permit to speak freely of sexuality has resulted only in the setting up of another shibboleth of sexual normality, gorged with dishonesty and kitsch. Women who understand their sexual experience in the way that Jackie Collins writes of it are irretrievably lost to themselves and their lovers:

> He took her to the bedroom and undressed her slowly, he made love to her beautifully. Nothing frantic, nothing rushed. He caressed her body as though there were nothing more important in the world. He took her to the edge of ecstasy and back again, keeping her hovering, sure of every move he made. Her breasts grew under his touch, swelling, becoming even larger and firmer. She floated on a suspended plane, a complete captive to his hands and body. He had amazing control, stopping at just the right moment. When it did happen it was only because he wanted it to, and they came in complete unison. She had never

experienced *that* before, and she clung to him, words tumbling out of her mouth about how much she loved him. Afterwards they lay and smoked and talked. "You're wonderful," he said. "You're a clever woman making me wait until after we were married!"

Miss Collins's heroine is prudish, passive, calculating, selfish and dull, despite her miraculous expanding tits. When her husband grows tired of playing on this sexual instrument she can have no recourse but must continue to loll on her deflated airbed, wondering what went wrong. There is no mention of genitals: everything happens in a swoon or a swamp of undifferentiated sensation. He labors for her pleasure like a eunuch in the harem. Sex is harnessed in the service of counterrevolution.

What Jackie Collins is expressing is the commonest romantic ideal of the perfect fuck. It shows how deeply we believe in the concept of male mastery. Miss Collins's heroine was manipulating her mate's colonizing sexual urge, making him wait, as long as his importunacy lasts, until she is ready. In manipulating his violent impulses she exercised an illusory superiority, for she is tender, sentimental and modest, loving not for her own gratification, but in expression of esteem, trust and true love, until she could civilize him into marriage and the virtuoso sexual performance. The complicated psychic aspect of his love is undervalued; she is still alone, egotistical, without libido to desire him or bring him to new pleasure in her. Jackie Collins and the sex-books show that we still make love to organs and not people: that so far from realizing that people are never more idiosyncratic, never more totally *there* than when they make love, we are never more incommunicative, never more alone.

5. Potency and the Sexual Revolution

MYRON BRENTON

"Today, millions of women, freed by technology from many household tasks, given by technology many 'aids to romance,' have become pioneers, with men, on the frontier of sex. As they become knowing consumers, the anxiety of men lest they fail to satisfy the women also grows—but at the same time this is another test that attracts men who, in their character, want to be judged by others."—DAVID RIESMAN, *The Lonely Crowd.*

"The basic fact is that they're all babies. . . . They just don't seem to have true masculine qualities. They're always and forever deferring *to you. They never make up their own blinking minds about where to eat, where to go, what to do. It drives one dotty. . . . They even ask you, under the most propitious circumstances, if they may kiss you. Fancy a European or an Englishman ever doing that. . . . From all my observations, and those of all the girls I know here, it's the fault of the American woman. She babies him and wears the pants. It's as absurdly simple as that."*—An English secretary working in New York City.

New Light on an Old Standard

The contemporary American male as lover is caught up in a welter of contradictions. The masculine stereotype demands that he be sexually virile and attentive, but he devotes most of his psychic and physical energies to making a success of himself in the breadwinning role. To make love freely and spontaneously, he must acknowledge his sexual partner erotically; yet too often his stereotyped view of her gets in the way of real eroticism. He lives in a society that exposes him to an unceasing array of sexual stimuli, yet severely limits his response to them. He expects to be the dominant figure in the sexual relationship, but the social and sexual patterns he follows tend to make his woman the controlling figure. He enjoys bragging a bit about how much he likes the girls, but many of his attitudes reflect rather more hostility—or at least suspicion—than they do liking. He considers himself a pretty sexy fellow, but in some of his actions he betrays a fear of, and antagonism toward, sex.

The contradictions are either engendered or exacerbated by a phenomenon of the profoundest importance in the sexual relationship between the sexes: the

American male is witness to, and sometimes unwilling participant in, the breakdown of the sexual double standard. As a result, many of his comfortable notions about female sexuality are turning out to be will-o'-the-wisps, and insofar as women are concerned, he faces even greater challenges in the bedroom than in the world outside. Indeed, this is the crux of the sexual revolution so often and so indiscriminately discussed these days—the slow, erratic, anguish-filled, but implacable march of women toward sexual equality and the changes this is bringing about.

The woman's sexual revolution demands adjustments and adaptations on the part of both sexes. However, since the male has always insisted on his freedom and since—in terms of visible trends, at least—the American woman is now insisting on hers, the burden of adjustment and adaptation falls on him. In some ways he likes this new state of affairs. He has more sexual partners available; they participate actively, instead of conforming to a sexual ideal of passivity; in marriage, he and his wife achieve a sexual adjustment much sooner than in the past; the sexual climate is much freer and much more healthy than it was during the Victorian gloom. But in other significant ways the woman's sexual revolution is proving highly disconcerting to him—and to her as well. Equality implies choice of action; choice implies responsibility; responsibility demands perspective. The old ways of the sexual double standard were easier; they were less demanding.

On an intellectual level a majority of better-educated American men may say that sexual equality is fair and just and may nod approvingly over the continuing erosion of the double standard. But when they are faced with this equality on a more starkly personal basis, their reaction often is emphatically unequalitarian. This is to be expected. The American male does not, after all, live isolated from any of the traditional patterns in the relationship between the sexes, and the sexual double standard has been in existence for thousands of years. It has had currency in primitive societies and in highly developed civilizations, in sophisticated centers and in remote parts of the world. It is by far the predominant sexual pattern in the relationship between men and women. In effect, the history of the interaction between men and women almost everywhere in the world and far back into the reaches of time includes overwhelming and sometimes really extraordinary measures on the part of men to dominate or to control the female's sexual behavior or to allow uncontrolled behavior only under conditions socially degrading to her.

It would be a surprise if the contemporary male, having the weight of this pattern on his psychic shoulders and being, moreover, the product of an antisexual Victorian culture, were to feel at ease about the sexual equality of a woman who meant something to him. By and large he's not at ease. Any random conversation on the subject at a cocktail party bears this out, and so do a variety of professional observations.

Scrutinizing adolescent dating patterns in ten Northern high schools, sociologist James S. Coleman found that the double standard still is very much institutionalized there. Another social scientist, Ira L. Reiss, surveyed premarital sexual standards on the college campus and found that most college men still adhere closely to at least some facets of the double standard. Perry J. Gangloff, executive director of the Family Service Bureau of Broome County, New York, made an illuminating comment on the subject of infidelity and the double standard: Wives are apt to accept unfaithfulness in their husbands if they otherwise carry on within their families as usual. Husbands, on the other hand, are much less tolerant; they "tend to bring their unfaithful wives to the agency for counseling, expecting that the agency will persuade the wife to stop her unfaithful behavior."

Curiously, a host of psychiatrists and family service counselors presented me with virtually the same casework material regarding married couples whose wives, as well as husbands, had had premarital sexual experience. During the counseling session it's usually the husband who comments on his wife's premarital affairs, not the other way around. Despite the fact that he brought up the subject in the first place, he's likely to hide his real feelings by assuring the caseworker that he's not at all bothered by his wife's lack of chastity at marriage. He'll also say that it plays no part in their present marital difficulties, although this is clearly not the case. Often he's markedly suspicious of his wife's fidelity to him, even when suspicion isn't in the least warranted.

Such men are in the clinical population, but the apprehensions they unconsciously feel about their wives' premarital and extramarital sexual experience are no different from those overtly voiced by men everywhere for many centuries. Why has the female rarely been entrusted with her own sexuality? A number of plausible answers have been forthcoming. It takes little imagination to realize that the male, being bigger and more muscular than she is and not being encumbered by pregnancy and childbearing, would among preliterate peoples and in the beginnings of civilization establish himself as the dominant —therefore controlling—figure in all aspects of life between the sexes. Having established his superiority over the female, he viewed her as more or less a servant, much as he did his cattle and other effects. He required her to be intact upon acquisition. Afterward, she was to be available for his use only—unless, of course, he wanted to use his prerogative of sharing her with others, as is the case in some cultures.

As for the woman, she really had little choice, not only because she was weaker and needed his superior strength to protect her, but also because she needed protection for her children. In effect, she was trading her freedom for male protection.

As for the offspring themselves, they're another factor often mentioned in any discussion of the double standard, for closely allied to the notion of property is the notion of inheritance. After all, paternity is inferential. Males in patriarchal societies—where inheritance always passes from father to son —had to establish some degree of certainty that the chosen sons were actually their own. This reinforced the proscription against extramarital sexual activity for wives. Still another reason advanced for the establishment of the sexual double standard is that unbridled sex for everyone in the community would lead to so much rivalry and jealousy as to threaten the community's very existence, and it has always proved easier to control the sexual desire of women than that of men.

These are reasonable explanations for the formation of the sexual double standard, and all may have played a part in it. Yet it's difficult to believe that repressive measures of the kind directed against women, so sharply focused on her sexual behavior and so consistently applied for so many centuries, do not, in addition, have a more fundamental reason behind them—a reason perhaps buried in the unconscious mind of the male. Analyzing primitive man's virginity taboos, Freud wrote: "Where primitive man instituted a taboo, there he fears a danger; and it cannot be disputed that the general principle underlying all these regulations and avoidances is a dread of women." Analyzing the meaning of feminine purity, a favorite double-standard concept often used over the past 125 years both as a sop to woman and as a lever to make her conform, psychiatrist Abram Kardiner wrote:

> It connotes either, "You, the woman, shall have no pleasure at all," or "I alone shall give you pleasure," or "I don't care whether you have pleasure or not; you shall give me pleasure and me alone."

Why the dread of woman? Why this obsessive concern about her sexual pleasure? Maybe the puzzle of the sexual double standard and its longevity over these thousands of years take on more clarity if one narrows on one of the elemental and irrevocable biological differences between the sexes—the penis compared with the cunnus. During coitus, his penis puts the male to the test in a unique way—a way the female isn't tested. She can pretend arousal; he must obtain an erection. She can think of totally nonsexual matters and still carry on with the sexual act; he has to be in a specifically erotic frame of mind to sustain erection. She can pretend pleasure; for him, little pretense is possible. If she's so inclined, she can mask failure to reach an orgasm with make-believe; he can't: his sexual success is highly visible, and so—humiliatingly—is his failure. Furthermore, sexual functioning can occur without her active participation; it cannot without his. Upon reaching an orgasm, she doesn't ejaculate; that he loses semen (unconsciously equated with strength) is a very obvious matter. In his case a multiple orgasm is a relatively rare phenomenon; in hers, not at all. He's subject to detumescence, the loss of sexual capacity, very soon after reaching an orgasm; she can, if she wishes, simply keep on going. This leads to an age-old fear in man that she can't be satisfied and either drains him dry or turns to other men, once thoroughly awakened. The sum of these differences in male and female sexuality has, it would seem, given men a tendency to anxiety in relation to the female.

This anxiety comes sharply into focus when we take into account the two diametrically opposed—yet strikingly similar—viewpoints that men have always held regarding the female sex drive. Most of the time they've taken her to be an insatiable creature, whose power it is to make putty of otherwise grown males—the conclusion being that she had best be kept in check. This held true for the Hebrews, Romans, early Christians, and Arabs. For instance, a study of historical changes in sexual attitudes, *Sex in History,* quotes a little-known passage from Ecclesiastes: "Women are overcome by the spirit of fornication more than men and in their heart they plot against men." The Victorians, however, disregarded the hitherto consistent view of supercharged female sexuality. In that time of great social and economic change, attitudes toward sex underwent a profound alteration: Sex went underground. Convention had it that woman's sex drive was far weaker than man's, if it existed at all, and that decent women neither enjoyed sexual intercourse nor were aroused by it. Actually, when one follows the two historical trains of thought about female sexuality to their logical conclusions, they wind up at the same safe spot. If woman is insatiable, she can't be satisfied; if woman is unmoved by sex—well, then she can't be satisfied. Either way the male is, sexually speaking, off the hook.

That the sexual double standard is—at least in part—based on the male's anxiety about the unique sexual testing process to which he's subject doesn't mean the female isn't also put to a sexual test. At the very minimum she has to draw the male's interest, if not actually make a bold attempt to excite him sexually. She must, as one psychoanalyst picturesquely explained, "find ways of making this place of hers attractive for the man." The testing she's subjected to clearly engenders its own anxieties. But men have generally recognized the fact that the greater responsibility for, and greater proof of, sexual readiness is theirs. And they have interpreted this biological fact as a challenge, a trial of manliness.

It's precisely at this point, the point at which the male's copulatory ability becomes tied up with his notions about himself as a man, that concern about his potency begins. A vigorously competitive society in which particular emphasis is placed not on how well a person does, but on how well he or she does in relation to others, intensifies these associations between sex and male pride and increases the resultant anxiety. The male is forced to keep comparing his performance with that of other men. The American boy of seventeen who still hasn't toted up his first sexual experience feels much less self-assured than his more experienced classmates, feels that there must be something wrong with him. So does the married man twice his age who is perfectly content with the quantity and quality of sex he and his wife have had until he learns of another man's having twice that amount of sex. Prompted by his newly crystallized anxieties, he may go to his doctor and seek drugs to increase his potency. This kind of request is hardly uncommon in physicians' offices these days. When the first two Kinsey volumes on sexual behavior were publsihed, some social scientists kept exclaiming in surprise over the fact that the books were so popular with the general public despite their profusion of dry statistical data and tables. It was precisely this data that was so fascinating—and potentially anxiety-provoking—for one could compare one's own scores against the tables and come away with a sexual rating of sorts.

In the sexual revolution of the twentieth century, women are beginning to emerge victoriously from the sad, twisted anti-sexualism of the Victorian era to affirm the force and equality of their sex drives. For many a beleaguered American male the growing emergence of the sexually emancipated woman is more than a profound threat; it's a definite distortion of the natural order of things. Yet nature doesn't bear him out as he would like it to. Although the female sex drive isn't as constant as the man's and although it's more easily inhibited, once it has the freedom to express itself and is awakened, it proves fully as strong as the man's—if not stronger than his. The female animal in heat expresses her sexuality with unmistakable vigor, and in the few cultures where women are allowed full sexual freedom, they are as sexually inclined and as initiating as the men.

Yet, in a curious way, the beleaguered male is perfectly correct. A distortion does exist—because sexual equality, as it's shaping up in America, is no equality at all. Not when the pendulum has swung all the way 'round, and as with the ancient Hebrews, Romans, early Christians, and Arabs, the contemporary male's plaint, increasingly heard these days, is that his female counterpart is sexually far too grasping, greedy, and aggressive.

The Modern Woman's Demand for Sexual Pleasure

What is working the most fundamental change in the sexual relationship between the sexes—what is making the greatest impact on the male and giving vent to accusations of sexual aggressiveness—is the fact that the vast majority of American women now want the sex act to be pleasurable for themselves, as well as for the men.

This expectation holds true for virgins and nonvirgins alike, for women in every age group and all social classes. It is the inevitable result of the wedding between the feminist movement and the libido and sexual repression theories of Freud, and it is given further impetus by the commercialization of sex. The image of the plodding, unimaginative, selfish husband who rolls on a wife more dutiful than responsive for a quick act of sex—and who then rolls over and falls asleep, sexually sated, while she tosses and turns for a long time—is an enduring one in American sexual folklore. But it's obsolete in spirit—although not, of course, in fact. Women know that there's sexual pleasure to be had for the female of the species, and they hope to get—or, increasingly, insist on getting—it for themselves. It's to be expected that the middle- and upper-middle-class women, the ones most exposed to—and the most sophisticated about—the sexual revolution, would emphasize their own sexuality. But so pervasive has the woman's-right-to-sexual-pleasure movement become that it's being emphasized in blue-collar reading material as well. More and more sin-suffer-and-repent stories in the confession magazines, mostly read by women from a low-income group, accent what one confession-magazine editor described to me as "the thrills sex gives women" and sex scenes emphasizing women's "rapturous response." Articles in these magazines also reflect concern for women's sexual pleasure; they deal with frigidity, impotence, wedding-night problems, and the like. In her *Blue-Collar Marriage,* Dr. Mirra Komarovsky notes that most wives "think that men are more highly sexed than women," but even though it's sometimes communicated indirectly "there is no mistaking their feeling that ideally wives should also experience sexual enjoyment."

The recognition that the woman, too, has the right to pleasurable sex is a rewarding one for men. It means that their partners are more responsive than they were before. It means the freedom to experiment in the conjugal bedroom with the less conventional forms of sex, rather than to look to the bordello (as the Victorian men did) for sexual spice and variety. But the positive side of the picture is marred by the new responsibilities the male faces and the new image of womanhood he must get used to. For many men it's a difficult adjustment. They discover that women's sexual freedom means not only the right to respond but also the right to initiate. And more girls are becoming less shy about initiating, less veiled about their desires, than they were before.

To a man whose yardstick is the traditional, somewhat inhibited girl who, even if she is experienced, always waits for the male to be the clear-cut, direct initiator and aggressor—that is to say, if he's like most males—the girl who is candid about her own sex desires appears sexually menacing, rather than sexually exciting. Drs. Phyllis and Eberhard Kronhausen, conducting a sex study of American college men, noticed that a number of them gained their initial experience with older women but that some were so taken aback by the spectacle of a female frankly wanting sex that they rejected the invitation. The same thing occurred on the campuses themselves when a girl made her sexual interest in a boy too plain for (his) comfort.

The Kronhausen assessment was made in 1960. Four years later, author Gael Greene, doing a study of sex and the college girl, found the situation unchanged. Conceding that "a girl's perception will, of course, be distorted by her own fears and prejudices," Miss Greene had to admit, upon taking stock of the current campus scene:

> One of the most striking characteristics of sex on the campus in the sixties is the widening gap between the conservatism of the college boy and the increasing sophistication of the coed. It plagues the girls. It threatens and paralyzes the boys.

At least some of the boys evade the issue in much the same way that their adult counterparts do—by concentrating on outside achievement for confirmation of masculine identity. In 1963, at a time when there was a great deal of furor about campus sex, a large northeastern all-male university considered liberalizing its rules regarding visiting rights. The powers-that-be consulted one of the professors, asking him whether, in his opinion, such liberalization would result in orgies. He told me that he had replied, "Orgies? A lot of these students don't even know how to hold hands, they're so focused on intellectual activities!"

But the campus is only a segment of America, after all, and the American woman's growing reputation as a sexual aggressor springs only partly from what goes on behind the walls of ivy. It's a reputation confined—so far— mostly to the middle class, and it bids fair to supplant the American woman's earlier reputation for Momism—that is, in the late 1940's she was reputed to devour her sons emotionally; in the mid-1960's, to devour her menfolk sexually.

There *is* a parallel. Most of the more virulent critics of the domineering Mom barely mentioned the man she was married to; he wasn't even important enough to criticize, although his passivity was partly responsible for her ravaging her sons emotionally. Similarly, the critics of the sexually emancipated woman of the 1960's find plenty to say about her supposed rapacity, but for the most part they refrain from placing the problem in a wider framework that encompasses both sexes. When psychoanalyst Theodor Reik tells a *Playboy* panel that he's astonished by the way "women, more and more, are taking over the active roles in sex, which was not so before," he prophesies that the men are finally going to resent it, but it behooves us to at least wonder whether *any* activity on the part of the sex with the supposedly lesser sex drive would unnerve some men and whether the women are becoming increasingly active because the men are becoming increasingly inactive. When author-raconteur Alexander King tells the same panel that sexual equality has gone too far, "so that women are sitting like district attorneys to see what the man can or cannot perform," and adds that this has put men tremendously on the defensive, we're entitled to question this assumption that the sexually emancipated woman has run wild with her newfound power and to ask whether the entire patterning of male-female relationships today actually forces women into a dominant position sexually.

We can certainly infer that a sexual vacuum of sorts is being created and that the patterning isn't at all conducive to sexual equality by considering the change in the nature of sexual complaints over a period of several decades. This qualitative change has been tremendous, and a number of the authorities with whom I discussed the American male had something to say about it. A quarter of a century ago the typical female patient complained that she didn't like sex and couldn't achieve sexual satisfaction. The typical male patient complained of premature ejaculation or outright impotence. Both sexes were somewhat in the same plight: they wanted sex but couldn't have it. Today, increasingly, the women are saying, "My husband doesn't try hard enough. He doesn't want it often enough." And the men are saying, "What can I do with this woman? She's so demanding. Why doesn't she let me alone?" Dr. Ralph Greenson's conclusion is that men "seem to have become more security-minded, rather than pleasure-minded."

One of the recurrent themes the experts I interviewed voiced time and again was the reluctance (or inability) of many American husbands to accept any sexual condition other than male control and male supremacy. They function perfectly well within the limits defined by the sexual stereotypes of masculinity and femininity. But if their wives, perhaps carried away during a moment of passion, take some of the sexual initiative, they become offended. For such men, too, any coital position that places the woman symbolically or actually in the dominant position is anathema. Voicing her dilemma in the face of such male sensitivity, one middle-class wife among my interviewees said, "I want to please my husband. I want to make him feel comfortable. But sometimes I feel like I'm having to walk on eggshells."

In point of fact, clinicians are finding that in a number of their cases involving frigid women the problem is by no means all it seems to be on the surface. It's not a simple matter of a sexually inhibited woman frustrating her sexually eager husband, although both partners may see it that way. The clinicians are discovering that in these particular cases the woman certainly has her own problems, but so does the man. Without realizing it, he gives her to understand—either consciously or unconsciously—that he would be terribly threatened were she to respond freely to his ardor. A psychiatrist in New York City told me of one frigid female patient who articulated this feeling beautifully after she had been in therapy for a number of months. She said, "You know, I don't trust my husband. I'm afraid to let myself go. If I did, I really don't think he could take it." To judge from my interviews, many American wives are secretly afraid—justifiably or not—that their husbands can't take it.

A Quest for the Sexual Ideal

Does the foregoing mean that a man can't function adequately and give his sexual partner pleasure under a system of sexual equalitarianism? This is the opinion of a number of observers, who view with dismay the unfortunate consequences of equalitarianism to date. The authors of a study of esoteric Eastern and African sexual practices summed up this pessimistic viewpoint that either men or women must dominate—that equality is impossible:

> Feminine equality may only be achieved by masculine abdication and at the price of masculine subjugation. The sexual consequences of the subjugation by the "equal" female are well defined and have often been described: the male, in varying ways and degrees, is "unmanned." It would seem that a great many men, and quite likely the majority of men, are able to function at peak level sexually only with women who are submissive and who willingly accept, or skillfully pretend to accept, the domination of the male.

The trends developing in the United States and beginning to develop in Europe would seem to bear this out. Yet it is a degrading portrait that is painted—that of a male so weak that he can only function adequately at the price of female inferiority—and it overlooks one very important factor. *There must be congruity between role expectation and the preparation for the role.* It's perfectly reasonable to expect a man and woman to engage in vigorous, mutually satisfying sex and to do so under conditions of equality—provided that circumstances are congenial to this expectation. Some couples do enjoy precisely this kind of sex life within an equalitarian setting. Many do not, however, because the conditions are not at all conducive to it.

There are a number of reasons to explain this. Although they certainly don't apply equally to every man, in the aggregate they account for the difficulties the male has in coping with the sexual revolution.

The Old Stereotypes—The American male has to keep adjusting his stereotyped images of what a woman is and isn't with the realities he comes face to face with in everyday life. In effect, the more beleaguered he feels himself in the nonsexual aspects of his relationships with women, the less chance he has of being the relaxed self-assured lover he's expected to be. He has to adjust, for instance, to the fact that in early childhood he's taught girls need to be protected—and that later he finds them competing scholastically with him for grades, achievements, and the like. He's taught that women are the more virtuous sex, and he can't help feeling a bit shocked whenever they turn out otherwise. He's taught that certain tasks are masculine and women show no talent for them, then feels threatened when he meets women who do. He's taught that women are "naturally" homemakers and mothers, and he finds it incomprehensible that there's a growing problem centering on women who find little fulfillment in being exclusively housewives and mothers. He's taught that his primary function—earning a living—is what makes the world go round, then finds out the "little woman" thinks her problems are equal in importance to his.

In short, he has to grapple with the fact that women are refusing to conform to the stereotypes. Since his masculine identity is at least partly based on the validity of these stereotypes—since he confirms his maleness at least as much by what women *aren't* as by what men *are*—the whole thing is apt to have a fairly unsettling effect on him.

Antagonism Toward Women—Nor does it help in his role as lover if, when he was a youngster, his parents poured on the pressure to make sure he was acting in a properly masculine fashion. The greater the emphasis on masculinity, the greater the likelihood that the child will develop an unconscious antagonism toward anything resembling feminity—including women themselves. A man who has learned to be defensive about things female is hardly apt to be relaxed and confident about females in a sexual situation.

Early dating, one of the ways boys are supposed to show their budding masculinity these days, is a case in point. The boy whose mother and whose peer group pushes him into a parody of adolescent dating when he's only nine, ten, or eleven, before he really has an inclination to date, is put into a precarious position. According to Oscar Rabinowitz, the practice sets up a distorted basis for future heterosexual relationships. The preadolescent who dates because he's supposed to, because this is the way a man should behave, will still be dating for this reason when he's twenty-five. Frequently, when he takes out girls, such a man's attitude is: "What can I get out of her?"

Bodies: The Social Context of Sexuality

51

Defensiveness about and antagonism toward women are developed in boys who grow up in households in which the mother is clearly the dominant figure and the father is passive in the areas of influence having to do with home and family. According to Dr. Josselyn:

> However he may conceive of the important role of the father figure out of the home, that is of minor significance to him during childhood as long as the father is so relatively unimportant in the home. As a boy, he cannot feel adequate if he accepts an anemic image of himself as an imitation of the powerful mother figure. Rather he prefers to make a noise as if it were the man that is powerful in spite of the fact that to him, in childhood, reality would imply that the woman is the real power.

So he repeats the pattern he was exposed to as a child, seeking to become active and important outside the family unit and remaining relatively passive in it. It shouldn't be assumed, however, that a passive man is simply and uncomplicatedly a meek, unaggressive individual. He may be timid, yes, but Caspar Milquetoast often has some unexpected dimensions. Underneath the surface meekness lives an angry man, a man resentful of what women (in effect, his mother) have done to him. His hostile aggression is negative, circuitous: He provokes his wife into dominating him; he uses adroit ways of stalling her when she wants him to do something around the house; he becomes very efficient in the use of "Yes, dear," without really listening to her at all; he makes fun of her in public, slyly hitting her in the weak spots. Nor should it be assumed that the passive man is necessarily sexually inactive. His wife or girl friend is likely to take the initiative most of the time—in effect, to lead him to bed. When he has a mistress, he's apt to be even more dependent on her than on his wife. But as long as he doesn't feel threatened, he can maintain an erection, functioning fairly adequately in sex. Of course, he feels threatened more readily than more assertive men do. And if his dependency on his wife becomes too great, he's apt to see her more as mother than as wife and, consequently, fail to be aroused by her. Impotence is one means a passive man has of showing indirect aggression. "Every time you see one of these impotence cases clinically," says research associate Jay Haley, "you find that although the man expresses great distress about his misfortune, he also finds a little pleasure in it. He has a way of really hooking his wife; she can't get a response from him, can't get an erection from him."

The Idealized Mother—The mother who's both powerful in the home and greatly idealized—the female head of the patriarchal household—presents even greater danger to her son from the standpoint of his potency than his wife does. It might actually be said that the more a man has been taught to idealize his mother, to invest her extravagantly with concepts of purity and goodness, to focus on her very narrowly as a maternal-housewife figure in the typical double-standard way, the less likelihood there is that he'll be an adequate lover with his wife, especially when she herself becomes a mother. In his mind there occurs a confusion that has its roots in the incest taboo; mother and wife become in a sense merged in his mind. For him, more than for most men, the world is divided into good women and bad, virgins and nonvirgins, women who engage in sexual intercourse primarily for procreation and women who engage in it for pleasure. The good woman for such a man resembles his mother (and possibly his sister); he marries her, but since he concentrates so much on her housewife and mother roles, it's extremely difficult for him to view her in a sexual way as well. For sex (which he considers dirty) he's drawn to the "bad" woman—the one so unlike his mother that there's no chance his incest fears will be activated.

Double-Standard Dating—The fact that all statistics show the sexual double standard to be breaking down steadily shouldn't obscure two important facts: (1) The bulk of the population still adheres to double-standard attitudes, particularly when it comes to premarital and extramarital sex, and (2) no matter how many girls engage in sex before marriage or even do so at increasingly younger ages, most start out dating on a double-standard basis. The issue to be taken up here is not the familiar one of chasity versus sexual liberalism, but the relationship hazards that present themselves when the two sexes have such divergent aims and attitudes as the double standard imposes on them.

For one thing, girls still, much more than boys, are imbued with guilt feelings about sex. If these guilt feelings prompt a girl to repress her sexual urges, it may take her many years of living with her husband and growing secure enough as a person before she can shed her inhibitions, before she can feel herself free enough really to enjoy sex relations. By then her husband may very well be preoccupied with his work, devoting the major portion of his energy and attention to it, and far less interested in sex than his newly awakened wife is. Here, then, is another factor to account for the contemporary American woman's growing reputation as a sexual aggressor. Unlike her counterpart in Victorian times, not only does she shed her inhibitions and learn to enjoy sex, but she also learns that it's her right to expect and demand it.

Strong guilt feelings don't necessarily keep a girl from engaging in coitus before marriage, of course. Even so, these guilt feelings can work their destructive magic after the wedding day. Clinicians often see women who insist that they enjoyed sex before marriage but find it dull and themselves unresponsive once they marry. One frequent reason is that what such a woman really enjoyed during her single status wasn't sex itself but its forbidden-fruits aspect.

Again, it's still girls, much more than boys, who are saturated with notions of illusory romance, who are encouraged to make marriage their primary goal in life and to seek in family life the justification for their being, who are taught that sex is an expression of love. A number of studies of adolescents show that until they go steady or become engaged, most girls don't enjoy necking or petting as much as they pretend to their boyfriends. Their overriding concern is: "How far shall I let him go?" The result is that responsibility for the extent of a couple's sexual intimacies rests primarily or exclusively with the girl, while the boy's responsibilities are largely confined to his own needs and desires. It also means that this dichotomy creates a tendency in many girls—consciously or unconsciously, maybe with a little subtle assist from mother—to use sex as a manipulative device to get the boy to the altar. As for the boys, it creates a tendency to pretend love and a desire for marriage in order to get the girl to have sex. And, once marriage has taken place, sex is apt to mean something quite different for the husband and the wife; for instance, he may see it more in physical terms while she views it more as a demonstration of love.

It has often been said that the American dating pattern is a kind of sexual ritual: the boy tries to get all he can; the girl puts her budding femininity to work, keeping his sexual interest high and his sexual accomplishments low. It isn't as grim as it seems in cold print, of course. More often than not, the ritual is carried out with the softening effects of humor. Moreover, the girl would be slightly insulted if he didn't try, while the boy might just possibly be a bit relieved if she stopped him—depending on how far along they were in their relationship—at the point of kissing, necking, or petting. Sociologist James S. Coleman has pointed out that the girl uses the hint of sex to gain dates and to "keep the boy partly at her bidding." Sex is a currency, which she uses to exercise some kind of control over him; thus, when she's too free with her favors, she debases the currency. As for the boy, it's just the opposite: the more currency he accumulates, or the more sexual conquests he makes, the more status he gains as a manly figure. Although the girl has the primary responsibility for deciding how far they will go sexually, the boy is apt to use her need for dates as a lever. According to a study on teen-agers made by Grace and Fred Hechinger, dating has become a "social 'must,' the expected way of teenage life," and popularity is "the big prize and an obsession." So the boys are in an excellent position to dictate some of the terms; girls say it's not uncommon for them to be warned that if they don't pet on the second or third date, they will be dropped.

Boys and girls need to test themselves against each other in their growing-up years, but the very divergent attitudes created or reinforced by the double standard make sex far too much a manipulative, exploitative, competitive tool. It's not surprising, then, that often, later on, sex is used as a controlling or competitive device by marital partners who have not matured and in whom these patterns remain ingrained. There is, for instance, the common example of the wife who wheedles a favor or a present out of her husband by the artful use of sexual denial or sexual promise. There is the example of the wife who uses sex systematically as a way of doling out rewards and punishments: if "Hubby" has been a good boy in her eyes, he can have it; if not, he'll just have to do without until he behaves himself. There is the example of the husband who remains faithful to his wife just so long as he doesn't feel threatened, but when he faces trouble, maybe on the job, he finds another woman to sleep with because a sexual conquest boosts his sagging ego. And there is the example of the husband who absolutely insists on having sex with his wife when he feels that she has paid too much attention to another man at a party or has otherwise made him feel insecure, and he must prove his dominance over her.

These examples could go on indefinitely; the irony is that whenever sex is consistently used in an exploitative of competitive manner—as a weapon—it's less sexy. The erotic element is diluted, and eventually there's likely to occur some impairment of sexual functioning. This may mean impotence, curtailment of sexual interest, compulsive sexuality, or simply a mechanized, joyless coupling that leaves one somehow unfulfilled.

The Sex Bombardment—The ceaseless emphasis on and the commercialization of sex—via the mass media, songs, dances, advertising, and even the social sciences—are a powerful force in intensifying the competitive aspects of sex and are destructive in other ways as well. This sex-obsession feature of contemporary American culture is frequently attacked on humanistic and moralistic grounds—*i.e.,* it leads to sexual depersonalization and has unpleasantly voyeuristic connotations. Actually, the obsession with matters sexual is a perfectly understandable phenomenon. Since one extreme reaction usually invites another, the Victorian denial of sex and the current compulsive affirmation of it are simply two sides of the same well-worn coin. If any proof is needed that the American psyche is still imbued with a heavy dose of fear and guilt about sex, this compulsive need to affirm it—to show ourselves "liberated"—is sufficient evidence. Contemporary America is no more sexually liberated than the Don Juan who has to sleep with every woman crossing his path or the self-styled pornography policeman who sees hard-core smut wherever he turns. Parenthetically but not insignificantly, despite all the so-called sexual freedom, there's still no realistic, comprehensive sex-education program for young people in the nation's schools.

The constant preoccupation with sex does more than demonstrate how much fear and guilt still surround it. In another ironic turn, the very preoccupation has a decidedly negative effect on having a good time in bed, quite apart from the possibly castrating effects of the fear-guilt syndrome itself. I use the phrase "having a good time in bed" advisedly. The remarkable increase in leisure time has given rise to the fun approach to life and to a number of studies and surveys which show that Puritanical impulses still cause Americans to transform fun into work. Nowhere is this more evident than in sex. We're told, over and over again, in a truly remarkable multiplicity of approaches by the mass media, professional sexologists, and even some members of the clergy, that sex should be fun. Indeed, sex *should* be fun, among other things. More to the point, it should be a joyful, lusty act performed in fun—that is, performed at least somewhat spontaneously. Spontaneity, one might say, is the life-blood of the libido. The less spontaneous a male is allowed to be, the less potent he *can* be. If his sexual expression is severely over-regularized, his ability to function sexually may easily disappear altogether. In somewhat different form this is also true of a woman; she *can* have sex all the time, of course, since she need not produce an erection, but the more inhibitory rules and regulations are woven around her sexuality, the less able she is to reach orgasm or, for that matter, to enjoy the sex act in any sense.

But the incessant barrage of sexual symbolism that emanates from books, magazines, television, motion pictures, radio, and newspapers destroys real spontaneity. All of it is a cornucopia of sexual stimuli, a never-ending reminder that sex is fun, fun is sex, sex is for people, people ought to be sexy, sex will make you free. Yet the very constancy and the never-endingness of it rob sexuality of freedom. In effect, both sexes are brainwashed. The female is obliged to walk around in a perpetual state of half expectancy (only "half" because the double standard still exerts its inhibitory influence); the male is obliged to walk around with a perpetual psychic erection. And he does this under the most erotically depressing conditions. He's continually reminded that he has to measure up to a certain norm of attractiveness if he's to wind up with the prettiest girl, for not winding up with her constitutes a failure of masculinity on his part. One might say, on reflection, that he's not so much kept in a state of psychic erection as in a state of fear that he doesn't have what it takes sexually, that the girl isn't pretty enough, that the erection won't be adequate, that other men are more virile than he is, or that, way down somewhere in the nether regions of his self, may lurk a homosexual.

Exploiting Male Anxieties—David Riesman has pointed out that college men these days are much more fearful of possibly being homosexual than they were in earlier generations; actually, this fear is pervasive in the middle class generally. The many homosexual jokes that keep making the rounds, each one accompanied by peals of laughter at once uneasy and relieved, are one indication. The continual speculations that are made about classmates or co-workers who don't exude 100 percent Grade A virility—*Is he or isn't he?*—are another. Some men find themselves subtly motivated to marry in order to prove their heterosexuality or are pressured to do so by their employers. While researching a study on the erosion of privacy in the United States, I came across numerous instances in which corporate pressure was quietly put on bright—but single —young men to marry. The reason the employers usually gave was that married men are "more stable." Stability, in this sense, means there's less likelihood of married employees being homosexuals.

The advertisers have not overlooked the sales possibilities in male anxiety, thereby expanding both sales and anxiety. As Philip Wylie noted a considerable time ago, all the fashion and cosmetic advertisements directed at the yearning female seduce her with the simple, unmistakable message "Madam, are you a good lay?" It was only a matter of time, obviously, until the manufacturers and advertisers woke up to the fact that feelings of sexual inadequacy know no sex. Thus, the message from Madison Avenue is now: "Mister, can you lay 'em good?" And, increasingly, the advertisers play on that other deep-seated fear of the American male: "Mister, sure you're not a homosexual?" In a stroke of genius, this anxiety is being manipulated to excellent effect in an area where it might be least expected to—the male cosmetics industry. The secret of this particular success seems to lie in a reverse twist: any connotation of effeminacy on the part of the consumer is ingeniously avoided by presenting the product as so "gutsy" that only a real man would dare use it.

For example, an ad for Fabergé's Brut, a new shaving lotion, ran: "Now comes bold new Brut for men. By Fabergé." And underneath, in the same heavy type, the ad read: "If you have any doubts about yourself, try something else."

Competitive Sex—The competitiveness with which sex is imbued today presents the worst possible condition for real sexual enjoyment, whether in marriage or out of it, whether in a love relationship or not. There's great concern among some social scientists over the increase in the practice commonly referred to as sex-for-sex's-sake—that is, sex had solely within the framework of desire, not of love or affection. But much of what passes for sex (even in so-called love relationships) is really a way of proving something, a way of being competitive, a way of rationalizing fears, a means of controlling, a device used for exploitation, and a technique for not being left out of things, so that it's essentially removed from love, affection, *or* desire. This is really the most extreme dehumanization of sex.

It's by no means uncommon these days, for instance, for people to go to bed with each other not because they really *want* to, not because they really desire each other, but because if they didn't perform sexually, they would somehow be left feeling too vulnerable—too much at the mercy of the internalized voice of anxiety, asking, "Just what is the matter with you? Aren't you like other people? Aren't you normal?" The outer-directed man who wants to be judged by others and is therefore attracted by the test of satisfying a modern sexually knowledgeable woman provides another example. What he's doing is more akin to entering a competitive meet than to engaging in an act meant to be enjoyable, meant to be a physical release and a form of communication. If he loses, defeat is ego-shattering. If he wins—well, under the rules of the game, he's only as good as his last sexual performance.

Even with sexual preoccupation rampant, then, there seems to be lacking a real appreciation for sexual intercourse, a genuine savoring of it. What is tragically absent, despite all the concern about sex-for-sex's-sake, is a true gusto for sex.

The Fifty-Fifty Orgasm—Surely gusto for sex cannot be shown as long as every act of sexual intercourse is expected to send both partners into transports of maddening delight, marriage-manual fashion, with the bells ringing and the flags flying. When the rigidities of the past were shattered and it was recognized that both men and women had the right to sexual pleasure, the feminists and the sexologists did exactly what they might have been expected to. They rushed from one black and white situation to another. They equated the male and female orgasms as though they were exactly alike, demanding that sex become a fifty-fifty proposition—one for you, one for me. In doing so, however, they failed to take into account the facts that there's a tremendous variation in orgasmic response during coitus in women; that the female orgasm—unlike the male one—is a learned, rather than a reflexive, response; that it's subject to hormonal fluctuations; that it's more diffuse and more easily inhibited than the male orgasm; and that women who don't feel under competitive pressure to attain a coital orgasm on every single occasion are apt to feel satisfied (by the closeness with the man that the sexual act engenders) even when they don't make it all the time.

This physiologically unrealistic demand men and women were led to make on themselves and on each other came to be further codified. Thus, it wasn't sufficient to recognize the right of the American female to sexual pleasure—a realistic and admirable ideal flexible enough to allow for a wide range of possibilities, making both the type of pleasure and the means of reaching it an individual matter. Instead, there has come into being a sort of sexual standard which defines female sexual satisfaction solely in terms of the orgasm—not only the orgasm, but the orgasm every time; not only the orgasm every time, but the orgasm attained solely via coitus; not only the orgasm reached every time strictly during coitus itself but an explosive kind of orgasm closely approximating the male's; and not only an explosive orgasm achieved directly as a result of intercourse on every occasion that intercourse takes place, but this selfsame orgasm achieved simultaneously with the man's climax.

Let it be acknowledged at once that the average couple doesn't engage in the sex act fully determined, do or die fashion, to achieve every last item on this strict sexual agenda. Let it be acknowledged, too, that some of the social scientists—seeing too many men intimidated and too many women left frustrated by the frenetic or futile quest for the female orgasm, seeing too many couples less concerned with sex than with technique—now advise a more relaxed and individualistic approach.

"We've looked on sex as a panacea—'get them adjusted sexually'—because we're an inhibited society," one psychotherapist told me. "We've emphasized sex too much in our initial concern for marital adjustment. Hopefully the woman will reach orgasm, but there's no guarantee she will every time she engages in the sex act, and there's no biological urgency for her to." Nevertheless, sexual equalitarianism—with its narrow concentration on the fifty-fifty orgasm—is working a profound and dismaying change in what might be called the sexual self-image of the American male.

The Tyranny of the Female Orgasm—In point of fact, the male's sexual self-image is no longer based on the self. It is based on the response evoked from the sexual partner. Now, there's nothing unusual in the fact that a man takes pride in and joy from having brought his partner to the heights of erotic ecstasy. It has always been thus. Her excitement both feeds his ego and is itself erotically stimulating to him. Therefore, the purveyors of advice on sexual matters from Roman times to ours have told wives to simulate rapture even if they didn't really feel it. The experienced prostitute, wise to the ways that she can enhance her professional reputation, has at hand a whole repertoire of sighs, moans, and little screams, which are, to her thrilled clients, the mirror of their virility. But there's a subtle—if highly significant—difference between gaining ego gratification from the response one is able to evoke in one's sexual partner and basing one's entire sexual self-image on this response. Yet this, in terms of noticeable trends, is what is happening to the American male. More and more, not only does he feel that he must prove himself sexually, but he also bases the sexual test primarily or exclusively on his partner's pleasure and satisfaction. In other words, his sexual success or failure is *dependent* on her. If she figuratively gives him an *A,* he's a real man. Any lesser grade, as measured by her response, leaves him somewhat doubtful of his sexual capabilities.

"Some men begin to wonder if they're sexually potent enough when they don't get the same kind of performance out of their wives that the gamekeeper got out of Constance Chatterley," Dr. Dan W. Dodson commented when we discussed the suburban sexual scene. He added that there's tremendous pressure to make sex the mark of masculinity—and to make it, under the most difficult conditions, what it's idealized as being in the media.

In many cases, of course, the male isn't alone in expecting to elicit such a performance. The woman too measures both her femininity and his masculinity by the degree to which she responds. But even if she has a more relaxed, less mechanistic view of sex and doesn't insist on the orgasm for herself, the male still is apt to be unhappy unless her orgasm occurs to confirm his sexual capabilities. In the Komarovsky study of the blue-collar marriage this came through clearly in the replies of many of the respondents, male and female. For instance, a taxi driver's wife said, "It's no fun for him unless I come across, so I try." And a plumber's wife commented, "You can't enjoy it all the time. . . . He gets all let down when it's blaa."

To be sure, such replies don't indicate pure self-concern on the male's part. Another element is involved, particularly when there's affection or love between the sexual partners. This element is sexual sharing. The man wants his partner to share his enjoyment, wants her to have pleasure for her own sake. But as a result of the tremendous emphasis placed on the female orgasm, it's the lesser motivation. One might say he really isn't being given psychic room to want to share spontaneously. As clinical psychologist Joseph Stein expressed it, "Her orgasm is important to his own feelings of adequacy. He is never quite sure that he is a thrilling lover until her arousal culminates in this climax." As a result, in many cases sexual technique preempts sexual spontaneity and feeling.

It was inevitable, too, for the pendulum to swing from one extreme to the other in this respect: for the American male to make the incredible shift from a Victorian preoccupation exclusively with his own pleasure to a present-day preoccupation with his partner's orgasm. However, this is a self-conscious approach, and if there's anything that reduces sexual adequacy for either sex, it's self-consciousness about it.

A case in point, a common one, concerns the man who concentrates on a variety of techniques to delay orgasm and who does so, not to prolong pleasure, but exclusively on behalf of a very inhibited partner who requires an extremely lengthy buildup before she's able to achieve a coital orgasm. When these delaying tactics develop into a regular and unvarying routine (especially with the same woman) and when, as Dr. Stein put it, "both cater to her inhibited state," then the whole thing eventually becomes a chore and the man impairs "his spontaneous ability to arouse the female and become aroused himself."

Another pattern increasingly seen by clinicians is the reverse of the traditional one in which the husband insists on his sexual rights regardless of his wife's inclinations. Among some middle-class couples it's now the wife who insists on *her* sexual rights irrespective of her husband's mood or feelings. She wrongly takes it for granted that men are always and instantly in the mood to have sex anytime the female is. She makes little or no effort to stimulate him, or she becomes insulted and incensed if her efforts to arouse him don't always succeed. In short, her definition of sexual equality is naïvely literal, and she confuses sexual imperiousness with sexual initiative. She forgets that there can be delicacy in the sexual relationship even between equals. The result, more often than not, is the direct opposite of what she intended: by commanding an erection, she psychologically emasculates the male. Not that the man in question is necessarily blameless. He intensifies the situation by his reluctance to be candid about what is wrong. It's difficult for him to admit that he isn't in a perpetual state of sexual readiness, for to admit this would be to go against the stereotype. to seem less the man.

The male for whom the pressures of the sexual revolution have become too great may be driven into actual impotence. More likely, he severely curtails his sexual activity, explaining he has simply lost interest in sex, a curtailment which may not, however, prevent him from resuming mastubatory practices. Then again, he may turn to brief homosexual encounters, affairs with other women, or visits to call girls.

The Whore in Every Woman—That sex with their wives has become a duty, rather than a pleasure, is seen by the marked change in the reasons that men give for going to prostitutes and call girls. Men once blamed unresponsive wives or wives unwilling to participate in a specific sexual technique. But these are the days of the sexual revolution, and increasingly, the men who require the services of prostitutes say that they have wives who are *too* responsive and demanding. In effect, the pressure of having to please has become too great; the men "cop out." They prefer a one-sided arrangement with themselves on the receiving end. " 'It burns them up not to be lords and masters in their own beds, and so they try to make believe they are in ours,' " a perceptive call girl is quoted as saying in a recent study on prostitution in New York. She observed that her sole task is to make her clients feels good, and that unlike their wives she's not concerned about getting anything but money in return. " 'Take this two-hundred-and-fifty dollar baby comes to see me one or two times a week. Always says he enjoys being with me instead of his wife, because when he's with her he's so busy trying to please her he hardly has time to think about himself.' "

Is the prostitute significant solely in terms of the haven she provides for men who feel cornered by their wives? Or does her attraction for such men—for all men who seek her out—have something more fundamental and general to say about the sexual relationship between men and women? I noticed a curious reaction during my off-the-cuff interviews with men. When the conversation turned to sex and we ruminated on female response during intercourse, many of my interviewees came up with the same insight, which they expressed in almost identical words: "Way down deep, there's a bit of the whore in every woman." Nor is the concept unfamiliar in psychoanalysis. Helen Deutsch, Karl Abrams, Harold Greenwald, and others in the field have indicated the existence of prostitution fantasies in ordinary women. Many psychoanalysts relate these fantasies to the masochistic tendencies supposedly found in all females. However, the men I spoke with—both blue-collar and middle-class —didn't seem to have masochism in mind. The way they spoke made it evident that they were less concerned with female psychology than in projecting their own wishes: They *wanted* women to want to be treated like whores.

Why should they want this? The answer lies in what it is that the whore represents. She represents sex in its primitive sense, untrammeled and un-diluted by feelings of guilt, fear, sentimental love, respect, and competition. In short, she represents pure eroticism: men sleep with her solely for her sexual self. Never mind that in reality most prostitutes are actually frigid with their clients. Never mind that many of the men who patronize call girls and prosti-tutes suffer from sexual disturbances of one kind or another. It's the pros-titute's *image* that counts, and the image the prostitute holds in the public eye is that of a person focused on the erotic in herself and in her clients.

This focus on sheer sexuality—this relinquishing of the self to sex—is surely at the bottom of the woman's wish to be a whore and the man's wish to have her be one. What it shows is this: Even if she's unable to acknowledge it consciously, she wants to feel that her man is aroused by, consumed by, possessed by, and compelled into the sexual act by her sexual desirability and her desire. She wants to feel that it's his sexual love of *her*—uncomplicated by the fact that she's his wife and the mother of his children—that triggers of his dramatic primitive urges. I'm not suggesting that she doesn't also want the man to care for her on an affectional level; of course, she does. At its best, in a mature relationship, sex involves a healthy interchange of feeling, as well as physical passion. But what stimulates her desire is to be desired sexually, as well as soulfully. And she wants to return this earthy sexual love in kind.

As for the man who expresses his belief in the whore in every woman, a parallel situation applies. He's confirming his own deep-down wish to be simply and directly and primitively sexual when he's in the sexual situation. He wants her to be the whore so that he can act with her as unself-consciously as he imagines he acts (or would act) with the genuine prostitute. It's not at all uncommon, when one refers to the sexual revolution, to point out that these days a man can have *with his wife* the varieties of sex he used to have only in a brothel. This is an interesting rephrasing of the old statement about the whore in every woman. But he cannot have these kinds of varieties of sexual experience—at least not with any real sense of fulfillment—unless he and his partner respond primitively to each other.

Bodies: The Social Context of Sexuality   **61**

Furthermore, the emphasis our culture places on explicit sex obscures the fact that an erotic interchange isn't circumscribed by the dimensions of the bedroom. A look, a touch, walking along the street together, or enjoying a meal together—all such acts can evoke a sensuousness, quite satisfying in itself, in two persons free enough within themselves and aware enough of each other to allow such a basic response. The emphasis on sexual intercourse—the close association between sex and masculinity—often causes the American male to forget that sexuality isn't limited to coitus. When I asked the clinicians to tell me what is the chief complaint of wives about their husbands, the most common reply was: "'He doesn't look at me as a woman. He doesn't make me feel like a woman.'" Needless to say, many such wives complain bitterly about their lack of a sex life. But much more than sex is involved when they are sexually ignored. Their main feeling is one of being rejected as women. When the husbands begin to pay them more attention and overtly acknowledge their wives as desirable females, the women themselves often become much less concerned about actually engaging in sexual intercourse. They no longer cast doubts on their husbands' potency or keep badgering them to exhibit it.

Yet a free, spontaneous, primitive sexual response between men and women who look on each other as individuals, rather than as walking stereotypes, is enormously difficult to evoke. We have seen the many factors responsible. Actually, these factors cannot be isolated from one another. So interrelated and interconnected are they that only in their complex, conjoined state do they really make sense. The problems of potency facing the American male in the midst of the sexual revolution aren't sexual problems pure and simple; they involve all aspects of his relationship to himself and to the opposite sex at a time when the patriarchal sources of his masculine identity are seriously weakened or disappearing altogether.

Words

We must remember that the gesture is there only in its relationship to the response, to the attitude. One would not have words unless there were such responses. Language would never have arisen as a set of bare arbitrary terms which were attached to certain stimuli. Words have arisen out of a social interrelationship.

GEORGE HERBERT MEAD

Still, a man hears what he wants to hear, and disregards the rest.

SIMON AND GARFUNKLE

ANGELA: There are at least two aspects of language that I think are important to us here. The first is the social context of language, how language reflects the value system of the group that speaks it. One selection I wanted to use was about variations of language that are used by Blacks in urban areas, the inner cities. But the main point is that speech is modified to suit the needs of the speakers. We could just as well look at linguistic variations based on class differences or geographic differences.

DEMA: I remember you saying once how pancakes are called hotcakes in some parts of the country, griddle cakes in other parts.

ANGELA: Yes, but there are better examples of how people change language to fit their social context; technical or occupational variations, for instance. Strippers and golfers and sociologists all have definite differences in their speech. The other aspect of language I wanted to deal with is the linguistic interaction between just two or three people. The thing that I think is interesting in interpersonal linguistic usage is the variety of interpretations that can be given words by the speaker and the listener. Molly, I remember once you pointed out in class that if someone says "I'm happy," you can only understand him if what *you* think is "happy" and what *he* thinks is "happy" happen to be the same thing.

DEMA: And there's no way of telling if they happen to be the same thing. It's amazing we understand each other at all.

MOLLY: It's like when someone asks you, "What does 'far out' mean?", and you say, "Well, it means the same thing that 'wow' used to mean."

6. "Rapping" in the Black Ghetto

THOMAS KOCHMAN

"Rapping," "shucking," "jiving," "running it down," "gripping," "copping
a plea," "signifying" and "sounding" are all part of the black ghetto idiom and
describe different kinds of talking. Each has its own distinguishing features of
form, style, and function; each is influenced by, and influences, the speaker,
setting, and audience; and each sheds light on the black perspective and the
black condition—on those orienting values and attitudes that will cause a
speaker to speak or perform in his own way within the social context of the
black community.

I was first introduced to black idiom in New York City, and, as a professional linguist interested in dialects, I began to compile a lexicon of such
expressions. My real involvement, however, came in Chicago, while preparing
a course on black idiom at the Center for Inner City studies, the southside
branch of Northeastern Illinois State College.

Here I began to explore the full cultural significance of this kind of verbal
behavior. My students and informants within black Chicago, through their
knowledge of these terms, and their ability to recognize and categorize the
techniques, and to give examples, gave me much reliable data. When I turned
for other or better examples to the literature—such as the writings of Malcolm
X, Robert Conot, and Iceberg Slim—my students and informants were able
to recognize and confirm their authenticity.

While often used to mean ordinary conversation, rapping is distinctively a
fluent and a lively way of talking, always characterized by a high degree of
personal style. To one's own group, rapping may be descriptive of an interesting narration, a colorful rundown of some past event. An example of this kind
of rap is the answer from a Chicago gang member to a youth worker who asked
how his group became organized:

> Now I'm goin tell you how the jive really started. I'm goin to tell you how the
> club got this big. 'Bout 1956 there used to be a time when the Jackson Park show
> was open and the Stony show was open. Sixty-six street, Jeff, Gene, all of 'em,
> little bitty dudes, little bitty . . . Gene wasn't with 'em then. Gene was cribbin
> (living) over here. Jeff, all of 'em, real little bitty dudes, you dig? All of us were
> little.

Sixty-six (the gang on sixty-sixth street), they wouldn't allow us in the Jackson Park show. That was when the parky (?) was headin it. Everybody say, If we want to go to the show, we go! One day, who was it? Carl Robinson. He went up to the show . . . and Jeff fired on him. He came back and all this was swelled up 'bout yay big, you know. He come back over to the hood (neighborhood). He told (name unclear) and them dudes went up there. That was when mostly all the main sixty-six boys was over here like Bett Riley. All of 'em was over here. People that quit gang-bangin (fighting, especially as a group), Marvell Gates, people like that.

They went on up there, John, Roy and Skeeter went in there. And they start humbuggin (fighting) in there. That's how it all started. Sixty-six found out they couldn't beat us, at *that* time. They couldn't *whup* seven-o. Am I right Leroy? You was cribbin over here then. Am I right? We were dynamite! Used to be a time, you ain't have a passport, Man, you couldn't walk through here. And if didn't nobody know you it was worse than that. . . ."

Rapping to a woman is a colorful way of "asking for some pussy." "One needs to throw a lively rap when he is 'putting the make' on a broad." (John Horton, "Time and Cool People," *trans*action, April, 1967.)

According to one informant the woman is usually someone he has just seen or met, looks good, and might be willing to have sexual intercourse with him. My informant says the term would not be descriptive of talk between a couple "who have had a relationship over any length of time." Rapping then, is used at the beginning of a relationship to create a favorable impression and be persuasive at the same time. The man who has the reputation for excelling at this is the pimp, or mack man. Both terms describe a person of considerable status in the street hierarchy, who, by his lively and persuasive rapping ("macking" is also used in this context) has acquired a stable of girls to hustle for him and give him money. For most street men and many teenagers he is the model whom they try to emulate. Thus, within the community you have a pimp walk, pimp style boots and clothes, and perhaps most of all "pimp talk," is a colorful literary example of a telephone rap. One of my informants regards it as extreme, but agrees that it illustrates the language, style and technique of rapping. "Blood" is rapping to an ex-whore named Christine in an effort to trap her into his stable:

Now try to control yourself baby. I'm the tall stud with the dreamy bedroom eyes across the hall in four-twenty. I'm the guy with the pretty towel wrapped around his sexy hips. I got the same hips on now that you X-rayed. Remember that hump of sugar your peepers feasted on?

She said, "Maybe, but you shouldn't call me. I don't want an incident. What do you want? A lady doesn't accept phone calls from strangers."

I said, "A million dollars and a trip to the moon with a bored, trapped, beautiful bitch, you dig? I'm no stranger. I've been popping the elastic on your panties ever since you saw me in the hall. . . ."

Rapping between men and women often is competitive and leads to a lively repartee with the women becoming as adept as the men. An example follows:

BASICS: PEOPLE

A man coming from the bathroom forgot to zip his pants. An unescorted party of women kept watching him and laughing among themselves. The man's friends "hip" (inform) him to what's going on. He approaches one woman—"Hey baby, did you see that big black Cadillac with the full tires? ready to roll in action just for you." She answers—"No mother-fucker, but I saw a little gray Volkswagen with two flat tires." Everybody laughs. His rap was "capped" (Excelled, topped).

When "whupping the game" on a "trick" or "lame" (trying to get goods or services from someone who looks like he can be swindled), rapping is often descriptive of the highly stylized verbal part of the maneuver. In well established "con games" the rap is carefully prepared and used with great skill in directing the course of the transaction. An excellent illustration came from an adept hustler who was playing the "murphy" game on a white trick. The "murphy" game is designed to get the *trick* to give his money to the hustler, who in this instance poses as a "steerer" (one who directs or steers customers to a brothel), to keep the whore from stealing it. The hustler then skips with the money.

Look Buddy, I know a fabulous house not more than two blocks away. Brother you ain't never seen more beautiful, freakier broads than are in that house. One of them, the prettiest one, can do more with a swipe than a monkey can with a banana. She's like a rubber doll; she can take a hundred positions."

At this point the sucker is wild to get to this place of pure joy. He entreats the con player to take him there, not just direct him to it.

The "murphy" player will prat him (pretend rejection) to enhance his desire. He will say, "Man, don't be offended, but Aunt Kate, that runs the house don't have nothing but highclass white men coming to her place. . . . You know, doctors, lawyers, big-shot politicians. You look like a clean-cut white man, but you ain't in that league are you? (Iceberg Slim, *Pimp: The Story of My Life*)

After a few more exchanges of the "murphy" dialogue, "the mark is separated from his scratch."

An analysis of rapping indicates a number of things.

■ For instance, it is revealing that one raps *to* rather than *with* a person supporting the impression that rapping is to be regarded more as a performance than verbal exchange. As with other performances, rapping projects the personality, physical appearance and style of the performer. In each of the examples given, the intrusive "I" of the speaker was instrumental in contributing to the total impression of the rap.

■ The combination of personality and style is usually best when "asking for some pussy." It is less when "whupping the game" on someone or "running something down."

In "asking for some pussy" for example, where personality and style might be projected through non-verbal means: stance, clothing, walking, looking, one can speak of a "silent rap." The woman is won here without the use of words, or rather, with words being implied that would generally accompany the non-verbal components.

■ As a lively way of "running it down" the verbal element consists of personality and style plus information. To someone *reading* my example of the gang member's narration, the impression might be that the information would be more influential in directing the listener's response. The youth worker might be expected to say "So that's how the gang got so big," instead of "Man, that gang member is *bad* (strong, brave)" in which instance he would be responding to the personality and style of the rapper. However, if the reader would *listen* to the gang member on tape or could have been present when the gang member spoke he more likely would have reacted more to personality and style as my informants did.

Remember that in attendance with the youth worker were members of the gang who *already knew* how the gang got started (e.g. "Am I right Leroy? You was cribbin' over here then") and for whom the information itself would have little interest. Their attention was held by the *way* the information was presented.

■ The verbal element in "whupping the game" on someone, in the preceding example, was an integral part of an overall deception in which information and personality-style were skillfully manipulated for the purpose of controlling the "trick's" response. But again, greater weight must be given to personality-style. In the "murphy game" for example, it was this element which got the trick to trust the hustler and leave his money with him for "safe-keeping."

The function of rapping in each of these forms is *expressive*. By this I mean that the speaker raps to project his personality onto the scene or to evoke a generally favorable response. When rapping is used to "ask for some pussy" or to "whup the game" on someone its function is *directive*. By this I mean that rapping becomes an instrument to manipulate and control people to get them to give up or to do something. The difference between rapping to a "fox" (pretty girl) for the purpose of "getting inside her pants" and rapping to a "lame" to get something from him is operational rather than functional. The latter rap contains a concealed motivation where the former does not.

"Shucking," "shucking it," "shucking and jiving," "S-ing" and "J-ing" or just "jiving," are terms that refer to language behavior practiced by the black when confronting "the Man" (the white man, the establishment, or *any* authority figure), and to another form of language behavior practiced by blacks with each other on the peer group level.

In the South, and later in the North, the black man learned that American society had assigned to him a restrictive role and status. Among whites his behavior had to conform to this imposed station and he was constantly reminded to "keep his place." He learned that it was not acceptable in the presence of white people to show feelings of indignation, frustration, discontent, pride, ambition, or desire; that real feelings had to be concealed behind a mask of innocence, ignorance, childishness, obedience, humility and deference. The terms used by the black to describe the role he played before white folks in the South was "tomming" or "jeffing." Failure to accommodate the white Southerner in this respect was almost certain to invite psychological and often physical brutality. A description related by a black psychiatrist, Alvin F. Poussaint, is typical and revealing:

> Once last year as I was leaving my office in Jackson, Miss., with my Negro secretary, a white policeman yelled, "Hey, boy! Come here!" Somewhat bothered, I retorted: "I'm no boy!" He then rushed at me, inflamed, and stood towering over me, snorting "What d'ja say, boy?" Quickly he frisked me and demanded, "What's your name boy?" Frightened, I replied, "Dr. Poussaint. I'm a physician." He angrily chuckled and hissed, "What's your first name, boy?" When I hesitated he assumed a threatening stance and clenched his fists. As my heart palpitated, I muttered in profound humiliation, "Alvin."
>
> He continued his psychological brutality, bellowing, "Alvin, the next time I call you, you come right away, you hear? You hear?" I hesitated. "You hear me, boy?" My voice trembling with helplessness, but *following my instincts of self-preservation,* I murmured, "Yes, sir." *Now fully satisfied that I had performed and acquiesced to my "boy" status,* he dismissed me with, "Now, boy, go on and get out of here or next time we'll take you for a little ride down to the station house! (Alvin F. Poussaint, "A Negro Psychiatrist Explains the Negro Psyche," *The New York Times Magazine,* August 20, 1967), (emphasis mine).

In the northern cities the black encountered authority figures equivalent to Southern "crackers": policemen, judges, probation officers, truant officers, teachers and "Mr. Charlies" (bosses), and soon learned that the way to get by and avoid difficulty was to shuck. Thus, he learned to accommodate "the Man," to use the total orchestration of speech, intonation, gesture and facial expression for the purpose of producing whatever appearance would be acceptable. It was a technique and ability that was developed from fear, a respect for power, and a will to survive. This type of accommodation is exemplified by the Uncle Tom with his "Yes sir, Mr. Charlie," or "Anything you say, Mr. Charlie."

Through accommodation, many blacks became adept at concealing and controlling their emotions and at assuming a variety of postures. They became competent actors. Many developed a keen perception of what affected, motivated, appeased or satisfied the authority figures with whom they came into contact. Shucking became an effective way for many blacks to stay out of trouble, and for others a useful artifice for avoiding arrest or getting out of trouble when apprehended. Shucking it with a judge, for example, would be to feign repentance in the hope of receiving a lighter or suspended sentence. Robert Conot reports an example of shucking in his book, *Rivers of Blood, Years of Darkness:* Joe was found guilty of possession of narcotics. But he did an excellent job of shucking it with the probation officer.

The probation officer interceded for Joe with the judge: "His own attitude toward the present offense appears to be serious and responsible and it is believed that the defendant is an excellent subject for probation."

Some field illustrations of shucking to get out of trouble came from some seventh grade children from an inner-city school in Chicago. The children were asked to talk their way out of a troublesome situation.
■ You are cursing at this old man and your mother comes walking down the stairs. She hears you.
To "talk your way out of this":
"I'd tell her that I was studying a scene in school for a play."
■ What if you were in a store stealing something and the manager caught you?
"I would start stuttering. Then I would say, 'Oh, Oh, I forgot. Here the money is.' "

A literary example of shucking comes from Iceberg Slim's autobiography. Iceberg, a pimp, shucks before "two red-faced Swede rollers (detectives)" who catch him in a motel room with his whore. My italics identify which elements of the passage constitute the shuck.

> I put my shaking hands into the pajama pockets . . . *I hoped I was keeping the fear out of my face. I gave them a wide toothy smile.* They came in and stood in the middle of the room. Their eyes were racing about the room. Stacy was open mouthed in the bed.
> I said, *"Yes gentlemen, what can I do for you?"*
> Lanky said, "We wanta see your I.D."
> I went to the closet and got the phony John Cato Fredrickson I.D. I put it in his palm. I felt cold sweat running down my back. They looked at it, then looked at each other.
> Lanky said, "You are in violation of the law. You signed the motel register improperly. Why didn't you sign your full name? What are you trying to hide? What are you doing here in town? It says here you're a dancer. We don't have a club in town that books entertainers."
> I said, *"Officers, my professional name is Johnny Cato. I've got nothing to hide. My full name had always been too long for the marquees. I've fallen into the habit of using the shorter version.*
> *"My legs went out last year. I don't dance anymore. My wife and I decided to go into business. We are making a tour of this part of the country. We think that in your town we've found the ideal site for a Southern fried chicken shack. My wife has a secret recipe that should make us rich up here."* (Iceberg Slim, *Pimp: The Story of My Life*)

Another example of shucking was related to me by a colleague. A black gang member was coming down the stairway from the club room with seven guns on him and encountered some policemen and detectives coming up the same stairs. If they stopped and frisked him he and others would have been arrested. A paraphrase of his shuck follows: "Man, I gotta get away from up there. There's gonna be some trouble and I don't want no part of it." This shuck worked on the minds of the policemen. It anticipated their questions as to why he was leaving the club room, and why he would be in a hurry. He also gave *them* a reason for wanting to get up to the room fast.

BASICS: PEOPLE

It ought to be mentioned at this point that there was not uniform agreement among my informants in characterizing the above examples as shucking. One informant used shucking only in the sense in which it is used among peers, e.g., bull-shitting, and characterized the above examples as jiving or whupping game. Others however, identified the above examples as shucking, and reserved jiving and whupping game for more offensive maneuvers. In fact, one of the apparent features of shucking is that the posture of the black when acting with members of the establishment be a *defensive* one.

Frederick Douglass, in telling of how he taught himself to read, would challenge a white boy with whom he was playing, by saying that he could write as well as he. Whereupon he would write down all the letters he knew. The white boy would then write down more letters than Douglass did. In this way, Douglass eventually learned all the letters of the alphabet. Some of my informants regarded the example as whupping game. Others regarded it as shucking. The former were perhaps focusing on the manuever rather than the language used. The latter may have felt that any maneuvers designed to learn to read were justifiably defensive. One of my informants said Douglass was "shucking *in order to* whup the game." This latter response seems to be the most revealing. Just as one can rap to whup the game on someone, so one can shuck or jive for the same purpose; that is, assume a guise or posture or perform some action in a certain way that is designed to work on someone's mind to get him to give up something.

"Whupping Game" to Con Whitey

The following examples from Malcolm X illustrate the shucking and jiving in this context though jive is the term used. Today, whupping game might also be the term used to describe the operation. Whites who came at night got a better reception; the several Harlem nightclubs they patronized were geared to entertain and jive (flatter, cajole) the night white crowd to get their money. (Malcolm X, *The Autobiography of Malcolm X*)

The maneuvers involved here are clearly designed to obtain some benefit or advantage.

> Freddie got on the stand and went to work on his own shoes. Brush, liquid polish, brush, paste wax, shine rag, lacquer sole dressing . . . step by step, Freddie showed me what to do.
>
> "But you got to get a whole lot faster. You can't waste time!" Freddie showed me how fast on my own shoes. Then because business was tapering off, he had time to give me a demonstration of how to make the shine rag pop like a firecracker. "Dig the action?" he asked. He did it in slow motion. I got down and tried it on his shoes. I had the principle of it. "Just got to do it, faster," Freddie said. *"It's a jive noise, that's all. Cats tip better, they figure you're knocking yourself out!"* (Malcolm X, *The Autobiography of Malcolm X*)

An eight year old boy whupped the game on me one day this way:

> My colleague and I were sitting in a room listening to a tape. The door to the room was open and outside was a soda machine. Two boys came up in the elevator, stopped at the soda machine, and then came into the room.
>
> "Do you have a dime for two nickels?" Presumably the soda machine would not accept nickels. I took out the change in my pocket, found a dime and gave it to the boy for two nickels.
>
> After accepting the dime, he looked at the change in my hand and asked, "Can I have two cents? I need carfare to get home." I gave him the two cents.

At first I assumed the verbal component of the maneuver was the rather weak, transparently false reason for wanting the two cents. Actually, as was pointed out to me later, the maneuver began with the first question which was designed to get me to show my money. He could then ask me for something that he knew I had, making my refusal more difficult. He apparently felt that the reason need not be more than plausible because the amount he wanted was small. Were the amount larger, he would no doubt have elaborated on the verbal element of the game. The form of the verbal element could be in the direction of rapping or shucking and jiving. If he were to rap the eight-year old might say, "Man, you know a cat needs to have a little bread to keep the girls in line." Were he to shuck and jive he might make the reason for needing the money more compelling, look hungry, etc.

The function of shucking and jiving as it refers to blacks and "the Man" is designed to work on the mind and emotions of the authority figure for the purpose of getting him to feel a certain way or give up something that will be to the other's advantage. Iceberg showed a "toothy smile" which said to the detective, "I'm glad to see you" and "Would I be glad to see you if I had something to hide?" When the maneuvers seem to be *defensive* most of my informants regarded the language behavior as shucking. When the maneuvers were *offensive* my informants tended to regard the behavior as 'whupping the game.'

Also significant is that the first form of shucking described, which developed out of accommodation, is becoming less frequently used today by many blacks, because of a new found self-assertiveness and pride, challenging the system. The willingness on the part of many blacks to accept the psychological and physical brutality and general social consequences of not "keeping one's place" is indicative of the changing self-concept of the black man. Ironically, the shocked reaction of some whites to the present militancy of the black is partly due to the fact that the black was so successful at "putting Whitey on" via shucking in the past. This new attitude can be seen from a conversation I recently had with a shoe shine attendant at O'Hare airport in Chicago.

I was having my shoes shined and the black attendant was using a polishing machine instead of the rag that was generally used in the past. I asked whether the machine made his work any easier. He did not answer me until about ten seconds had passed and then responded in a loud voice that he "never had a job that was easy," that he would give me "one hundred dollars for any *easy* job" I could offer him, that the machine made his job "faster" but not "easier." I was startled at the response because it was so unexpected and I realized that here was a new "breed of cat" who was not going to shuck for a big tip or ingratiate himself with "Whitey" anymore. A few years ago his response probably would have been different.

The contrast between this "shoe-shine" scene and the one illustrated earlier from Malcolm X's autobiography, when "shucking Whitey" was the common practice, is striking.

Shucking, jiving, shucking and jiving, or S-ing and J-ing, when referring to language behavior practiced by blacks, is descriptive of the talk and gestures that are appropriate to "putting someone on" by creating a false impression. The terms seem to cover a range from simply telling a lie, to bullshitting, to subtly playing with someone's mind. An important difference between this form of shucking and that described earlier is that the same talk and gestures that are deceptive to the "the Man" are often transparent to those members of one's own group who are able practitioners at shucking themselves. As Robert Conot has pointed out, "The Negro who often fools the white officer by 'shucking it' is much less likely to be successful with another Negro. . . ." Also, S-ing and J-ing within the group often has play overtones in which the person being "put on" is aware of the attempts being made and goes along with it for enjoyment or in appreciation of the style.

"Running it down" is the term used by speakers in the ghetto when it is their intention to give information, either by explanation, narrative, or giving advice. In the following literary example, Sweet Mac is "running this Edith broad down" to his friends:

> Edith is the "saved" broad who can't marry out of her religion . . . or do anything else out of her religion for that matter, especially what I wanted her to do. A bogue religion, man! So dig, for the last couple weeks I been quoting the Good Book and all that stuff to her; telling her I am now saved myself, you dig. (Woodie King, Jr., "The Game," *Liberator,* August, 1965)

The following citation from Claude Brown uses the term with the additional sense of giving advice:

> If I saw him (Claude's brother) hanging out with cats I knew were weak, who might be using drugs sooner or later, I'd run it down to him.

It seems clear that running it down has simply an informative function, that of telling somebody something that he doesn't already know.

"Gripping" is of fairly recent vintage, used by black high school students in Chicago to refer to the talk and facial expression that accompanies a *partial* loss of face or self-possession, or showing of fear. Its appearance alongside "copping a plea," which refers to a total loss of face, in which one begs one's adversary for mercy, is a significant new perception. In linking it with the street code which acclaims the ability to "look tough and inviolate, fearless, secure, 'cool,' " it suggests that even the slightest weakening of this posture will be held up to ridicule and contempt. There are always contemptuous overtones attached to the use of the term when applied to the others' behavior. One is tempted to link it with the violence and toughness required to survive on the street. The intensity of both seems to be increasing. As one of my informants noted, "Today, you're *lucky* if you end up in the hospital"—that is, are not killed.

Reaction to Fear and Superior Power

Both gripping and copping a plea refer to behavior produced from fear and a respect for superior power. An example of gripping comes from the record *"Street and Gangland Rhythms"* (Band 4 Dumb Boy). Lennie meets Calvin and asks him what happened to his lip. Calvin says that a boy named Pierre hit him for copying off him in school. Lennie, pretending to be Calvin's brother, goes to confront Pierre. Their dialogue follows:

> Lennie: "Hey you! What you hit my little brother for?"
> Pierre: "Did he tell you what happen man?"
> Lennie: "Yeah, he told me what happened."
> Pierre: "But you . . . but you . . . but you should tell your people to teach him to go to school, man." (Pause) I, I know, I know I didn't have a right to hit him."

Pierre, anticipating a fight with Lennie if he continued to justify his hitting of Calvin, tried to avoid it by "gripping" with the last line.

Copping a plea, originally meant "To plead guilty to a lesser charge to save the state the cost of a trial," (with the hope of receiving a lesser or suspended sentence) but is now generally used to mean 'to beg,' 'plead for mercy,' as in the example "Please cop, don't hit me. I give." (*Street and Gangland Rhythms,* Band 1 "Gang Fight"). This change of meaning can be seen from its use by Piri Thomas in *Down These Mean Streets.*

> The night before my hearing, I decided to make a prayer. It had to be on my knees, 'cause if I was gonna cop a plea to God, I couldn't play it cheap.

The function of gripping and copping a plea is obviously to induce pity or to acknowledge the presence of superior strength. In so doing, one evinces noticeable feelings of fear and insecurity which also result in a loss of status among one's peers.

Signifying is the term used to describe the language behavior that, as Abrahams has defined it, attempts to "imply, goad, beg, boast by indirect verbal or gestural means." (Roger D. Abrahams, *Deep Down in the Jungle*)

In Chicago it is also used as a synonym to describe language behavior more generally known as "sounding" elsewhere.

Some excellent examples of signifying as well as of other forms of language behavior come from the well-known "toast" (narrative form) "The Signifying Monkey and the Lion" which was collected by Abrahams from Negro street corner bards in Philadelphia. In the above toast the monkey is trying to get the lion involved in a fight with the elephant:

> Now the lion came through the jungle one peaceful day,
> When the signifying monkey stopped him, and that is what he started to say:
> He said, "Mr. Lion," he said, "A bad-assed mother-fucker down your way,"
> He said, "Yeah! The way he talks about your folks is a certain shame.
> "I even heard him curse when he mentioned your grandmother's name."
> The lion's tail shot back like a forty-four
> When he went down that jungle in all uproar.

Thus the monkey has goaded the lion into a fight with the elephant by "signifying," that is, indicating that the elephant has been "sounding on" (insulting) the lion. When the lion comes back, thoroughly beaten up, the monkey again "signifies" by making fun of the lion:

> . . . lion came back through the jungle more dead than alive,
> When the monkey started some more of that signifying jive.
> He said, "Damn, Mr. Lion, you went through here yesterday, the jungle rung.
> Now you come back today, damn near hung."

The monkey, of course, is delivering this taunt from a safe distance away on the limb of a tree when his foot slips and he falls to the ground, at which point,

> Like a bolt of lightning, a stripe of white heat,
> The lion was on the monkey with all four feet.

In desperation the monkey quickly resorts to "copping a plea":

> The monkey looked up with a tear in his eyes,
> He said, "Please, Mr. Lion, I apologize."

His "plea" however, fails to move the lion to show any mercy so the monkey tries another verbal ruse, "shucking":

> He said, "You lemme get my head out of the sand, ass out the grass, I'll fight you like a natural man."

In this he is more successful as,

> The lion jumped back and squared for a fight.
> The motherfucking monkey jumped clear out of sight.

A safe distance away again, the monkey returns to "signifying":

> He said, "Yeah, you had me down, you had me at last,
> But you left me free, now you can still kiss my ass."

This example illustrates the methods of provocation, goading and taunting artfully practiced by a signifier.

Interestingly, when the *function* of signifying is *directive* the *tactic* employed is *indirection,* i.e., the signifier reports or repeats what someone else has said about the listener; the "report" is couched in plausible language designed to compel belief and arouse feelings of anger and hostility. There is also the implication that if the listener fails to do anything about it—what has to be "done" is usually quite clear—his status will be seriously compromised. Thus the lion is compelled to vindicate the honor of his family by fighting or else leave the impression that he is afraid, and that he is not "king" of the jungle. When used for the purpose of directing action, "signifying" is like "shucking" in also being deceptive and subtle in approach and depending for success on the naivete or gullibility of the person being "put on."

When the function of signifying is to arouse feelings of embarrassment, shame, frustration or futility, to diminish someone's status, the tactic employed is direct in the form of a taunt, as in the example where the monkey is making fun of the lion.

"Sounding" to Relieve Tensions

Sounding is the term which is today most widely known for the game of verbal insult known in the past as "Playing the Dozens," "The Dirty Dozens," or just "The Dozens." Other current names for the game have regional distribution: Signifying or "Sigging" (Chicago), Joning (Washington, D.C.), Screaming (Harrisburg), etc. In Chicago, the term "sounding" would be descriptive of the initial remarks which are designed to sound out the other person to see whether he will play the game. The verbal insult is also subdivided, the term "signifying" applying to insults which are hurled directly at the person and the dozens applying to results hurled at your opponent's family, especially, the mother.

Sounding is often catalyzed by signifying remarks referred to earlier such as "Are you going to let him say that about your mama" to spur an exchange between members of the group. It is begun on a relatively low key and built up by verbal exchanges. The game goes like this:

> One insults a member of another's family; others in the group make disapproving sounds to spur on the coming exchange. The one who has been insulted feels at this point that he must reply with a slur on the protagonist's family which is clever enough to defend his honor (And therefore that of his family). This, of course, leads the other (once again, more due to pressure from the crowd than actual insult) to make further jabs. This can proceed until everyone is bored with

the whole affair, until one hits the other (fairly rare), or until some other subject comes up that interrupts the proceedings (the usual state of affairs). (Roger D. Abrahams, "Playing the Dozens," *Journal of American Folklore,* July-September, 1962)

Mack McCormick describes the dozens as a verbal contest:

in which the players strive to bury one another with vituperation. In the play, the opponent's mother is especially slandered . . . Then, in turn fathers are identified as queer and syphilitic. Sisters are whores, brothers are defective, cousins are "funny" and the opponent is himself diseased. (Mack McCormick, "The Dirty Dozens," book jacket in the record album *The Unexpurgated Folksongs of Men,* Arhoolie Records).

An example of the "game" collected by one of my students goes:

Frank looked up and saw Leroy enter the Outpost. Leroy walked past the room where Quinton, "Nap," "Pretty Black," "Cunny," Richard, Haywood, "Bull" and Reese sat playing cards. As Leroy neared the T.V. room, Frank shouted to him.

Frank: "Hey Leroy, your mama—calling you man."

Leroy turned and walked toward the room where the sound came from. He stood in the door and looked at Frank.

Leroy: "Look motherfuckers, I don't play that shit."

Frank (signifying): "Man, I told you cats 'bout that mama jive" (as if he were concerned about how Leroy felt)

Leroy: "That's all right Frank; you don't have to tell these funky motherfuckers nothing; I'll fuck me up somebody yet."

Frank's face lit up as if he were ready to burst his side laughing. "Cunny" became pissed at Leroy.

"Cunny": "Leroy, you stupid bastard, you let Frank make a fool of you. He said that 'bout your mama."

"Pretty Black": "Aw, fat ass head 'Cunny' shut up."

"Cunny": "Ain't that some shit. This black slick head motor flicker got nerve 'nough to call somebody 'fathead.' Boy, you so black, you sweat Permalube Oil."

This eased the tension of the group as they burst into loud laughter.

"Pretty Black": "What 'chu laughing 'bout 'Nap,' with your funky mouth smelling like dog shit."

Even Leroy laughed at this.

"Nap": "Your mama motherfucker."

"Pretty Black": "Your funky mama too."

"Nap": (strongly) "It takes twelve barrels of water to make a steamboat run; it takes an elephant's dick to make your Grandmammy come; she been elephant fucked, camel fucked and hit side the head with your Grandpappy's nuts."

Reese: "Godorr-damn; go on and rap motherfucker."

Reese began slapping each boy in his hand, giving his positive approval of "Naps" comment. "Pretty Black" in an effort not to be outdone, but directing his verbal play elsewhere stated:

Words   79

"Pretty Black": "Reese, what you laughing 'bout? You so square, you shit bricked shit."
Frank: "Whoooowee!"
Reese (sounded back): "Square huh, what about your nappy ass hair before it was stewed; that shit was so bad till, when you went to bed at night, it would leave your head and go on the corner and meddle."
The boys slapped each other in the hand and cracked up.
"Pretty Black": "On the streets meddling, bet Dinky didn't offer me no pussy and I turned it down."
Frank: "Reese scared of pussy."
"Pretty Black": "Hell yeah; the greasy mother rather fuck old ugly, funky cock Sue Willie than get a piece of ass from a decent broad."
Frank: "Godorr-damn! Not Sue Willie."
"Pretty Black": "yeah ol meat-beating Reese rather screw that cross-eyed, clapsy bitch, who when she cry, tears rip down her ass."
Haywood: "Don't be so mean, Black."
Reese: "Aw shut up, you half-white bastard."
Frank: "Wait man, Haywood ain't gonna hear much more of that half-white shit; he's a brother too."
Reese: "Brother, my black ass; that white ass landlord gotta be this motherfuck-er's paw."
"Cunny": "Man, you better stop foolin with Haywood; he's turning red."
Haywood: "Fuck yall. (as he withdrew from the "sig" game.)
Frank: "Yeah, fuck yall; let's go to the stick hall."
The group left enroute to the billiard hall. (James Maryland, "Signifying at the Outpost," unpublished term paper for the course *Idiom of the Negro Ghettos,* January 1967)

The above example of sounding is an excellent illustration of the "game" as played by 15-17-year-old Negro boys, some of whom have already acquired the verbal skill which for them is often the basis for having a high "rep." Ability with words is apparently as highly valued as physical strength. In the sense that the status of one of the participants in the game is diminished if he has to resort to fighting to answer a verbal attack, verbal ability may be even more highly regarded than physical ability.

The relatively high value placed on verbal ability must be clear to most black boys at early age. Most boys begin their activity in sounding by compiling a repertoire of "one liners." When the game is played the one who has the greatest number of such remarks wins. Here are some examples of "one liners" collected from fifth and sixth grade black boys in Chicago:

Yo mama is so bowlegged, she looks like the bit out of a donut.

Yo mama sent her picture to the lonely hearts club, and they sent it back and said "We ain't that lonely!"

Your family is so poor the rats and roaches eat lunch out.

Your house is so small the roaches walk single file.

I walked in your house and your family was running around the table. I said, "Why you doin that?" Your mama say, "First one drops, we eat."

Real proficiency in the game comes to only a small percentage of those who play it. These players have the special skill in being able to turn around what their opponents have said and attack them with it. Thus, when someone indifferently said "fuck you" to Concho, his retort was immediate and devastating: "Man, you haven't even kissed me yet."

The "best talkers" from this group often become the successful street-corner, barber shop, and pool hall story tellers who deliver the long, rhymed, witty, narrative stories called "toasts." They are, as Roger D. Abrahams has described, the traditional "men of words" and have become on occasion entertainers such as Dick Gregory and Redd Fox, who are virtuosos at repartee, and preachers, whose verbal power has been traditionally esteemed.

The function of the "dozens" or "sounding" is to borrow status from an opponent through an exercise of verbal power. The opponent feels compelled to regain his status by "sounding" back on the speaker or other group member whom he regards as more vulnerable.

The presence of a group seems to be especially important in controlling the game. First of all, one does not "play" with just anyone since the subject matter is concerned with things that in reality one is quite sensitive about. It is precisely *because* "Pretty Black" has a "black slick head" that makes him vulnerable to "Cunny's" barb, especially now when the Afro-American "natural" hair style is in vogue. Without the control of the group "sounding" will frequently lead to a fight. This was illustrated by a tragic epilogue concerning Haywood, when Haywood was being "sounded" on in the presence of two girls by his best friend (other members of the group were absent), he refused to tolerate it. He went home, got a rifle, came back and shot and killed his friend. In the classroom from about the fourth grade on fights among black boys invariably are caused by someone "sounding" on the other person's mother.

Significantly, the subject matter of sounding is changing with the changing self-concept of the black with regard to those physical characteristics that are characteristically "Negro," and which in the past were vulnerable points in the black psyche: blackness and "nappy" hair. It ought to be said that for many blacks, blackness was always highly esteemed and it might be more accurate to regard the present sentiment of the black community toward skin color as reflecting a shifted attitude for only a *portion* of the black community. This suggests that "sounding" on someone's light skin color is not new. Nevertheless, one can regard the previously favorable attitude toward light skin color and "good hair" as the prevailing one. "Other things being equal, the more closely a woman approached her white counterpart, the more attractive she was considered to be, by both men and women alike. "Good hair" (hair that is long and soft) and light skin were the chief criteria." (Elliot Liebow, *Tally's Corner*)

The dozens has been linked to the over-all psychosocial growth of the black male. McCormick has stated that a "single round of a dozen or so exchanges frees more pent-up aggressions than will a dose of sodium pentothal." The fact that one permits a kind of abuse within the rules of the game and within the confines of the group which would otherwise not be tolerated, is filled with psychological import. It seems also important, however, to view its function from the perspective of the non-participating members of the group. Its function for them may be to incite and prod individual members of the group to combat for the purpose of energizing the elements, of simply relieving the boredom of just "hanging around" and the malaise of living in a static and restrictive environment.

A summary analysis of the different forms of language behavior which have been discussed above permit the following generalizations:

The prestige norms which influence black speech behavior are those which have been successful in manipulating and controlling people and situations. The function of all of the forms of language behavior discussed above, with the exception of "running it down," was to project personality, assert oneself, or arouse emotion, frequently with the additional purpose of getting the person to give up or do something which will be of some benefit to the speaker. Only running it down has its primary function to communicate information and often here too, the personality and style of the speaker in the form of rapping is projected along with the information.

The purpose for which language is used suggests that the speaker views the social situations into which he moves as consisting of a series of transactions which require that he be continually ready to take advantage of a person or situation or defend himself against being victimized. He has absorbed what Horton has called "street rationality." As one of Horton's respondents put it: "The good hustler . . . conditions his mind and must never put his guard too far down, to relax, or he'll be taken."

I have carefully avoided limiting the group within the black community of whom the language behavior and perspective of their environment is characteristic. While I have no doubt that it is true of those whom are generally called "street people" I am uncertain of the extent to which it is true of a much larger portion of the black community, especially the male segment. My informants consisted of street people, high school students, and blacks, who by their occupation as community and youth workers, possess what has been described as a "sharp sense of the streets." Yet it is difficult to find a black male in the community who has *not* witnessed or participated in the dozens or heard of signifying, or rapping, or shucking and jiving at some time during his growing up. It would be equally difficult to imagine a high school student in a Chicago inner city school not being touched by what is generally regarded as "street culture."

In conclusion, by blending style and verbal power, through rapping, sounding and running it down, the black in the ghetto establishes his personality; through shucking, gripping and copping a plea, he shows his respect for power; through jiving and signifying he stirs up excitement. With all of the above, he hopes to manipulate and control people and situations to give himself a winning edge.

Interactions

> We don't start from certain words, but from certain occasions or activities.
>
> LUDWIG WITTGENSTEIN

> It is the very rules of transformation that are of interest to me—not the message, but the code.
>
> GREGORY BATESON

DEMA: The whole thing is so insane when you stop to think about it. Here's a couple of people, or even a group of people like us, and no one knows if anyone knows what anyone else is saying!

MOLLY: Not only that, but just all the other trips that are there when you're rapping with someone else. I mean, just all those other trips, getting in the way.

JOHN: No, they don't get in the way . . . that's just it. If they got in the way, we'd notice them.

RICH: Wait a minute! If *what* got in the way?

DEMA: The way you try to come across to other people, the impression you try to give them. It's like Shakespeare, "All the world's a stage," you know?

PAT: Oh, I think Laing has written about that, about the images we try to create of ourselves and other people.

ANGELA: Do you think we should put that in?

PAT: Well, it's really short and to the point. But Laing can be confusing. That might not be so good.

SCOTT: Laing would be great, but that's getting into psychology; we'd better stick to sociology. *(Laughter)*

DEMA: Yeah, we have to observe territoriality. *(Laughter)*

7. The Presentation of Self in Everyday Life

ERVING GOFFMAN*

> *All the world's a stage,*
> *And all the men and women merely players.*
> *They have their exits and their entrances;*
> *And one man in his time plays many parts.*

WILLIAM SHAKESPEARE
As You Like It, Act 2, Scene 7

This quotation from Shakespeare could well serve as the keynote for this selection in our book. Taking seriously Shakespeare's statement, Goffman presents a dramaturgical (theatrical) model of human life and utilizes it as the conceptual framework for understanding "life-in-society." In this view the stage is wherever people are interacting, the actors comprise all people, the audience consists of those persons who observe the behavior of others, the parts are the roles that people are called upon to play (whether they are occupational, familial, friendship roles or whatever), and the costuming consists of whatever clothing happens to be in style. In applying this perspective, you might consider the costuming differences in our society between the social classes, between age groups, and between the sexes. (Note also the importance of clothing for daily interaction as analyzed in the subsequent three selections.)

Goffman's insightful analysis provides us with a framework from which we can gain a different perspective of both our own interactions and those of our fellow man. However, when properly understood, you may find that this approach to understanding human behavior can be disturbing. For example, if we are all actors playing roles on the stage of life, where is the "self" of the individual? If the dramaturgical point of view is correct, are people ever serious? Or, is all of life merely a "put-on?" Doesn't this theoretical framework for understanding human interaction present what is essentially a manipulative approach to life, a sort of "Machiavellianism-for-the-common-man"?

*Erving Goffman is Director of the Center for Urban Ethnography at the University of Pennsylvania. His books include *Stigma, Interaction Ritual, Encounters, Asylums, Behavior in Public Places, Strategic Interaction,* and the book from which this selection is taken.

In developing this model for understanding human interaction, Goffman does not intend to claim that people are not sincere in their interactions, that they do not mean what they are doing, or that they are not "involved" in their daily activities. He means rather that all of us have an idea of what and who we are, an idea of or feeling about our "self," and that we are concerned with presenting this "idea-of-the-self" to others as we go about our everyday lives. All of us are concerned that others receive or maintain an idea or view of our "self" that is somewhat compatible with the view that we have of ourselves. In order to manage the impression that others have of us we manipulate various aspects of our lives, including such things as the words we use and the clothing we wear. As such, Goffman says that we are actors on a stage, that we are always "on," continually presenting an image to an audience. The difference between everyday life and the theater itself is that in everyday life we believe the various roles to which we are assigned by our position in society.

For further analysis of the performances that we constantly present to others, of the ways by which we attempt to manage the impressions that others have of us, I urge you to read in its entirety the remarkable book from which this selection is taken.

When an individual enters the presence of others, they commonly seek to acquire information about him or to bring into play information about him already possessed. They will be interested in his general socio-economic status, his conception of self, his attitude toward them, his competence, his trustworthiness, etc. Although some of this information seems to be sought almost as an end in itself, there are usually quite practical reasons for acquiring it. Information about the individual helps to define the situation, enabling others to know in advance what he will expect of them and what they may expect of him. Informed in these ways, the others will know how best to act in order to call forth a desired response from him.

For those present, many sources of information become accessible and many carriers (or "sign-vehicles") become available for conveying this information. If unacquainted with the individual, observers can glean clues from his conduct and appearance which allow them to apply their previous experience with individuals roughly similar to the one before them or, more important, to apply untested stereotypes to him. They can also assume from past experience that only individuals of a particular kind are likely to be found in a given social setting. They can rely on what the individual says about himself or on documentary evidence he provides as to who and what he is. If they know, or know of, the individual by virtue of experience prior to the interaction, they can rely on assumptions as to the persistence and generality of psychological traits as a means of predicting his present and future behavior.

However, during the period in which the individual is in the immediate presence of the others, few events may occur which directly provide the others with the conclusive information they will need if they are to direct wisely their own activity. Many crucial facts lie beyond the time and place of interaction or lie concealed within it. For example, the "true" or "real" attitudes, beliefs, and emotions of the individual can be ascertained only indirectly, through his avowals or through what appears to be involuntary expressive behavior. Similarly, if the individual offers the others a product or service, they will often find that during the interaction there will be no time and place immediately available for eating the pudding that the proof can be found in. They will be forced to accept some events as conventional or natural signs of something not directly available to the senses. In Ichheiser's terms,[1] the individual will have to act so that he intentionally or unintentionally *expresses* himself, and the others will in turn have to be *impressed* in some way by him.

The expressiveness of the individual (and therefore his capacity to give impressions) appears to involve two radically different kinds of sign activity: the expression that he *gives,* and the expression that he *gives off.* The first involves verbal symbols or their substitutes which he uses admittedly and solely to convey the information that he and the others are known to attach to these symbols. This is communication in the traditional and narrow sense. The second involves a wide range of action that others can treat as symptomatic of the actor, the expectation being that the action was performed for reasons other than the information conveyed in this way. As we shall have to see, this distinction has an only initial validity. The individual does of course intentionally convey misinformation by means of both of these types of communication, the first involving deceit, the second feigning.

Taking communication in both its narrow and broad sense, one finds that when the individual is in the immediate presence of others, his activity will have a promissory character. The others are likely to find that they must accept the individual on faith, offering him a just return while he is present before them in exchange for something whose true value will not be established until after he has left their presence. (Of course, the others also live by inference in their dealings with the physical world, but it is only in the world of social interaction that the objects about which they make inferences will purposely facilitate and hinder this inferential process.) The security that they justifiably feel in making inferences about the individual will vary, of course, depending on such factors as the amount of information they already possess about him, but no amount of such past evidence can entirely obviate the necessity of acting on the basis of inferences. As William I. Thomas suggested:

> It is also highly important for us to realize that we do not as a matter of fact lead our lives, make our decisions, and reach our goals in everyday life either statistically or scientifically. We live by inference. I am, let us say, your guest. You do not know, you cannot determine scientifically, that I will not steal your money or your spoons. But inferentially I will not, and inferentially you have me as a guest.[2]

[1]Gustav Ichheiser, "Misunderstandings in Human Relations," Supplement to *The American Journal of Sociology,* 55 (September, 1949): 6-7.
[2]Quoted in E. H. Volkart, editor, *Social Behavior and Personality,* Contributions of W. I. Thomas to Theory and Social Research (New York: Social Science Research Council, 1951), p. 5.

Let us now turn from the others to the point of view of the individual who presents himself before them. He may wish them to think highly of him, or to think that he thinks highly of them, or to perceive how in fact he feels toward them, or to obtain no clear-cut impression; he may wish to ensure sufficient harmony so that the interaction can be sustained, or to defraud, get rid of, confuse, mislead, antagonize, or insult them. Regardless of the particular objective which the individual has in mind and of his motive for having this objective, it will be in his interests to control the conduct of the others, especially their responsive treatment of him.[3] This control is achieved largely by influencing the definition of the situation which the others come to formulate, and he can influence this definition by expressing himself in such a way as to give them the kind of impression that will lead them to act voluntarily in accordance with his own plan. Thus, when an individual appears in the presence of others, there will usually be some reason for him to mobilize his activity so that it will convey an impression to others which it is in his interests to convey. Since a girl's dormitory mates will glean evidence of her popularity from the calls she receives on the phone, we can suspect that some girls will arrange for calls to be made, and Willard Waller's finding can be anticipated:

> It has been reported by many observers that a girl who is called to the telephone in the dormitories will often allow herself to be called several times, in order to give all the other girls ample opportunity to hear her paged.[4]

Of the two kinds of communication—expressions given and expressions given off—this report will be primarily concerned with the latter, with the more theatrical and contextual kind, the non-verbal, presumably unintentional kind, whether this communication be purposely engineered or not. As an example of what we must try to examine, I would like to cite at length a novelistic incident in which Preedy, a vacationing Englishman, makes his first appearance on the beach of his summer hotel in Spain:

> But in any case he took care to avoid catching anyone's eye. First of all, he had to make it clear to those potential companions of his holiday that they were of no concern to him whatsoever. He stared through them, round them, over them—eyes lost in space. The beach might have been empty. If by chance a ball was thrown his way, he looked surprised; then let a smile of amusement lighten his face (Kindly Preedy), looked round dazed to see that there *were* people on the beach, tossed it back with a smile to himself and not a smile *at* the people, and then resumed carelessly his nonchalant survey of space.

[3]Here I owe much to an unpublished paper by Tom Burns of the University of Edinburgh. He presents the argument that in all interaction a basic underlying theme is the desire of each participant to guide and control the responses made by the others present. A similar argument has been advanced by Jay Haley in a recent unpublished paper, but in regard to a special kind of control, that having to do with defining the nature of the relationship of those involved in the interaction.

[4]Willard Waller, "The Rating and Dating Complex," *American Sociological Review,* 2: 730.

Interactions   **89**

But it was time to institute a little parade, the parade of the Ideal Preedy. By devious handlings he gave any who wanted to look a chance to see the title of his book—a Spanish translation of Homer, classic thus, but not daring, cosmopolitan too—and then gathered together his beach-wrap and bag into a neat sand-resistant pile (Methodical and Sensible Preedy), rose slowly to stretch at ease his huge frame (Big-Cat Preedy), and tossed aside his sandals (Carefree Preedy, after all).

The marriage of Preedy and the sea! There were alternative rituals. The first involved the stroll that turns into a run and a dive straight into the water, thereafter smoothing into a strong splashless crawl towards the horizon. But of course not really to the horizon. Quite suddenly he would turn on to his back and thrash great white splashes with his legs, somehow thus showing that he could have swum further had he wanted to, and then would stand up a quarter out of water for all to see who it was.

The alternative course was simpler, it avoided the cold-water shock and it avoided the risk of appearing too high-spirited. The point was to appear to be so used to the sea, the Mediterranean, and this particular beach, that one might as well be in the sea as out of it. It involved a slow stroll down and into the edge of the water—not even noticing his toes were wet, land and water all the same to *him!*—with his eyes up at the sky gravely surveying portents, invisible to others, of the weather (Local Fisherman Preedy).[5]

The novelist means us to see that Preedy is improperly concerned with the extensive impressions he feels his sheer bodily action is giving off to those around him. We can malign Preedy further by assuming that he has acted merely in order to give a particular impression, that this is a false impression, and that the others present receive either no impression at all, or, worse still, the impression that Preedy is affectedly trying to cause them to receive this particular impression. But the important point for us here is that the kind of impression Preedy thinks he is making is in fact the kind of impression that others correctly and incorrectly glean from someone in their midst.

I have said that when an individual appears before others his actions will influence the definition of the situation which they come to have. Sometimes the individual will act in a thoroughly calculating manner, expressing himself in a given way solely in order to give the kind of impression to others that is likely to evoke from them a specific response he is concerned to obtain. Sometimes the individual will be calculating in his activity but be relatively unaware that this is the case. Sometimes he will intentionally and consciously express himself in a particular way, but chiefly because the tradition of his group or social status require this kind of expression and not because of any particular response (other than vague acceptance or approval) that is likely to be evoked from those impressed by the expression. Sometimes the traditions of an individual's role will lead him to give a well-designed impression of a particular kind and yet he may be neither consciously nor unconsciously disposed to create such an impression. The others, in their turn, may be

[5]William Sansom, *A Contest of Ladies* (London: Hogarth, 1956), pp. 230-32.

BASICS: PEOPLE

suitably impressed by the individual's efforts to convey something, or may misunderstand the situation and come to conclusions that are warranted neither by the individual's intent nor by the facts. In any case, in so far as the others act *as if* the individual had conveyed a particular impression, we may take a functional or pragmatic view and say that the individual has "effectively" projected a given definition of the situation and "effectively" fostered the understanding that a given state of affairs obtains.

There is one aspect of the others' response that bears special comment here. Knowing that the individual is likely to present himself in a light that is favorable to him, the others may divide what they witness into two parts: a part that is relatively easy for the individual to manipulate at will, being chiefly his verbal assertions, and a part in regard to which he seems to have little concern or control, being chiefly derived from the expressions he gives off. The others may then use what are considered to be the ungovernable aspects of his expressive behavior as a check upon the validity of what is conveyed by the governable aspects. In this a fundamental asymmetry is demonstrated in the communication process, the individual presumably being aware of only one stream of his communication, the witnesses of this stream and one other. For example, in Shetland Isle one crofter's wife, in serving native dishes to a visitor from the mainland of Britain, would listen with a polite smile to his polite claims of liking what he was eating; at the same time she would take note of the rapidity with which the visitor lifted his fork or spoon to his mouth, the eagerness with which he passed food into his mouth, and the gusto expressed in chewing the food, using these signs as a check on the stated feelings of the eater. The same woman, in order to discover what one acquaintance (A) "actually" thought of another acquaintance (B), would wait until B was in the presence of A but engaged in conversation with still another person (C). She would then covertly examine the facial expressions of A as he regarded B in conversation with C. Not being in conversation with B, and not being directly observed by him, A would sometimes relax usual constraints and tactful deceptions, and freely express what he was "actually" feeling about B. This Shetlander, in short, would observe the unobserved observer.

Now given the fact that others are likely to check up on the more controllable aspects of behavior by means of the less controllable, one can expect that sometimes the individual will try to exploit this very possibility, guiding the impression he makes through behavior felt to be reliably informing.[6] For example, in gaining admission to a tight social circle, the participant observer may not only wear an accepting look while listening to an informant, but may also be careful to wear the same look when observing the informant talking to others; observers of the observer will then not as easily discover where he actually stands. A specific illustration may be cited from Shetland Isle. When

---

[6]The widely read and rather sound writings of Stephen Potter are concerned in part with signs that can be engineered to give a shrewd observer the apparently incidental cues he needs to discover concealed virtues the gamesman does not in fact possess.

a neighbor dropped in to have a cup of tea, he would ordinarily wear at least a hint of an expectant warm smile as he passed through the door of the cottage. Since lack of physical obstructions outside the cottage and lack of light within it usually made it possible to observe the visitor unobserved as he approached the house, islanders sometimes took pleasure in watching the visitor drop whatever expression he was manifesting and replace it with a sociable one just before reaching the door. However, some visitors, in appreciating that this examination was occurring, would blindly adopt a social face a long distance from the house, thus ensuring the projection of a constant image.

This kind of control upon the part of the individual reinstates the symmetry of the communication process, and sets the stage for a kind of information game—a potentially infinite cycle of concealment, discovery, false revelation, and rediscovery. It should be added that since the others are likely to be relatively unsuspicious of the presumably unguided aspect of the individual's conduct, he can gain much by controlling it. The others of course may sense that the individual is manipulating the presumably spontaneous aspects of his behavior, and seek in this very act of manipulation some shading of conduct that the individual has not managed to control. This again provides a check upon the individual's behavior, this time his presumably uncalculated behavior, thus re-establishing the asymmetry of the communication process. Here I would like only to add the suggestion that the arts of piercing an individual's effort at calculated unintentionality seem better developed than our capacity to manipulate our own behavior, so that regardless of how many steps have occurred in the information game, the witness is likely to have the advantage over the actor, and the initial asymmetry of the communication process is likely to be retained.

When we allow that the individual projects a definition of the situation when he appears before others, we must also see that the others, however passive their role may seem to be, will themselves effectively project a definition of the situation by virtue of their response to the individual and by virtue of any lines of action they initiate to him. Ordinarily the definitions of the situation projected by the several different participants are sufficiently attuned to one another so that open contradiction will not occur. I do not mean that there will be the kind of consensus that arises when each individual present candidly expresses what he really feels and honestly agrees with the expressed feelings of the others present. This kind of harmony is an optimistic ideal and in any case not necessary for the smooth working of society. Rather, each participant is expected to suppress his immediate heartfelt feelings, conveying a view of the situation which he feels the others will be able to find at least temporarily acceptable. The maintenance of this surface of agreement, this veneer of consensus, is facilitated by each participant concealing his own wants behind statements while asserting values to which everyone present feels obliged to give lip service. Further, there is usually a kind of division of definitional labor. Each participant is allowed to establish the tentative official ruling regarding matters which are vital to him but not immediately important to others, e.g., the rationalizations and justifications by which he accounts for his past activity. In exchange for this courtesy he remains silent or non-committal on matters important to others but not immediately important to him. We have then a kind of interactional *modus vivendi.* Together the participants contribute to a single over-all definition of the situation which involves not so much a real agreement as to what exists but rather a real agreement as to whose claims concerning what issues will be temporarily honored. Real agreement will also exist concerning the desirability of avoiding an open conflict of definitions of the situation.[7] I will refer to this level of agreement as a "working consensus." It is to be understood that the working consensus established in one interaction setting will be quite different in content from the working consensus established in a different type of setting. Thus, between two friends at lunch, a reciprocal show of affection, respect, and concern for the other is maintained. In service occupations, on the other hand, the specialist often maintains an image of disinterested involvement in the problem of the client, while the client responds with a show of respect for the competence and integrity of the specialist. Regardless of such differences in content, however, the general form of these working arrangements is the same.

In noting the tendency for a participant to accept the definitional claims made by the others present, we can appreciate the crucial importance of the information that the individual *initially* possesses or acquires concerning his fellow participants, for it is on the basis of this initial information that the individual starts to define the situation and starts to build up lines of responsive action. The individual's initial projection commits him to what he is proposing to be and requires him to drop all pretenses of being other things. As the interaction among the participants progresses, additions and modifications in this initial informational state will of course occur, but it is essential that these later developments be related without contradiction to, and even built up from, the initial positions taken by the several participants. It would seem that an individual can more easily make a choice as to what line of treatment to demand from and extend to the others present at the beginning of an encounter than he can alter the line of treatment that is being pursued once the interaction is underway.

In everyday life, of course, there is a clear understanding that first impressions are important. Thus, the work adjustment of those in service occupations will often hinge upon a capacity to seize and hold the initiative in the service relation, a capacity that will require subtle aggressiveness on the part of the

[7]An interaction can be purposely set up as a time and place for voicing differences in opinion, but in such cases participants must be careful to agree not to disagree on the proper tone of voice, vocabulary, and degree of seriousness in which all arguments are to be phrased, and upon the mutual respect which disagreeing participants must carefully continue to express toward one another. This debaters' or academic definition of the situation may also be invoked suddenly and judiciously as a way of translating a serious conflict of views into one that can be handled within a framework acceptable to all present.

Interactions   **93**

server when he is of lower socio-economic status than his client. W. F. Whyte suggests the waitress as an example:

> The first point that stands out is that the waitress who bears up under pressure does not simply respond to her customers. She acts with some skill to control their behavior. The first question to ask when we look at the customer relationship is, "Does the waitress get the jump on the customer, or does the customer get the jump on the waitress?" The skilled waitress realizes the crucial nature of this question. . . .
> The skilled waitress tackles the customer with confidence and without hesitation. For example, she may find that a new customer has seated himself before she could clear off the dirty dishes and change the cloth. He is now leaning on the table studying the menu. She greets him, says, "May I change the cover, please?" and, without waiting for an answer, takes his menu away from him so that he moves back from the table, and she goes about her work. The relationship is handled politely but firmly, and there is never any question as to who is in charge.[8]

When the interaction that is initiated by "first impressions" is itself merely the initial interaction in an extended series of interactions involving the same participants, we speak of "getting off on the right foot" and feel that it is crucial that we do so. Thus, one learns that some teachers take the following view:

> You can't ever let them get the upper hand on you or you're through. So I start out tough. The first day I get a new class in, I let them know who's boss . . . You've got to start off tough, then you can ease up as you go along. If you start out easy-going, when you try to be tough, they'll just look at you and laugh.[9]

Similarly, attendants in mental institutions may feel that if the new patient is sharply put in his place the first day on the ward and made to see who is boss, much future difficulty will be prevented.[10]

Given the fact that the individual effectively projects a definition of the situation when he enters the presence of others, we can assume that events may occur within the interaction which contradict, discredit, or otherwise throw doubt upon this projection. When these disruptive events occur, the interaction itself may come to a confused and embarrassed halt. Some of the assumptions upon which the responses of the participants had been predicated become untenable, and the participants find themselves lodged in an interaction for which the situation has been wrongly defined and is now no longer defined. At such moments the individual whose presentation has been discredited may

[8]W. F. Whyte, "When Workers and Customers Meet," Chap. VII, *Industry and Society,* ed. W. F. Whyte (New York: McGraw-Hill, 1946), pp. 132–33.
[9]Teacher interview quoted by Howard S. Becker, "Social Class Variations in the Teacher-Pupil Relationship," *Journal of Educational Sociology,* 25: 459.
[10]Harold Taxel, "Authority Structure in a Mental Hospital Ward" (unpublished Master's thesis, Department of Sociology, University of Chicago, 1953).

feel ashamed while the others present may feel hostile, and all the participants may come to feel ill at ease, nonplussed, out of countenance, embarrassed, experiencing the kind of anomy that is generated when the minute social system of face-to-face interaction breaks down.

In stressing the fact that the initial definition of the situation projected by an individual tends to provide a plan for the co-operative activity that follows —in stressing this action point of view—we must not overlook the crucial fact that any projected definition of the situation also has a distinctive moral character. It is this moral character of projections that will chiefly concern us in this report. Society is organized on the principle that any individual who possesses certain social characteristics has a moral right to expect that others will value and treat him in an appropriate way. Connected with this principle is a second, namely that an individual who implicitly or explicitly signifies that he has certain social characteristics ought in fact to be what he claims he is. In consequence, when an individual projects a definition of the situation and thereby makes an implicit or explicit claim to be a person of a particular kind, he automatically exerts a moral demand upon the others, obliging them to value and treat him in the manner that persons of his kind have a right to expect. He also implicitly forgoes all claims to be things he does not appear to be[11] and hence forgoes the treatment that would be appropriate for such individuals. The others find, then, that the individual has informed them as to what is and as to what they *ought* to see as the "is."

One cannot judge the importance of definitional disruptions by the frequency with which they occur, for apparently they would occur more frequently were not constant precautions taken. We find that preventive practices are constantly employed to avoid these embarrassments and that corrective practices are constantly employed to compensate for discrediting occurrences that have not been successfully avoided. When the individual employs these strategies and tactics to protect his own projections, we may refer to them as "defensive practices"; when a participant employs them to save the definition of the situation projected by another, we speak of "protective practices" or "tact." Together, defensive and protective practices comprise the techniques employed to safeguard the impression fostered by an individual during his presence before others. It should be added that while we may be ready to see that no fostered impression would survive if defensive practices were not employed, we are less ready perhaps to see that few impressions could survive if those who received the impression did not exert tact in their reception of it.

In addition to the fact that precautions are taken to prevent disruption of projected definitions, we may also note that an intense interest in these disruptions comes to play a significant role in the social life of the group. Practical jokes and social games are played in which embarrassments which are to be

---

[11]This role of the witness in limiting what it is the individual can be has been stressed by Existentialists, who see it as a basic threat to individual freedom. See Jean-Paul Sartre, *Being and Nothingness,* trans. by Hazel E. Barnes (New York: Philosophical Library, 1956), p. 365 ff.

taken unseriously are purposely engineered.[12] Fantasies are created in which devastating exposures occur. Anecdotes from the past—real, embroidered, or fictitious—are told and retold, detailing disruptions which occurred, almost occurred, or occurred and were admirably resolved. There seems to be no grouping which does not have a ready supply of these games, reveries, and cautionary tales, to be used as a source of humor, a catharsis for anxieties, and a sanction for inducing individuals to be modest in their claims and reasonable in their projected expectations. The individual may tell himself through dreams of getting into impossible positions. Families tell of the time a guest got his dates mixed and arrived when neither the house nor anyone in it was ready for him. Journalists tell of times when an all-too-meaningful misprint occurred, and the paper's assumption of objectivity or decorum was humorously discredited. Public servants tell of times a client ridiculously misunderstood form instructions, giving answers which implied an unanticipated and bizarre definition of the situation.[13] Seamen, whose home away from home is rigorously he-man, tell stories of coming back home and inadvertently asking mother to "pass the fucking butter."[14] Diplomats tell of the time a near-sighted queen asked a republican ambassador about the health of his king.[15]

To summarize, then, I assume that when an individual appears before others he will have many motives for trying to control the impression they receive of the situation.

---

[12]Goffman, *op. cit.,* pp. 319–27.

[13]Peter Blau, "Dynamics of Bureaucracy" (Ph.D. dissertation, Department of Sociology, Columbia University, forthcoming, University of Chicago Press), pp. 127–29.

[14]Walter M. Beattie, Jr., "The Merchant Seaman" (unpublished M.A. Report, Department of Sociology, University of Chicago, 1950), p. 35.

[15]Sir Frederick Ponsonby, *Recollections of Three Reigns* (New York, Dutton, 1952), p. 46.

8. The Family as a Company of Players

ANNABELLE B. MOTZ*

All the world's a stage, and we are all players.

Erving Goffman in his *The Presentation of Self in Everyday Life* views our everyday world as having both front stage and back. Like professionals, we try to give a careful and superior performance out front. Back stage we unzip, take off our masks, complain of the strain, think back over the last act, and prepare anxiously for the next.

Sometimes the "on stage" performances are solos; sometimes we act in teams or groups. The roles may be carefully planned, rehearsed, and executed; or they may be spontaneous or improvised. The presentation can be a hit; or it can flop badly.

Picture a theater starring the family. The "stars" are the husband, wife, and children. But the cast includes a wide range of persons in the community—fellow workers, friends, neighbors, delivery-men, shop-keepers, doctors, and everyone who passes by. Usually husband and wife are the leads; and the appeal, impact, and significance of their performances vary with the amount of time on stage, the times of day and week, the circumstances of each presentation, and the moods of the audience.

Backstage for the family members is generally to be found in their homes, as suggested by the expression, "a man's home is his castle." The front stage is where they act out their dramatic parts in schools, stores, places of employment, on the street, in the homes of other persons; or, as when entertaining guests, back in their own homes.

My aim is to analyze the performances of family members before the community audience—their *front stage* appearances. The behavior conforms to the rules and regulations that society places upon its members; perhaps the analysis of the family life drama will provide insights into the bases of the problems for which an increasing number of middle-class persons are seeking professional help.

*Annabelle B. Motz is Associate Professor of Sociology at American University, Washington, D.C.

Many years ago, Thorstein Veblen noted that although industrialization made it possible for the American worker to live better than at any previous time in history, it made him feel so insignificant that he sought ways to call attention to himself. In *The Theory of the Leisure Class,* Veblen showed that all strata of society practiced "conspicuous consumption"—the ability to use one's income for non-essential goods and services in ways readily visible to others. A man's abilities were equated with his monetary worth and the obvious command he had in the marketplace to purchase commodities beyond bare necessities. Thus, a family that lives more comfortably than most must be a "success."

While conspicuous consumption was becoming an essential element of front stage performance, the ideal of the American as a completely rational person —governed and governing by reason rather than emotion—was being projected around the world. The writings of the first four decades of this century stress over and over again the importance of the individual and individual opinion. (The growth of unionism, the Social Security program, public opinion polling, and federal aid to education are a few examples of the trend toward positive valuation of each human being—not to mention the impact of Freud and Dewey and their stress on individual worth.) The desirability of rule by majority and democratic debate and voting as the best means of reaching group decisions—all these glorified rationality.

As population, cities, and industry grew, so also did anonymity and complexity; and rationality in organizations (more properly known as bureaucratization) had to keep pace. The individual was exposed to more and more people he knew less and less. The face to face relationships of small towns and workshops declined. Job requirements, duties and loyalties, hiring and firing, had to "go by the book." Max Weber has described the bureaucratic organization: each job is explicitly defined, the rights of entry and exit from the organization can be found in the industry's manual, and the rights and duties of the worker and of the organization toward the worker are rationally defined; above all, the worker acts as a rational being on the job—he is never subject to emotional urges.

With the beams and bricks of "front" and rationality the middle-class theater is built; with matching props the stage is set.

There are two basic scenes. One revolves about family and close personal relationships. It takes place in a well-furnished house—very comfortable, very stylish, but not "vulgar." The actors are calm, controlled, reasonable.

The other scene typically takes place in a bureaucratic anteroom cluttered with physical props and with people treated like physical props. The actors do not want the audience to believe that they *are* props—so they attract attention to themselves and dramatize their individuality and worth by spending and buying far more than they need.

What does this mean in the daily life of the family stars?

Take first the leading lady, wife, and mother. She follows Veblen and dramatizes her husband's success by impressing any chance on-lookers with her

BASICS: PEOPLE

efficient house management. How does one run a house efficiently? All must be reasoned order. The wife-housekeeper plans what has to be done and does it simply and quickly. Kitchen, closets, and laundry display department store wares as attractively as the stores themselves. The house is always presentable, and so is she. Despite her obviously great labors, she does not seem to get flustered, over-fatigued, or too emotional. (What would her neighbors or even a passing door-to-door salesman think if they heard her screaming at the children?) With minimal household help she must appear the gracious hostess, fresh and serene—behind her a dirty kitchen magically cleaned, a meal effortlessly prepared, and husband and children well behaved and helpful.

Outside the home, too, she is composed and rational. She does not show resentment toward Johnny's teacher, who may irritate her or give Johnny poor marks. She does not yawn during interminable and dull PTA programs (what would they think of her and her family?). At citizen meetings she is the embodiment of civic-minded, responsible, property-ownership (even if the mortgage company actually owns the property). Her supermarket cart reflects her taste, affluence, efficiency, and concern. At church she exhibits no un-churchly feelings. She prays that her actions and facial expression will not give away the fact that her mind has wandered from the sermon; she hopes that as she greets people, whether interested in them or not, she will be able to say the "right" thing. Her clothes and car are extremely important props—the right make, style, finish; and they project her front stage character, giving the kind of impression she thinks she and the other members of the family want her to give.

Enter Father Center Stage

The male lead is husband, father, and man-of-affairs. He acts in ways that, he hopes, will help his status, and that of his family. At all times he must seem to be in relaxed control of difficult situations. This often takes some doing. For instance, he must be both unequal and equal to associates; that is, he is of course a good fellow and very democratic, but the way he greets and handles his superiors at work is distinctly, if subtly, different from the way he speaks to and handles inferiors. A superior who arrives unexpectedly must find him dynamically at work, worth every cent and more of his income; an inferior must also find him busy, demonstrating how worthy he is of superior status and respect. He must always be in control. Even when supposedly relaxing, swapping dirty jokes with his colleagues, he must be careful to avoid any that offend their biases. He has to get along; bigots, too, may be able to do him good or harm.

Sometimes he cannot give his real feelings release until he gets behind the wheel—and the savage jockeying which takes place during evening rush may reflect this simultaneous discharge by many drivers.

The scene shifts back to the home. The other stars greet him—enter loving wife and children. He may not yet be ready or able to re-establish complete emotional control—after all, a man's home is his backstage—and the interplay of the sub-plots begins. If his wife goes on with her role, she will be the dutiful spouse, listening sympathetically, keeping the children and her temper quiet. If she should want to cut loose at the same time, collision will probably still be avoided because both have been trained to restrain themselves and present the right front as parents to their children—if not to each other.

Leisure is not rest. At home father acts out his community role of responsible family head. The back yard is kept up as a "private" garden; the garage as a showroom for tools on display. He must exhibit interest—but not too much enthusiasm—in a number of activities, some ostensibly recreational, retaining a nice balance between appearing a dutiful husband and a henpecked one. Reason must rule emotion.

The children of old vaudevillians literally were born and reared in the theater—were nursed between acts by mothers in spangles, trained as toddlers to respond to footlights as other children might to sunlight. The young in the middle-class family drama also learn to recognize cues and to perform.

Since "front" determines the direction and content of the drama, they are supposed to be little ladies and gentlemen. Proper performances from such tyros require much backstage rehearsal. Unfortunately, the middle-class backstage is progressively disappearing, and so the children too must be prepared to respond appropriately to the unexpected—whether an unwanted salesman at the door who must be discreetly lied to about mother's whereabouts or a wanted friend who must not be offended. They are taught rationality and democracy in family councils—where they are also taught what behavior is expected of them. Reason is, rife; even when they get out of hand the parents "reason" with them. As Dorothy Barclay says when discussing household chores and the child, "Appealing to a sense of family loyalty and pride in maturity is the tack most parents take first in trying to overcome youngsters' objections (to household chores). Offering rewards come second, arguing and insisting third."

"Grown-up" and "good" children do family chores. They want the house to look "nice"; they don't tell family secrets when visitors are present, and even rush to close closet and bedroom doors when the doorbell rings unexpectedly.

The child, of course, carries the family play into school, describing it in "show and tell" performances and in his deportment and dress. Part of the role of responsible parenthood includes participation in PTA and teacher conferences, with the child an important player, even it offstage.

To the child, in fact, much of the main dynamic of the play takes place in the dim realm of offstage (not always the same as backstage)—his parents' sex activities, their real income and financial problems, and many other things, some of them strange and frightening, that "children are not old enough to understand."

They early learn the fundamental lesson of front stage: be prepared; know your lines. Who knows whether the neighbors' windows are open? The parent who answers a crying child with, "Calm down now, let's sit down and talk this over," is rehearsing him in stage presence, and in his character as middle-class child and eventually middle-class adult.

Often the family acts as a team. The act may be rehearsed, but it must appear spontaneous. Watch them file in and out of church on Sunday mornings. Even after more than an hour of sitting, the children seem fresh and starched. They do not laugh or shout as on the playground. The parents seem calm, in complete control. Conversations and postures are confined to those appropriate for a place of worship.

Audience reaction is essential to a play. At church others may say, "What nice children you have!" or, "We look forward to seeing you next Sunday." Taken at face value, these are sounds of audience approval and applause; the performers may bask in them. Silence or equivocal remarks may imply disapproval and cause anxiety. What did they really mean? What did we do wrong? Sometimes reaction is delayed, and the family will be uncertain of their impression. In any case, future performances will be affected.

Acting a role, keeping up a front, letting the impressions and expectations of other people influence our behavior, does result in a great deal of good. Organized society is possible only when there is some conformity to roles and rules. Also a person concerned with the impression others have of him feels that he is significant to them and they to him. When he polishes his car because a dirty one would embarrass him, when his wife straightens her make-up before answering the door, both exhibit a sense of their importance and personal dignity in human affairs. Those who must, or want to, serve as models or examplars must be especially careful of speech and performance—they are always on stage. When people keep up appearances they are identifying themselves with a group and its standards. They need it; presumably it needs them.

Moreover, acting what seems a narrow role may actually broaden experience and open doors. To tend a lawn, or join a PTA, social club, or art group —"to keep up appearances"—may result in real knowledge and understanding about horticulture, education, or civic responsibility.

For the community, front produces the positive assets of social cohesion. Well-kept lawns, homes, cars, clean children and adults have definite aesthetic, financial, and sanitary value. People relate to one another, develop common experiences. People who faithfully play their parts exhibit personal and civic responsibility. The rules make life predictable and safe, confine ad-libs within acceptable limits, control violence and emotional tangents, and allow the show to go on and the day's work to be done. Thus, the challenging game of maintaining front relates unique personalities to one another and unites them in activity and into a nation.

So much for the good which preoccupation with front and staging accomplishes; what of the bad?

First, the inhibition of the free play of emotion must lead to frustration. Human energies need outlets. If onstage acting does not allow for release of tension, then the escape should take place backstage. But what if there is virtually no backstage? Perhaps then the releases will be found in the case histories of psychiatrists and other counselors. Communication between husband and wife may break down because of the contrast between the onstage image each has of the other as a perfect mate and the unmasked actuality backstage. Perhaps when masks crumble and crack, when people can no longer stand the strain of the front, then what we call nervous breakdown occurs.

Growing up with Bad Reviews

And how does the preoccupation with front affect the growth and development of the child? How can a child absorb and pattern himself after models which are essentially unreal? A mother may "control" her emotions when a child spills milk on her freshly scrubbed floor, and "reason" with him about it; she may still retain control when he leaves the refrigerator open after repeated warnings; but then some minor thing such as loud laughter over the funnies may suddenly blow off the lid, and she will "let him have it, but good!" What can he learn from such treatment? To respect his mother's hard work at keeping the house clean? To close the refrigerator door? Not to laugh loudly when reading the comics? That mother is a crab? Or, she's always got it in for him? Whatever he has learned, it is doubtful it was what his mother wanted! Whatever it was it will probably not clarify his understanding of such family values as pride in work, reward for effort, consideration of other people, or how to meet problems. Too, since the family's status is vitally linked with the maintenance of fronts, any deviance by the child, unless promptly rectified, threatens family standing in the community. This places a tremendous burden on a child actor.

Moreover, a concentration on front rather than content must result in a leveling and deadening of values and feelings. If a man buys a particular hat primarily because of what others may think, then its intrinsic value as a hat —in fact, even his own judgement and feelings about it—become secondary. Whether the judgment of those whose approval he covets is good or bad is unimportant—just so they approve. Applause has taken the place of value.

A PTA lecture on "The Future of America" will call for the same attentive front from him as a scientist's speech on the "Effects of Nuclear Warfare on Human Survival." Reading a newspaper on a crowded bus, his expression undergoes little change whether he is reading about nuclear tests, advice of the lovelorn, or Elizabeth Taylor's marital problems. To his employer he presents essentially the same bland, non-argumentative, courteous front whether he has just been refused a much deserved pay raise or told to estimate the cost of light bulbs. He seems impartial, objective, rational—and by so doing he also seems to deny that there is any difference to him between the pay raise and the light bulbs, as well as to deny his feelings.

The Price of Admission

What price does the community pay for its role as audience?

The individual human talents and energies are alienated from assuming responsibility for the well-being and survival of the group. The exaggerated self-consciousness of individuals results in diluted and superficial concern with the community at a time when deep involvement, new visions, and real leadership are needed. Can the world afford to have over-zealous actors who work so hard on their lines that they forget what the play is all about?

It is probable that this picture will become more general in the near future and involve more and more people—assuming that the aging of the population continues, that the Cold War doesn't become hot and continues to need constant checks on loyalty and patriotism, that automation increases man's leisure at the same time as it keeps up or increases the production of consumer goods, and that improved advertising techniques make every home a miniature department store. The resulting conformity, loyalty, and patriotism may foster social solidarity. It may also cause alienation, immaturity, confusion, and much insecurity when new situations, for which old fronts are no longer appropriate, suddenly occur. Unless people start today to separate the important from the tinsel and to assume responsibility for community matters that are vital, individual actors will feel even more isolated; and the society may drift ever further from the philosophy that values every person.

Tomorrow's communities will need to provide new backstages, as the home, work place, and recreation center become more and more visible. Psychiatrists, counselors, confessors, and other professional listeners must provide outlets for actors who are exhausted and want to share their backstage thoughts. With increased leisure, business men will probably find it profitable to provide backstage settings in the form of resorts, rest homes, or retreats.

The state of the world is such today that unless the family and the community work together to evaluate and value the significant and direct their energies accordingly, the theater with its actors, front stage, backstage, and audience may end in farce and tragedy.

9. Knots

R. D. LAING

Narcissus fell in love with his image, taking it to be another

Jack falls in love with Jill's image of Jack, taking it to be himself.
She must not die, because then he would lose himself.
He is jealous in case any one else's image is reflected in her mirror.

Jill is a distorting mirror to herself.
Jill has to distort herself to appear undistorted to herself.

To undistort herself, she finds Jack to distort her distorted image
    in his distorting mirror
She hopes that his distortion of her distortion may undistort her
    image without her having to distort herself.

Part 11
Breakdowns:
Institutional

Breakdown: American Culture

Breakdown: American Culture

ANGELA: The basic idea I wanted to explore in this section was the breakdown of everything, the disintegration of American, or Western, society as we know it. The breakdown of bonding for the culture . . .

SCOTT: Oh, but there's still some bonding . . .

ANGELA: . . . and the rise of subcultures and subgroups.

SCOTT: But there's still a form of bonding. Fragmenting is a pattern of growth too, you know. When you grow you become millions of specialized cells. Just in this room, look at all the differences among us!

ANGELA: But what form does the bonding take? How do we recognize it?

SCOTT: Well, the government's still here . . . *(Laughter)* I still vote here, right? And stuff like that, where you go to work, where you live . . . that keeps things together in a basic way. Things are going to be bonded a lot differently from the way they were . . .

DANA: But the act of bonding will still be there.

SCOTT: Right. Somehow people are going to keep things so they can get along.

MOLLY: You know, there's another article by Wolfe we could stick in here, about how the old class system is breaking down and many different styles of living are popping up all over. It's kind of dated, though; his book was written a couple of years ago.

ANGELA: I don't know about this . . . we already have an article by him.

MOLLY: It's just an idea. I mean, it's a lot more fun to read Tom Wolfe than it is to read Alvin Toffler, and in this case they would say virtually the same thing anyway. You know, when I was first studying sociology, I got tired of writers who had a safe, objective way of saying things. I prefer Wolfe because he seems to be involved with his subject as he writes.

ANGELA: Well, let's take a look at this article and talk about it later, okay?

FRED: Getting back to this idea of breakdown. Sometimes I think that everything's always been going crazy. I'm not sure that there has ever been a time when things *weren't* going crazy.

DANA: But maybe we're the first people who ever recognized that they were flipped out.

RICH: And *that's* why we're flipped out! Oh, far out! We're the first society to ever realize that we're all bananas! *(Laughter)*

10. The American Malaise

HERBERT J. GANS*

Last summer, President Nixon, while commenting on the pseudoclassical architecture of American public buildings, went on to suggest that America might be heading for the same fate as ancient Greece and Rome. "As they became wealthy, as they lost their will to live, to improve," he pointed out, "they became subject to the decadence that destroys the civilization. The United States is reaching that period."

Somewhat earlier, Andrew Hacker, an eminent political scientist, wrote a book entitled "The End of the American Era," and since then other intellectuals and journalists have come to similar pessimistic conclusions. This feeling is not limited to scholars and those in the media, however, for several recent polls have reported a widespread mood of malaise about the future of America.

I shall leave it to the classical historians to comment upon Mr. Nixon's analysis of the decline of Greece and Rome, but the American malaise has nothing to do with too much affluence, a loss of will to improve, or for that matter, with decadence. Indeed, just the opposite: Two decades of American affluence have only reinforced the historic urge of Americans to improve themselves, and the malaise has come about because of the realization that improvement is no longer as easy as it once was. Their will for improvement remains strong, however, and whether America declines or falls apart depends in large part on what kinds of improvement are made in the years to come.

If there is any American malaise about our evident decline as a world power it is hardly intense, but then many Americans have never been particularly enthusiastic about improving the world, either through foreign aid or war. And while the national pride of other Americans was hurt by the outcome of the Vietnam war, their hurt does not seem to be intense, for even erstwhile hawks are now eager to end the war completely.

In fact, the American malaise is almost entirely domestic, and although the President seems to believe that it stems from too much wealth and easy living, it has actually developed in part out of the inability of people to further

*Herbert J. Gans, a sociology professor at Columbia University, is a senior research associate at the Center for Policy Research.

Breakdown: American Culture   **109**

improve their standard of living. Specifically, it has resulted from two phenomena: the closing of the gap between people's aspirations and expectations, and a recent widening of the gap between these expectations and their achievement.

Until after World War II, most Americans were still so busy making ends meet that they could only *aspire* to improving their standard of living. In the last 10 years or so, however, many have come to *expect* that improvement and increasing numbers have begun to *demand* it. Most of these expectations still have to do with personal and material improvement, although this is less an expression of materialism than a desire for more comfort and convenience. New expectations have also emerged, however; people now want more autonomy in their lives and are less willing than in the past to be bossed around by superiors or by antiquated and arbitrary rules, both at work and in the community. The demand for equal rights which began in the ghettos and the élite universities has spread, more quietly, to many others. College and high-school students want more freedom—and education—in their schools; blue-collar, white-collar and professional workers want more control over their work and working conditions; women are demanding equality with men.

In addition, Americans are expecting more from their institutions. Whereas people once griped only among themselves about shoddy goods, they now expect businessmen to cut fewer corners in their products, pricing policies and advertising; and the demand for a cleaner environment has outdistanced recent increases in pollution. People also expect a better performance from public services; they seem to be less tolerant than before about traffic congestion, good garbage pickup and governmental red tape, and they also complain more about the offerings of the mass media. Many of these dissatisfactions have been around a long time, but larger numbers are voicing them than before.

All this has been accompanied by a higher public morality; a 6 per cent unemployment rate is no longer considered tolerable, and there is somewhat more unhappiness than in the past with conditions in American mental hospitals and prisons—not only among the prisoners—and with the brutality of war. Although the Vietnam war is hardly the first war in which atrocities have been committed by Americans, it is the first one in which they have become a public issue. In part this is a result of the war's unpopularity and its coverage by television, but it also reflects the rise in public standards about how wars ought to be fought.

Yet perhaps the most significant upturn in expectations concerns the role of Government; people now ask for more responsiveness, accountability and honesty than before. The traditional faith in the ability of private enterprise to run the nation's economy has declined, and people now routinely expect Government to be the solver of last resort of America's problems.

When aspirations rise and people begin to hope for a better way of life, they are only hoping, but when expectations heighten, people become more impatient, more critical of their society when expectations are not realized, and eventually, more active politically. All of these reactions emerged during the nineteen-sixties, and show no signs of abating. Of course, the most visible criticism and political action has come from the blacks and other darker-skinned minorities, the educated young and more recently, educated women, and most Americans have not yet become significantly more active politically. However, protest and demonstration are largely strategies of minorities, of people who have no other access to Government; more populous interest groups can make their demands felt more silently. The fact that they have done so is perhaps best illustrated by the actions of Government itself—for example, by the President's recent conversion to neo-Keynesian economic policies, the Congressional pressure for a national health program, day care, greater subsidies to higher education and the courts' objections to the property tax, to mention only a few.

To be sure, the new public expectations are still quite modest, and public morality remains too tolerant—for example of the continued heavy bombing of Indochinese civilians. Nor is it clear how intensively these expectations, so far voiced largely by upper-middle-class people, are felt by the lower-middle and working classes of Middle America. Even so, I suspect that it is this population, the majority of Americans, whose expectations are on the move, and that it is their silent pressure on elected politicians which is responsible for the changes in governmental policy and rhetoric now taking place.

Common sense suggests that the upturn in expectations should have been accompanied by feelings of optimism about the future, but obviously just the reverse is happening. One reason is that when aspirations rise, people are often optimistic; but when new expectations develop, and people assume they can get what they previously only hoped for, they are easily disappointed when expectations and achievements diverge. Nevertheless, the major reason for the malaise is that expectations are not being achieved. Much of today's pessimism began when it became apparent that the Vietnam war was causing havoc in the American economy, and that the dissent about the war was spilling over into other issues, showing many Americans for the first time that the country was seriously divided about many matters.

But the malaise also resulted from the new expectations themselves, and might have come about even without the war. The plain fact is that not all the expectations can possibly be attained and their very existence has created a variety of economic and political consequences which may have a lasting effect on the character and mood of American life. Even if the war can be ended and the difficulties that came in its wake removed, there remains the problem of which and whose expectations can be achieved, and whose not. The difficulty —or perhaps the impossibility—of solving this problem promises no early end to the malaise it produces.

One obvious limit to the achievement of expectations is natural and technological; the bounties of nature, we now know, are not infinite and technology is not the perfect substitute for nature it was once thought to be. Even nonpolluting inventions bring new problems with them, and even the cleanest source of new energy must heat up or otherwise disturb climatic conditions. The extent of nature's limits is still being debated but the debate might never even have been initiated had it not been for the rise in expectations for clean air and water and open space.

There are also economic and social limits to the achievement of all expectations. As long as economic expectations remained modest, we could believe that we lived in an affluent society, but now that they have risen, it becomes obvious that there is not enough affluence for everybody. If all families shared equally in reported family income, they would earn about $11,000 a year, just above what the Bureau of Labor Statistics considers an adequate but modest standard of living. That figure would rise only by $1,000 to $2,000 if tax loopholes were eliminated and corporate profits shared more widely, although if the annual gross national product were divided among all Americans a family of four would currently receive about $19,000.

Moreover, when high expectations are translated into high wages, which allow others to demand yet higher prices and profits, the result is an expensive society that creates problems even for the rich. Moderate income groups are more deprived, however, for high overhead and labor costs have made the repair of goods uneconomic and new housing is now so expensive that it is out of reach for almost two-thirds of the population.

Of course, the poor suffer more than anybody in a high-wage/high-price society, for their income, whether from wages or welfare benefits, does not rise as quickly as other people's. But as the more affluent become increasingly unhappy about their own economic situation, they become less willing to heed the suffering of the poor. Higher expectations also complicate solutions to the race problem, for many poor blacks, themselves more expectant, are no longer willing to be kept down in a castelike underclass, and many whites are just as reluctant to let them out if it means any sacrificing of their expectations. Moreover, while in the past some whites were willing to live in partially integrated neighborhoods—as long as blacks "knew their place"—they now expect to be able to segregate themselves residentially, both from people of lower status and darker skin.

The most recent important consequences of the rise in expectations are political, however, and they probably contribute the largest share of the malaise. For one thing, the increasing demand for governmental action to realize these expectations has begun to politicize the entire society, for government decisions now affect more and more of everyday life, and issues that were once considered to be above politics or nonpolitical are fought out in the political arena. As a result, matters previously decided by fiat, consensus, or by the application of traditional values now have to be negotiated, and in many ways, America has become a negotiating society.

The onset of the negotiating society is perhaps most apparent in the economy; prices and wages are now matters of public policy to be decided by business, labor and "the public" in Washington. In social life, whites must now often negotiate with blacks, teachers with students, parents with children, and even officers must sometimes consult with enlisted men before issuing orders. Political decisions once made by a handful of politicians in the White House and the Congress (or in City Hall) with the advice and consent of a few lobbyists and experts must increasingly take even nonvocal constituents into account, and L.B.J. lost his job partly because he failed to do so when he escalated the Vietnam war.

Politicization and the demand for negotiation not only complicate the life of the political decision-maker but also contribute to the malaise. They bring political conflict out in the open, raising popular awareness of the conflict, and increasing the dissatisfaction of those on the losing end. Once upon a time, the price of New York City's subway token was settled quietly by meetings between Mayor Wagner and union chief Michael Quill—and before that, no one even conceived that subway employees might be entitled to higher wages—but today, almost every voter in New York State knows about the issue, and is unhappy about the outcome.

In addition, when people have higher expectations, and want their interests represented politically, more interests and interest groups must be considered in every political decision, so that decisions are harder to reach, particularly those that can satisfy everybody. The indecision and inaction that come with the greater demand for participation also add to the malaise, and evoke memories of allegedly good old days when decision-making was easier.

The greater demands placed on Government have also led to the realization that Government cannot do as much as is expected of it. Although the New Deal nurtured the belief that social problems could be solved through governmental action, Daniel Patrick Moynihan and others have pointed out that Government is good at appropriating funds but not always able to deliver services. Often, this inability is a result of sabotage by local governments or power-holders, and even Federal funds are sometimes diverted by them for other purposes, so that the true abilities of the Federal Government have not yet been properly tested. But whatever the causes, the limits of governmental effectiveness also help to frustrate the achievement of higher expectations.

The final and perhaps most important reason for the malaise is that the new expectations are developing in an old economic and political system which cannot really deal with them. We are, after all, still a very unequal society, in which income and power are highly centralized. Though everyone's income has risen in the last 20 years, 5 per cent of the people still earn about 22 per cent of the annual income; 1 per cent own more than a third of the nation's total assets, and the 200 largest corporations do a majority of the nation's business. Government is equally centralized; it is more responsive to its own bureaucracies and to the most well-funded and highly organized interest groups than to other citizens; more to businessmen than consumers; and more to suppliers of military hardware than to advocates of peaceful software.

This state of affairs is less a result of conspiracy than of past arrangements; it reflects an older society in which popular expectations were lower and few people expected either the economy or the Government to meet their wishes and needs. Consequently, they remained politically inactive, and both the corporations and the Government responded mainly to groups which already had high expectations, developing centralized decision-making routines which they are now not always able or willing to change.

Ralph Nader and others are fighting hard to make the corporate and governmental apparatuses more accountable to the general public, and their success so far could not have been achieved without the favorable climate in which they are working. At the same time, greater success is held back in part by some traditional attitudes that support the existing centralization. For one thing, many people do not care how public decisions are made as long as these decisions benefit them. Others still believe sufficiently in *laissez-faire* to oppose public intervention in the operations of business, although this belief is much less intense than it was only a few years ago. And many more doubt that even a more accountable Government could improve their standard of living, for they continue to see it as their enemy, which demands taxes for wasteful expenditures which do not benefit them and which they would rather spend privately.

Still, there is enough public dissatisfaction about centralization to create a feeling among people that they are powerless and increasingly so, that they cannot bring about change even if they want to—and this too contributes to malaise. To some extent, their judgment is accurate; as bureaucracies become more important and corporations larger, the centers of power are harder to reach and, of course, as more people want a voice, each voice must, by simple arithmetic, become less powerful. Nevertheless, some of the feelings of powerlessness are themselves a consequence of higher expectations. When people did not demand power, they did not realize how powerless they were, and only now that they want it do they feel that they are powerless—and unhappy.

The rise in expectations has also been accompanied by reactions which are often described as a new wave of conservatism in American life, but are actually attempts by economic and other interest groups opposed to the realization of these expectations to nip them in the bud.

These reactions take several forms, the main one being a counsel for more modest expectations and a return to traditional values which themselves call for modest expectations and for less negotiation. Such reactions are deemed necessary to uphold the social order and keep America from falling apart. Already conservative politicans and intellectuals are arguing that too many people are becoming overly permissive and are asking for too much, that wages are high enough—and that profits are not—that rising payrolls for public services are bankrupting the cities, and that antipoverty programs are making the poor too demanding and too scornful of the traditional work ethic.

Many of the people who put forth these ideas to save the society are themselves quite affluent, both in income and power, and having achieved their own expectations are now asking less affluent people to tighten their belts. Even so, they are not likely to persuade the people for whom their appeals are intended, for revolutions of rising expectations are not easily reversed. Nor should they be reversed—at least in a society that remains as unequal as ours—despite the difficulty of realizing all the expectations.

I do not want to suggest that the demand for conservatism comes only from the affluent. It also comes from some moderate-income Americans who exaggerate and resent the modest rise in income and power experienced by the poor and the blacks during the nineteen-sixties, and from all groups used to relatively unilateral authority, who resent the demand for negotiation and are unhappy with the concurrent politicization of their constituents or clients.

Likewise, adults are complaining about the rising expectations of the young. Although the so-called generation gap has come about mainly because many educated young people are advocating economic and social values that are diametrically opposed to those of Middle America, nonaffluent adults are also angry because affluent young people seem to be having it easier all the time and obtaining more of the pleasures of life to boot. Indeed, their anger seems to have mounted just as their own expectations began to be frustrated.

The new ways in which young people are pursuing pleasure were presumably what the President had in mind when he warned that decadence might destroy American civilization, and adults have traditionally offered such warnings when young people rejected their values. Still, there is no evidence that America is becoming decadent. Marijuana does not appear to drive its users into a life of sloth and fantasy as much as alcohol, and the liberalization of sexual values has not brought about a decline in public morality or social order. In fact, the same students who now sleep together more readily are also the most insistent pressure group for a higher morality in public life.

Actually, sex is one area of life in which high expectations can be achieved painlessly, which is all the more frustrating to people whose nonsexual expectations are not being realized. Moreover, while economic and political change usually have far-reaching consequences, sexual change does not. The fact that young people now take off their clothes more readily, or see films and plays in which actors and actresses take off theirs, has not increased their economic or political power, which is why the new eroticism can ultimately be tolerated more easily than the right of 18-year-olds to vote, which might change some election outcomes in 1972.

Finally, the frustration of expectations has produced a wave of nostalgia, a renewed celebration of the good old days when traditonal values were still intact, consensus was the informal law of the land and politicization and negotiation had not yet emerged to escalate political conflict. The current nostalgia for the nineteen-forties is not coincidental, for that decade is being romanticized as free from political conflict and polluting technology, dominated by a popular and just war, and characterized by innocuous love songs and movies in which sex—and politics—never reared their heads. Needless to say, the real nineteen-forties were not like that at all, but then societies tend to remember only the pleasant past.

The future of the American malaise depends largely upon the outcome of the clash between rising expectations and an economic and political system which is still geared to a society of lower expectations; that outcome is impossible to predict. If the new expectations are as widespread and intensely felt as

I have suggested, one could argue that the status quo cannot long persist, and that the system must change—by becoming more responsive and accountable, and by bringing about at least some redistribution of income and power to satisfy those with rising expectations. On the other hand, it is also possible that the centralization of the economy and the Government has gone so far that corporate and political leaders have sufficient control over the available resources and power to ward off large-scale change. Or, they may resort to more totalitarian measures to maintain current centralization and inequality both, even if this brings about what Bertram Gross has called "friendly fascism."

I am inclined to think that over the long run the system will change, because it has always changed just enough to survive, although the change will be far slower and less complete than the new expectations demand. Meanwhile, only three guesses about the future can be made with any assurance. First, expectations will continue to rise—or at least not decrease—and the voices of those who will advocate reducing expectations and returning to traditional values will become louder. Second, there may be more overt political conflict over the distribution of income and power—that is, who gets what—and although almost all political issues have ultimately revolved around this question, people will be more aware of it, which may in turn affect their political attitudes and actions.

The conflict over who gets what is now manifesting itself over the President's New Economic Program, which like most previous wage and price control programs, tends to perpetuate the status quo, making it difficult for less affluent groups to improve their fortunes. Similar distribution questions will come up in the debate over other issues—for example, the national health program, the financing of the next housing boom, the Federal subsidy of schools and colleges —and tax policy, probably the quickest device for altering income distribution. One current question is whether the Nixon Administration will levy a new regressive tax, such as the value-added (or sales) tax, or whether there will finally be a concerted attempt to make the Federal income tax truly progressive.

Similar issues will be fought out over the distribution of power. For example a workable lid on and the nationalization of campaign expenditures would reduce the power of fat-cat contributors on candidates. The real power lies elsewhere, however, and cannot be redistributed without considerably increasing the accountability of the corporations and the Federal bureaucracies, as well as Congress and the White House—and democratizing those state and local governmental bodies still dominated by business interests, lobbyists and unrepresentative political machines.

The 1972 election may provide some clues about the future of these distributional issues, for several Presidential candidates have at least begun to speak out on them. Of course, what politicians say before an election and do afterward differs, and even the most dedicated President cannot significantly alter the distribution of income and power by himself. He needs the help of a like-minded Congress and Supreme Court (which he will not have), but they too can act only if there is widespread and intense public demand for action. This does not exist now and may not develop until subsequent election years, if then. Its coming may be hastened, however, if the economy does not regain its health, for then, as in the Depression, people and politicians alike would be ready for drastic change.

The third guess about the future is that it is quite possible that the poor, the black and other minorities will not be able to improve their economic and political position significantly, partly because they are minorities, partly because until the Middle-American majority realizes its expectations it will not be inclined to support more effective antipoverty efforts. This in turn will probably lead to more unrest, particularly in the ghettos, and more crime in middle-class neighborhoods, for theft and burglary are, at least in part, methods of income redistribution to which the poor resort when society pays no attention to their expectations. More poor individuals will probably make it out of the slums and the black middle class will further increase in size, but those who are left behind will therefore be even more highly motivated to lash out against society—and against themselves through the pathologies associated with poverty and powerlessness.

This will make life harder in the cities, but then life will get harder for everybody. Even if good economic times return and even if there is some redistribution of income and power, the struggle over whose expectations will be met and whose not, and the continuing politicization of society, will increase the amount and intensity of public conflict. But since Americans are not really used to solving distributional struggles or living with political conflict, the current malaise may well become permanent.

Nevertheless, the phenomena I have described and the predictions I have ventured do not justify the conclusion that America is declining or falling, or even falling apart. Societies do not decline because they are too rich, as President Nixon would have it, but because their people are unable to find a proper way of dividing up the available wealth and power. This is also the case in America, and no one can tell how and when Americans will find that way.

The past 20 years have seen a rise in the expectations of the poor and the Middle Americans, who are now beginning to demand a larger share of the pie of wealth and power. This is hardly a sign of decline or decadence, but of vitality and the very will to improve which Mr. Nixon thinks is disappearing. And if America adapts to the rise in expectations, it is even a sign that justifies some optimism about the future. Of course, if Middle America tries to obtain its share of the pie by further squeezing the poor, and if the poor fight back, then it is possible that America will one day fall apart from internal strife— and not just in its cities alone. But if both the poor and the Middle Americans obtain a larger share—mainly from the rich, and from the economic growth that lies ahead—then America may become a somewhat more egalitarian society than it has been in the past. To some, particularly among the rich, this may signify the end of America, but it is only the end of an America that should have disappeared earlier.

11. The Fractured Family

ALVIN TOFFLER

The flood of novelty about to crash down upon us will spread from universities and research centers to factories and offices, from the marketplace and mass media into our social relationships, from the community into the home. Penetrating deep into our private lives, it will place absolutely unprecedented strains on the family itself.

The family has been called the "giant shock absorber" of society—the place to which the bruised and battered individual returns after doing battle with the world, the one stable point in an increasingly flux-filled environment. As the super-industrial revolution unfolds, this "shock absorber" will come in for some shocks of its own.

Social critics have a field day speculating about the family. The family is "near the point of complete extinction," says Ferdinand Lundberg, author of *The Coming World Transformation.* "The family is dead except for the first year or two of child raising," according to psychoanalyst William Wolf. "This will be its only function." Pessimists tell us the family is racing toward oblivion —but seldom tell us what will take its place.

Family optimists, in contrast, contend that the family, having existed all this time, will continue to exist. Some go so far as to argue that the family is in for a Golden Age. As leisure spreads, they theorize, families will spend more time together and will derive great satisfaction from joint activity. "The family that plays together, stays together," etc.

A more sophisticated view holds that the very turbulence of tomorrow will drive people deeper into their families. "People will marry for stable structure," says Dr. Irwin M. Greenberg, Professor of Psychiatry at the Albert Einstein College of Medicine. According to this view, the family serves as one's "portable roots," anchoring one against the storm of change. In short, the more transient and novel the environment, the more important the family will become.

It may be that both sides in this debate are wrong. For the future is more open than it might appear. The family may neither vanish *nor* enter upon a new Golden Age. It may—and this is far more likely—break up, shatter, only to come together again in weird and novel ways.

BREAKDOWNS: INSTITUTIONAL

The Mystique of Motherhood

The most obviously upsetting force likely to strike the family in the decades immediately ahead will be the impact of the new birth technology. The ability to pre-set the sex of one's baby, or even to "program" its IQ, looks and personality traits, must now be regarded as a real possibility. Embryo implants, babies grown *in vitro,* the ability to swallow a pill and guarantee oneself twins or triplets or, even more, the ability to walk into a "babytorium" and actually purchase embryos—all this reaches so far beyond any previous human experience that one needs to look at the future through the eyes of the poet or painter, rather than those of the sociologist or conventional philosopher.

It is regarded as somehow unscholarly, even frivolous, to discuss these matters. Yet advances in science and technology, or in reproductive biology alone, could, within a short time, smash all orthodox ideas about the family and its responsibilities. When babies can be grown in a laboratory jar what happens to the very notion of maternity? And what happens to the self-image of the female in societies which, since the very beginnings of man, have taught her that her primary mission is the propagation of and nurture of the race?

Few social scientists have begun as yet to concern themselves with such questions. One who has is psychiatrist Hyman G. Weitzen, director of Neuropsychiatric Service at Polyclinic Hospital in New York. The cycle of birth, Dr. Weitzen suggests, "fulfills for most women a major creative need . . . Most women are proud of their ability to bear children . . . The special aura that glorifies the pregnant woman has figured largely in the art and literature of both East and West."

What happens to the cult of motherhood, Weitzen asks, if "her offspring might literally not be hers, but that of a genetically 'superior' ovum, implanted in her womb from another woman, or even grown in a Petri dish?" If women are to be important at all, he suggests, it will no longer be because they alone can bear children. If nothing else, we are about to kill off the mystique of motherhood.

Not merely motherhood, but the concept of parenthood itself may be in for radical revision. Indeed, the day may soon dawn when it is possible for a child to have more than two biological parents. Dr. Beatrice Mintz, a developmental biologist at the Institute for Cancer Research in Philadelphia, has grown what are coming to be known as "multi-mice"—baby mice each of which has more than the usual number of parents. Embryos are taken from each of two pregnant mice. These embryos are placed in a laboratory dish and nurtured until they form a single growing mass. This is then implanted in the womb of a third female mouse. A baby is born that clearly shares the genetic characteristics of both sets of donors. Thus a typical multi-mouse, born of two pairs of parents, has white fur and whiskers on one side of its face, dark fur and whiskers on the other, with alternating bands of white and dark hair covering the rest of the body. Some 700 multi-mice bred in this fashion have already produced more than 35,000 offspring themselves. If multi-mouse is here, can "multi-man" be far behind?

Under such circumstances, what or who is a parent? When a woman bears in her uterus an embryo conceived in another woman's womb, who is the mother? And just exactly who is the father?

If a couple can actually purchase an embryo, then parenthood becomes a legal, not a biological matter. Unless such transactions are tightly controlled, one can imagine such grotesqueries as a couple buying an embryo, raising it *in vitro,* then buying another in the name of the first, as though for a trust fund. In that case, they might be regarded as legal "grandparents" before their first child is out of its infancy. We shall need a whole new vocabulary to describe kinship ties.

Furthermore, if embryos are for sale, can a corporation buy one? Can it buy ten thousand? Can it resell them? And if not a corporation, how about a non-commercial research laboratory? If we buy and sell living embryos, are we back to a new form of slavery? Such are the nightmarish questions soon to be debated by us. To continue to think of the family, therefore, in purely conventional terms is to defy all reason.

Faced by rapid social change and the staggering implications of the scientific revolution, super-industrial man may be forced to experiment with novel family forms. Innovative minorities can be expected to try out a colorful variety of family arrangements. They will begin by tinkering with existing forms.

The Streamlined Family

One simple thing they will do is streamline the family. The typical pre-industrial family not only had a good many children, but numerous other dependents as well—grandparents, uncles, aunts, and cousins. Such "extended" families were well suited for survival in slow-paced agricultural societies. But such families are hard to transport or transplant. They are immobile.

Industrialism demanded masses of workers ready and able to move off the land in pursuit of jobs, and to move again whenever necessary. Thus the extended family gradually shed its excess weight and the so-called "nuclear" family emerged—a stripped-down, portable family unit consisting only of parents and a small set of children. This new style family, far more mobile than the traditional extended family, became the standard model in all the industrial countries.

Super-industrialism, however, the next stage of eco-technological development, requires even higher mobility. Thus we may expect many among the people of the future to carry the streamlining process a step further by remaining childless, cutting the family down to its most elemental components, a man and a woman. Two people, perhaps with matched careers, will prove more efficient at navigating through education and social shoals, through job changes and geographic relocations, than the ordinary child-cluttered family. Indeed, anthropologist Margaret Mead has pointed out that we may already be moving toward a system under which, as she puts it, "parenthood would

BREAKDOWNS: INSTITUTIONAL

be limited to a smaller number of families whose principal functions would be childrearing," leaving the rest of the population "free to function—for the first time in history—as individuals."

A compromise may be the postponement of children, rather than childlessness. Men and women today are often torn in conflict between a commitment to career and a commitment to children. In the future, many couples will sidestep this problem by deferring the entire task of raising children until after retirement.

This may strike people of the present as odd. Yet once childbearing is broken away from its biological base, nothing more than tradition suggests having children at an early age. Why not wait, and buy your embryos later, after your work career is over? Thus childlessness is likely to spread among young and middle-aged couples; sexagenarians who raise infants may be far more common. The post-retirement family could become a recognized social institution.

Bio-Parents and Pro-Parents

If a smaller number of families raise children, however, why do the children have to be their own? Why not a system under which "professional parents" take on the childrearing function for others?

Raising children, after all, requires skills that are by no means universal. We don't let "just anyone" perform brain surgery or, for that matter, sell stocks and bonds. Even the lowest ranking civil servant is required to pass tests proving competence. Yet we allow virtually anyone, almost without regard for mental or moral qualification, to try his or her hand at raising young human beings, so long as these humans are biological offspring. Despite the increasing complexity of the task, parenthood remains the greatest single preserve of the amateur.

As the present system cracks and the super-industrial revolution rolls over us, as the armies of juvenile delinquents swell, as hundreds of thousands of youngsters flee their homes, and students rampage at universities in all the techno-societies, we can expect vociferous demands for an end to parental dilettantism.

There are far better ways to cope with the problems of youth, but professional parenthood is certain to be proposed, if only because it fits so perfectly with the society's overall push toward specialization. Moreover, there is a powerful, pent-up demand for this social innovation. Even now millions of parents, given the opportunity, would happily relinquish their parental responsibilities—and not necessarily through irresponsibility or lack of love. Harried, frenzied, up against the wall, they have come to see themselves as inadequate to the tasks. Given affluence and the existence of specially-equipped and licensed professional parents, many of today's biological parents would not only gladly surrender their children to them, but would look upon it as an act of love, rather than rejection.

Parental professionals would not be therapists, but actual family units assigned to, and well paid for, rearing children. Such families might be multigenerational by design, offering children in them an opportunity to observe and learn from a variety of adult models, as was the case in the old farm homestead. With the adults paid to be professional parents, they would be freed of the occupational necessity to relocate repeatedly. Such families would take in new children as old ones "graduate" so that age-segregation would be minimized.

Thus newspapers of the future might well carry advertisements addressed to young married couples: "Why let parenthood tie you down? Let us raise your infant into a responsible, successful adult. Class A Pro-family offers: father age 39, mother, 36, grandmother, 67. Uncle and aunt, age 30, live in, hold part-time local employment. Four-child-unit has opening for one, age 6–8. Regulated diet exceeds government standards. All adults certified in child development and management. Bio-parents permitted frequent visits. Telephone contact allowed. Child may spend summer vacation with bio-parents. Religion, art, music encouraged by special arrangement. Five year contract, minimum. Write for further details."

The "real" or "bio-parents" could, as the ad suggests, fill the role presently played by interested godparents, namely that of friendly and helpful outsiders. In such a way, the society could continue to breed a wide diversity of genetic types, yet turn the care of children over to mother-father groups who are equipped, both intellectually and emotionally, for the task of caring for kids.

Communes and Homosexual Daddies

Quite a different alternative lies in the communal family. As transience increases the loneliness and alienation in society, we can anticipate increasing experimentation with various forms of group marriage. The banding together of several adults and children into a single "family" provides a kind of insurance against isolation. Even if one to two members of the household leave, the remaining members have one another. Communes are springing up modeled after those described by psychologist B. F. Skinner in *Walden Two* and by novelist Robert Rimmer in *The Harrad Experiment and Proposition 31.* In the latter work, Rimmer seriously proposes the legalization of a "corporate family" in which from three to six adults adopt a single name, live and raise children in common, and legally incorporate to obtain certain economic and tax advantages.

According to some observers, there are already hundreds of open or covert communes dotting the American map. Not all, by any means, are composed of young people or hippies. Some are organized around specific goals—like the group, quietly financed by three East Coast colleges—which has taken as its function the task of counseling college freshmen, helping to orient them to campus life. The goals may be social, religious, political, even recreational. Thus we shall before long begin to see communal families of surfers dotting the beaches of California and Southern France, if they don't already. We shall see the emergence of communes based on political doctrines and religious faiths. In Denmark, a bill to legalize group marriage has already been introduced in the Folketing (Parliament). While passage is not imminent, the act of introduction is itself a significant symbol of change.

In Chicago, 250 adults and children already live together in "family-style monasticism" under the auspices of a new, fast growing religious organization, the Ecumenical Institute. Members share the same quarters, cook and eat together, worship and tend children in common, and pool their incomes. At least 60,000 people have taken "EI" courses and similar communes have begun to spring up in Atlanta, Boston, Los Angeles and other cities. "A brand-new world is emerging," says Professor Joseph W. Mathews, leader of the Ecumenical Institute, "but people are still operating in terms of the old one. We seek to re-educate people and give them the tools to build a new social context."

Still another type of family unit likely to win adherents in the future might be called the "geriatric commune"—a group marriage of elderly people drawn together in a common search for companionship and assistance. Disengaged from the productive economy that makes mobility necessary, they will settle in a single place, band together, pool funds, collectively hire domestic or nursing help, and proceed—within limits—to have the "time of their lives."

Communalism runs counter to the pressure for ever greater geographical and social mobility generated by the thrust toward super-industrialism. It presupposes groups of people who "stay put." For this reason, communal experiments will first proliferate among those in the society who are free from the industrial discipline—the retired population, the young, the dropouts, the students, as well as among self-employed professional and technical people. Later, when advanced technology and information systems make it possible for much of the work of society to be done at home via computer-telecommunication hookups, communalism will become feasible for larger numbers.

We shall, however, also see many more "family" units consisting of a single unmarried adult and one or more children. Nor will all of these adults be women. It is already possible in some places for unmarried men to adopt children. In 1965 in Oregon, for example, a thirty-eight-year-old musician named Tony Piazza became the first unmarried man in that state, and perhaps in the United States, to be granted the right to adopt a baby. Courts are more readily granting custody to divorced fathers, too. In London, photographer Michael Cooper, married at twenty and divorced soon after, won the right to raise his infant son, and expressed an interest in adopting other children. Observing that he did not particularly wish to remarry, but that he liked children, Cooper mused aloud: "I wish you could just ask beautiful women to have babies for you. Or any woman you liked, or who had something you admired. Ideally, I'd like a big house full of children—all different colors, shapes and sizes." Romantic? Unmanly? Perhaps. Yet attitudes like these will be widely held by men in the future.

Two pressures are even now softening up the culture, preparing it for acceptance of the idea of childrearing by men. First, adoptable children are in oversupply in some places. Thus, in California, disc jockeys blare commercials: "We have many wonderful babies of all races and nationalities waiting to bring love and happiness to the right families ... Call the Los Angeles County Bureau of Adoption." At the same time, the mass media, in a strange non-conspiratorial fashion, appear to have decided simultaneously that men who raise children hold special interest for the public. Extremely popular television shows in recent seasons have glamorized womanless households in which men scrub floors, cook, and, most significantly, raise children. *My Three Sons, The Rifleman, Bonanza* and *Bachelor Father* are four examples.

As homosexuality becomes more socially acceptable, we may even begin to find families based on homosexual "marriages" with the partners adopting children. Whether these children would be of the same or opposite sex remains to be seen. But the rapidity with which homosexuality is winning respectability in the techno-societies distinctly points in this direction. In Holland not long ago a Catholic priest "married" two homosexuals, explaining to critics that "they are among the faithful to be helped." England has rewritten its relevant legislation; homosexual relations between consenting adults are no longer considered a crime. And in the United States a meeting of Episcopal clergymen concluded publicly that homosexuality might, under certain circumstances, be adjudged "good." The day may also come when a court decides that a couple of stable, well educated homosexuals might make decent "parents."

We might also see the gradual relaxation of bars against polygamy. Polygamous families exist even now, more widely than generally believed, in the midst of "normal" society. Writer Ben Merson, after visiting several such families in Utah where polygamy is still regarded as essential by certain Mormon fundamentalists, estimated that there are some 30,000 people living in underground family units of this type in the United States. As sexual attitudes loosen up, as property rights become less important because of rising affluence, the social repression of polygamy may come to be regarded as irrational. This shift may be facilitated by the very mobility that compels men to spend considerable time away from their present homes. The old male fantasy of the Captain's Paradise may become a reality for some, although it is likely that, under such circumstances, the wives left behind will demand extramarital sexual rights. Yesterday's "captain" would hardly consider this possibility. Tomorrow's may feel quite differently about it.

Still another family form is even now springing up in our midst, a novel childrearing unit I call the "aggregate family"—a family based on relationships between divorced and remarried couples, in which all the children become part of "one big family." Though sociologists have paid little attention as yet to this phenomenon, it is already so prevalent that it formed the basis for a hilarious scene in a recent American movie entitled *Divorce American Style*. We may expect aggregate families to take on increasing importance in the decades ahead.

Childless marriage, professional parenthood, post-retirement childrearing, corporate families, communes, geriatric group marriages, homosexual family units, polygamy—these, then, are a few of the family forms and practices with which innovative minorities will experiment in the decades ahead. Not all of us, however, will be willing to participate in such experimentation. What of the majority?

The Odds Against Love

Minorities experiment; majorities cling to the forms of the past. It is safe to say that large numbers of people will refuse to jettison the conventional idea of marriage or the familiar family forms. They will, no doubt, continue searching for happiness within the orthodox format. Yet, even they will be forced to innovate in the end, for the odds against success may prove overwhelming.

The orthodox format presupposes that two young people will "find" one another and marry. It presupposes that the two will fulfill certain psychological needs in one another, and that the two personalities will develop over the years, more or less in tandem, so that they continue to fulfill each other's needs. It further presupposes that this process will last "until death do us part."

These expectations are built deeply into our culture. It is no longer respectable, as it once was, to marry for anything but love. Love has changed from a peripheral concern of the family into its primary justification. Indeed, the pursuit of love through family life has become, for many, the very purpose of life itself.

Love, however, is defined in terms of this notion of shared growth. It is seen as a beautiful mesh of complementary needs, flowing into and out of one another, fulfilling the loved ones, and producing feelings of warmth, tenderness and devotion. Unhappy husbands often complain that they have "left their wives behind" in terms of social, educational or intellectual growth. Partners in successful marriages are said to "grow together."

This "parallel development" theory of love carries endorsement from marriage counsellors, psychologists and sociologists. Thus, says sociologist Nelson Foote, a specialist on the family, the quality of the relationship between husband and wife is dependent upon "the degree of matching in their phases of distinct but comparable development."

If love is a product of shared growth, however, and we are to measure success in marriage by the degree to which matched development actually occurs, it becomes possible to make a strong and ominous prediction about the future.

It is possible to demonstrate that, even in a relatively stagnant society, the mathematical odds are heavily stacked against any couple achieving this ideal of parallel growth. The odds for success positively plummet, however, when the rate of change in society accelerates, as it now is doing. In a fast-moving society, in which many things change, not once, but repeatedly, in which the husband moves up and down a variety of economic and social scales, in which the family is again and again torn loose from home and community, in which individuals move further from their parents, further from the religion of origin, and further from traditional values, it is almost miraculous if two people develop at anything like comparable rates.

If, at the same time, average life expectancy rises from, say, fifty to seventy years, thereby lengthening the term during which this acrobatic feat of matched development is supposed to be maintained, the odds against success become absolutely astronomical. Thus, Nelson Foote writes with wry understatement: "To expect a marriage to last indefinitely under modern conditions is to expect a lot." To ask love to last indefinitely is to expect even more. Transience and novelty are both in league against it.

Temporary Marriage

It is this change in the statistical odds against love that accounts for the high divorce and separation rates in most of the techno-societies. The faster the rate of change and the longer the life span, the worse these odds grow. Something has to crack.

In point of fact, of course, something has already cracked—and it is the old insistence on permanence. Millions of men and women now adopt what appears to them to be a sensible and conservative strategy. Rather than opting for some offbeat variety of the family, they marry conventionally, they attempt to make it "work," and then, when the paths of the partners diverge beyond an acceptable point, they divorce or depart. Most of them go on to search for a new partner whose developmental stage, at that moment, matches their own.

As human relationships grow more transient and modular, the pursuit of love becomes, if anything, more frenzied. But the temporal expectations change. As conventional marriage proves itself less and less capable of delivering on its promise of lifelong love, therefore, we can anticipate open public acceptance of temporary marriages. Instead of wedding "until death do us part," couples will enter into matrimony knowing from the first that the relationship is likely to be short-lived.

They will know, too, that when the paths of husband and wife diverge, when there is too great a discrepancy in developmental stages, they may call it quits —without shock or embarrassment, perhaps even without some of the pain that goes with divorce today. And when the opportunity presents itself, they will marry again . . . and again . . . and again.

Serial marriage—a pattern of successive temporary marriages—is cut to order for the Age of Transience in which all man's relationships, all his ties with the environment, shrink in duration. It is the natural, the inevitable outgrowth of a social order in which automobiles are rented, dolls traded in, and dresses discarded after one-time use. It is the mainstream marriage pattern of tomorrow.

In one sense, serial marriage is already the best kept family secret of the techno-societies. According to Professor Jessie Bernard, a world-prominent family sociologist, "Plural marriage is more extensive in our society today than it is in societies that permit polygamy—the chief difference being that we have institutionalized plural marriage serially or sequentially rather than contemporaneously." Remarriage is already so prevalent a practice that nearly one out of every four bridegrooms in America has been to the altar before. It is so prevalent that one IBM personnel man reports a poignant incident involving a divorced woman, who, in filling out a job application, paused when she came to the question of marital status. She put her pencil in her mouth, pondered for a moment, then wrote: "Unremarried."

Transience necessarily affects the durational expectancies with which persons approach new situations. While they may yearn for a permanent relationship, something inside whispers to them that it is an increasingly improbable luxury.

Even young people who most passionately seek commitment, profound involvement with people and causes, recognize the power of the thrust toward transience. Listen, for example, to a young black American, a civil-rights worker, as she describes her attitude toward time and marriage:

"In the white world, marriage is always billed as 'the end'—like in a Hollywood movie. I don't go for that. I can't imagine myself promising my whole lifetime away. I might want to get married now, but how about next year? That's not disrespect for the institution [of marriage], but the deepest respect. In The [civil rights] Movement, you need to have a feeling for the temporary —of making something as good as you can, while it lasts. In conventional relationships, time is a prison."

Such attitudes will not be confined to the young, the few, or the politically active. They will whip across nations as novelty floods into the society and catch fire as the level of transience rises still higher. And along with them will come a sharp increase in the number of temporary—then serial—marriages.

The idea is summed up vividly by a Swedish magazine, *Svensk Damtidning,* which interviewed a number of leading Swedish sociologists, legal experts, and others about the future of man-woman relationships. It presented its findings in five photographs. They showed the same beautiful bride being carried across the threshold five times—by five different bridegrooms.

Marriage Trajectories

As serial marriages become more common, we shall begin to characterize people not in terms of their present marital status, but in terms of their marriage career or "trajectory." This trajectory will be formed by the decisions they make at certain vital turning points in their lives.

For most people, the first such juncture will arrive in youth, when they enter into "trial marriage." Even now the young people of the United States and Europe are engaged in a mass experiment with probationary marriage, with or without benefit of ceremony. The staidest of United States universities are beginning to wink at the practice of co-ed housekeeping among their students.

Acceptance of trial marriage is even growing among certain religious philosophers. Thus we hear the German theologian Siegfried Keil of Marburg University urge what he terms "recognized premarriage." In Canada, Father Jacques Lazure has publicly proposed "probationary marriages" of three to eighteen months.

In the past, social pressures and lack of money restricted experimentation with trial marriage to a relative handful. In the future, both these limiting forces will evaporate. Trial marriage will be the first step in the serial marriage "careers" that millions will pursue.

A second critical life juncture for the people of the future will occur when the trial marriage ends. At this point, couples may choose to formalize their relationship and stay together into the next stage. Or they may terminate it and seek out new partners. In either case, they will then face several options. They may prefer to go childless. They may choose to have, adopt or "buy" one or more children. They may decide to raise these children themselves or to farm them out to professional parents. Such decisions will be made, by and large, in the early twenties—by which time many young adults will already be well into their second marriages.

A third significant turning point in the marital career will come, as it does today, when the children finally leave home. The end of parenthood proves excruciating for many, particularly women who, once the children are gone, find themselves without a *raison d'être*. Even today divorces result from the failure of the couple to adapt to this traumatic break in continuity.

Among the more conventional couples of tomorrow who choose to raise their own children in the time-honored fashion, this will continue to be a particularly painful time. It will, however, strike earlier. Young people today already leave home sooner than their counterparts a generation ago. They will probably depart even earlier tomorrow. Masses of youngsters will move off, whether into trial marriage or not, in their mid-teens. Thus we may anticipate that the middle and late thirties will be another important breakpoint in the marital careers of millions. Many at that juncture will enter into their third marriage.

This third marriage will bring together two people for what could well turn out to be the longest uninterrupted stretch of matrimony in their lives—from, say, the late thirties until one of the partners dies. This may, in fact, turn out to be the only "real" marriage, the basis of the only truly durable marital relationship. During this time two mature people, presumably with well-matched interests and complementary psychological needs, and with a sense of being at comparable stages of personality development, will be able to look forward to a relationship with a decent statistical probability of enduring.

Not all these marriages will survive until death, however, for the family will still face a fourth crisis point. This will come, as it does now for so many, when one or both of the partners retires from work. The abrupt change in daily routine brought about by this development places great strain on the couple. Some couples will go the path of the post-retirement family, choosing this moment to begin the task of raising children. This may overcome for them the vacuum that so many couples now face after reaching the end of their occupational lives. (Today many women go to work when they finish raising children; tomorrow many will reverse that pattern, working first and childrearing next.) Other couples will overcome the crisis of retirement in other ways, fashioning both together a new set of habits, interests and activities. Still others will find the transition too difficult, and will simply sever their ties and enter the pool of "in-betweens"—the floating reserve of temporarily unmarried persons.

Of course, there will be some who, through luck, interpersonal skill and high intelligence, will find it possible to make long-lasting monogamous marriages work. Some will succeed, as they do today, in marrying for life and finding durable love and affection. But others will fail to make even sequential marriages endure for long. Thus some will try two or even three partners within, say, the final stage of marriage. Across the board, the average number of marriages per capita will rise—slowly but relentlessly.

Most people will probably move forward along this progression, engaging in one "conventional" temporary marriage after another. But with widespread familial experimentation in the society, the more daring or desperate will make side forays into less conventional arrangements as well, perhaps experimenting with communal life at some point, or going it alone with a child. The net result will be a rich variation in the types of marital trajectories that people will trace, a wider choice of life-patterns, an endless opportunity for novelty of experience. Certain patterns will be more common than others. But temporary marriage will be a standard feature, perhaps the dominant feature, of family life in the future.

The Demands of Freedom

A world in which marriage is temporary rather than permanent, in which family arrangements are diverse and colorful, in which homosexuals may be acceptable parents and retirees start raising children—such a world is vastly different from our own. Today all boys and girls are expected to find life-long partners. In tomorrow's world, being single will be no crime. Nor will couples be forced to remain imprisoned, as so many still are today, in marriages that have turned rancid. Divorce will be easy to arrange, so long as responsible provision is made for children. In fact, the very introduction of professional parenthood could touch off a great liberating wave of divorces by making it easier for adults to discharge their parental responsibilities without necessarily remaining in the cage of a hateful marriage. With this powerful external pressure removed, those who stay together would be those who wish to stay together, those for whom marriage is actively fulfilling—those, in short, who are in love.

We are also likely to see, under this looser, more variegated family system, many more marriages involving partners of unequal age. Increasingly, older men will marry young girls or vice versa. What will count will not be chronological age, but complementary values and interests and, above all, the level of personal development. To put it another way, partners will be interested not in age, but in stage.

Children in this super-industrial society will grow up with an ever enlarging circle of what might be called "semi-siblings"—a whole clan of boys and girls brought into the world by their successive sets of parents. What becomes of such "aggregate" families will be fascinating to observe. Semi-sibs may turn out to be like cousins, today. They may help one another professionally or in time of need. But they will also present the society with novel problems. Should semi-sibs marry, for example?

Surely, the whole relationship of the child to the family will be dramatically altered. Except perhaps in communal groupings, the family will lose what little remains of its power to transmit values to the younger generation. This will further accelerate the pace of change and intensify the problems that go with it.

Looming over all such changes, however, and even dwarfing them in significance is something far more subtle. Seldom discussed, there is a hidden rhythm in human affairs that until now has served as one of the key stabilizing forces in society: the family cycle.

We begin as children; we mature; we leave the parental nest; we give birth to children who, in turn, grow up, leave and begin the process all over again. This cycle has been operating so long, so automatically, and with such implacable regularity, that men have taken it for granted. It is part of the human landscape. Long before they reach puberty, children learn the part they are expected to play in keeping this great cycle turning. This predictable succession of family events has provided all men, of whatever tribe or society, with a sense of continuity, a place in the temporal scheme of things. The family cycle has been one of the sanity-preserving constants in human existence.

Today this cycle is accelerating. We grow up sooner, leave home sooner, marry sooner, have children sooner. We space them more closely together and complete the period of parenthood more quickly. In the words of Dr. Bernice Neugarten, a University of Chicago specialist on family development, "The trend is toward a more rapid rhythm of events through most of the family cycle."

But if industrialism, with its faster pace of life, has accelerated the family cycle, super-industrialism now threatens to smash it altogether. With the fantasies that the birth scientists are hammering into reality, with the colorful familial experimentation that innovative minorities will perform, with the likely development of such institutions as professional parenthood, with the increasing movement toward temporary and serial marriage, we shall not merely run the cycle more rapidly; we shall introduce irregularity, suspense, unpredictability—in a word, novelty—into what was once as regular and certain as the seasons.

When a "mother" can compress the process of birth into a brief visit to an embryo emporium, when by transferring embryos from womb to womb we can destroy even the ancient certainty that childbearing took nine months, children will grow up into a world in which the family cycle, once so smooth and sure, will be jerkily arhythmic. Another crucial stabilizer will have been removed from the wreakage of the old order, another pillar of sanity broken.

There is, of course, nothing inevitable about the developments traced in the preceding pages. We have it in our power to shape change. We may choose one future over another. We cannot, however, maintain the past. In our family forms, as in our economics, science, technology and social relationships, we shall be forced to deal with the new.

The Super-industrial Revolution will liberate men from many of the barbarisms that grew out of the restrictive, relatively choiceless family patterns of the past and present. It will offer to each a degree of freedom hitherto unknown. But it will exact a steep price for that freedom.

As we hurtle into tomorrow, millions of ordinary men and women will face emotion-packed options so unfamiliar, so untested, that past experience will offer little clue to wisdom. In their family ties, as in all other aspects of their lives, they will be compelled to cope not merely with transience, but with the added problem of novelty as well.

Thus, in matters both large and small, in the most public of conflicts and the most private of conditions, the balance between routine and non-routine, predictable and non-predictable, the known and the unknown, will be altered. The novelty ratio will rise.

In such an environment, fast-changing and unfamiliar, we shall be forced, as we wend our way through life, to make our personal choices from a diverse array of options. And it is to the third central characteristic of tomorrow, *diversity,* that we must now turn. For it is the final convergence of these three factors—transience, novelty and diversity—that sets the stage for the historic crisis of adaptation that is the subject of this book: future shock.

12. How to Write Your Own Marriage Contract

SUSAN EDMISTON*

First we thought marriage was when Prince Charming came and took you away with him. Then we thought that marriage was orange blossoms and Alençon lace and silver patterns. Then we thought that marriage—at least—was when you couldn't face signing the lease on the new apartment in two different names.

But most of us never even suspected the truth. Nobody ever so much as mentioned that what marriage is, at its very heart and essence, is a contract. When you say "I do," what you are doing is not, as you thought, vowing your eternal love, but rather subscribing to a whole system of rights, obligations and responsibilities that may very well be anathema to your most cherished beliefs.

Worst of all, you never even get to read the contract—to say nothing of the fine print. If you did, you probably wouldn't agree to it. Marriage, as it exists today, is a peculiarly vague, and yet inflexible, arrangement of institutionalized inequality which goes only one step beyond the English common-law concept of husband and wife as one, and, as the saying goes, "that 'one' is the husband." We have progressed from the notion of wife as legal nonentity to the notion of wife as dependent and inferior.

In recent years, many people have taken to writing their own marriage ceremonies in a desperate attempt to make the institution more relevant to their own lives. But ceremonies, they are finding, do not reach the heart of the matter. So some couples are now taking the logical next step of drawing up their own contracts. These agreements may delineate any of the financial or personal aspects of the marriage relationship—from who pays which bills to who uses what birth control. Though many of their provisions may not be legally binding, at the very least they can help us to examine the often inchoate assumptions underlying our relationships, help us come to honest and equita-

*Susan Edmiston is a writer, editor, columnist and contributor to many national magazines. She is now at work on a book, "A Literary Guide to New York."

ble terms with one another, and provide guidelines for making our marriages what we truly want them to be.

Before their first child was born, Alix Kates Shulman and her husband had an egalitarian, partnership marriage. Alix worked full time as an editor in New York, and both shared the chores involved in maintaining their small household. After two children, however, the couple found that they had automatically fallen into the traditional sex roles: he went out and worked all day to support his family; she stayed home and worked from 6 a.m. to 9 p.m. taking care of children and housework. Unthinkingly, they had agreed not only to the legalities of marriage but to the social contract as well.

After six years at home—six years of chronic dissatisfaction—Alix became involved in the Women's Liberation movement and realized that it might be possible to change the contract under which she and her husband lived. The arrangement they worked out (see page 146), basically a division of household duties and child care, rejected "the notion that the work which brings in more money is more valuable. The ability to earn . . . money is a privilege which must not be compounded by enabling the larger earner to buy out of his/her duties."

Sitting down and writing out a contract may seem a cold and formal way of working out an intimate relationship, but often it is the only way of coping with the ghosts of 2,000 years of tradition lurking in our definitions of marriage. Now, after three years, Alix has written six books, and both Shulmans find that their agreement is a new way of life rather than a document to be followed legalistically.

No less an antagonist than Norman Mailer has attacked the Shulmans' contract. After describing it in *The Prisoner of Sex,* he writes (in his characteristic third person): "No, he would not be married to such a woman. If he were obliged to have a roommate he would pick a man. . . . He could love a woman and she might even sprain her back before a hundred sinks of dishes in a month, but he would not be happy to help her if his work should suffer, no, not unless her work were as valuable as his own." Mailer's comment makes the issues clear: under the old contract the work of childrearing and housekeeping is assumed to be less important than the work a man does—specifically, here, the career of self-aggrandizement Mailer has cut out for himself —and a wife, unless she is able to prove otherwise, is the one who must do the housework.

The Shulmans' contract renegotiates husband's and wife's roles as far as the care of children and home are concerned. Psychologists Barbara and Myron Koltuv took their agreement one step further.

"We agreed in the beginning that since I didn't care a bit about the house, he would do a lot of cleaning and I would do a lot of cooking," says Barbara. "He does a lot of the shopping, too, because he likes to buy things and I don't. Whenever either of us feels 'I'm doing all the drudge work and you're not doing anything,' we switch jobs. Gradually we've eliminated a lot of stuff neither of us wanted to do. In the early days, we'd cook dinner for people because we didn't feel it was hospitable to ask them to go out, but now we often go out instead.

"In the beginning we literally opened up separate bank accounts. We split our savings and checking accounts. At the time he made a third more money than I did. I deferred to him all the time, even though it was only a third. I felt that if he didn't spend so much money on the eight dozen book clubs he belongs to, I would only have to work about two hours a day. He would claim I wasn't being realistic, that I didn't know how much we had and was being tight.

"Each of us paid the bills alternate months. I thought this was the only way to prove to him I could handle money. After six months, when I figured out how much I was spending and how much of his money I was using, I decided to take on more patients to expand my practice. I found I was spending as much on cabs as he was on book clubs. Since that time we haven't had a single argument about money.

When the Koltuvs' child was born, they reopened negotiations. "We decided to split the care of our daughter between us equally. We knew there were certain hours we'd both be working so we found a woman to take care of her during these hours. Then I had the mornings and he had the evenings. The person whose time it was had to make all the decisions—whether or not she could have Pepsi-Cola, whether she could go to a friend's house, and so forth.

"The hardest thing was being willing to give up control. What we call responsibility is often control, power, being the boss. When I was really able to recognize that my husband's relationship with Hannah is his and mine is mine, everything was all right. He's going to do it differently but he's going to do it all right. We've been teaching her all along that different people are different."

Agreements to disagree with the common marriage mores are nothing new. They have their roots in a fine old tradition that probably began with Mary Wollstonecraft, that first feminist of us all, who in 1792 wrote *A Vindication of the Rights of Women.* Though Mary and her husband, English essayist and political theorist William Godwin, submitted to marriage, it was on their own terms. Godwin took an apartment about twenty doors from the couple's house to which he "repaired" every morning. A letter of the time describes this arrangement: "In order to give the connection as little as possible the appearance of such a vulgar and debasing tie as matrimony, the parties have established separate establishments, and the husband only visits his mistress like a lover when each is dressed, rooms in order, etc." The couple agreed that it was wrong for husband and wife to have to be together whenever they went out into "mixed society" and therefore, as Godwin writes, "rather sought occasions of deviating from, than of complying with, this rule."

The principle of separate quarters, which recently cropped up again in reports of a contract between Jacqueline Kennedy and Aristotle Onassis (see page 140), also appears in the agreement birth-control pioneer Margaret

Sanger signed with her husband, J. Noah H. Slee. Their contract stated that they would have separate homes and, later, separate quarters within the same house. Neither was to have the slightest influence over the business affairs of the other, and, when both were busy, communications were to be exchanged through their secretaries. They also agreed that Margaret Sanger would continue to use her own name. (Sanger, in fact, was the name of her first husband, but she had already made it a famous one.)

The ultimate feminist contract, however, was the one Lucy Stone and Henry Blackwell wrote when they married in 1855. Their agreement is a concise catalogue of the legal inequities of marriage in America at that time:

"While we acknowledge our mutual affection by publicly assuming the relationship of husband and wife," they wrote, "we deem it a duty to declare that this act on our part implies no sanction of, nor promise of voluntary obedience to, such of the present laws of marriage as refuse to recognize the wife as an independent, rational being, while they confer upon the husband an injurious and unnatural superiority." The contract went on to protest especially against the laws which gave the husband custody of the wife's person, the sole ownership of her personal property and the use of her real estate, the absolute right to the product of her industry and the exclusive control and guardianship of the couple's children. Finally, they protested against "the whole system by which 'the legal existence of the wife is suspended during marriage' so that, in most States, she neither has a legal part in the choice of her residence, nor can she make a will, nor sue or be sued in her own name, nor inherit property."

While it is obvious that we have made some progress since Lucy Stone's day, in many ways we are still living under the heritage of the kind of laws she deplored. The American institution of marriage derives from English common law, which developed a peculiar concept, unknown on the Continent, called the "unity of spouses." As Blackstone put it, "By marriage, the husband and wife are one person in law; that is, the very being or legal existence of the woman is suspended during marriage, or at least is incorparated or consolidated into that of the husband."

Beginning in 1839, one version or another of what was called the Married Women's Property Act was passed in each state of the Union, correcting some of the gross injustices of marriage. Most of these laws granted married women the right to contract, to sue and be sued without joining their husbands, to manage and control the property they brought with them to marriage, to engage in gainful employment and retain the earnings derived from it. Like a case of bad genes, however, the fiction of the unity of the spouses has never quite gone away. Husband and wife today are like Siamese twins: although largely separate persons under the law, they are still joined together in one spot or another. In one state, the wife's ability to contract may still be impaired; in another, she may not have full freedom to use her maiden name; in a third, she may not be considered capable of conspiracy with her husband.

These vestiges of the unity of spouses, however, are not the only ways in which marriage treats man and woman unequally, for we have evolved a different—but still unequal—concept of marriage. Today we regard husband as head of household and wife as housewife; husband as supporter and wife as dependent; husband as authority and wife as faithful helpmeet. This concept of marriage has not been *created* by the law but is an expression of culturally shared values which are *reflected* in the law. It is the conventional notion of marriage consciously embraced or unthinkingly accepted by many, if not most, Americans today.

The Onassis Marriage Contract

According to Christian Kafarakis, former chief steward on Aristotle Onassis' yacht, the marriage contract between Onassis and Jacqueline Bouvier Kennedy contains 170 clauses, covering every possible detail of their marital life.

There have been charges and countercharges, proofs and refutations flying ever since the contract was printed in *The People*, a Sunday newspaper in England. Does the contract exist? Was it created by an ex-steward with great legal imagination? Was Christian Kafarakis even a steward?

Truth or hoax, the document works more to support the current system of wife-as-prostitute than to equalize men and women. But it does spur our imaginations to greater possibilities of contract-making.

Separate bedrooms are stipulated, according to Mr. Kafarakis, for instance. He feels this may explain why Jackie O. has her own house on the island of Skorpios and stays in her Fifth Avenue apartment rather than in Onassis' floor-through at the Hotel Pierre.

So that Mrs. Onassis may be "sheltered from want," the Greek millionaire is supposed to have contracted for $600,000 a year in maintenance.

More, according to Mr. Kafarakis:

"If Onassis should ever part from Jackie, he will have to give her a sum amounting to nearly £4.2 million [$9.6 million] for every year of their marriage.

"If she leaves him, her payoff will be a lump sum in the neighborhood of £7.5 million [$18 million], which is a highly desirable neighborhood. That is, if the parting comes before five years.

"If she sticks it out longer, she will receive, in addition to the £7.5 million, an alimony of £75,000 a year for ten years.

"If Onassis dies while they are still married, she will inherit the staggering sum of £42 million [$100 million]."

What's wrong with it? The responsibility of support is commonly thought to favor women at the expense of men; I leave it for men to document how this notion injures them and will only deal here with the disabilities from a woman's point of view. Like all commonly held notions, the idea of marriage as a relationship between supporter and dependent is so much a part of our very atmosphere that it is hard to see it objectively. (To counter this difficulty, many women's groups are suggesting that people wishing to get a marriage license should have to take a test on the laws, as they do to get a driver's license.) Basically, the bargain in today's unwritten marriage contract is that the husband gets the right to the wife's services in return for supporting her. Whereas under common law the husband had "the absolute right to the product of the wife's industry," today the husband has only the absolute right to the product of the wife's industry *within the home.* "The wife's services and society are so essential a part of what the law considers the husband entitled to as part of the marriage," says Harriet Pilpel in *Your Marriage and the Law,* "that it will not recognize any agreement between the spouses which provides that the husband is to pay for such services or society."

The concept of the husband as supporter and wife as dependent underlies all the current legal inequalities of married women. To cite some specific examples:

Property. In common-law property states—like New York—husband and wife each exercise full control of what they own before, or acquire during, the marriage. But the woman who works only inside the home never has a chance to acquire property of her own, and therefore may never have any legitimate interest in, or control of, the family assets. (The only way she can acquire property is by gift, which makes her subject to her husband's patronage.) As John Gay said in *The Beggar's Opera,* "The comfortable estate of widowhood is the only hope that keeps up a wife's spirits." Her situation is improved by her husband's death; in every common-law property state, each spouse has a non-barrable interest in the estate of the other. However, this sometimes adds up to very little. For instance, in New Jersey, a wife only has "dower rights"; if her husband dies, she is entitled to one-third of the income from his real property. If the couple lived in an apartment and didn't own any real estate, the law guarantees her nothing.

Even in six of the eight community-property states where the spouses share equally in the property acquired during the marriage, the husband is given management control. Thus a woman may earn as much as her husband and have no say in how her money is spent. In the two exceptions, Washington and Texas, husband and wife have separate control of the property each acquires. Even this arrangement leaves the non-earning spouse without any control of the purse strings.

Name. In many states the law deprives the wife of full freedom to use her own name: in Illinois in 1965 when a woman sought the right to vote although she had not registered under her married name, the Appellate Court said she couldn't. In a recent case, a three-judge Federal court upheld the Alabama law requiring a woman to assume her husband's surname upon marriage by ruling that a married woman does not have a right to have her driver's license issued in her maiden name. In Michigan, if a man changes his last name his wife must also change hers; she may not contest the change, although the couple's minor children over the age of sixteen may do so.

Domicile. Domicile is a technical term sometimes defined as a "place where a person has a settled connection for certain legal purposes." (You can live in one place and be domiciled in another.) Domicile affects various legal rights and obligations, including where a person may vote, hold public office, serve on juries, receive welfare, qualify for tuition advantages at state educational institutions, be liable for taxes, have his or her estate administered, and file for divorce. In general, a wife's domicile automatically follows that of her husband and she has no choice in the matter. (NOW members are currently challenging this law in North Carolina.)

The husband, generally, also has had the right to decide where he and his wife live, although recently he has been required to make a reasonable decision taking her wishes into account. The burden of proving she is reasonable, however, still rests with the wife.

To some women the loss of these rights may seem a small price to pay for support. In fact, the arrangement works out differently depending on economic class. The higher up the ladder her husband is, the better a woman is supported and the fewer services she gives in return. For the many millions of women who work outside the home, on the other hand, the bargain is not a terribly good one: in reality all they earn for the services they give their husbands is the responsibility of working outside the home as well as in it to help their families survive. These women learn another price they pay for the illusion of support—the low salaries they receive compared with men's are ironically justified by the argument that the "men have families to feed." This is not the fault of husbands but of a society that has structured its economy on the unpaid services of women.

But the heaviest price those women who accept the role of dependent pay is a psychological one. Economic dependency is in itself corrupting, as can be seen in rawest form in country-and-Western songs of the "I-know-he's-being-untrue-but-I-never-confront-him-with-it-because-if-he-left-me-who-would-support-the-children" variety. And economic dependency breeds other kinds of dependency. The woman who has no established legal right in the family income fares better or worse depending on how well she pleases the head of the household. In the attempt to please she may surrender her own tastes, her own opinions, her own thoughts. If she habitually defers to or depends on her husband's decisions she will eventually find herself incapable of making her own.

The solution is not that wives should never work in the home or that husbands should not share their incomes with them. The solution is that we must begin to recognize that the work wives do belongs to them, not their husbands, and should be accorded a legitimate value. If wives make the contribution of full partners in their marriages, they should receive the rights of partners—not only, like slaves, the right to be housed, clothed and fed, or in other words, supported. This is hardly a new idea: in 1963 the Report of the President's Commission on the Status of Women recommended that "during marriage each spouse should have a legally defined right in the earnings of the other, in the real and personal property acquired through these earnings, and in their management."

There is, however, hope of progress. Although the Uniform Marriage and Divorce Act drafted by the National Conference of Commissioners on Uniform State Laws has not yet been adopted anywhere (Colorado has adopted the divorce portion of the law), it embraces some of the principles of marriage as partnership. It would make irremediable breakdown of the marriage the only ground for divorce, institute a division of property based on the assumption that husband and wife have contributed equally to the marriage, and determine custody according to the best interests of the child without the traditional bias in favor of the mother.

Should the Equal Rights Amendment be passed, it may require that most of the inequalities in the marriage relationship be abolished. According to an analysis published recently in *The Yale Law Journal,* the amendment should give women the freedom to use any name they wish, give them the same independent choice of domicile that married men have now, invalidate laws vesting management of community property in the husband alone, and prohibit enforcement of sex-based definitions of conjugal function. "Courts would not be able to assume for any purpose that women had a legal obligation to do housework, or provide affection and companionship, or to be available for sexual relations, unless men owed their wives exactly the same duties. Similarly, men could not be assigned the duty to provide financial support simply because of their sex." Even should the amendment pass, however, it will take years of action in the courts to implement it. Meanwhile, perhaps the best we can do is to say with Lucy Stone and Henry Blackwell that while we wish to acknowledge our mutual affection by publicly assuming the relationship of husband and wife, we do not promise obedience to those laws that discriminate against us. And perhaps, by writing our own contracts we can modify the effect of the laws upon us.

The problem with a husband and wife sitting down together and drafting a legal contract incorporating their beliefs concerning marriage is that the state immediately horns its way into the act. Marriage, contrary to popular belief, is more *ménage à trois* than *folie à deux.* It is a contract to which the state is a third party, and though you and your spouse may be in perfect accord, there are certain things the state will not tolerate. Most of these things are against what is known as public policy. Under public policy, according to

The Utopian Marriage Contract

1. The wife's right to use her maiden name or any other name she chooses.

2. What surname the children will have: husband's, wife's, a hyphenated combination, a neutral name or the name the children choose when they reach a certain age.

3. Birth control: Whether or not, what kind and who uses it. (One couple—the wife can't use the Pill—splits the responsibility 50-50. Half the time she uses a diaphragm, the other half he uses a condom.)

4. Whether or not to have children, or to adopt them, and if so how many.

5. How the children will be brought up.

6. Where the couple will live: Will the husband be willing to move if the wife gets a job offer she wants to take? Separate bedrooms? Separate apartments?

7. How child care and housework will be divided: The spouse who earns less should not be penalized for the inequities of the economic world by having to do a larger share.

8. What financial arrangement will the couple embrace? If husband and wife are both wage-earners, there are three basic possibilities:

a) Husband and wife pool their income, pay expenses and divide any surplus. (This was Leonard and Virginia Woolf's arrangement. At the end of the year, after payment of expenses, they divided the surplus between them equally so each had what they called a personal "hoard.")

b) Husband and wife pay shares of expenses proportional to their incomes. Each keeps whatever he or she has left.

c) Husband and wife each pay 50 per cent of expenses. Each keeps whatever he or she has left.

If husband earns significantly more than wife, the couple might consider a) that the disparity is a result of sexist discrimination in employment and there should perhaps be some kind of "home reparations program" to offset this inequity, and b) whether the couple really has an equal partnership if one has greater economic strength, and therefore possibly greater power psychologically, in the relationship.

9. Sexual rights and freedoms. Although any arrangement other than monogamy would clearly be against public policy, in practice some people make arrangements such as having Tuesdays off from one another.

10. The husband might give his consent to abortion in advance.   —S. E.

Harriet Pilpel, "the courts, in many states, will not enforce any agreement which attempts to free the husband from the duty of support to the wife. . . . Nor will the courts uphold any agreement which attempts to limit or eliminate the personal or conjugal rights of marriage as distinguished from property rights. An agreement that the parties will not live together after marriage is void. So is an agreement not to engage in sexual intercourse or not to have children. One court has even held that it is against public policy for an engaged couple to agree that they will live in whatever place the wife chooses. Under the law, said the court, that is the "husband's prerogative and he cannot relinquish it." Public policy also forbids contracts which anticipate divorce in any way. Agreements defining what will happen if a couple divorces or the conditions under which they will divorce are seen as facilitating the dissolution of marriages.

There are certain contracts, called antenuptial agreements, that the state clearly permits us to make. These contracts, according to Judith Boies, a matrimonial and estates lawyer with the New York law firm Paul, Weiss, Rifkind, Wharton & Garrison, may concern property owned before marriage, property acquired after marriage by gift or inheritance, and property rights in each other's estates. A wife cannot waive support, but she can waive interest in her husband's estate.

Some lawyers believe that people should be able to make whatever marriage contracts they like with one another. "Why should marriage be any different from any other contract?" asks constitutional lawyer Kristin Booth Glen, who teaches a course in women's rights at New York University Law School. She believes that the state's intervention in people's marriages may be in violation of Article I, Section 10, of the United States Constitution, which says that the states are forbidden to pass laws "impairing the obligation of contracts." Other lawyers feel that we don't really know which of the contracts we might wish to make concerning marriage would be enforceable. "There will have to be some litigation first," says Kathleen Carlsson, a lawyer for the Lucy Stone League. "In the light of the new feminist atmosphere, the decisions rendered today might not be the same as those rendered twenty years ago."

Judith Boies concurs with this view and feels that couples should begin right now to make whatever contracts suit their needs. If both spouses are wage-earners, they should contract how money and expenses will be divided. If they decide to have any joint bank accounts, they should sign a written agreement defining in what proportions the money in the account belongs to them. Then if one party cleans out the account—a frequent if unfortunate prelude to divorce—the contract would establish how they had intended to share the property.

Wives often assume—erroneously—that everything their husbands own belongs to them. In the common-law property states, property belongs to the person whose name it is in. When property is jointly owned, half presumably belongs to each spouse. However, this presumption is rebuttable. The husband

The Shulmans' Marriage Agreement

I. Principles

We reject the notion that the work which brings in more money is more valuable. The ability to earn more money is a privilege which must not be compounded by enabling the larger earner to buy out of his/her duties and put the burden on the partner who earns less or on another person hired from outside.

We believe that each partner has an equal right to his/her own time, work, values, choices. As long as all duties are performed, each of us may use his/her extra time any way he/she chooses. If he/she wants to use it making money, fine. If he/she wants to spend it with spouse, fine.

As parents we believe we must share all responsibility for taking care of our children and home—and not only the work but also the responsibility. At least during the first year of this agreement, *sharing responsibility* shall mean dividing the *jobs* and dividing the *time*.

II. Job Breakdown and Schedule

(A) Children

1. Mornings: Waking children; getting their clothes out; making their lunches; seeing that they have notes, homework, money, bus passes, books; brushing their hair; giving them breakfast (making coffee for us). Every other week each parent does all.
2. Transportation: Getting children to and from lessons, doctors, dentists (including making appointments), friends' houses, etc. Parts occurring between 3 and 6 p.m. fall to wife. She must be compensated by extra work from husband (see 10 below). Husband does all weekend transportation and pick-ups after 6.
3. Help: Helping with homework, personal questions; explaining things. Parts occurring between 3 and 6 p.m. fall to wife. After 6 p.m. husband does Tuesday, Thursday and Sunday; wife does Monday, Wednesday and Saturday. Friday is free for whoever has done extra work during the week.
4. Nighttime (after 6 p.m.): Getting children to take baths, brush their teeth, put away their toys and clothes, go to bed; reading with them; tucking them in and having nighttime talks; handling if they wake in the night. Husband does Tuesday, Thursday and Sunday. Wife does Monday, Wednesday and Saturday. Friday is split according to who has done extra work.
5. Baby sitters: Baby sitters must be called by the parent the sitter is to replace. If no sitter turns up, that parent must stay home.
6. Sick care: Calling doctors; checking symptoms; getting prescriptions filled; remembering to give medicine; taking days off to stay home with sick child, providing special activities. This must still be worked out equally, since now wife seems to do it all. In any case, wife must be compensated (see 10 below).
7. Weekends: All usual child care, plus special activities (beach, park, zoo). Split equally. Husband is free all Saturday, wife is free all Sunday.

(B) Housework

8. Cooking: Breakfasts during the week are divided equally; husband does all weekend breakfasts (including shopping for them and dishes). Wife does all dinners except Sunday nights. Husband does Sunday dinner and any other dinners on his nights of responsibility if wife isn't home. Whoever invites guests does shopping, cooking and dishes; if both invite them, split work.
9. Shopping: Food for all meals, housewares, clothing and supplies for children. Divide by convenience. Generally, wife does daily food shopping; husband does special shopping.
10. Cleaning: Husband does dishes Tuesday, Thursday and Sunday. Wife does Monday, Wednesday and Saturday. Friday is split according to who has done extra work during week. Husband does all the housecleaning in exchange for wife's extra child care (3 to 6 daily) and sick care.
11. Laundry: Home laundry, making beds, dry cleaning (take and pick up). Wife does home laundry. Husband does dry-cleaning delivery and pick-up. Wife strips beds, husband remakes them.

BREAKDOWNS: INSTITUTIONAL

can claim, for instance, that he and his wife only have a joint account so she can buy groceries.

The second kind of agreement couples might make is one in which the husband agrees to pay the wife a certain amount for domestic services. If there is no money to pay her, the debt accrues from year to year. When money becomes available, the wife would be a creditor and have first claim on it.

A third kind of financial contract could be made between husband and wife when one spouse puts the other through medical school or any other kind of education or training. The wife could agree to provide the husband with so much money per year to be paid back at a certain rate in subsequent years. This contract has a good chance of being enforceable, since even the tax laws recognize that husbands and wives make loans to one another.

"All these financial contracts have a reasonably good chance of standing up in court," says Judith Boies. The one with the least chance is the one providing payment for household services, although passage of the Equal Rights Amendment might strengthen its position. Since the financial contracts are more likely to be valid than those affecting personal aspects of the marriage, they should be made separately.

Judith Boies believes that, ideally, the personal contracts should also be valid. "The state shouldn't even marry people; it should just favor every contract that makes adequate provision for wife and children." The areas that might be covered in a comprehensive, total, utopian contract might include the wife's right to use the name she chooses, the children's names, division of housework and child care, finances, birth control, whether or not to have children and how many, the upbringing of the children, living arrangements, sexual rights and freedoms, and anything else of importance to the individual couple.

Since the marriage relationship is not a static one, any contract should permit the couple to solve their problems on a continuing basis. It should be amendable, revisable or renewable. One possibility is to draw up the first contract for a relatively short period of time, and renegotiate it when it expires.

Although current policy clearly makes any agreement concerning it invalid, our utopian contract might also cover divorce. After all, the court in California's Contra Costa County now permits couples to write their own divorce agreements and receive their decrees by mail.

At this point, many readers are probably thinking, "Why get married at all, why not just draw up a contract that covers all contingencies?" Again, the state got there first. Such an agreement would be considered a contract for the purpose of "meretricious relations," or in other words an illicit sexual relationship, and therefore would be invalid.

Other readers are probably thinking, "But we love each other, so why should we have a contract?" As Barbara Koltuv says, "Part of the reason for thinking out a contract is to find out what your problems are; it forces you to take charge of your life. Once you have the contract, you don't have to refer back to it. The process is what's important."

Whether these contracts are legally enforceable or not, just drawing them up may be of great service to many couples. What we are really doing in thrashing out a contract is finding out where we stand on issues, clearing up all the murky, unexamined areas of conflict, and unflinchingly facing up to our differences.

Reprint of the National Advisory Commission on Civil Disorders, U.S. Government Printing Office, 1968.

13. The Future of the Cities

NATIONAL ADVISORY COMMISSION
ON CIVIL DISORDERS

Introduction

We believe action of the kind outlined in preceding pages can contribute substantially to control of disorders in the near future. But there should be no mistake about the long run. The underlying forces continue to gain momentum.

The most basic of these is the accelerating segregation of low-income, disadvantaged Negroes within the ghettos of the largest American cities.

By 1985, the 12.1 million Negroes segregated within central cities today will have grown to approximately 20.3 million—an increase of 68 percent.

Prospects for domestic peace and for the quality of American life are linked directly to the future of these cities.

Two critical questions must be confronted: Where do present trends now lead? What choices are open to us?

The Key Trends

Negro population growth

The size of the Negro population in central cities is closely related to total national Negro population growth. In the past 16 years, about 98 percent of this growth has occurred within metropolitan areas, and 86 percent in the central cities of those areas.

A conservative projection of national Negro population growth indicates continued rapid increases. For the period 1966 to 1985, it will rise to a total of 30.7 million, gaining an average of 484,000 a year, or 7.6 percent more than the increase in each year from 1960 to 1966.

Central Cities.—Further Negro population growth in central cities depends upon two key factors: in-migration from outside metropolitan areas, and patterns of Negro settlement within metropolitan areas.

From 1960 to 1966, the Negro population of all central cities rose 2.4 million, 88.9 percent of total national Negro population growth. We estimate

Breakdown: American Culture   **145**

that natural growth accounted for 1.4 million, or 58 percent of this increase, and in-migration accounted for one million, or 42 percent.

As of 1966, the Negro population in all central cities totaled 12.1 million. By 1985, we have estimated that it will rise 68 percent to 20.3 million. We believe that natural growth will account for 5.2 million of this increase and in-migration for 3.0 million.

Without significant Negro out-migration, then, the combined Negro populations of central cities will continue to grow by an average of 274,000 a year through 1985, even if no further in-migration occurs.

Growth projected on the basis of natural increase and in-migration would raise the proportion of Negroes to whites in central cities by 1985 from the present 20.7 percent to between an estimated 31 and 34.7 percent.

Largest Central Cities.—These, however, are national figures. Much faster increases will occur in the largest central cities where Negro growth has been concentrated in the past two decades. Washington, D.C., Gary, and Newark are already over half Negro. A continuation of recent trends would cause the following 10 major cities to become over 50 percent Negro by the indicated dates:

New Orleans	1971	St. Louis	1978
Richmond	1971	Detroit	1979
Baltimore	1972	Philadelphia	1981
Jacksonville	1972	Oakland	1983
Cleveland	1975	Chicago	1984

These cities, plus Washington, D.C. (now over 66 percent Negro) and Newark, contained 12.6 million people in 1960, or 22 percent of the total population of all 224 American central cities. All 13 cities undoubtedly will have Negro majorities by 1985, and the suburbs ringing them will remain largely all white, unless there are major changes in Negro fertility rates,[1] in-migration, settlement patterns, or public policy.

Experience indicates that Negro school enrollment in these and other cities will exceed 50 percent long before the total population reaches that mark. In fact, Negro students already comprise more than a majority in the public elementary schools of 12 of the 13 cities mentioned above. This occurs because the Negro population in central cities is much younger and because a much higher proportion of white children attend private schools. For example, St. Louis' population was about 36 percent Negro in 1965; its public elementary school enrollment was 63 percent Negro. If present trends continue, many cities in addition to those listed above will have Negro school majorities by 1985, probably including:

Dallas	Louisville
Pittsburgh	Indianapolis
Buffalo	Kansas City, Mo.
Cincinnati	Hartford
Harrisburg	New Haven

[1] The fertility rate is the number of live births each year per 1,000 women aged 15 to 44.

Thus, continued concentration of future Negro population growth in large central cities will produce significant changes in those cities over the next 20 years. Unless there are sharp changes in the factors influencing Negro settlement patterns within metropolitan areas, there is little doubt that the trend toward Negro majorities will continue. Even a complete cessation of net Negro in-migration to central cities would merely postpone this result for a few years.

Growth of the young Negro population

We estimate that the Nation's white population will grow 16.6 million, or 9.6 percent, from 1966 to 1975, and the Negro population 3.8 million, or 17.7 percent, in the same period. The Negro age group from 15 to 24 years of age, however, will grow much faster than either the Negro population as a whole, or the white population in the same age group.

From 1966 to 1975, the total number of Negroes in this age group nationally will rise 1.6 million, or 40.1 percent. The white population aged 15 to 24 will rise 6.6 million, or 23.5 percent.

This rapid increase in the young Negro population has important implications for the country. This group has the highest unemployment rate in the Nation, commits a relatively high proportion of all crimes and plays the most significant role in civil disorders. By the same token, it is a great reservoir of underused human resources which are vital to the Nation.

The location of new jobs

Most new employment opportunities do not occur in central cities, near all-Negro neighborhoods. They are being created in suburbs and outlying areas —and this trend is likely to continue indefinitely. New office buildings have risen in the downtowns of large cities, often near all-Negro areas. But the out-flow of manufacturing and retailing facilities normally offsets this addition significantly—and in many cases has caused a net loss of jobs in central cities while the new white collar jobs are often not available to ghetto residents.

Providing employment for the swelling Negro ghetto population will require society to link these potential workers more closely with job locations. This can be done in three ways: By developing incentives to industry to create new employment centers near Negro residential areas; by opening suburban residential areas to Negroes and encouraging them to move closer to industrial centers; or by creating better transportation between ghetto neighborhoods and new job locations.

All three involve large public outlays.

The first method—creating new industries in or near the ghetto—is not likely to occur without Government subsidies on a scale which convinces private firms that it will pay them to face the problems involved.

The second method—opening up suburban areas to Negro occupancy— obviously requires effective fair housing laws. It will also require an extensive program of federally aided, low-cost housing in many suburban areas.

Breakdown: American Culture   147

The third approach—improved transportation linking ghettos and suburbs —has received little attention from city planners and municipal officials. A few demonstration projects show promise, but carrying them out on a large scale will be very costly.

Although a high proportion of new jobs will be located in suburbs, there are still millions of jobs in central cities. Turnover in those jobs alone can open up a great many potential positions for Negro central-city residents—if employers cease racial discrimination in their hiring and promotion practices.

Nevertheless, as the total number of Negro central-city jobseekers continues to rise, the need to link them with emerging new employment in the suburbs will become increasingly urgent.

The increasing cost of municipal services

Local governments have had to bear a particularly heavy financial burden in the two decades since the end of World War II. All U.S. cities are highly dependent upon property taxes that are relatively unresponsive to changes in income. Consequently, growing municipalities have been hard pressed for adequate revenues to meet rising demands for services generated by population increase. On the other hand, stable or declining cities have not only been faced with steady cost increases but also with a slow-growing, or even declining, tax base.

As a result of the population shifts of the postwar period, concentrating the middle class in residential suburbs while leaving the poor in the central cities, the increasing burden of municipal taxes frequently falls upon that part of the urban population least able to pay them.

Increasing concentrations of urban growth have called forth greater expenditures for every kind of public service: Education, health, police protection, fire protection, parks, sanitation, etc. These expenditures have strikingly outpaced tax revenues.

The story is summed up below:

LOCAL GOVERNMENT REVENUES, EXPENDITURES, AND DEBT
(Billions of dollars)

	1950	1966	Increase
Revenues	11.7	41.5	+29.8
Expenditures	17.0	60.7	+43.7
Debt outstanding	18.8	77.5	+58.7

Despite the growth of Federal assistance to urban areas under various grant-in-aid programs, the fiscal plight of many cities is likely to grow even more serious in the future. Local expenditures inevitably will continue to rise steeply as a result of several factors, including the difficulty of increasing productivity in the predominantly service activities of local governments, together with the rapid technologically induced increases in productivity in other economic sectors.

Traditionally, individual productivity has risen faster in the manufacturing, mining, construction, and agricultural sectors than in those involving personal services. However, since all sectors compete with each other for talent and personnel, wages and salaries in the service-dominated sectors generally must keep up, with those in the capital-dominated sectors. Since productivity in manufacturing has risen about 2.5 percent per year compounded over many decades, and even faster in agriculture, the basis for setting costs in the service-dominated sectors has gone up too.

In the postwar period, costs of the same units of output have increased very rapidly in certain key activities of local government. For example, education is the single biggest form of expenditure by local governments (including school districts), accounting for over 40 percent of their outlays. From 1947 to 1967, costs per pupil-day in U.S. public schools rose at a rate of 6.7 percent per year compounded—only slightly less than doubling every 10 years.[2] This major cost item is likely to keep on rising rapidly in the future, along with other government services like police, fire, and welfare activities.

Some increases in productivity may occur in these fields, and some economies may be achieved through use of assistants such as police and teachers' aides. Nevertheless, the need to keep pace with private sector wage scales will force local government costs to rise sharply.

This and other future cost increases are important to future relations between central cities and suburbs. Rising costs will inevitably force central cities to demand more and more assistance from the Federal Government. But the Federal Government can obtain such funds through the income tax only from other parts of the economy. Suburban governments are, meanwhile, experiencing the same cost increases along with the rising resentment of their constituents.

Choices for the Future

The complexity of American society offers many choices for the future of relations between central cities and suburbs and patterns of white and Negro settlement in metropolitan areas. For practical purposes, however, we see two fundamental questions:

■ Should future Negro population growth be concentrated in central cities, as in the past 20 years, thereby forcing Negro and white populations to become even more residentially segregated?
■ Should society provide greatly increased special assistance to Negroes and other relatively disadvantaged population groups?

[2]It is true that the average pupil-teacher ratio declined from 28 to about 25, and other improvements in teaching quality may have occurred. But they cannot account for anything approaching this rapid increase in costs.

For purposes of analysis, the Commission has defined three basic choices for the future embodying specific answers to these questions:

The present policies choice

Under this course, the Nation would maintain approximately the share of resources now being allocated to programs of assistance for the poor, unemployed and disadvantaged. These programs are likely to grow, given continuing economic growth and rising Federal revenues, but they will not grow fast enough to stop, let alone reverse, the already deteriorating quality of life in central-city ghettos.

This choice carries the highest ultimate price, as we will point out.

The enrichment choice

Under this course, the Nation would seek to offset the effects of continued Negro segregation and deprivation in large city ghettos. The enrichment choice would aim at creating dramatic improvements in the quality of life in disadvantaged central-city neighborhoods—both white and Negro. It would require marked increases in Federal spending for education, housing, employment, job training, and social services.

The enrichment choice would seek to lift poor Negroes and whites above poverty status and thereby give them the capacity to enter the mainstream of American life. But it would not, at least for many years, appreciably affect either the increasing concentration of Negroes in the ghetto or racial segregation in residential areas outside the ghetto.

The integration choice

This choice would be aimed at reversing the movement of the country toward two societies, separate and unequal.

The integration choice—like the enrichment choice—would call for large-scale improvement in the quality of ghetto life. But it would also involve both creating strong incentives for Negro movement out of central-city ghettos and enlarging freedom of choice concerning housing, employment, and schools.

The result would fall considerably short of full integration. The experience of other ethnic groups indicates that some Negro households would be scattered in largely white residential areas. Others—probably a larger number—would voluntarily cluster together in largely Negro neighborhoods. The integration choice would thus produce both integration and segregation. But the segregation would be voluntary.

Articulating these three choices plainly oversimplifies the possibilities open to the country. We believe, however, that they encompass the basic issues—issues which the American public must face if it is serious in its concern not only about civil disorder, but the future of our democratic society.

The Present Policies Choice

Powerful forces of social and political inertia are moving the country steadily along the course of existing policies toward a divided country.

This course may well involve changes in many social and economic programs—but not enough to produce fundamental alterations in the key factors of Negro concentration, racial segregation, and the lack of sufficient enrichment to arrest the decay of deprived neighborhoods.

Some movement toward enrichment can be found in efforts to encourage industries to locate plants in central cities, in increased Federal expenditures for education, in the important concepts embodied in the "War on Poverty," and in the Model Cities Program. But Congressional appropriations for even present Federal programs have been so small that they fall short of effective enrichment.

As for challenging concentration and segregation, a national commitment to this purpose has yet to develop.

Of the three future courses we have defined, the present policies choice—the choice we are now making—is the course with the most ominous consequences for our society.

The probability of future civil disorders

We believe that the present policies choice would lead to a larger number of violent incidents of the kind that have stimulated recent major disorders.

First, it does nothing to raise the hopes, absorb the energies, or constructively challenge the talents of the rapidly growing number of young Negro men in central cities. The proportion of unemployed or underemployed among them will remain very high. These young men have contributed disproportionately to crime and violence in cities in the past, and there is danger, obviously, that they will continue to do so.

Second, under these conditions, a rising proportion of Negroes in disadvantaged city areas might come to look upon the deprivation and segregation they suffer as proper justification for violent protest or for extending support to now isolated extremists who advocate civil disruption by guerrilla tactics.

More incidents would not necessarily mean more or worse riots. For the near future, there is substantial likelihood that even an increased number of incidents could be controlled before becoming major disorders, if society undertakes to improve police and National Guard forces so that they can respond to potential disorders with more prompt and disciplined use of force.

In fact, the likelihood of incidents mushrooming into major disorders would be only slightly higher in the near future under the present policies choice than under the other two possible choices. For no new policies or programs could possibly alter basic ghetto conditions immediately. And the announcement of new programs under the other choices would immediately generate new expectations. Expectations inevitably increase faster than performance. In the short run, they might even increase the level of frustration.

In the long run, however, the present policies choice risks a seriously greater probability of major disorders, worse, possibly, than those already experienced.

If the Negro population as a whole developed even stronger feelings of being wrongly "penned in" and discriminated against, many of its members might come to support not only riots, but the rebellion now being preached by only a handful. Large-scale violence, followed by white retaliation could follow. This spiral could quite conceivably lead to a kind of urban *apartheid* with semimartial law in many major cities, enforced residence of Negroes in segregated areas, and a drastic reduction in personal freedom for all Americans, particularly Negroes.

The same distinction is applicable to the cost of the present policies choice. In the short run, its costs—at least its direct cash outlays—would be far less than for the other choices.

Social and economic programs likely to have significant lasting effect would require very substantial annual appropriations for many years. Their cost would far exceed the direct losses sustained in recent civil disorders. Property damage in all the disorders we investigated, including Detroit and Newark, totaled less than $100 million.

But it would be a tragic mistake to view the present policies choice as cheap. Damage figures measure only a small part of the costs of civil disorder. They cannot measure the costs in terms of the lives lost, injuries suffered, minds and attitudes closed and frozen in prejudice, or the hidden costs of the profound disruption of entire cities.

Ultimately, moreover, the economic and social costs of the present policies choice will far surpass the cost of the alternatives. The rising concentration of impoverished Negroes and other minorities within the urban ghettos will constantly expand public expenditures for welfare, law enforcement, unemployment, and other existing programs without arresting the decay of older city neighborhoods and the breeding of frustration and discontent. But the most significant item on the balance of accounts will remain largely invisible and incalculable—the toll in human values taken by continued poverty, segregation, and inequality of opportunity.

Polarization

Another and equally serious consequence is the fact that this course would lead to the permanent establishment of two societies: one predominantly white and located in the suburbs, in smaller cities, and in outlying areas, and one largely Negro located in central cities.

We are well on the way to just such a divided nation.

This division is veiled by the fact that Negroes do not now dominate many central cities. But they soon will, as we have shown, and the new Negro mayors will be facing even more difficult conditions than now exist.

As Negroes succeed whites in our largest cities, the proportion of low-income residents in those cities will probably increase. This is likely even if both white and Negro incomes continue to rise at recent rates, since Negroes have much lower incomes than whites. Moreover, many of the ills of large central cities spring from their age, their location, and their obsolete physical structures. The deterioration and economic decay stemming from these factors have been proceeding for decades and will continue to plague older cities regardless of who resides in them.

These facts underlie the fourfold dilemma of the American city:

■ Fewer tax dollars come in, as large numbers of middle-income taxpayers move out of central cities and property values and business decline;
■ More tax dollars are required to provide essential public services and facilities, and to meet the needs of expanding lower income groups;
■ Each tax dollar buys less, because of increasing costs;
■ Citizen dissatisfaction with municipal services grows as needs, expectations and standards of living increase throughout the community.

These are the conditions that would greet the Negro-dominated municipal governments that will gradually come to power in many of our major cities. The Negro electorates in those cities probably would demand basic changes in present policies. Like the present white electorates there, they would have to look for assistance to two basic sources: the private sector and the Federal Government.

With respect to the private sector, major private capital investment in those cities might have ceased almost altogether if white-dominated firms and industries decided the risks and costs were too great. The withdrawal of private capital is already far advanced in most all-Negro areas of our large cities.

Even if private investment continued, it alone would not suffice. Big cities containing high proportions of low-income Negroes and block after block of deteriorating older property need very substantial assistance from the Federal Government to meet the demands of their electorates for improved services and living conditions.

It is probable, however, that Congress will be more heavily influenced by representatives of the suburban and outlying city electorate. These areas will comprise 40 percent of our total population by 1985, compared with 31 percent in 1960; and central cities will decline from 32 percent to 27 percent.[3]

Since even the suburbs will be feeling the squeeze of higher local government costs, Congress might resist providing the extensive assistance which central cities will desperately need.

Thus the present policies choice, if pursued for any length of time, might force simultaneous political and economic polarization in many of our largest metropolitan areas. Such polarization would involve large central cities— mainly Negro, with many poor, and nearly bankrupt—on the one hand and most suburbs—mainly white, generally affluent, but heavily taxed—on the other hand.

[3]Based on Census Bureau series D projections.

Some areas might avoid political confrontation by shifting to some form of metropolitan government designed to offer regional solutions for pressing urban problems such as property taxation, air and water pollution, refuse disposal, and commuter transport. Yet this would hardly eliminate the basic segregation and relative poverty of the urban Negro population. It might even increase the Negro's sense of frustration and alienation if it operated to prevent Negro political control of central cities.

The acquisition of power by Negro-dominated governments in central cities is surely a legitimate and desirable exercise of political power by a minority group. It is in an American political tradition exemplified by the achievements of the Irish in New York and Boston.

But such Negro political development would also involve virtually complete racial segregation and virtually complete spatial separation. By 1985, the separate Negro society in our central cities would contain almost 21 million citizens. That is almost 68 percent larger than the present Negro population of central cities. It is also larger than the current population of every Negro nation in Africa except Nigeria.

If developing a racially integrated society is extraordinarily difficult today when 12.1 million Negroes live in central cities, then it is quite clearly going to be virtually impossible in 1985 when almost 21 million Negroes—still much poorer and less educated than most whites—will be living there.

Can present policies avoid extreme polarization?

There are at least two possible developments under the present policies choice which might avert such polarization. The first is a faster increase of incomes among Negroes than has occurred in the recent past. This might prevent central cities from becoming even deeper "poverty traps" than they now are. It suggests the importance of effective job programs and higher levels of welfare payments for dependent families.

The second possible development is migration of a growing Negro middle class out of the central city. This would not prevent competition for Federal funds between central cities and outlying areas, but it might diminish the racial undertones of that competition.

There is, however, no evidence that a continuation of present policies would be accompanied by any such movement. There is already a significant Negro middle class. It grew rapidly from 1960 to 1966. Yet in these years, 88.9 percent of the total national growth of Negro population was concentrated in central cities—the highest in history. Indeed, from 1960 to 1966, there was actually a net total in-migration of Negroes from the urban fringes of metropolitan areas into central cities.[4] The Commission believes it unlikely that this

[4]Although Negro population on the urban fringe of metropolitan areas did increase slightly (0.2 million) from 1960 to 1966, it is safe to assume an actual net in-migration to central cities from these areas based upon the rate of natural increase of the Negro population.

trend will suddenly reverse itself without significant changes in private attitudes and public policies.

The Enrichment Choice

The present policies choice plainly would involve continuation of efforts like Model Cities, manpower programs, and the War on Poverty. These are in fact enrichment programs, designed to improve the quality of life in the ghetto.

Because of their limited scope and funds, however, they constitute only very modest steps toward enrichment—and would continue to do so even if these programs were somewhat enlarged or supplemented.

The premise of the enrichment choice is performance. To adopt this choice would require a substantially greater share of national resources—sufficient to make a dramatic, visible impact on life in the urban Negro ghetto.

The effect of enrichment on civil disorders

Effective enrichment policies probably would have three immediate effects on civil disorders.

First, announcement of specific large-scale programs and the demonstration of a strong intent to carry them out might persuade ghetto residents that genuine remedies for their problems were forthcoming, thereby allaying tensions.

Second, such announcements would strongly stimulate the aspirations and hopes of members of these communities—possibly well beyond the capabilities of society to deliver and to do so promptly. This might increase frustration and discontent, to some extent canceling the first effect.

Third, if there could be immediate action on meaningful job training and the creation of productive jobs for large numbers of unemployed young people, they would become much less likely to engage in civil disorders.

Such action is difficult now, when there are about 585,000 young Negro men aged 14 to 24 in the civilian labor force in central cities—of whom 81,000 or 13.8 percent, are unemployed and probably two or three times as many are underemployed. It will not become easier in the future. By 1975, this age group will have grown to approximately 700,000.

Given the size of the present problem, plus the large growth of this age group, creation of sufficient meaningful jobs will require extensive programs, begun rapidly. Even if the Nation is willing to embark on such programs, there is no certainly that they can be made effective soon enough.

Consequently, there is no certainty that the enrichment choice would do much more in the near future to diminish violent incidents in central cities than would the present policies choice. However, if enrichment programs can succeed in meeting the needs of residents of disadvantaged areas for jobs, education, housing, and city services, then over the years this choice is almost certain to reduce both the level and frequency of urban disorder.

The Negro middle class

One objective of the enrichment choice would be to help as many disadvantaged Americans as possible—of all races—to enter the mainstream of American prosperity, to progress toward what is often called middle-class status. If the enrichment choice were adopted, it could certainly attain this objective to a far greater degree than would the present policies choice. This could significantly change the quality of life in many central-city areas.

It can be argued that a rapidly enlarging Negro middle class would also promote Negro out-migration, and that the enrichment choice would thus open up an escape hatch from the ghetto. This argument, however, has two weaknesses.

The first is experience. Central cities already have sizable and growing numbers of middle-class Negro families. Yet only a few have migrated from the central city. The past pattern of white ethnic groups gradually moving out of central-city areas to middle-class suburbs has not applied to Negroes. Effective open-housing laws will help make this possible, but it is probably that other more extensive changes in policies and attitudes will be required—and these would extend beyond the enrichment choice.

The second weakness in the argument is time. Even if enlargement of the Negro middle class succeeded in encouraging movement out of the central city, it could not do so fast enough to offset the rapid growth of the ghetto. To offset even *half* the growth estimated for the ghetto by 1975 an out-migration from central cities of 217,000 persons a year would be required. This is eight times the annual increase in suburban Negro population—including natural increase—that occurred from 1960 to 1966. Even the most effective enrichment program is not likely to accomplish this.

A corollary problem derives from the continuing migration of poor Negroes from the Southern to Northern and Western cities. Adoption of the enrichment choice would require large-scale efforts to improve conditions in the South sufficiently to remove the pressure to migrate. Under present conditions, slightly over a third of the estimated increase in Negro central-city population by 1985 will result from in-migration—3.0 million out of total increase of 8.2 million.

Negro self-development

The enrichment choice is in line with some of the currents of Negro protest thought that fall under the label of "Black Power." We do not refer to versions of Black-Power ideology which promote violence, generate racial hatred, or advocate total separation of the races. Rather, we mean the view which asserts that the American Negro population can assume its proper role in society and overcome its feelings of powerlessness and lack of self-respect only by exerting power over decisions which directly affect its own members. A fully integrated society is not thought possible until the Negro minority within the ghetto has developed political strength—a strong bargaining position in dealing with the rest of society.

In short, this argument would regard predominantly Negro central cities and predominantly white outlying areas not as harmful, but as an advantageous future.

Proponents of these views also focus on the need for the Negro to organize economically as well as politically, thus tapping new energies and resources for self-development. One of the hardest tasks in improving disadvantaged areas is to discover how deeply deprived residents can develop their own capabilities by participating more fully in decisions and activities which affect them. Such learning-by-doing efforts are a vital part of the process of bringing deprived people into the social mainstream.

Separate but equal societies

The enrichment choice by no means seeks to perpetuate racial segregation. In the end, however, its premise is that disadvantaged Negroes can achieve equality of opportunity with whites while continuing in conditions of nearly complete separation.

This premise has been vigorously advocated by Black-Power proponents. While most Negroes originally desired racial integration, many are losing hope of ever achieving it because of seemingly implacable white resistance. Yet they cannot bring themselves to accept the conclusion that most of the millions of Negroes who are forced to live racially segregated lives must therefore be condemned to inferior lives—to inferior educations, or inferior housing, or inferior status.

Rather, they reason, there must be some way to make the quality of life in the ghetto areas just as good—or better—than elsewhere. It is not surprising that some Black-Power advocates are denouncing integration and claiming that, given the hypocrisy and racism that pervade white society, life in a black society is, in fact, morally superior. This argument is understandable, but there is a great deal of evidence that it is unrealistic.

The economy of the United States and particularly the sources of employment are preponderantly white. In this circumstance, a policy of separate but equal employment could only relegate Negroes permanently to inferior incomes and economic status.

The best evidence regarding education is contained in recent reports of the Office of Education and Civil Rights Commission which suggest that both racial and economic integration are essential to educational equality for Negroes. Yet critics point out that certainly until integration is achieved, various types of enrichment programs must be tested, and that dramatically different results may be possible from intensive educational enrichment—such as far smaller classes, or greatly expanded preschool programs, or changes in the home environment of Negro children resulting from steady jobs for fathers.

Still others advocate shifting control over ghetto schools from professional administrators to local residents. This, they say, would improve curricula, give students a greater sense of their own value, and thus raise their morale and educational achievement. These approaches have not yet been tested sufficiently. One conclusion, however, does seem reasonable: Any real improvement in the quality of education in low-income, all-Negro areas will cost a great deal more money than is now being spent there—and perhaps more than is being spent per pupil anywhere. Racial and social class integration of schools may produce equal improvement in achievement at less total cost.

Whether or not enrichment in ghetto areas will really work is not yet known, but the enrichment choice is based on the yet-unproven premise that it will. Certainly, enrichment programs could significantly improve existing ghetto schools if they impelled major innovations. But "separate but equal" ghetto education cannot meet the long-run fundamental educational needs of the central-city Negro population.

The three basic educational choices are: Providing Negro children with quality education in integrated schools; providing them with quality education by enriching ghetto schools; or continuing to provide many Negro children with inferior education in racially segregated school systems, severely limiting their lifetime opportunities.

Consciously or not, it is the third choice that the Nation is now making, and this choice the Commission rejects totally.

In the field of housing, it is obvious that "separate but equal" does not mean really equal. The enrichment choice could greatly improve the quantity, variety, and environment of decent housing available to the ghetto population. It could not provide Negroes with the same freedom and range of choice as whites with equal incomes. Smaller cities and suburban areas together with the central city provide a far greater variety of housing and environmental settings than the central city alone. Programs to provide housing outside central cities, however, extend beyond the bounds of the enrichment choice.

In the end, whatever its benefits, the enrichment choice might well invite a prospect similar to that of the present policies choice: separate white and black societies.

If enrichment programs were effective, they could greatly narrow the gap in income, education, housing, jobs, and other qualities of life between the ghetto and the mainstream. Hence the chances of harsh polarization—or of disorder—in the next 20 years would be greatly reduced.

Whether they would be reduced far enough depends on the scope of the programs. Even if the gap were narrowed from the present, it still could remain as a strong source of tension. History teaches that men are not necessarily placated even by great absolute progress. The controlling factor is relative progress—whether they still perceive a significant gap between themselves and others whom they regared as no more deserving. Widespread perception of such a gap—and consequent resentment—might well be precisely the situation 20 years from now under the enrichment choice, for it is essentially another way of choosing a permanently divided country.

The Integration Choice

The third and last course open to the Nation combines enrichment with programs designed to encourage integration of substantial numbers of Negroes into the society outside the ghetto.

Enrichment must be an important adjunct to any integration course. No matter how ambitious or energetic such a program may be, relatively few Negroes now living in central-city ghettos would be quickly integrated. In the meantime, significant improvement in their present environment is essential.

The enrichment aspect of this third choice should, however, be recognized as interim action, during which time expanded and new programs can work to improve education and earning power. The length of the interim period surely would vary. For some it may be long. But in any event, what should be clearly recognized is that enrichment is only a means toward the goal; it is not the goal.

The goal must be achieving freedom for every citizen to live and work according to his capacities and desires, not his color.

We believe there are four important reasons why American society must give this course the most serious consideration. First, future jobs are being created primarily in suburbs, while the chronically unemployed population is increasingly concentrated in the ghetto. This separation will make it more and more difficult for Negroes to achieve anything like full employment in decent jobs. But if, over time, these residents began to find housing outside central cities, they would be exposed to more knowledge of job opportunities, would have much shorter trips to reach jobs, and would have a far better chance of securing employment on a self-sustaining basis.

Second, in the judgment of this Commission, racial and social-class integration is the most effective way of improving the education of ghetto children.

Third, developing an adequate housing supply for low-income and middle-income families and true freedom of choice in housing for Negroes of all income levels will require substantial out-movement. We do not believe that such an out-movement will occur spontaneously merely as a result of increasing prosperity among Negroes in central cities. A national fair housing law is essential to begin such movement. In many suburban areas, a program combining positive incentives with the building of new housing will be necessary to carry it out.

Fourth, and by far the most important, integration is the only course which explicitly seeks to achieve a single nation rather than accepting the present movement toward a dual society. This choice would enable us at least to begin reversing the profoundly divisive trend already so evident in our metropolitan areas—before it becomes irreversible.

Conclusions

The future of our cities is neither something which will just happen nor something which will be imposed upon us by an inevitable destiny. That future will be shaped to an important degree by choices we make now.

We have attempted to set forth the major choices because we believe it is vital for Americans to understand the consequences of our present drift:

Three critical conclusions emerge from this analysis:

1. The nation is rapidly moving toward two increasingly separate Americas.

Within two decades, this division could be so deep that it would be almost impossible to unite:

■ a white society principally located in suburbs, in smaller central cities, and in the peripheral parts of large central cities; and

■ a Negro society largely concentrated within large central cities.

The Negro society will be permanently relegated to its current status, possibly even if we expend great amounts of money and effort in trying to "gild" the ghetto.

2. In the long run, continuation and expansion of such a permanent division threatens us with two perils.

The first is the danger of sustained violence in our cities. The timing, scale, nature, and repercussions of such violence cannot be foreseen. But if it occurred, it would further destroy our ability to achieve the basic American promises of liberty, justice, and equality.

The second is the danger of a conclusive repudiation of the traditional American ideals of individual dignity, freedom, and equality of opportunity. We will not be able to espouse these ideals meaningfully to the rest of the world, to ourselves, to our children. They may still recite the Pledge of Allegiance and say "one nation . . . indivisible." But they will be learning cynicism, not patriotism.

3. We cannot escape responsibility for choosing the future of our metropolitan areas and the human relations which develop within them. It is a responsibility so critical that even an unconscious choice to continue present policies has the gravest implications.

That we have delayed in choosing or, by delaying, may be making the wrong choice, does not sentence us either to separatism or despair. But we must choose. We will choose. Indeed, we are now choosing.

From *One Year Later*, Urban America, Inc. and The Urban Coalition, 1969. Reprinted by permission of Praeger Publishers, Inc.

14. "Conclusions" from *The Slums and Ghettos* and *One Society or Two?*

URBAN COALITION, INC.

From The Slums and Ghettos

"It is time now to turn with all the purpose at our command to the major unfinished business of this nation," the Commission said a year ago. It called on the nation "to mount programs on a scale equal to the dimension of the problems; to aim these programs for high impact in the immediate future in order to close the gap between promise and performance; to undertake new initiatives and experiments that can change the system of failure and frustration that now dominates the ghetto and weakens our society." The following summarizes the nation's response in relation to the elements of the system examined in the preceding pages.

Poverty

1. Employment and income have risen in the slum-ghetto in both absolute and relative terms. Poverty remains a pervasive fact of life there, however, and the continuing disparity between this poverty and the general affluence remains a source of alienation and discontent.

2. Further gains in employment and income in the slums and ghettos are dependent on continued prosperity. But prosperity alone will not upgrade the hard-core poor and unemployed. Specific programs are necessary to meet their special needs and problems.

3. The largest gap in these programs, as they affect employment, is lack of a public job-creation program to complement increased public-private job-training efforts.

4. Job discrimination remains a serious problem, reinforcing the concentration of minorities in low-pay, low-status occupations.

5. Increased attention has been given efforts to open business opportunities to minorities, but only limited progress has been made.

6. No progress has been made in reform of the welfare system. Judicial gains have been offset by the threat of backward steps posed by the 1967 amendments to federal welfare laws.

7. Development and public acceptance of an income-supplementation system is still not in sight.

Education

1. The major issue to emerge in the past year is that of decentralization or community control of schools. Its impact on the quality of slum-ghetto education cannot yet be evaluated.

2. Despite a turning away of some blacks from school integration as a goal, it has been pursued with some success in small- to moderate-size cities. There is no evidence of success in big cities with substantial minority populations.

3. Federal enforcement of laws and judicial rulings against school segregation has been of limited effectiveness in the South and is only beginning in the North.

4. Direct efforts to improve ghetto schools through compensatory programs are hampered by shortages of funds and by lack of means to measure precisely their effectiveness. Federal aid each year is spread more thinly and state aid is inequitably distributed.

5. Ghetto schools continue to fail. The small amount of progress that has been made has been counterbalanced by a growing atmosphere of hostility and conflict in many cities.

Environment

1. Two Presidential study groups have expanded and made more precise the nation's knowledge about housing need and how to meet it. Out of their work has come Congressional commitment to a well-documented housing production goal.

2. The Housing Act of 1968 substantially expanded the programmatic tools necessary to meet this goal. But appropriations cuts pushed its attainment far into the future.

3. Passage of a federal fair housing law represented the first essential step for opening new housing choices to residents of the slums and ghettos. Its impact will be hampered by inadequate appropriations for enforcement.

4. There are as yet no sufficient means to direct federal housing and community improvement programs toward opening extra-ghetto areas to the poor and minorities. In their absence, problems of finding acceptable sites also are likely to hamper seriously realization of the 1968 act's goal for construction of subsidized housing.

5. Rehabilitation has not fulfilled its promise as a means of improving the slum-ghetto environment. The model cities program, using a redirected approach to urban renewal, continues to offer promise limited only by its level of funding. At present, however, there are no programs that seriously threaten the continued existence of the slums.

Progress in dealing with the conditions of slum-ghetto life has been nowhere near in scale with the problems. Nor has the past year seen even a serious start toward the changes in national priorities, programs, and institutions advocated by the Commission. The sense of urgency in the Commission report has not been reflected in the nation's response.

From One Society or Two?

"The deepening racial division is not inevitable," the Commission said a year ago. "The movement apart can be reversed. Choice is still possible. Our principal task is to define that choice and to press for a national resolution." The following summarizes the national response to that task in relation to the issues examined in the preceding pages.

1. Civil disorders increased in number but declined in intensity in 1968. A significant drop in the death rate was due primarily to more sophisticated response by police and the military, resulting directly from the work of the Commission.

2. A wave of disorder struck the nation's high schools in 1968–69 and is continuing. At the same time, turbulence on college and university campuses has taken on an increasingly racial character.

3. A genuinely alarming increase in crimes of violence contributed to an atmosphere of fear inside and out of the slums and ghettos. There was little evidence of change or reform in the criminal justice system sufficient to stem this increase.

4. Incidents involving the police continued to threaten the civil peace in the slums and ghettos. There was some evidence of a hardening of police attitudes and a weakening of traditional civil controls over their activities.

5. Structural change in local government to make it more responsive was rare. The number of black elected officials increased substantially throughout the nation and particularly in the South, but remained disproportionately low.

6. There was no evidence that any more than a small minority of the nation's Negro population was prepared to follow militant leaders toward separatism or the tactical use of violence. This minority, however, continued to have an impact beyond its numbers, particularly on the young.

7. There was striking evidence of a deepening of the movement toward black pride, black identity, and black control and improvement of ghetto neighborhoods. There were repeated suggestions that efforts toward community control and self-help had been a major contribution to the relative quiet of the summer, 1968.

8. White concern with the problems of the slums and ghettos mounted with the Commission report, the assasination of Martin Luther King, and the April disorders. It was subsumed by concern for law and order in the months following the assassination of Sen. Robert F. Kennedy, and continued to decline during the Presidential campaign. Outright resistance to slum-ghetto needs and demands intensified during the same months.

9. Black and white Americans remained far apart in their perception of slum-ghetto problems and the meaning of civil disorders. The gap probably had widened by the end of the year.

10. The physical distance between the places where blacks and whites lived did not diminish during the past year and threatens to increase with population growth. The most recent trend showed a virtual stoppage in black immigration and a sharp increase in the rate of white departure; the ghettos, meanwhile, were growing in area while declining in population density. There was an increase in suburban Negro population, but there also were indications of growth in suburban ghettos.

The nation has not reversed the movement apart. Blacks and whites remain deeply divided in their perceptions and experiences of American society. The deepening of concern about conditions in the slums and ghettos on the part of some white persons and institutions has been counterbalanced—perhaps overbalanced—by a deepening aversion and resistance on the part of others. The mood of the blacks, wherever it stands precisely in the spectrum between militancy and submission, is not moving in the direction of patience. The black neighborhoods in the cities remain slums, marked by poverty and decay; they remain ghettos, marked by racial concentration and confinement. The nation has not yet made available—to the cities or the blacks themselves—the resources to improve these neighborhoods enough to make a significant change in their residents' lives. Nor has it offered those who might want it the alternative of escape.

Neither has the nation made a choice among the alternative futures described by the Commission, which is the same as choosing what the Commission called "present policies." The present policies alternative, the Commission said, "may well involve changes in many social and economic programs—but not enough to produce fundamental alterations in the key factors of Negro concentration, racial segregation, and the lack of sufficient enrichment to arrest the decay of deprived neighborhoods."

It is worth looking again at the Commission's description of where this choice would lead:

"We believe that the present policies choice would lead to a larger number of violent incidents of the kind that have stimulated recent major disorders.

"First, it does nothing to raise the hopes, absorb the energies, or constructively challenge the talents of the rapidly growing number of young Negro men in central cities. The proportion of unemployed or underemployed among them will remain very high. These young men have contributed disproportionately to crime and violence in cities in the past, and there is danger, obviously, that they will continue to do so.

"Second, under these conditions, a rising proportion of Negroes in disadvantaged city areas might come to look upon the deprivation and segregation they suffer as proper justification for violent protest or for extending support to now isolated extremists who advocate civil disruption by guerrilla tactics.

"More incidents would not necessarily mean more or worse riots. For the near future, there is substantial likelihood that even an increased number of incidents could be controlled before becoming major disorders, if society undertakes to improve police and National Guard forces so that they can respond to potential disorders with more prompt and disciplined use of force.

"In fact, the likelihood of incidents mushrooming into major disorders would be only slightly higher in the near future under the present policies choice than under the other two possible choices. For no new policies or programs could possibly alter basic ghetto conditions immediately. And the announcement of new programs under the other choices would immediately generate new expectations. Expectations inevitably increase faster than performance. In the short run, they might even increase the level of frustration.

"In the long run, however, the present policies choice risks a seriously greater probability of major disorders, worse, possibly, than those already experienced.

"If the Negro population as a whole developed even stronger feelings of being wrongly 'penned in' and discriminated against, many of its members might come to support not only riots, but the rebellion now being preached by only a handful. Large-scale violence, followed by white retaliation, could follow. This spiral could quite conceivably lead to a kind of urban *apartheid* with semimartial law in many major cities, enforced residence of Negroes in segregated areas, and a drastic reduction in personal freedom for all Americans, particularly Negroes."

The Commission's description of the immediate consequences of the present policies choice sounds strikingly like a description of the year since its report was issued: some change but not enough; more incidents but less full-scale disorder because of improved police and military response; a decline in expectations and therefore in short-run frustrations. If the Commission is equally correct about the long run, the nation in its neglect may be sowing the seeds of unprecedented future disorder and division. For a year later, we are a year closer to being two societies, black and white, increasingly separate and scarcely less unequal.

Daniel J. Elazar, "Are We a Nation of Cities?" *The Public Interest,* No. 4 (Summer 1966), pp. 42–58. Copyright © National Affairs Inc., 1966.

15. Are We a Nation of Cities?

DANIEL J. ELAZAR

It is generally agreed that the United States is now "a nation of cities,"— to use a phrase popularized by Lyndon B. Johnson—and that this has given rise to a unique and dramatic "urban problem." When a proposition of this kind receives general assent, however, it may be just the right moment to look at it critically and skeptically. . . .

Proponents of the current myths may argue that most small city growth has taken place within the nation's metropolitan areas. While they are technically correct, they are wrong to assume that "the metropolitan area" is just some kind of bigger city, lacking only a single government to formalize reality. The independent suburban townships and smaller cities exist for real reasons, not by historical accident. In fact, the larger the metropolitan area, the more likely the small cities within it are to value their autonomy and their separate identities. Moreover, while the rise of small cities originally created the contemporary metropolitan pattern, their continued growth—together with the stagnation of the central city—is now working to replace that pattern with one which dilutes the supposed "extended city" character of metropolitanism, replacing it with a pattern of extended urban settlement based on a whole ménage of cities of varying sizes and degrees of inter-relationship. . . . In short, what is developing in the United States is the spread of a relatively low-density population engaged in urban economic pursuits; many of these American-style city dwellers actually live on plots of land that would look large to a Chinese or Indian farmer.

American urban living is further complicated by the vast difference in the life-styles of residents of American cities, depending on each city's size and location. It should not be difficult to visualize the differences between cities of 20,000 on the fringes of Boston and those of the same population in the heart of the Rockies, between a Philadelphia of two million people in the shadow of New York and a Denver of half a million which serves as the "capital" of a region that ranges five hundred or more miles in any direction. Yet the picture of urbanized America that is implicit in most contemporary discussion depicts all urbanized Americans a living in the same kind of environment and facing the same, or at least very similar, problems. . . .

[A]ccording to the myth, we face a newly urbane population frustrated because it cannot easily get to the concert halls, the art museums, and the theaters; a population that is forced, against its will, to live in sprawling suburbs; forced to depend upon the family automobile; forced to maintain lawns, raise flowers, and rake leaves. The *Life* double-issue of December, 1965, devoted to "The City," provides the most recent comprehensive example of this myth, presented in its most universally accepted form. . . .

This composite of myths about American urban reality has led to the conclusion that our cities have failed us and that we face an urban crisis. This, in turn, has led to the development of certain models for urban improvement which are based on another set of myths, derived from the classic European stereotype of the city, either directly or as translated into modern terms by social scientists. . . .

Whatever changes the American people seem to be seeking, they are not directed toward the enhancement of the facilities that lead to an urbane or citified life, but rather to the introduction into the city of qualities associated with the rural life—whether trees, cleaner air and water, larger parks, or new family-style dwellings to reduce the overall density of population. . . . No doubt this response also reflects a mythology—but it is a mythology that must be considered when we seek to understand American attitudes toward the city. The historical record confirms this American desire to gain the economic benefits of urbanization while resisting the way of life usually associated with living in cities. It might be said that the American people persist in maintaining an implicit distinction between urbanization and citification, willingly accepting the former while seeking to avoid the latter.

In understanding the reasons for the rejection of citification we can understand the real character of the American city and of the "American way of urbanization." *The American urban place is preeminently an "anti-city,"* implicitly developed to reflect a basic American life-style which has repeatedly emphasized agrarian elements from the days of the first colonists to our own. The underlying character of the American urban place is shaped by three basic phenomena: agrarianism, metropolitanism, and nomadism. . . .

Nobody conversant with American history need be reminded of the rural roots of American civilization. Articulate Americans consistently viewed the rural life as the good life, or, indeed, the best life, where the vices inherent in man by virtue of Adam's fall would be least likely to flourish. . . .

From an ideology which looked upon rural living (either in separated farms or in agricultural villages) as the best way to limit individual sin, the agrarian doctrine was translated into positive terms to become part of the world view of the 18th-century enlightenment. . . . The city was seen as the source of social corruption even more than individual corruption; the city was to be avoided as a source of inequality, class distinction, and social disorganization that could lead to tyranny in one form or another.

Even when the agrarian myth was in full flower, Americans had begun to flock to the cities, primarily to gain economic advantage; and the cities had become the pace-setters in American life. But, while they desired to gain economically and socially by exploiting the benefits of urban concentration, the new city-dwellers rejected the classically urban styles of living (as developed in Old World cities). Accepting the necessity and even the value of urbanization for certain purposes, in particular, economic ones, Americans have characteristically tried to have their cake and eat it, too, by bringing the old agrarian ideals into the urban setting and by reinterpreting them through the establishment of a modified pattern of "rural"-style living within an urban context. The result has been the conversion of *urban* settlements into *metropolitan* ones, whose very expansiveness provides the physical means for combining something like rural and urban life-styles into a new pattern which better suits the American taste. . . .

As part of this effort, sets of institutions and symbolic actions have been developed, partially by design, which are meant to evoke rural and small-town America and its traditional way of life. Limited and fragmented local government is one of these. The creation of many smaller cities—the *bête noire* of most professional city-planners—in place of a single large metropolis reflects this desire for maintenance of the small community, both as an abstract principle and in order to control such crucial local functions as zoning and police, which in a direct or derivative sense embody the traditions of local control. We see this in the continued emphasis on political autonomy for suburban communities, and in their resistance to any efforts, real or imagined, to absorb them into the political sphere of the central city. . . .

It is generally known by now that suburbia has become the equal of small-town America as the symbol of the country's "grass-roots" and as the fountainhead of what is distinctive about "the American way of life." This is so regardless of whether suburbia is praised or condemned for its role. (The Chicago *Tribune,* traditional champion of the agrarian virtues as it perceives them, now features suburban settings for its "rural virtue" cartoons.) . . .

While urbanization and metropolitanization in other nations have led to the development of official policies to encourage high-density living, federal, state, and even local policies (other than the property tax) in the United States are heavily weighted in favor of the homeowner and low-density development. . . . The foundations for today's widespread home ownership were laid during the 1930's by the New Deal, as part of the New Dealers' over-all efforts to translate the ideals and values of traditional American agrarianism into terms appropriate to the new urban setting. . . .

The trend to owner-occupied housing has revived such symbolically rural occupations as gardening and "do-it-yourself" home maintenance. The public response to these activities—state and county fairs (not to mention home and garden shows) outdraw art galleries in annual attendance *even in the largest cities,* and the greater share of adult education courses deal with home-related activities—indicates that they are, in effect, an urban recrudescence of a significant "vernacular" cultural tradition long associated with rural and small-town life. . . .

Similarly, the impact that private maintenance of lawns and gardens has on the maintenance of the aesthetic qualities of American urban areas has generally been ignored by students of urbanization. In the days of "Great Society" beautification programs it would serve us well to recall that the private expenditure for lawn and garden maintenance far exceeds the public expenditures for parks, tree plantings, and similar efforts at urban beautification. . . .

Metropolitanism of settlement, as well as metropolitanism of commerce, began with the very birth of cities in the United States. Urbanization and suburbanization went hand in hand. Even as the rate of urban growth began to accelerate after the War of 1812, a counter, almost anti-urban, trend began to develop alongside it. As fast as some Americans moved to the city, others who were able to do so moved out, while maintaining their ties with it. The process of suburbanization can be traced throughout the 19th century. After 1820, the nation's largest cities, such as New York, Boston, Philadelphia, Baltimore, and New Orleans, began to experience an out-migration to newly created suburban areas. Though most of these early suburbs were later annexed by their central cities, the suburbanization process continued after each set of annexations, gaining new impetus as new means of transportation were developed and made possible movement out of the city for people who worked in the city. First the railroad, then the electric trolley, and finally the automobile stimulated suburbanization past the "horse and buggy" stage.

By 1920, over half the nation lived in "urban places," and nearly a third lived in cities of over 100,000. However, no sooner did the big city become the apparent embodiment of the American style of life, then it began to be replaced by a less citified style in turn. *The upward trend in the growth of big cities came to an end during the depression,* then gave way to the development of medium- and smaller-size cities on the fringes of the big cities themselves. . . . Newly-settled suburbs and smaller cities were annexed to already large cities because their residents, or at least those who made the decisions locally, felt reasonably confident that their suburban style of life would be maintained, even within the city limits. When this became no longer possible, metropolitanism then became firmly fixed as suburbanization, with the semi-city becoming more important than the city as the locus of growth in area after area.

This trend is additionally encouraged by the penchant toward nomadism which has always characterized Americans. With a population that is so highly mobile that one family in five moves every year, the older European notion of the city as a stable, self-perpetuating community could not apply in the New World. . . . Consequently, the city, like every other local government subdivision, has become a politically defined entity populated to a great extent by different groups in every generation. . . .

This, in turn, significantly alters the meaning of moving from farm to city, and from central city to suburb, in the United States. . . . In the United States the . . . movement . . . has been no more than one of a continual series that originally propelled European immigrants across the seas; then, as Americans, westward and into cities; and now from city to suburb. . . .

The American city ... has its classic antecedent in the pattern of Israelite city-building described in the Bible, as befits the cities of an agrarian republic produced by the heirs of the Bible-inspired Reformation. Like the cities of ancient Israel, the American city is located within territorial political jurisdictions that take precedence over it—in its case, the state rather than the tribe, and in both cases, the nation above that. Thus, the city in this country, as in ancient Israel, developed not as the equivalent of the State, but to serve certain functions for an existing civil society which could best be served by bringing men together in relatively dense population groups where they could interact socially and commercially. ...

Unlike the more or less self-contained Classical city, the American and Biblical cities have developed economically through a relationship with their hinterlands in a special pattern of suburbanization which can be considered unique and characteristic. In both cases, the urban center has been surrounded by satellites—villages or cities—that stand in what we would call a metropolitan relationship to the center. ... Both the American and Biblical cities were designed to serve an agrarian ideal. This means, in particular, that the life of the city has been subordinated to the values of society rather than being given a free hand to shape those values along "sophisticated" lines. In the second place, both kinds of cities have served mobile populations; the Biblical city served an agricultural population that migrated with its flocks within the city's hinterland along set patterns, while the American city increasingly serves a population that migrates from center to peripheries and back ... the average resident changing location several times during his life. ...

The contemporary American city, with its shopping centers located in such a way as to attract both suburban and urban people without regard to their relationship to the city's center, is simply a contemporary expression of the same pattern. Americans wish *private* convenience in shopping, first and foremost; hence the failure of downtown enthusiasts to recentralize that function. ...

The American urban place is a non-city because Americans wish it to be just that. Our age has been the first in history even to glimpse the possibility of having the economic advantages of the city while rejecting the previously inevitable conditions of citified living, and Americans apparently intend to take full advantage of the opportunity. If we wish to make a realistic approach to our real urban problems, we would be wise to begin with that fact of American life.

Reprinted from *Report of the President's Task Force on Suburban Problems.*

16. Report of the President's Task Force on Suburban Problems

On October 11, 1967, President Johnson directed the creation of a Task Force on Suburban Problems. In the letter setting forth the mandate of the group, he requested a report on:

—The nature of the enduring economic, social and physical problems of suburbs and of the people who live there, especially older suburbs and newer areas experiencing rapid residential growth.

—The scope and impact of current federal policies and programs on the development of suburbia.

—The policy leadership and programmatic and financial responsibility which the Federal Government should assume in the future with respect to addressing the problems of suburbs and suburban dwellers.

In responding to this request, our report develops recommendations and proposals for assuring the orderly development of the suburbs, for contributing to the quality of suburban life, and for securing harmony between the suburbs and the central cities to which they are related.

The main conclusions we have reached about the nature of suburban problems are these:

First, the already vast and rapidly growing suburbs of the United States are *in a state of quiet, slowly-building crisis.* Nearly 66 million Americans now live in them, and by 1985 another 58 million will reside there. They are the burgeoning American frontier in the second half of the twentieth century. And they are aching with social, physical and economic strains caused by their incredible changes of recent years. They need organized help to help themselves—from local, state and federal governments—if the needs of their many millions of residents, and multi-millions of future arrivals are to be served.

Second, the suburban crisis in *an indivisible part of the urban crisis.* The suburbs do not stand alone: they are an integral part of the great metropolitan areas of the United States where two of three Americans already live. Help to the troubled central city and the suburbs must move in parallel. Without the improvement of both, all will suffer. Pollution, crime and decay are no respecters of municipal boundaries; the economic productivity of the urban region will be crippled; and the quality and diversity of life for all will corrode.

The suburbs need help, but only that help which is part of a wise and comprehensive program for the metropolitan area as a whole. We are struck again by the wisdom of Learned Hand, who reminded us of "a satisfaction in the sense that we are all engaged in a common venture." To continue to deal with cities on a piecemeal basis will be only to worsen the effects of the present crazy-quilt of overlapping and inefficient jurisdictions.

Third, dealt with in this framework and spirit, *the suburbs present a vast and exciting opportunity,* not merely another problem. Help now, before their troubles reach the point of disaster, is timely, feasible and financable. There does not exist a more promising or more major opportunity for political leadership and public understanding to serve the fundamental interests of the unity, safety, well-being and progress of the United States than help now to the suburban fraction of the urban crisis.

The Task Force, therefore, proposes that such help be made available along eight lines of action:

First, a series of measures to insure that what must be done *can be financed* and that the local and state agencies which must carry the major responsibilities for action are not bankrupted in the process—*including the establishment of an Urban Development Bank (URBANK)* to do for our urban areas what the World Bank is accomplishing for global economic development;

Second, a series of measures to open the *doors of opportunity* to ease the disadvantages suffered by certain special groups—Vietnam veterans, Negroes, the poor and the aged;

Third, creation of new institutions *to insure the intelligent planning and use of land on the urban frontiers,*—extending the multi-purpose and "piggybacking" successes achieved by some natural resource developments to the suburban scene—land being the central resource of the future if our urban areas are to accommodate new millions of inhabitants and remain habitable;

Fourth, a series of measures *to improve the environment of the suburbs*—to reduce crime; to combat noise and pollution; and to increase water conservation, park lands and community centers;

Fifth, measures to facilitate *creation of new planned communities* of diversified character which, at the same time, can help relieve population pressures on the central city, serve as models and yardsticks for the improvement of existing communities, and provide a realistic alternative to continued mass production of suburbia;

Sixth, measures *to improve transportation between central cities and the suburbs, and among the suburbs,* thereby improving the productivity of the entire urban area and making its opportunities—for housing, jobs and recreation—more fully accessible to all its residents;

Seventh, measures to help fill the future need for planners, administrators and scientists capable of bringing to bear modern technology in the management of our urban conglomerates;

Eighth, sharp increase in funds for research and development to increase the efficiency and economy of urban facilities and services on a metropolitan basis. We as a nation have the resources to do what must be done. We now must develop the understanding, the will, the commitment and the leadership to do it. The welfare of most Americans is directly at stake; and ultimately of all citizens and the nation itself.

Part III
Beginnings

Beginnings: Protest

Beginnings: The New Consciousness

Beginnings: Places - Communes and Cities

Beginnings: The Rise of Global Consciousness

Beginnings: Planning

       Architecture and Design

       Technology

       People

Beginnings: Protest

As a rule both rulers and rules uphold the internalized power structure as "legitimate" by right and usually the shattering of this belief in legitimacy has far-reaching ramifications.

MAX WEBER

Oh God said to Abraham, kill me a son, Abe says man, you must be puttin' me on.

BOB DYLAN

RICH: The only problem with this section is that all these people did most of their protesting ten years ago. They were prophets for a lot of things. They were prophets for this book, in a way, but Marcuse is still pretty much in the same place, Malcolm X is dead, C. Wright Mills is dead . . .

DEMA: That's like protest now; the whole concept seems to be dead.

JOHN: I was just going to say, doesn't it seem like mass demonstrations are obsolete? I mean, that sort of anti-war protesting just doesn't seem to be happening anymore.

ANGELA: What you're saying is that either we shouldn't have the section on protest at all, or . . .

JOHN: It would be a good historical section, but the new type of protest seems to be taking place in the voting booth.

ANGELA: The protest movement seems to be focusing on community work, community organization, things like that.

DEMA: And that doesn't make headlines.

ANGELA: What?

DEMA: Well, when there were thousands of screaming kids, that made a lot of good copy for the headlines—you could see them every night with Walter Cronkite. But this new thing is more silent, less spectacular. People like Dana are organizing community agencies, but quietly.

MOLLY: Yeah, you just can't change the world, so I think everyone just got a little more pragmatic and started doing things they could really *do*.

SCOTT: That's education for you. Education in this country just sort of goes off at a right angle from what's really happening, just takes you off into never-never land for a couple of years, and when it finally pops you back into reality . . .

MOLLY: What a shock!

SCOTT: Right, well, that's what happened with protest. I mean, I come out of home with mommy and daddy, and go to college from high school, and find out what's happening in the world, and I scream, "Stop it!" I expect it to stop, just like that. And that's really never-never land stuff. I could act like that because I was in a never-never land at the time, namely, college. And when you finally get out of the never-never land machine, you see that the only things you can really *do* are little things, in your own back yard.

17. After the Bombing

MALCOLM X

Now what effect does [the struggle over Africa] have on us? Why should the black man in America concern himself since he's been away from the African continent for three or four hundred years? Why should we concern ourselves? What impact does what happens to them have upon us? Number one, you have to realize that up until 1959 Africa was dominated by the colonial powers. Having complete control over Africa, the colonial powers of Europe projected the image of Africa negatively. They always project Africa in a negative light: jungle savages, cannibals, nothing civilized. Why then naturally it was so negative that it was negative to you and me, and you and I began to hate it. We didn't want anybody telling us anything about Africa, much less calling us Africans. In hating Africa and in hating the Africans, we ended up hating ourselves, without even realizing it. Because you can't hate the roots of a tree, and not hate the tree. You can't hate your origin and not end up hating yourself. You can't hate Africa and not hate yourself.

You show me one of these people over here who has been thoroughly brainwashed and has a negative attitude toward Africa, and I'll show you one who has a negative attitude toward himself. You can't have a positive attitude toward yourself and a negative attitude toward Africa at the same time. To the same degree that your understanding of and attitude toward Africa become positive, you'll find that your understanding of and your attitude toward yourself will also become positive. And this is what the white man knows. So they very skillfully make you and me hate our African identity, our African characteristics.

You know yourself that we have been a people who hated our African characteristics. We hated our heads, we hated the shape of our nose, we wanted one of those long dog-like noses, you know; we hated the color of our skin, hated the blood of Africa that was in our veins. And in hating our features and our skin and our blood, why, we had to end up hating ourselves. And we hated ourselves. Our color became to us a chain—we felt that it was holding us back; our color became to us like a prison which we felt was keeping us confined, not letting us go this way or that way. We felt that all of these

Beginnings: Protest 179

restrictions were based solely upon our color, and the psychological reaction to that would have to be that as long as we felt imprisoned or chained or trapped by black skin, black features and black blood, that skin and those features and that blood holding us back automatically had to become hateful to us. And it became hateful to us.

It made us feel inferior; it made us feel inadequate; made us feel helpless. And when we fell victims to this feeling of inadequacy or inferiority or helplessness, we turned to somebody else to show us the way. We didn't have confidence in another black man to show us the way, or black people to show us the way. In those days we didn't. We didn't think a black man could do anything except play some horns—you know, make some sound and make you happy with some songs and in that way. But in serious things, where our food, clothing, shelter and education were concerned, we turned to the man. We never thought in terms of bringing these things into existence for ourselves, we never thought in terms of doing things for ourselves. Because we felt helpless. What made us feel helpless was our hatred for ourselves. And our hatred for ourselves stemmed from our hatred for things African. . . .

After 1959 the spirit of African nationalism was fanned to a high flame and we then began to witness the complete collapse of colonialism. France began to get out of French West Africa, Belgium began to make moves to get out of the Congo, Britain began to make moves to get out of Kenya, Tanganyika, Uganda, Nigeria and some of these other places. And although it looked like they were getting out, they pulled a trick that was colossal.

When you're playing ball and they've got you trapped, you don't throw the ball away—you throw it to one of your teammates who's in the clear. And this is what the European powers did. They were trapped on the African continent, they couldn't stay there—they were looked upon as colonial and imperialist. They had to pass the ball to someone whose image was different, and they passed the ball to Uncle Sam. And he picked it up and has been running it for a touchdown ever since. He was in the clear, he was not looked upon as one who had colonized the African continent. At that time, the Africans couldn't see that though the United States hadn't colonized the African continent, it had colonized 22 million blacks here on this continent. Because we're just as thoroughly colonized as anybody else.

When the ball was passed to the United States, it was passed at the time when John Kennedy came into power. He picked it up and helped to run it. He was one of the shrewdest backfield runners that history has ever recorded. He surrounded himself with intellectuals—highly educated, learned and well-informed people. And their analysis told him that the government of America was confronted with a new problem. And this new problem stemmed from the fact that Africans were now awakened, they were enlightened, they were fearless, they would fight. This meant that the Western powers couldn't stay there by force. Since their own economy, the European economy and the American economy, was based upon their continued influence over the African continent, they had to find some means of staying there. So they used the friendly approach.

They switched from the old openly colonial imperialistic approach to the benevolent approach. They came up with some benevolent colonialism, philanthropic colonialism, humanitarianism, or dollarism. Immediately everything was Peace Corps, Operation Crossroads, "We've got to help our African brothers." Pick up on that: Can't help us in Mississippi. Can't help us in Alabama, or Detroit, or out here in Dearborn where some real Ku Klux Klan lives. They're going to send all the way to Africa to help. I know Dearborn; you know, I'm from Detroit, I used to live out here in Inkster. And you had to go through Dearborn to get to Inkster. Just like driving through Mississippi when you got to Dearborn. Is it still that way? Well, you should straighten it out.

So, realizing that it was necessary to come up with these new approaches, Kennedy did it. He created an image of himself that was skilfully designed to make the people on the African continent think that he was Jesus, the great white father, come to make things right. I'm telling you, some of these Negroes cried harder when he died than they cried for Jesus when he was crucified. From 1954 to 1964 was the era in which we witnessed the emerging of Africa. The impact that this had on the civil-rights struggle in America has never been fully told.

For one thing, one of the primary ingredients in the complete civil-rights struggle was the Black Muslim movement. The Black Muslim movement took no part in things political, civic—it didn't take too much part in anything other than stopping people from doing this drinking, smoking, and so on. Moral reform it had, but beyond that it did nothing. But it talked such a strong talk that it put the other Negro organizations on the spot. Before the Black Muslim movement came along, the NAACP was looked upon as radical; they were getting ready to investigate it. And then along came the Muslim movement and frightened the white man so hard that he began to say, "Thank God for old Uncle Roy, and Uncle Whitney and Uncle A. Philip and Uncle"—you've got a whole lot of uncles in there; I can't remember their names, they're all older than I so I call them "uncle." Plus, if you use the word "Uncle Tom" nowadays, I hear they can sue you for libel, you know. So I don't call any of them Uncle Tom anymore. I call them Uncle Roy.

One of the things that made the Black Muslim movement grow was its emphasis upon things African. This was the secret to the growth of the Black Muslim movement. African blood, African origin, African culture, African ties. And you'd be surprised—we discovered that deep within the subconscious of the black man in this country, he is still more African than he is American. He *thinks* that he's more American than African, because the man is jiving him, the man is brainwashing him every day. He's telling him, "You're an American, you're an American." Man, how could you think you're an American when you haven't ever had any kind of an American treat over here? You have never, never. Ten men can be sitting at a table eating, you know, dining, and I can come and sit down where they're dining. They're dining; I've got a plate in front of me, but nothing is on it. Because all of us are sitting at the same table, are all of us diners? I'm not a diner until you let me dine. Just being at the table with others who are dining doesn't make me a diner, and this is what you've got to get in your head here in this country.

Just because you're in this country doesn't make you an American. No, you've got to go farther than that before you can become an American. You've got to enjoy the fruits of Americanism. You haven't enjoyed those fruits. You've enjoyed the thorns. You've enjoyed the thistles. But you have not enjoyed the fruits, no sir. You have fought harder for the fruits than the white man has, you have worked harder for the fruits than the white man has, but you've enjoyed less. When the man put the uniform on you and sent you abroad, you fought harder than they did. Yes, I know you—when you're fighting for them, you can fight.

The Black Muslim movement did make that contribution. They made the whole civil-rights movement become more militant, and more acceptable to the white power structure. He would rather have them than us. In fact, I think we forced many of the civil-rights leaders to be even more militant than they intended. I know some of them who get out there and "boom, boom, boom" and don't mean it. Because they're right on back in their corner as soon as the action comes.

John F. Kennedy also saw that it was necessary for a new approach among the American Negroes. And during his entire term in office, he specialized in how to psycho the American Negro. Now, a lot of you all don't like my saying that—but I wouldn't ever take a stand on that if I didn't know what I was talking about. By living in this kind of society, pretty much around them, and you know what I mean when I say "them," I learned to study them. You can think that they mean you some good ofttimes, but if you look at it a little closer you'll see that they don't mean you any good. That doesn't mean there aren't some of them who mean good. But it does mean that most of them don't mean good.

Kennedy's new approach was pretending to go along with us in our struggle for civil rights. He was another proponent of rights. But I remember the expose that *Look* magazine did on the Meredith situation in Mississippi. *Look* magazine did an expose showing that Robert Kennedy and Governor Barnett had made a deal, wherein the Attorney General was going to come down and try to force Meredith into school, and Barnett was going to stand at the door, you know, and say, "No, you can't come in." He was going to get in anyway, but it was all arranged in advance and then Barnett was supposed to keep the support of the white racists, because that's who he was upholding, and Kennedy would keep the support of the Negroes, because that's who he'd be upholding. It was a cut-and-dried deal. And it's not a secret; it was written, they write about it. But if that's a deal, how many other deals do you think go down? What you think is on the level is crookeder, brothers and sisters, than a pretzel, which is most crooked.

So in my conclusion I would like to point out that the approach that was used by the administration right up until today was designed skilfully to make it appear they were trying to solve the problem when they actually weren't. They would deal with the conditions, but never the cause. They only gave us tokenism. Tokenism benefits only a few. It never benefits the masses, and the masses are the ones who have the problem, not the few. That one who benefits from tokenism, he doesn't want to be around us anyway—that's why he picks up on the token. . . .

The masses of our people still have bad housing, bad schooling and inferior jobs, jobs that don't compensate with sufficient salaries for them to carry on their life in this world. So that the problem for the masses has gone absolutely unsolved. The only ones for whom it has been solved are people like Whitney Young, who is supposed to be placed in the cabinet, so the rumor says. He'll be the first black cabinet man. And that answers where he's at. And others have been given jobs, like Carl Rowan, who was put over the USIA, and is very skilfully trying to make Africans think that the problem of black men in this country is all solved.

The worst thing the white man can do to himself is to take one of these kinds of Negroes and ask him, "How do your people feel, boy?" He's going to tell that man that we are satisfied. That's what they do, brothers and sisters. They get behind the door and tell the white man we're satisfied. "Just keep on keeping me up here in front of them, boss, and I'll keep them behind you." That's what they talk when they're behind closed doors. Because, you see, the white man doesn't go along with anybody who's not for him. He doesn't care are you for right or wrong, he wants to know are you for him. And if you're for him, he doesn't care what else you're for. As long as you're for him, then he puts you up over the Negro community. You become a spokesman.

In your struggle it's like standing on a revolving wheel; you're running, but you're not going anywhere. You run faster and faster and the wheel just goes faster and faster. You don't ever leave the spot that you're standing in. So, it is very important for you and me to see that our problem has to have a solution that will benefit the masses, not the upper class—so-called upper class. Actually, there's no such thing as an upper-class Negro, because he catches the same hell as the other class Negro. All of them catch the same hell, which is one of things that's good about this racist system—it makes us all one. . . .

If you'd tell them right now what is in store for 1965, they'd think you crazy for sure. But 1965 will be the longest and hottest and bloodiest year of them all. It has to be, not because you want it to be, or I want it to be, or we want it to be, but because the conditions that created these explosions in 1963 are still here; the conditions that created explosions in 1964 are still here. You can't say that you're not going to have an explosion when you leave the conditions, the ingredients, still here. As long as those explosive ingredients remain, then you're going to have the potential for explosion on your hands.

And, brothers and sisters, let me tell you, I spend my time out there in the streets with people, all kinds of people, listening to what they have to say. And they're dissatisfied, they're disillusioned, they're fed up, they're getting to the point of frustration where they begin to feel, "What do we have to lose?" When you get to that point, you're the type of person who can create a very dangerously explosive atmosphere. This is what's happening in our neighborhoods, to our people.

I read in a poll taken by *Newsweek* magazine this week, saying that Negroes are satisfied. Oh, yes, *Newsweek,* you know, supposed to be a top magazine with a top pollster, talking about how satisfied Negroes are. Maybe I haven't met the Negroes he met. Because I know he hasn't met the ones that I've met. And this is dangerous. This is where the white man does himself the most harm. He invents statistics to create an image, thinking that that image is going to hold things in check. You know why they always say Negroes are lazy? Because they want Negroes to be lazy. They always say Negroes can't unite because they don't want Negroes to unite. And once they put this thing in the Negro's mind, they feel that he tries to fulfill their image. If they say you can't unite black people, and then you come to them to unite them, they won't unite because it's been said that they're not supposed to unite. It's a psycho that they work, and it's the same way with these statistics.

When they think that an explosive era is coming up, then they grab their press again and begin to shower the Negro public, to make it appear that all Negroes are satisfied. Because if you know you're dissatisfied all by yourself and ten others aren't, you play it cool; but if you know that all ten of you are dissatisifed, you get with it. This is what the man knows. The man knows that if these Negroes find out how dissatisfied they really are—even Uncle Tom is dissatisfied, he's just playing his part for now—this is what makes the man frightened. It frightens them in France and frightens them in England, and it frightens them in the United States.

And it is for this reason that it is so important for you and me to start organizing among ourselves, intelligently, and try to find out: "What are we going to do if this happens, that happens or the next thing happens?" Don't think that you're going to run to the man and say, "Look, boss, this is me." Why, when the deal goes down, you'll look just like me in his eyesight; I'll make it tough for you. Yes, when the deal goes down, he doesn't look at you in any better light than he looks at me. . . .

I point these things out, brothers and sisters, so that you and I will know the importance in 1965 of being in complete unity with each other, in harmony with each other, and not letting the man maneuver us into fighting one another. The situation I have been maneuvered into right now, between me and the Black Muslim movement, is something that I really deeply regret, because I don't think anything is more destructive than two groups of black people fighting each other. But it's something that can't be avoided because it goes deep down beneath the surface, and these things will come up in the very near future.

I might say this before I sit down. If you recall, when I left the Black Muslim movement, I stated clearly that it wasn't my intention to even continue to be aware that they existed; I was going to spend my time working in the non-Muslim community. But they were fearful if they didn't do something that perhaps many of those who were in the [Black Muslim] mosque would leave it and follow a different direction. So they had to start doing a takeoff on me, plus, they had to try and silence me because of what they know that I know. I think that they should know me well enough to know that they certainly can't frighten me. But when it does come to the light—excuse me for keeping coughing like that, but I got some of that smoke last night—there are some things involving the Black Muslim movement which, when they come to light, will shock you.

The thing that you have to understand about those of us in the Black Muslim movement was that all of us believed 100 per cent in the divinity of Elijah Muhammad. We believed in him. We actually believed that God, in Detroit by the way, that God had taught him and all of that. I always believed that he believed it himself. And I was shocked when I found out that he himself didn't believe it. And when that shock reached me, then I began to look everywhere else and try and get a better understanding of the things that confront all of us so that we can get together in some kind of way to offset them.

I want to thank you for coming out this evening. I think it's wonderful that as many of you came out, considering the blackout on the meeting that took place. Milton Henry and the brothers who are here in Detroit are very progressive young men, and I would advise all of you to get with them in any way that you can to try and create some kind of united effort toward common goals, common objectives. Don't let the power structure maneuver you into a time-wasting battle with others when you could be involved in something that is constructive and getting a real job done. . . .

I say again that I'm not a racist, I don't believe in any form of segregation or anything like that. I'm for brotherhood for everybody, but I don't believe in forcing brotherhood upon people who don't want it. Let us practice brotherhood among ourselves, and then if others want to practice brotherhood with us, we're for practicing it with them also. But I don't think that we should run around trying to love somebody who doesn't love us. Thank you.

18. The New Forms of Control

HERBERT MARCUSE

A comfortable, smooth, reasonable, democratic unfreedom prevails in advanced industrial civilization, a token of technical progress. Indeed, what could be more rational than the suppression of individuality in the mechanization of socially necessary but painful performances; the concentration of individual enterprises in more effective, more productive corporations; the regulation of free competition among unequally equipped economic subjects; the curtailment of prerogatives and national sovereignties which impede the international organization of resources. That this technological order also involves a political and intellectual coordination may be a regrettable and yet promising development.

The rights and liberties which were such vital factors in the origins and earlier stages of industrial society yield to a higher stage of this society: they are losing their traditional rationale and content. Freedom of thought, speech, and conscience were—just as free enterprise, which they served to promote and protect—essentially *critical* ideas, designed to replace an obsolescent material and intellectual culture by a more productive and rational one. Once institutionalized, these rights and liberties shared the fate of the society of which they had become an integral part. The achievement cancels the premises.

To the degree to which freedom from want, the concrete substance of all freedom, is becoming a real possibility, the liberties which pertain to a state of lower productivity are losing their former content. Independence of thought, autonomy, and the right of political opposition are being deprived of their basic critical function in a society which seems increasingly capable of satisfying the needs of the individuals through the way in which it is organized. Such a society may justly demand acceptance of its principles and institutions, and reduce the opposition to the discussion and promotion of alternative policies *within* the status quo. In this respect, it seems to make little difference whether the increasing satisfaction of needs is accomplished by an authoritarian or a non-authoritarian system. Under the conditions of a rising standard of living, non-conformity with the system itself appears to be socially useless, and the more so when it entails tangible economic and political disadvantages and threatens the smooth operation of the whole. Indeed, at least in so far as the necessities of life are involved, there seems to be no reason why the production and distribution of goods and services should proceed through the competitive concurrence of individual liberties.

Freedom of enterprise was from the beginning not altogether a blessing. As the liberty to work or to starve, it spelled toil, insecurity, and fear for the vast majority of the population. If the individual were no longer compelled to prove himself on the market, as a free economic subject, the disappearance of this kind of freedom would be one of the greatest achievements of civilization. The technological processes of mechanization and standardization might release individual energy into a yet uncharted realm of freedom beyond necessity. The very structure of human existence would be altered; the individual would be liberated from the work world's imposing upon him alien needs and alien possibilities. The individual would be free to exert autonomy over a life that would be his own. If the productive apparatus could be organized and directed toward the satisfaction of the vital needs, its control might well be centralized; such control would not prevent individual autonomy, but render it possible.

This is a goal within the capabilities of advanced industrial civilization, the "end" of technological rationality. In actual fact, however, the contrary trend operates: the apparatus imposes its economic and political requirements for defense and expansion on labor time and free time, on the material and intellectual culture. By virtue of the way it has organized its technological base, contemporary industrial society tends to be totalitarian. For "totalitarian" is not only a terroristic political coordination of society, but also a non-terroristic economic-technical coordination which operates through the manipulation of needs by vested interests. It thus precludes the emergence of an effective opposition against the whole. Not only a specific form of government or party rule makes for totalitarianism, but also a specific system of production and distribution which may well be compatible with a "pluralism" of parties, newspapers, "countervailing powers," etc.

Today political power asserts itself through its power over the machine process and over the technical organization of the apparatus. The government of advanced and advancing industrial societies can maintain and secure itself only when it succeeds in mobilizing, organizing, and exploiting the technical, scientific, and mechanical productivity available to industrial civilization. And this mobilizes society as a whole, above and beyond any particular individual or group interests. The brute fact that the machine's physical (only physical?) power surpasses that of the individual, and of any particular group of individuals, makes the machine the most effective political instrument in any society whose basic organization is that of the machine process. But the political trend may be reversed; essentially the power of the machine is only the stored-up and projected power of man. To the extent to which the work world is conceived of as a machine and mechanized accordingly, it becomes the *potential* basis of a new freedom for man.

Contemporary industrial civilization demonstrates that it has reached the stage at which "the free society" can no longer be adequately defined in the traditional terms of economic political, and intellectual liberties, not because these liberties have become insignificant, but because they are too significant to be confined within the traditional forms. New modes of realization are needed, corresponding to the new capabilities of society.

Such new modes can be indicated only in negative terms because they would amount to the negation of the prevailing modes. Thus economic freedom would mean freedom *from* the economy—from being controlled by economic forces and relationships; freedom from the daily struggle for existence, from earning a living. Political freedom would mean liberation of the individuals *from* politics over which they have no effective control. Similarly, intellectual freedom would mean the restoration of individual thought now absorbed by mass communication and indoctrination, abolition of "public opinion" together with its makers. The unrealistic sound of these propositions is indicative, not of their utopian character, but of the strength of the forces which prevent their realization. The most effective and enduring form of warfare against liberation is the implanting of material and intellectual needs that perpetuate obsolete forms of the struggle for existence.

The intensity, the satisfaction and even the character of human needs, beyond the biological level, have always been preconditioned. Whether or not the possibility of doing or leaving, enjoying or destroying, possessing or rejecting something is seized as a *need* depends on whether or not it can be seen as desirable and necessary for the prevailing societal institutions and interests. In this sense, human needs are historical needs and, to the extent to which the society demands the repressive development of the individual, his needs themselves and their claim for satisfaction are subject to overriding critical standards.

We may distinguish both true and false needs. "False" are those which are superimposed upon the individual by particular social interests in his repression: the needs which perpetuate toil, aggressiveness, misery, and injustice. Their satisfaction might be most gratifying to the individual, but this happiness is not a condition which has to be maintained and protected if it serves to arrest the development of the ability (his own and others) to recognize the disease of the whole and grasp the chances of curing the disease. The result then is euphoria in unhappiness. Most of the prevailing needs to relax, to have fun, to behave and consume in accordance with the advertisements, to love and hate what others love and hate, belong to this category of false needs.

Such needs have a societal content and function which are determined by external powers over which the individual has no control; the development and satisfaction of these needs is heteronomous. No matter how much such needs may have become the individual's own, reproduced and fortified by the conditions of his existence; no matter how much he identifies himself with them and finds himself in their satisfaction, they continue to be what they were from the beginning—products of a society whose dominant interest demands repression.

The prevalence of repressive needs is an accomplished fact, accepted in ignorance and defeat, but a fact that must be undone in the interest of the happy individual as well as all those whose misery is the price of his satisfaction. The only needs that have an unqualified claim for satisfaction are the vital ones—nourishment, clothing, lodging at the attainable level of culture. The satisfaction of these needs is the prerequisite for the realization of *all* needs, of the unsublimated as well as the sublimated ones.

For any consciousness and conscience, for any experience which does not accept the prevailing societal interest as the supreme law of thought and behavior, the established universe of needs and satisfactions is a fact to be questioned—questioned in terms of truth and falsehood. These terms are historical throughout, and their objectivity is historical. The judgment of needs and their satisfaction, under the given conditions, involves standards of *priority*—standards which refer to the optimal development of the individual, of all individuals, under the optimal utilization of the material and intellectual resources available to man. The resources are calculable. "Truth" and "falsehood" of needs designate objective conditions to the extent to which the universal satisfaction of vital needs and, beyond it, the progressive alleviation of toil and poverty, are universally valid standards. But as historical standards, they do not only vary according to area and stage of development, they also can be defined only in (greater or lesser) *contradiction* to the prevailing ones. What tribunal can possibly claim the authority of decision?

In the last analysis, the question of what are true and false needs must be answered by the individuals themselves, but only in the last analysis; that is, if and when they are free to give their own answer. As long as they are kept incapable of being autonomous, as long as they are indoctrinated and manipulated (down to their very instincts), their answer to this question cannot be taken as their own. By the same token, however, no tribunal can justly arrogate to itself the right to decide which needs should be developed and satisfied. Any such tribunal is reprehensible, although our revulsion does not do away with the question: how can the people who have been the object of effective and productive domination by themselves create the conditions of freedom?

The more rational, productive, technical, and total the repressive administration of society becomes, the more unimaginable the means and ways by which the administered individuals might break their servitude and seize their own liberation. To be sure, to impose Reason upon an entire society is a paradoxical and scandalous idea—although one might dispute the righteousness of a society which ridicules this idea while making its own population into objects of total administration. All liberation depends on the consciousness of servitude and the emergence of this consciousness is always hampered by the predominance of needs and satisfactions which, to a great extent, have become the individual's own. The process always replaces one system of precondition-ing by another; the optimal goal is the replacement of false needs by true ones, the abandonment of repressive satisfaction.

The distinguishing feature of advanced industrial society is its effective suffocation of those needs which demand liberation—liberation also from that which is tolerable and rewarding and comfortable—while it sustains and ab-solves the destructive power and repressive function of the affluent society. Here, the social controls exact the overwhelming need for the production and consumption of waste; the need for stupefying work where it is no longer a real necessity; the need for modes of relaxation which soothe and prolong this stupefication; the need for maintaining such deceptive liberties as free competi-tion at administered prices, a free press which censors itself, free choice be-tween brands and gadgets.

Under the rule of a repressive whole, liberty can be made into a powerful instrument of domination. The range of choice open to the individual is not the decisive factor in determining the degree of human freedom, but *what* can be chosen and what *is* chosen by the individual. The criterion for free choice can never be an absolute one, but neither is it entirely relative. Free election of masters does not abolish the masters or the slaves. Free choice among a wide variety of goods and services does not signify freedom if these goods and services sustain social controls over a life of toil and fear—that is, if they sustain alienation. And the spontaneous reproduction of superimposed needs by the individual does not establish autonomy; it only testifies to the efficacy of the controls.

Our insistence on the depth and efficacy of these controls is open to the objection that we overrate greatly the indoctrinating power of the "media," and that by themselves the people would feel and satisfy the needs which are now imposed upon them. The objection misses the point. The preconditioning does not start with the mass production of radio and television and with the centralization of their control. The people enter this stage as preconditioned receptacles of long standing; the decisive difference is in the flattening out of the contrast (or conflict) between the given and the possible, between the satisfied and the unsatisfied needs. Here, the so-called equalization of class distinctions reveals its ideological function. If the worker and his boss enjoy the same television program and visit the same resort places, if the typist is as attractively made up as the daughter of her employer, if the Negro owns a Cadillac, if they all read the same newspaper, then this assimilation indicates not the disappearance of classes, but the extent to which the needs and satisfac-tions that serve the preservation of the Establishment are shared by the under-lying population.

Indeed, in the most highly developed areas of contemporary society, the transplantation of social into individual needs is so effective that the difference between them seems to be purely theoretical. Can one really distinguish be-tween the mass media as instruments of information and entertainment, and as agents of manipulation and indoctrination? Between the automobile as nuisance and as convenience? Between the horrors and the comforts of functional architecture? Between the work for national defense and the work for corporate gain? Between the private pleasure and the commercial and political utility involved in increasing the birth rate?

We are again confronted with one of the most vexing aspects of advanced industrial civilization: the rational character of its irrationality. Its productivity and efficiency, its capacity to increase and spread comforts, to turn waste into need, and destruction into construction, the extent to which this civilization transforms the object world into an extension of man's mind and body makes the very notion of alienation questionable. The people recognize themselves in their commodities; they find their soul in their automobile, hi-fi set, split-level home, kitchen equipment. The very mechanism which ties the individual to his society has changed, and social control is anchored in the new needs which it has produced.

The prevailing forms of social control are technological in a new sense. To be sure, the technical structure and efficacy of the productive and destructive apparatus has been a major instrumentality for subjecting the population to the established social division of labor throughout the modern period. Moreover, such integration has always been accompanied by more obvious forms of compulsion: loss of livelihood, the administration of justice, the police, the armed forces. It still is. But in the contemporary period, the technological controls appear to be the very embodiment of Reason for the benefit of all social groups and interests—to such an extent that all contradiction seems irrational and all counteraction impossible.

No wonder then that, in the most advanced areas of this civilization, the social controls have been introjected to the point where even individual protest is affected at its roots. The intellectual and emotional refusal "to go along" appears neurotic and impotent. This is the socio-psychological aspect of the political event that marks the contemporary period: the passing of the historical forces which, at the preceding stage of industrial society, seemed to represent the possibility of new forms of existence.

But the term "introjection" perhaps no longer describes the way in which the individual by himself reproduces and perpetuates the external controls exercised by his society. Introjection suggests a variety of relatively spontaneous processes by which a Self (Ego) transposes the "outer" into the "inner." Thus introjection implies the existence of an inner dimension distinguished from and even antagonistic to the external exigencies—an individual consciousness and an individual unconscious *apart from* public opinion and behavior.[1] The idea of "inner freedom" here has its reality: it designates the private space in which man may become and remain "himself."

Today this private space has been invaded and whittled down by technological reality. Mass production and mass distribution claim the *entire* individual, and industrial psychology has long since ceased to be confined to the factory.

[1]The change in the function of the family here plays a decisive role: its "socializing" functions are increasingly taken over by outside groups and media. See my *Eros and Civilization* (Boston: Beacon Press, 1955), p. 96 ff.

The manifold processes of introjection seem to be ossified in almost mechanical reactions. The result is, not adjustment but *mimesis:* an immediate identification of the individual with *his* society and, through it, with the society as a whole.

This immediate, automatic identification (which may have been characteristic of primitive forms of association) reappears in high industrial civilization; its new "immediacy," however, is the product of a sophisticated, scientific management and organization. In this process, the "inner" dimension of the mind in which opposition to the status quo can take root is whittled down. The loss of this dimension, in which the power of negative thinking—the critical power of Reason—is at home, is the ideological counterpart to the very material process in which advanced industrial society silences and reconciles the opposition. The impact of progress turns Reason into submission to the facts of life, and to the dynamic capability of producing more and bigger facts of the same sort of life. The efficiency of the system blunts the individuals' recognition that it contains no facts which do not communicate the repressive power of the whole. If the individuals find themselves in the things which shape their life, they do so, not by giving, but by accepting the law of things—not the law of physics but the law of their society.

I have just suggested that the concept of alienation seems to become questionable when the individuals identify themselves with the existence which is imposed upon them and have in it their own development and satisfaction. This identification is not illusion but reality. However, the reality constitutes a more progressive stage of alienation. The latter has become entirely objective; the subject which is alienated is swallowed up by its alienated existence. There is only one dimension, and it is everywhere and in all forms. The achievements of progress defy ideological indictment as well as justification; before their tribunal, the "false consciousness" of their rationality becomes the true consciousness.

This absorption of ideology into reality does not, however, signify the "end of ideology." On the contrary, in a specific sense advanced industrial culture is *more* ideological than its predecessor, inasmuch as today the ideology is in the process of production itself.[2] In a provocative form, this proposition reveals the political aspects of the prevailing technological rationality. The productive apparatus and the goods and services which it produces "sell" or impose the social system as a whole. The means of mass transportation and communication, the commodities of lodging, food, and clothing, the irresistible output of the entertainment and information industry carry with them prescribed attitudes and habits, certain intellectual and emotional reactions which bind the consumers more or less pleasantly to the producers and, through the latter, to the whole. The products indoctrinate and manipulate; they promote a false consciousness which is immune against its falsehood. And

[2]Theodor W. Adorno, *Prismen. Kulturkritik und Gesellschaft.* (Frankfurt: Suhrkamp, 1955), p. 24 f.

as these beneficial products become available to more individuals in more social classes, the indoctrination they carry ceases to be publicity; it becomes a way of life. It is a good way of life—much better than before—and as a good way of life, it militates against qualitative change. Thus emerges a pattern of *one-dimensional thought and behavior* in which ideas, aspirations, and objectives that, by their content, transcend the established universe of discourse and action are either repelled or reduced to terms of this universe. They are redefined by the rationality of the given system and of its quantitative extension.

The trend may be related to a development in scientific method: operationalism in the physical, behaviorism in the social sciences. The common feature is a total empiricism in the treatment of concepts; their meaning is restricted to the representation of particular operations and behavior. The operational point of view is well illustrated by P. W. Bridgman's analysis of the concept of length:[3]

> We evidently know what we mean by length if we can tell what the length of any and every object is, and for the physicist nothing more is required. To find the length of an object, we have to perform certain physical operations. The concept of length is therefore fixed when the operations by which length is measured are fixed: that is, the concept of length involves as much and nothing more than the set of operations by which length is determined. In general, we mean by any concept nothing more than a set of operations; *the concept is synonymous with the corresponding set of operations.*

Bridgman has seen the wide implications of this mode of thought for the society at large:[4]

> To adopt the operational point of view involves much more than a mere restriction of the sense in which we understand 'concept,' but means a far-reaching change in all our habits of thought, in that we shall no longer permit ourselves to use as tools in our thinking concepts of which we cannot give an adequate account in terms of operations.

Bridgman's prediction has come true. The new mode of thought is today the predominant tendency in philosophy, psychology, sociology, and other fields. Many of the most seriously troublesome concepts are being "eliminated" by showing that no adequate account of them in terms of operations or behavior can be given. The radical empiricist onslaught (I shall subsequently, in chap-

---

[3]P. W. Bridgman, *The Logic of Modern Physics* (New York: Macmillan, 1928), p. 5. The operational doctrine has since been refined and qualified. Bridgman himself has extended the concept of "operation" to include the "paper-and-pencil" operations of the theorist (in Philipp J. Frank, *The Validation of Scientific Theories* [Boston: Beacon Press, 1954], Chap. II). The main impetus remains the same: it is "desirable" that the paper-and-pencil operations "be capable of eventual contact, although perhaps indirectly, with instrumental operations."
[4]P. W. Bridgman, *The Logic of Modern Physics,* loc. cit., p. 31.

ters VII and VIII, examine its claim to be empiricist) thus provides the methodological justification for the debunking of the mind by the intellectuals —a positivism which, in its denial of the transcending elements of Reason, forms the academic counterpart of the socially required behavior.

Outside the academic establishment, the "far-reaching change in all our habits of thought" is more serious. It serves to coordinate ideas and goals with those exacted by the prevailing system, to enclose them in the system, and to repel those which are irreconcilable with the system. The reign of such a one-dimensional reality does not mean that materialism rules, and that the spiritual, metaphysical, and bohemian occupations are petering out. On the contrary, there is a great deal of "Worship together this week," "Why not try God," Zen, existentialism, and beat ways of life, etc. But such modes of protest and transcendence are no longer contradictory to the status quo and no longer negative. They are rather the ceremonial part of practical behaviorism, its harmless negation, and are quickly digested by the status quo as part of its healthy diet.

One-dimensional thought is systematically promoted by the makers of politics and their purveyors of mass information. Their universe of discourse is populated by self-validating hypotheses which, incessantly and monopolistically repeated, become hypnotic definitions or dictations. For example, "free" are the institutions which operate (and are operated on) in the countries of the Free World; other transcending modes of freedom are by definition either anarchism, communism, or propaganda. "Socialistic" are all encroachments on private enterprises not undertaken by private enterprise itself (or by government contracts), such as universal and comprehensive health insurance, or the protection of nature from all too sweeping commercialization, or the establishment of public services which may hurt private profit. This totalitarian logic of accomplished facts has its Eastern counterpart. There, freedom is the way of life instituted by a communist regime, and all other transcending modes of freedom are either capitalistic, or revisionist, or leftist sectarianism. In both camps, non-operational ideas are non-behavioral and subversive. The movement of thought is stopped at barriers which appear as the limits of Reason itself.

Such limitation of thought is certainly not new. Ascending modern rationalism, in its speculative as well as empirical form, shows a striking contrast between extreme critical radicalism in scientific and philosophic method on the one hand, and an uncritical quietism in the attitude toward established and functioning social institutions. Thus Descartes' *ego cogitans* was to leave the "great public bodies" untouched, and Hobbes held that "the present ought always to be preferred, maintained, and accounted best." Kant agreed with Locke in justifying revolution *if and when* it has succeeded in organizing the whole and in preventing subversion.

However, these accommodating concepts of Reason were always contradicted by the evident misery and injustice of the "great public bodies" and the effective, more or less conscious rebellion against them. Societal conditions existed which provoked and permitted real dissociation from the established state of affairs; a private as well as political dimension was present in which dissociation could develop into effective opposition, testing its strength and the validity of its objectives.

With the gradual closing of this dimension by the society, the self-limitation of thought assumes a larger significance. The interrelation between scientific-philosophical and societal processes, between theoretical and practical Reason, asserts itself "behind the back" of the scientists and philosophers. The society bars a whole type of oppositional operations and behavior; consequently, the concepts pertaining to them are rendered illusory or meaningless. Historical transcendence appears as metaphysical transcendence, not acceptable to science and scientific thought. The operational and behavioral point of view, practiced as a "habit of thought" at large, becomes the view of the established universe of discourse and action, needs and aspirations. The "cunning of Reason" works, as it so often did, in the interest of the powers that be. The insistence on operational and behavioral concepts turns against the efforts to free thought and behavior *from* the given reality and *for* the suppressed alternative. Theoretical and practical Reason, academic and social behaviorism meet on common ground: that of an advanced society which makes scientific and technical progress into an instrument of domination.

"Progress" is not a neutral term; it moves toward specific ends, and these ends are defined by the possibilities of ameliorating the human condition. Advanced industrial society is approaching the stage where continued progress would demand the radical subversion of the prevailing direction and organization of progress. This stage would be reached when material production (including the necessary services) becomes automated to the extent that all vital needs can be satisfied while necessary labor time is reduced to marginal time. From this point on, technical progress would transcend the realm of necessity, where it served as the instrument of domination and exploitation which thereby limited its rationality; technology would become subject to the free play of faculties in the struggle for the pacification of nature and of society.

Such a state is envisioned in Marx's notion of the "abolition of labor." The term "pacification of existence" seems better suited to designate the historical alternative of a world which—through an international conflict which transforms and suspends the contradictions within the established societies—advances on the brink of a global war. "Pacification of existence" means the development of man's struggle with man and with nature, under conditions where the competing needs, desires, and aspirations are no longer organized by vested interests in domination and scarcity—an organization which perpetuates the destructive forms of this struggle.

Today's fight against this historical alternative finds a firm mass basis in the underlying population, and finds its ideology in the rigid orientation of thought and behavior to the given universe of facts. Validated by the accomplishments of science and technology, justified by its growing productivity, the status quo defies all transcendence. Faced with the possibility of pacification on the grounds of its technical and intellectual achievements, the mature industrial society closes itself against this alternative. Operationalism, in theory and practice, becomes the theory and practice of *containment*. Underneath its obvious dynamics, this society is a throughly static system of life: self-propelling in its oppressive productivity and in its beneficial coordination. Containment of technical progress goes hand in hand with its growth in the established direction. In spite of the political fetters imposed by the status quo, the more technology appears capable of creating the conditions for pacification, the more are the minds and bodies of man organized against this alternative.

The most advanced areas of indusı ial society exhibit throughout these two features: a trend toward consummation of technological rationality, and intensive efforts to contain this trend within the established institutions. Here is the internal contradiction of this civilization: the irrational element in its rationality. It is the token of its achievements. The industrial society which makes technology and science its own is organized for the ever-more-effective domination of man and nature, for the ever-more-effective utilization of its resources. It becomes irrational when the success of these efforts opens new dimensions of human realization. Organization for peace is different from organization for war; the institutions which served the struggle for existence cannot serve the pacification of existence. Life as an end is qualitatively different from life as a means.

Such a qualitatively new mode of existence can never be envisaged as the mere by-product of economic and political changes, as the more or less spontaneous effect of the new institutions which constitute the necessary prerequisite. Qualitative change also involves a change in the *technical* basis on which this society rests—one which sustains the economic and political institutions through which the "second nature" of man as an agressive object of administration is stabilized. The techniques of industrialization are political techniques; as such, they prejudge the possibilities of Reason and Freedom.

To be sure, labor must precede the reduction of labor, and industrialization must precede the development of human needs and satisfactions. But as all freedom depends on the conquest of alien necessity, the realization of freedom depends on the *techniques* of this conquest. The highest productivity of labor can be used for the perpetuation of labor, and the most efficient industrialization can serve the restriction and manipulation of needs.

When this point is reached, domination—in the guise of affluence and liberty —extends to all spheres of private and public existence, integrates all authentic opposition, absorbs all alternatives. Technological rationality reveals its political character as it becomes the great vehicle of better domination, creating a truly totalitarian universe in which society and nature, mind and body are kept in a state of permanent mobilization for the defense of this universe.

Beginnings: The New Consciousness

I'd rather be a sparrow than a snail.

SIMON AND GARFUNKLE

I invented adventures for myself and made up a life, so as to at least live in some way.

DOSTOEVSKY

ANGELA: ... native Americans, black Americans, Mexican Americans, women, youth, aged, poor, silent majority, Puerto Ricans and Asian Americans.

RICH: Homosexuals, do you have any homosexuals?

ANGELA: No, I forgot. We'll have to add a reading there.

MOLLY: Do you know what this reminds me of? We went to an anti-war march down on Wilshire Boulevard in Los Angeles a few months ago. We hadn't gone to an anti-war march for a long time and we thought it'd be neat to go. So, we go and march around and it's a drag and then we go to the park and listen to the speakers and I swear to God! It's anti-war, right? ... and everyone is against the war, everyone agreed on that. Okay? Now the speakers ... first you listen to the black speaker, Bobby Seale, then you listen to the Armenians ...

RICH: Armenians?

MOLLY: Then you listen to the lesbians, then you listen to gay liberation, then you listen to the Chicanos, then you listen to women's liberation, and after awhile, you just o.d. on all these speakers. I mean, wow, you just ... get ... crazy!

SCOTT: Sometimes I think people are just like Hobbits, they just like it short and sweet. Every time a speaker would shout "Power to the People!" everyone would jump up and yell "Power to the People!" and the rest of the time we were all bored. *(Laughter)*

ANGELA: See? You guys have the same feeling that I do about this section.

MOLLY: Well, in a case like this, when Rich said we left out the homosexuals, it hits you right in the face ... oh, God, we're sure to leave out *somebody.*

ANGELA: Well, I don't know what to do about this.

SCOTT: I don't like this section at all.

DICK: Are you saying there should be nothing on minority groups?

JOHN: Well, it's not that, it's just that this seems to be the wrong way to go about doing the section. I see this kind of stuff all the time, and it's fine, but what *I'd* like to see is something that tells me why my dad is a racist. But I can't find anything like that.

MOLLY: That's the kind of stuff I'd like to see, too.

DANA: Well, you'll probably have to write it yourself; professional academicians just don't write like that. As long as we have to choose from the available writings, I think we'll have to have this kind of presentation. And I *do* think we should have this section. I think it's essential to recognize the growth of this sort of awareness. This section isn't for the people at anti-war rallies, it's to let people in the classroom know what the anti-war rally is all about. I think we have to offer this as some sort of background for what's going on in the country.

19. Stereotyping

VINE DELORIA, JR.

One reason that Indian people have not been heard from until recently is that we have been completely covered up by movie Indians. Western movies have been such favorites that they have dominated the public's conception of what Indians are. It is not all bad when one thinks about the handsome Jay Silverheels bailing the Lone Ranger out of a jam, or Ed Ames rescuing Daniel Boone with some clever Indian trick. But the other mythologies that have wafted skyward because of the movies have blocked out any idea that there might be real Indians with real problems.

Other minority groups have fought tenaciously against stereotyping, and generally they have been successful. Italians quickly quashed the image of them as mobsters that television projected in *The Untouchables.* Blacks have been successful in getting a more realistic picture of the black man in a contemporary setting because they have had standout performers like Bill Cosby and Sidney Poitier to represent them.

Since stereotyping was highlighted by motion pictures, it would probably be well to review the images of minority groups projected in the movies in order to understand how the situation looks at present. Perhaps the first aspect of stereotyping was the tendency to exclude people on the basis of their inability to handle the English language. Not only were racial minorities excluded, but immigrants arriving on these shores were soon whipped into shape by ridicule of their English.

Traditional stereotypes pictured the black as a happy watermelon-eating darky whose sole contribution to American society was his indiscriminate substitution of the "d" sound for "th." Thus a black always said "dis" and "dat," as in "lift dat bale." The "d" sound carried over and was used by white gangsters to indicate disfavor with their situation, as in "dis is de end, ya rat." The important thing was to indicate that blacks were like lisping children not yet competent to undertake the rigors of economic opportunities and voting.

Mexicans were generally portrayed as shiftless and padded out for siesta, without any redeeming qualities whatsoever. Where the black had been handicapped by his use of the "d," the Mexican suffered from the use of the double "e." This marked them off as a group worth watching. Mexicans, according to the stereotype, always said "theenk," "peenk," and later "feenk." Many advertisements today still continue this stereotype, thinking that it is cute and cuddly.

These groups were much better off than Indians were. Indians were always devoid of any English whatsoever. They were only allowed to speak when an important message had to be transmitted on the screen. For example, "many pony soldiers die" was meant to indicate that Indians were going to attack the peaceful settlers who happened to have broken their three hundredth treaty moments before. Other than that Indian linguistic ability was limited to "ugh" and "kemo sabe" (which means honky in some obscure Indian language).

The next step was to acknowledge that there was a great American dream to which any child could aspire. (It was almost like the train in the night that Richard Nixon heard as a child anticipating the dream fairy.) The great American dream was projected in the early World War II movies. The last reel was devoted to a stirring proclamation that we were going to win the war and it showed factories producing airplanes, people building ships, and men marching in uniform to the transports. There was a quick pan of a black face before the scene shifted to scenes of orchards, rivers, Mount Rushmore, and the Liberty Bell as we found out what we were fighting for.

The new images expressed a profound inability to understand why minority groups couldn't "make it" when everybody knew what America was all about —freedom and equality. By projecting an image of everyone working hard to win the war, the doctrine was spread that America was just one big happy family and that there really weren't any differences so long as we had to win the war.

It was a rare war movie in the 1940s that actually showed a black or a Mexican as a bona fide fighting man. When they did appear it was in the role of cooks or orderlies serving whites. In most cases this was a fairly accurate statement of their situation, particularly with respect to the Navy.

World War II movies were entirely different for Indians. Each platoon of red-blooded white American boys was equipped with its own set of Indians. When the platoon got into trouble and was surrounded, its communications cut off except for one slender line to regimental headquarters, and that line tapped by myriads of Germans, Japanese, or Italians, the stage was set for the dramatic episode of the Indians.

John Wayne, Randolph Scott, Sonny Tufts, or Tyrone Power would smile broadly as he played his ace, which until this time had been hidden from view. From nowhere, a Navajo, Commanche, Cherokee, or Sioux would appear, take the telephone, and in some short and inscrutable phraseology communicate such a plenitude of knowledge to his fellow tribesman (fortunately situated at the general's right hand) that fighting units thousands of miles away would instantly perceive the situation and rescue the platoon. The Indian would disappear as mysteriously as he had come, only to reappear the next week in a different battle to perform his esoteric rites. Anyone watching war movies during the 40s would have been convinced that without Indian telephone operators the war would have been lost irretrievably, in spite of John Wayne.

Indians were America's secret weapon against the forces of evil. The typing spoke of a primitive gimmick, and it was the strangeness of Indians that made them visible, not their humanity. With the Korean War era and movies made during the middle 50s, other minority groups began to appear and Indians were pushed into the background. This era was the heyday of the "All-American Platoon." It was the ultimate conception of intergroup relations. The "All-American Platoon" was a "one each": one black, one Mexican, one Indian, one farm boy from Iowa, one Southerner who hated blacks, one boy from Brooklyn, one Polish boy from the urban slums of the Midwest, one Jewish intellectual, and one college boy. Every possible stereotype was included and it resulted in a portrayal of Indians as another species of human being for the first time in moving pictures.

The platoon was always commanded by a veteran of grizzled countenance who had been at every battle in which the United States had ever engaged. The whole story consisted in killing off the members of the platoon until only the veteran and the college boy were left. The Southerner and the black would die in each other's arms singing "Dixie." The Jewish intellectual and the Indian formed some kind of attachment and were curiously the last ones killed. When the smoke cleared, the college boy, with a prestige wound in the shoulder, returned to his girl, and the veteran reconciled with his wife and checked out another platoon in anticipation of taking the same hill in the next movie.

While other groups have managed to make great strides since those days, Indians have remained the primitive unknown quantity. Dialogue has reverted back to the monosyllabic grunt and even pictures that attempt to present the Indian side of the story depend upon unintelligible noises to present their message. The only exception to this rule is a line famed for its durability over the years. If you fall asleep during the Late Show and suddenly awaken to the words "go in peace my son," it is either an Indian chief bidding his son good-bye as the boy heads for college or a Roman Catholic priest forgiving Paul Newman or Steve McQueen for killing a hundred men in the preceding reel.

Anyone raising questions about the image of minority groups as portrayed in television and the movies is automatically suspect as an un-American and subversive influence on the minds of the young. The historical, linguistic, and cultural differences are neatly blocked out by the fad of portraying members of minority groups in roles which formerly were reserved for whites. Thus Burt Reynolds played a Mohawk detective busy solving the crime problem in New York City. Diahann Carroll played a well-to-do black widow with small child in a television series that was obviously patterned after the unique single-headed white family.

In recent years the documentary has arisen to present the story of Indian people and a number of series on Black America have been produced. Indian documentaries are singularly the same. A reporter and television crew hasten to either the Navajo or Pine Ridge reservation, quickly shoot reels on poverty conditions, and return East blithely thinking that they have captured the essence of Indian life. In spite of the best intentions, the eternal yearning to present an exciting story of a strange people overcomes, and the endless cycle of poverty-oriented films continues.

This type of approach continually categorizes the Indian as an incompetent boob who can't seem to get along and who is hopelessly mired in a poverty of his own making. Hidden beneath these documentaries is the message that Indians really WANT to live this way. No one has yet filmed the incredible progress that is being made by the Makah tribe, the Quinaults, Red Lake Chippewas, Gila River Pima-Maricopas, and others. Documentaries project the feeling that reservations should be eliminated because the conditions are so bad. There is no effort to present the bright side of Indian life.

With the rise of ethnic studies programs and courses in minority-group history, the situation has become worse. People who support these programs assume that by communicating the best aspects of a group they have somehow solved the major problems of that group in its relations with the rest of society. By emphasizing that black is beautiful or that Indians have cont ited the names of rivers to the road map, many people feel that they have done justice to the group concerned.

One theory of interpretation of Indian history that has arisen in the past several years is that all of the Indian war chiefs were patriots defending their lands. This is the "patriot chief" interpretation of history. Fundamentally it is a good theory in that it places a more equal balance to interpreting certain Indian wars as wars of resistance. It gets away from the tendency, seen earlier in this century, to classify all Indian warriors as renegades. But there is a tendency to overlook the obvious renegades, Indians who were treacherous and would have been renegades had there been no whites to fight. The patriot chiefs interpretation also conveniently overlooks the fact that every significant leader of the previous century was eventually done in by his own people in one way or another. Sitting Bull was killed by Indian police working for the government. Geronimo was captured by an army led by Apache scouts who sided with the United States.

If the weak points of each minority group's history are to be covered over by a sweetness-and-light interpretation based on what we would like to think happened rather than what did happen, we doom ourselves to decades of further racial strife. Most of the study programs today emphasize the goodness that is inherent in the different minority communities, instead of trying to present a balanced story. There are basically two schools of interpretation running through all of these efforts as the demand for black, red, and brown pride dominates the programs.

One theory derives from the "All-American Platoon" concept of a decade ago. Under this theory members of the respective racial minority groups had an important role in the great events of American history. Crispus Attucks, a black, almost single-handedly started the Revolutionary War, while Eli Parker, the Seneca Indian general, won the Civil War and would have concluded it sooner had not there been so many stupid whites abroad in those days. This is the "cameo" theory of history. It takes a basic "manifest destiny" white interpretation of history and lovingly plugs a few feathers, woolly heads, and sombreros into the famous events of American history. No one tries to explain what an Indian is who was helping the whites destroy his own people, since we are now all Americans and have these great events in common.

The absurdity of the cameo school of ethnic pride is self-apparent. Little Mexican children are taught that there were some good Mexicans at the Alamo. They can therefore be happy that Mexicans have been involved in the significant events of Texas history. Little is said about the Mexicans on the other side at the Alamo. The result is a denial of a substantial Mexican heritage by creating the feeling that "we all did it together." If this trend continues I would not be surprised to discover that Columbus had a Cherokee on board when he set sail from Spain in search of the Indies.

The cameo school smothers any differences that existed historically by presenting a history in which all groups have participated through representatives. Regardless of Crispus Attuck's valiant behavior during the Revolution, it is doubtful that he envisioned another century of slavery for blacks as a cause worth defending.

The other basic school of interpretation is a projection backward of the material blessings of the white middle class. It seeks to identify where all the material wealth originated and finds that each minority group *contributed* something. It can therefore be called the contribution school. Under this conception we should all love Indians because they contributed corn, squash, potatoes, tobacco, coffee, rubber, and other agricultural products. In like manner, blacks and Mexicans are credited with Carver's work on the peanut, blood transfusion, and tacos and tamales.

The ludicrous implication of the contribution school visualizes the minority groups clamoring to enter American society, lined up with an abundance of foods and fancies, presenting them to whites in a never-ending stream of generosity. If the different minority groups were given an overriding 2 percent royalty on their contributions, the same way whites have managed to give themselves royalties for their inventions, this school would have a more realistic impact on minority groups.

The danger with both of these types of ethnic studies theories is that they present an unrealistic account of the role of minority groups in American history. Certainly there is more to the story of the American Indian than providing cocoa and popcorn for Columbus' landing party. When the clashes of history are smoothed over in favor of a mushy togetherness feeling, then people begin to wonder what has happened in the recent past that has created the conditions of today. It has been the feeling of younger people that contemporary problems have arisen because community leadership has been consistently betraying them. Older statesmen are called Uncle Toms, and the entire fabric of accumulated wisdom and experience of the older generation of minority groups is destroyed.

Rising against the simplistic cameo and contribution schools is the contemporary desire by church leaders to make Christianity relevant to minority groups by transposing the entire Christian myth and archetypes into Indian, black, and Mexican terms. Thus Father Groppi, noted white-black priest, wants to have black churches show a black Christ. This is absurd, because Christ was, as everyone knows, a Presbyterian, and he was a white man. That is to say, for nearly two thousand years he has been a white man. To suddenly show him as black, Mexican, or Indian takes away the whole meaning of the myth.

The Indian counterpart of the black Christ is the Christmas card portraying the Holy Family living in a hogan in Monument Valley on the Navajo reservation. As the shepherds sing and gather their flocks, little groups of Navajo angels announce the birth of the Christchild. The scene is totally patronizing and unrealistic. If the Christchild was born on the Navajo reservation, his chances of surviving the first two years of life would be less than those of the original Jesus with Herod chasing him. (We have not yet reached the point of showing three officials from the Bureau of Indian Affairs coming up the canyon as the Three Wise Men, but someone with a keen sense of relevancy will try it sooner or later.)

This type of religious paternalism overlooks the fact that the original figures of religious myths were designed to communicate doctrines. It satisfies itself by presenting its basic figures as so universalized that anyone can participate at any time in history. Thus the religion that it is trying to communicate becomes ahistorical, as Mickey Mouse and Snow White are ahistorical.

If the attempted renovation of religious imagery is ever combined with the dominant schools of ethnic studies, the result will be the Last Supper as the gathering of the "All-American Platoon" highlighted by the contributions of each group represented. Instead of simple bread and wine the table will be overflowing with pizza, tamales, greens, peanuts, popcorn, German sausage, and hamburgers. Everyone will feel that they have had a part in the creation of the great American Christian social order. Godless Communism will be vanquished.

Under present conceptions of ethnic studies there can be no lasting benefit either to minority groups or to society at large. The pride that can be built into children and youth by acknowledgment of the validity of their group certainly cannot be built by simply transferring symbols and interpretations arising in white cultural history into an Indian, black, or Mexican setting. The result will be to make the minority groups bear the white man's burden by using his symbols and stereotypes as if they were their own.

There must be a drive within each minority group to understand its own uniqueness. This can only be done by examining what experiences were relevant to the group, not what experiences of white America the group wishes itself to be represented in. As an example, the discovery of gold in California was a significant event in the experience of white America. The discovery itself was irrelevant to the western Indian tribes, but the migrations caused by the discovery of gold were vitally important. The two histories can dovetail around this topic but ultimately each interpretation must depend upon its orientation to the group involved.

What has been important and continues to be important is the Constitution of the United States and its continual adaptation to contemporary situations. With the Constitution as a framework and reference point, it would appear that a number of conflicting interpretations of the experience of America could be validly given. While they might conflict at every point as each group defines to its own satisfaction what its experience has meant, recognition that within the Constitutional framework we are engaged in a living process of intergroup relationships would mean that no one group could define the meaning of American society to the exclusion of any other.

Self-awareness of each group must define a series of histories about the American experience. Manifest destiny has dominated thinking in the past because it has had an abstract quality that appeared to interpret experiences accurately. Nearly every racial and ethnic group has had to bow down before this conception of history and conform to an understanding of the world that it did not ultimately believe. Martin Luther King, Jr., spoke to his people on the basis of self-awareness the night before he died. He told them that they as a people would reach the promised land. Without the same sense of destiny, minority groups will simply be adopting the outmoded forms of stereotyping by which whites have deluded themselves for centuries.

We can survive as a society if we reject the conquest-oriented interpretation of the Constitution. While some Indian nationalists want the whole country back, a guarantee of adequate protection of existing treaty rights would provide a meaningful compromise. The Constitution should provide a sense of balance between groups as it has between conflicting desires of individuals.

As each group defines the ideas and doctrines necessary to maintain its own sense of dignity and identity, similarities in goals can be drawn that will have relevance beyond immediate group aspirations. Stereotyping will change radically because the ideological basis for portraying the members of any group will depend on that group's values. Plots in books and movies will have to show life as it is seen from within the group. Society will become broader and more cosmopolitan as innovative themes are presented to it. The universal sense of inhumanity will take on an aspect of concreteness. From the variety of cultural behavior patterns we can devise a new understanding of humanity.

The problem of stereotyping is not so much a racial problem as it is a problem of limited knowledge and perspective. Even though minority groups have suffered in the past by ridiculous characterizations of themselves by white society, they must not fall into the same trap by simply reversing the process that has stereotyped them. Minority groups must thrust through the rhetorical blockade by creating within themselves a sense of "peoplehood." This ultimately means the creation of a new history and not mere amendments to the historical interpretations of white America.

20. What America Would Be Like Without Blacks

RALPH ELLISON

The fantasy of an America free of blacks is at least as old as the dream of creating a truly democratic society. While we are aware that there is something inescapably tragic about the cost of achieving our democratic ideals, we keep such tragic awareness segregated to the rear of our minds. We allow it to come to the fore only during moments of great national crisis.

On the other hand, there is something so embarrassingly absurd about the notion of purging the nation of blacks that it seems hardly a product of thought at all. It is more like a primitive reflex, a throwback to the dim past of tribal experience, which we rationalize and try to make respectable by dressing it up in the gaudy and highly questionable trappings of what we call the "concept of race." Yet, despite its absurdity, the fantasy of a blackless America continues to turn up. It is a fantasy born not merely of racism but of petulance, of exasperation, of moral fatigue. It is like a boil bursting forth from impurities in the bloodstream of democracy.

In its benign manifestations, it can be outrageously comic—as in the picaresque adventures of Percival Brownlee who appears in William Faulkner's story *The Bear*. Exasperating to his white masters because his aspirations and talents are for preaching and conducting choirs rather than for farming, Brownlee is "freed" after much resistance and ends up as the prosperous proprietor of a New Orleans brothel. In Faulkner's hands, the uncomprehending drive of Brownlee's owners to "get shut" of him is comically instructive. Indeed, the story resonates certain abiding, indeed tragic themes of American history with which it is interwoven, and which are causing great turbulence in the social atmosphere today. I refer to the exasperation and bemusement of the white American with the black, the black American's ceaseless (and swiftly accelerating) struggle to escape the misconceptions of whites, and the continual confusing of the black American's racial background with his individual culture. Most of all, I refer to the recurring fantasy of solving one basic problem of American democracy by getting "shut" of the blacks through various wishful schemes that would banish them from the nation's bloodstream, from its social structure, and from its conscience and historical consciousness.

Sick to Prosper

This fantastic vision of a lily-white America appeared as early as 1713, with the suggestion of a white "native American," thought to be from New Jersey, that all the Negroes be given their freedom and returned to Africa. In 1777, Thomas Jefferson, while serving in the Virginia legislature, began drafting a plan for the gradual emancipation and exportation of the slaves. Nor were Negroes themselves immune to the fantasy. In 1815 Paul Cuffe, a wealthy merchant, shipbuilder and landowner from the New Bedford area, shipped and settled at his own expense 38 of his fellow Negroes in Africa. It was perhaps his example that led in the following year to the creation of the American Colonization Society, which was to establish in 1821 the colony of Liberia. Great amounts of cash and a perplexing mixture of motives went into the venture. The slaveowners and many Border-state politicians wanted to use it as a scheme to rid the country not of slaves but of the militant free Negroes who were agitating against the "peculiar institution." The abolitionists, until they took a lead from free Negro leaders and began attacking the scheme, also participated as a means of righting a great historical injustice. Many blacks went along with it simply because they were sick of the black and white American mess and hoped to prosper in the quiet peace of the old ancestral home.

Such conflicting motives doomed the Colonization Society to failure, but what amazes one even more than the notion that anyone could have believed in its success is the fact that it was attempted during a period when the blacks, slave and free, made up 18% of the total population. When we consider how long blacks had been in the New World and had been transforming it and being Americanized by it, the scheme appears not only fantastic, but the product of a free-floating irrationality. Indeed, a national pathology.

Plan to Purge

Nevertheless, some of the noblest of Americans were bemused. Not only Jefferson but later Abraham Lincoln was to give the scheme credence. According to Historian John Hope Franklin, Negro colonization seemed as important to Lincoln as emancipation. In 1862, Franklin notes, Lincoln called a group of prominent free Negroes to the White House and urged them to support colonization, telling them: "Your race suffers greatly, many of them by living among us, while ours suffers from your presence. If this is admitted, it affords a reason why we should be separated."

In spite of his unquestioned greatness, Abraham Lincoln was a man of his times and limited by some of the less worthy thinking of his times. This is demonstrated both by his reliance upon the concept of race in his analysis of the American dilemma and by his involvement in a plan of purging the nation of blacks as a means of healing the badly shattered ideals of democratic federalism. Although benign, his motive was no less a product of fantasy. It envisaged an attempt to relieve an inevitable suffering that marked the growing pains of the youthful body politic by an operation which would have amounted to the severing of a healthy and indispensable member.

Yet, like its twin, the illusion of secession, the fantasy of a benign amputation that would rid the country of black men to the benefit of a nation's health not only persists; today, in the form of neo-Garveyism, it fascinates black men no less than it once hypnotized whites. Both fantasies become operative whenever the nation grows weary of the struggle toward the ideal of American democratic equality. Both would use the black man as a scapegoat to achieve a national catharsis, and both would, by way of curing the patient, destroy him.

What is ultimately intriguing about the fantasy of "getting shut" of the Negro American is the fact that no one who entertains it seems ever to have considered what the nation would have become had Africans *not* been brought to the New World, and had their descendants not played such a complex and confounding role in the creation of American history and culture. Nor do they appear to have considered with any seriousness the effect upon the nation of having any of the schemes for exporting blacks succeed beyond settling some 15,000 or so in Liberia.

We are reminded that Daniel Patrick Moynihan, who has recently aggravated our social confusion over the racial issue while allegedly attempting to clarify it, is co-author of a work which insists that the American melting pot didn't melt because our white ethnic groups have resisted all assimilative forces that appear to threaten their identities. The problem here is that few Americans know who and what they really are. That is why few of these groups— or at least few of the children of these groups—have been able to resist the movies, television, baseball, jazz, football, drum-majoretting, rock, comic strips, radio commercials, soap operas, book clubs, slang, or any of a thousand other expressions and carriers of our pluralistic and easily available popular culture. And it is here precisely that ethnic resistance is least effective. On this level the melting pot did indeed melt, creating such deceptive metamorphoses and blending of identities, values and life-styles that most American whites are culturally part Negro American without even realizing it.

If we can resist for a moment the temptation to view everything having to do with Negro Americans in terms of their racially imposed status, we become aware of the fact that for all the harsh reality of the social and economic injustices visited upon them, these injustices have failed to keep Negroes clear of the cultural mainstream; Negro Americans are in fact one of its major tributaries. If we can cease approaching American social reality in terms of such false concepts as white and nonwhite, black culture and white culture, and think of these apparently unthinkable matters in the realistic manner of Western pioneers confronting the unknown prairie, perhaps we can begin to imagine what the U.S. would have been, or not been, had there been no blacks to give it—if I may be so bold as to say—color.

For one thing, the American nation is in a sense the product of the American language, a colloquial speech that began emerging long before the British colonials and Africans were transformed into Americans. It is a language that evolved from the king's English but, basing itself upon the realities of the American land and colonial institutions—or lack of institutions, began quite early as a vernacular revolt against the signs, symbols, manners and authority of the mother country. It is a language that began by merging the sounds of many tongues, brought together in the struggle of diverse regions. And whether it is admitted or not, much of the sound of that language is derived from the timbre of the African voice and the listening habits of the African ear. So there is a *de'z* and *do'z* of slave speech sounding beneath our most polished Harvard accents, and if there is such a thing as a Yale accent, there is a Negro wail in it—doubtlessly introduced there by Old Yalie John C. Calhoun, who probably got it from his mammy.

Whitman viewed the spoken idiom of Negro Americans as a source for a native grand opera. Its flexibility, its musicality, its rhythms, freewheeling diction and metaphors, as projected in Negro American folklore, were absorbed by the creators of our great 19th century literature even when the majority of blacks were still enslaved. Mark Twain celebrated it in the prose of *Huckleberry Finn;* without the presence of blacks, the book could not have been written. No Huck and Jim, no American novel as we know it. For not only is the black man a co-creator of the language that Mark Twain raised to the level of literary eloquence, but Jim's condition as American and Huck's commitment to freedom are at the moral center of the novel.

In other words, had there been no blacks, certain creative tensions arising from the cross-purposes of whites and blacks would also not have existed. Not only would there have been no Faulkner; there would have been no Stephen Crane, who found certain basic themes of his writing in the Civil War. Thus, also, there would have been no Hemingway, who took Crane as a source and guide. Without the presence of Negro American style, our jokes, our tall tales, even our sports would be lacking in the sudden turns, the shocks, the swift changes of pace (all jazz-shaped) that serve to remind us that the world is ever unexplored, and that while a complete mastery of life is mere illusion, the real secret of the game is to make life swing. It is its ability to articulate this tragic-comic attitude toward life that explains much of the mysterious power and attractiveness of that quality of Negro American style known as "soul." An expression of American diversity within unity, of blackness with whiteness, soul announces the presence of a creative struggle against the realities of existence.

Without the presence of blacks, our political history would have been otherwise. No slave economy, no Civil War; no violent destruction of the Reconstruction; no K.K.K. and no Jim Crow system. And without the disenfranchisement of black Americans and the manipulation of racial fears and prejudices, the disproportionate impact of white Southern politicians upon our domestic and foreign policies would have been impossible. Indeed, it is almost impossible to conceive of what our political system would have become without the snarl of forces—cultural, racial, religious—that makes our nation what it is today.

Absent, too, would be the need for that tragic knowledge which we try ceaselessly to evade: that the true subject of democracy is not simply material well-being but the extension of the democratic process in the direction of perfecting itself. And that the most obvious test and clue to that perfection is the inclusion—*not* assimilation—of the black man.

Since the beginning of the nation, white Americans have suffered from a deep inner uncertainty as to who they really are. One of the ways that has been used to simplify the answer has been to seize upon the presence of black Americans and use them as a marker, a symbol of limits, a metaphor for the "outsider." Many whites could look at the social position of blacks and feel that color formed an easy and reliable gauge for determining to what extent one was or was not American. Perhaps that is why one of the first epithets that many European immigrants learned when they got off the boat was the term "nigger"—it made them feel instantly American. But this is tricky magic. Despite his racial difference and social status, something indisputably American about Negroes not only raised doubts about the white man's value system but aroused the troubling suspicion that whatever else the true American is, he is also somehow black.

Geared to What Is

Materially, psychologically and culturally, part of the nation's heritage is Negro American, and whatever it becomes will be shaped in part by the Negro's presence. Which is fortunate, for today it is the black American who puts pressure upon the nation to live up to its ideals. It is he who gives creative tension to our struggle for justice and for the elimination of those factors, social and psychological, which make for slums and shaky suburban communities. It is he who insists that we purify the American language by demanding that there be a closer correlation between the meaning of words and reality, between ideal and conduct, our assertions and our actions. Without the black American, something irrepressibly hopeful and creative would go out of the American spirit, and the nation might well succumb to the moral slobbism that has ever threatened its existence from within.

When we look objectively at how the dry bones of the nation were hung together, it seems obvious that some one of the many groups that compose the U.S. had to suffer the fate of being allowed no easy escape from experiencing the harsh realities of the human condition as they were to exist under even so fortunate a democracy as ours. It would seem that some one group had to be stripped of the possibility of escaping such tragic knowledge by taking sanctuary in moral equivocation, racial chauvinism or the advantage of superior social status. There is no point in complaining over the past or apologizing for one's fate. But for blacks there are no hiding places down here, not in suburbia or in penthouses, neither in country nor in city. They are an American people who are geared to what *is* and who yet are driven by a sense of what it is possible for human life to be in this society. The nation could not survive being deprived of their presence because, by the irony implicit in the dynamics of American democracy, they symbolize both its most stringent testing and the possibility of its greatest human freedom.

21. The Myths of the Mexican American

GLEN GAVIGLIO

The Mexican Americans, or Chicanos," have been referred to as the forgotten minority. They are supposedly a quiet, docile, passive, somnolent, and satisfied group of fatalistic near peasants. Therefore they have been erased from the conscience of most Americans. They have been invisible; they have been wiped from history, like the Indians. Yet Chicanos have not lost themselves, even though they have lived in a hostile environment for decades. Why have they been overlooked, ignored, and oppressed?

This brief essay is an attempt to synthesize some of the major sociohistoric factors that have influenced the development of *La Raza*. For purposes of analysis, this essay is arranged into four deeply ingrained myths of the Mexican American: (1) The Myth of the Border, (2) The Myth of the Docile Peasant, (3) The Myth of Ethnic and Racial Assimilation, and (4) The Myth of Mexican American Similarity.

Myths are important for societies; they influence every individual's definition of reality. People act in relation to the mythology of their society. Therefore myths are significant behavior inducing and shaping devices. (The social reality of the mind comes in all flavors of distortion.) The influence of some of these distortions is examined in each of the following myths.

The Myth of the Border

Historically, cries of "Spic," "Greaser," "Wetback," or "Taco Bender, go home" were very typical of the American Southwest. The cries are more subdued and sophisticated now, but invariably eruptions occur. For example, in 1969 in the Santa Clara Valley, just south of San Francisco, a venerable judge publicly excoriated a Chicano youth in court, saying that Hitler had a good thing going with the Jews and that a similar program should be undertaken with Mexicans. (At this writing that judge is still on the bench.)

There is a political boundary separating Mexico and the United States, but the winds of change have modified that boundary immensely. In a very real sense that border does not exist. The border is totally artificial from a geographical perspective. It does not separate climatic or agricultural regions; in fact, it cuts across the natural topography of the area. The difference between Calexico and Mexicali, El Paso and Juarez, and Brownsville and Matamoros is economic and political, not geographical. The border does not really exist for the Chicano. It never has.

At one time the Southwest was part of Mexico. It was inhabited by a mixture of Spaniards and Indians; it was naturally an arid region that was sparsely settled. The region was the frontier or borderlands of Mexico, and it was never an integral part of that country. When the Spanish did come to settle this region, there actually were very few pure Spaniards in the expeditions. Most of the settlers who came north from Mexico were Mestizo and Indian. The Indians who were living in this area had already been strongly influenced by the Aztec civilization. On the eve of the Mexican-American War (1848), there were only about 82,000 Spanish-speaking people living in the Southwest, but they had been there for generations. (There were also an untabulated number of Indians and Mestizos in the area.) In California in 1848, there were 21,000 Spanish-speaking in a population of about 100,000. When California became a state (1850), the constitution was written in Spanish. This constitution, created in part by people of Spanish ancestry, established California as a bilingual state (and it remained bilingual until 1878). In southern California there were bilingual schools until the 1870's. In other words, California has gone from bilingual schools to denial to the Chicanos of the right to vote, because they cannot read the Constitution. (This has been recently changed by the California Supreme Court.)

When the United States wrested the Southwest from Mexico, many Spanish-speaking people automatically became residents of the United States. They did not immigrate from anywhere. Therefore, when an Anglo tells a Chicano to go home, he is less than amusing; he is grossly misinformed. The Chicano is more firmly rooted in the American past than an Anglo who may have just recently migrated from Europe.

The Treaty of Guadalupe Hidalgo (1848), which terminated the Mexican-American War, was supposed to protect and guarantee the rights of self-determination for the Spanish-speaking people in the newly acquired United States territory. In actuality the treaty did little to protect the rights of the Mexicans in this region. The Anglos immediately displayed a tremendous hostility and resentment toward these Hispanos. The creed of American racism became brutally apparent in the systematic oppression that followed. For example, in California the antagonism between Spanish-speaking and Yankee miners culminated with the Foreign Miners Tax Law of 1850, which effectively drove the Spanish-speaking from the gold fields. (Note the word *foreign*.) In 1851 the Federal Land Tenure Act was passed. This act made possible the systematic and gradual extraction of land from the hands of the Hispanos.

No Chicano is really an immigrant in America. When they "moved north," they felt that they were moving in an environment that was geographically, culturally, and historically familiar. I would even say that in a political sense the border has been a nebulous entity. There was no border patrol until 1924 and there was not even a quota on Mexican immigration until 1965. The reason the border did not exist in a political or economic manner for either the Anglo or Chicano was the need for cheap labor in the fields. As long as there was a ready supply of bodies toward the south, the indigenous labor force could not organize and demand higher wages. When the field workers did try to organize, their leaders were quickly "deported." The farm workers could not effectively unionize until the Bracero program was terminated in 1965. (The program allowed Mexican nationals to reside temporarily in the United States in order to harvest the crops.) The Delano movement still has not completely succeeded, because the border is still quite open. Migrant workers can enter both legally and illegally. "Green Card Holders" are now entering the United States to pick crops in times of emergency (meaning "during strikes"). In reality, the border has always been exactly what the United States has wanted it to be.

The Myth of the Docile Peasant

The Chicano has been stereotyped as a passive peasant. This is absurd on statistical grounds alone. Over 80 per cent of all Chicanos reside in urban areas and over 1 million Chicanos live in Los Angeles. The image of the Chicano is not really a static one. According to the stereotype, the Chicano can be either a fat and lazy peon, slumbering under a cactus and wearing his sombrero and poncho, or he can be a stinking, ferocious, foul-mouthed, greasy bandito. The stereotype of the Mexican American stems from two basic sources: (1) the popularized folk mythology of traditional American racism and (2) the distorted sociological image. We can expect the first; it bears no surprises, but the latter is more repulsive to us, because it comes from unbiased sociological sources.

There is nothing unique in saying that the Society of America is racist, but when we confront the historical record of past American racial atrocities, the present looks as though peace and brotherhood abound (if you choose to ignore Vietnam). American literature, with but few exceptions, is filled with condescending racist drivel. One example from *The Oregon Trail* by Francis Parkman (Doubleday, 1948) will provide the proper flavor:

> Two or three squalid Mexicans, with their broad hats, and their vile faces overgrown with hair, were lounging about the bank of the river in front of (the gate of the Pueblo). They disappeared as they saw us approach [p. 2𝑢𝑢].
> A few squaws and Spanish women, and a few Mexicans, as mean and miserable as the place itself, were lazily sauntering about [p. 260].
> There was another room beyond, less sumptuously decorated, and here three or four Spanish girls, one of them very pretty, were baking cakes at a mud fireplace in the corner [p. 261].
> The human race in this part of the world is separated into three divisions, arranged in the order of their merits: white men, Indians, and Mexicans; to the latter of whom the honorable title of "whites" is by no means conceded [p. 263].

Usually the racism is not even this "subtle." Our history is replete with speeches of major political figures proclaiming a hyprocritical and altruistic imperialism. We have always had an inclination to save the ignorant and backward colored masses of the world from themselves, witness this speech delivered by John C. Calhoun in the Senate on January 4, 1848 (after we had defeated Mexico in a war):

> We have never dreamt of incorporating into our Union any but the Caucasian race—the free white race. To incorporate Mexico, would be the very first instance of the kind, of incorporating an Indian race; for more than half of the Mexicans are Indians, and the other is composed chiefly of mixed tribes. I protest against such a union as that! Ours, sir, is the government of a white race. The greatest misfortunes of Spanish America are to be traced to the fatal error of placing these colored races on an equality with the white race. That error destroyed the social arrangement which formed the basis of society. The Portuguese and ourselves have escaped—the Portuguese at least to some extent— and we are the only people on this continent which had made revolutions without being followed by anarchy. And yet it is professed, and talked about, to erect these Mexicans into a territorial government, and place them on an equality with the people of the United States. I protest utterly against such a project. . . .
>
> But . . . suppose all these difficulties removed; suppose their people attached to our Union, and desirous of incorporating with us, ought we to bring them in? Are they fit to be connected with us? Are they fit for self-government and for governing you? Are you, any of you, willing that your states should be governed by these twenty-odd Mexican states, with a population of about only one million of your blood, and two or three million of mixed blood better informed—all the rest pure Indians, a mixed blood equally ignorant and unfit for liberty, impure races, not as good as the Cherokees or Choctaws?

Calhoun did not even believe in spreading the faith to the ignorant colored masses, because they were too inferior even to govern themselves and accept the gospel of Americanism.

The mythology of American racism has been updated and perfected since the heyday of blatant expansionism and imperialism. The myths may be a little more subtle but they are still extremely harmful. It can be effectively argued that the myths are even more destructive because of the pervasive influence in the mass media. The world is being turned into a McLuhanesque global village; therefore more people are influenced by the racist stereotypes portrayed in the mass media. At the moment one of the worst offenders is the advertising industry. One particularly offensive commercial was for Arrid deodorant. It shows a Mexican bandito spraying his underarm while a voice says, "If it works for him, it will work for you." Do Chicanos stink worse than blacks? Can you envision that same commercial with a sloppy, fat ghetto black wearing a dirty and torn T-shirt? Or is the black movement too powerful (or too violent) to allow that kind of defamation? There is a real battle in America to see who will be the new "niggers." The Chicanos or the Hippies?

Beginnings: The New Consciousness 217

These stereotypes are extremely important because people act upon these myths. Very insipid and disastrous self-fulfilling prophecies can be initiated by racial and cultural myths. If the dominant group treats the minority group as an inferior race or culture, the minority can become just that. In a political and economic sense racial oppression is very obvious, but it has more subtle manifestations. What happens in the school system when students are "tracked" or when the teacher has lower expectations for some students? What happens to the minds of minority group members? Can a people be taught to hate themselves? Can a minority group believe the myths the majority perpetrates? One of the most sickening aspects of race relations in America is that the preceding questions must be answered in a very negative manner.

Another form of stereotyping is of a more insidious variety because it is generated by the academic community and therefore carries with it scientific validity. In particular the work of Heller *(Mexican-American Youth),* Tuck *(Not with the Fist),* and Madsen *(Mexican-Americans of South Texas)* should be mentioned. The studies have some very major defects. The most obvious deficiency from a traditional sociological perspective is a methodological one, the authors over-generalize from a biased or partial sampling of Chicanos. These studies list "characteristics" or "attributes" of the typical Mexican American. Some of these characteristics seem like a sociological updating of racial mythology. Is being passive, accepting, and fatalistic much different from being lazy? Do all Chicanos display these traits? We cannot be sure of the limited regional sample of Chicanos in these studies. Another glaring omission in these studies is their completely historical nature. They speak of the Chicano as existing in the eternal present, as if his traditional culture were static and unchanging. The Chicano may not try to change his environment in the same manner as the robust and enterprising Anglo, for he has found that passive adjustment to his social milieu is necessary to his survival. This passiveness creates another blatantly false stereotype. Were those who rode with Villa and Zapata during the Mexican Revolution passively accepting their fate? Were the Chicanos who organized numerous strikes in the Southwest for the past seventy-five years accepting their fate? Are Reies Tijerina, Cesar Chavez, and Corky Gonsalez leaders of a passive and somnolent bunch of poncho-clad peasants?

The last significant error in these books is their tendency to equate and confuse ethnic and class characteristics. Many of the characteristics attributed to Mexican Americans in these studies are shared by all lower-class people. Cohen and Hodges, in a study done in California, found that lower-lower-class Chicanos, blacks, and Anglos all shared some basically similar characteristics: extended families, marked anti-intellectualism, *machismo* (a supermasculine, double-standard-type male), use of physical force, and a type of fatalism. Oscar Lewis has argued that throughout the world the lower classes generally share these traits. Lewis terms these characteristics a "culture of poverty"; he sees it as a functional adaptation to their oppressive social conditions. Therefore there is nothing unique in these traits that are supposedly typical of the

Mexican American. Some statistical validity resides in the fact that a fairly large percentage of Chicanos live below the poverty level (16 per cent of the Anglos, 27 per cent of the blacks, and 37 per cent of the Chicanos). These figures may understate the degree of Chicano poverty. That 37 per cent basically represents United States citizens. According to the U.S. Department of Immigration, there are 1.5 million alien residents and 4.5 million illegal aliens below the poverty level.

The concept of the culture of poverty can also be interpreted in a very negative manner. It can be used to conclude that the cultural characteristics of the poor people themselves are responsible for their socioeconomic status. For example, take the noted fatalism of the lower classes. They feel that they have little control over the institutions and events that shape their lives. It is very possible that the pessimism, apathy and fatalism of the lower classes is a valid adjustment to a historical social reality. The life chances of a minority group member have been severely and systematically restricted; these people have not had and still do not have very much control over the decisions that affect their lives. Is it really so hard to imagine accepting a religion, whether it is a folk Catholicism or a revivalist Protestantism, that promises an internal reward when the present and future look so bleak? When reality is unbearably ugly, fatalism may be the only answer among rotten alternatives.

It would be wise not to apply the concept of culture of poverty to minority groups unless its sociohistorical component is considered. Why is there a culture of poverty? How did it start? Why do so many different societies have subcultures of poverty with similar traits? The answer lies in an analysis of how people adjust to the conditions of poverty, racism, and oppression.

The Myth of Ethnic and Racial Assimilation

The huddled and hungry hordes of the world streamed to the shores of America, where golden opportunities awaited them. The saga of America is sometimes told as though it were a giant, bottomless cauldron where the oppressed masses of humanity mingled and produced an egalitarian and tolerant democratic society. This is the great myth of the melting pot. It is a romantic and nostalgic vision of the American past that does very little justice to reality. Assimilation in the American melting pot was meant for whites only. For example, Indians were almost exterminated like vermin, instead of being melted, and of course enough has been said recently of black Americans. The Chicano still forms an unassimilated and distinct cultural entity in America.

Glazer and Moynihan (*Beyond the Melting Pot,* 1963) argue that ethnic homogenization never completely took place in America. New York is a veritable hodge-podge of racial and ethnic groups that still function as political interest groups. Glazer and Moynihan succinctly conclude, "The point about the Melting Pot . . . is that it did not happen." Every act of racism and discrimination is a painful contradiction of the concept of the melting pot.

Why have the Chicanos not been assimilated into the American mainstream? The most obvious reason for this lack of assimilation is the dominant Anglo group itself; it has not been willing to let the Chicano assimilate. The Mexican American is in a caste position similar to that of the black man after emancipation. There are other factors that have contributed to the cultural distance between the Chicano and the Anglo. First, there is the fact that Mexico is adjacent to the United States. The homeland for many Chicanos is never far away. There is a continual cultural regeneration and reinforcement. Many Mexicans come to America "temporarily" and never psychologically divorce themselves from the values of Mexico. Then there is the continual immigration, both legal and illegal, from Mexico. There are also visits from relatives going in both directions. The communal and extended nature of the Chicano family further reinforces certain cultural values, like language. Three and four generations may live in the same household. This pattern can be contrasted with many white immigrant groups who left the homeland far behind in Europe, geographically if not psychologically.

Another reason why the Chicano has not been and may never be totally assimilated is that he does not want to be. Why accept the dominant culture? If Anglo youth rebellion is any indication of the viability of mainstream, middle-class American values, Chicanos may be correct in refusing to assimilate. In fact, many of the criticisms that young people level at America have been part of the Chicano cultural and historical tradition. Chicanos have never been "materialistic," or what the Anglo considers "property oriented." The land was usually for all to use or hold communally; their agricultural practices and use of the land were in harmony with nature. Chicanos have always displayed a sense of community, a tendency toward mutual aid, and a strong communal or extended family. They have always nurtured an emphasis on warm interpersonal relationships and a respect for people as individuals.

The Myth of Mexican American Similarity

As with most minority groups, the Mexican American has been stereotyped. The stereotype is usually one of a lower-lower-class Chicano, a rigid caricature which allows a minimum of diversity. The stereotype, as mentioned in a previous section, has negative and racist connotations, and as a valid characterization of social reality, it is sadly lacking.

There are some statistical generalizations that can be made in relation to Chicanos. Many have parents or grandparents who migrated from Mexico, and as a consequence, many speak Spanish, Pocho (a combination of Spanish and English), or English with an accent. As a group, Chicanos tend to be Catholic (easily over 50 per cent). As a population they tend to be young (twenty years of age). The average yearly income for the Mexican American family is the lowest in the nation, except for the income of the reservation Indian. There are more Chicanos (60 to 70 per cent) living in poverty and more Chicanos with less education than blacks (less than eight years, on the average, for those over twenty-five). Chicanos as a group share certain cultural values, but within the broad contours just mentioned there is immense variety.

There are many physical differences in the Chicano population. Although Chicanos tend to be darker than the Anglo population, they range from swarthy to light skinned. All types of ethnic and racial groups have mingled in Mexico with the indigenous people, from black slaves to French immigrants. There are also Filipinos and Puerto Ricans who are culturally Chicano. There are rural and urban differences, generational conflicts, geographical differences, and class differences between Chicanos. Who is a Mexican American? How can you really stereotype the Chicano?

Here lies the strength and weakness of the Chicano. On one hand he is confronted in America with a severe "identity crisis." He is the true marginal man caught between cultures. Historically, he represents the uneasy compromise between the Hispano and the Indian who was delivered into a hostile Anglo world. Yet as a people, *La Raza* has developed a deeply ingrained humanism. The term *La Raza* does not simply mean the race or people, but the community or the family. *La Raza* stands in striking contrast to the cold and impersonal Anglo world.

Bibliography

Casavantes, Edward J. *A New Look at the Attributes of the Mexican American.* Albuquerque, N.M.: Southwestern Education Laboratory, Inc. 1969.

Forbes, Jack D. *Mexican-Americans: A Handbook for Educators.* Berkeley: Far West Laboratory for Educational Research and Development, 1969.

Glazer, Nathan, and Daniel Patrick Moynihan. *Beyond the Melting Pot.* Cambridge, Mass.: M.I.T. Press, 1963.

Heller, Celia S. *Mexican American Youth: Forgotten Youth at the Crossroads.* New York: Random House, Inc., 1966.

Madsen, William. *The Mexican-American of South Texas.* New York: Holt, Rinehart and Winston, Inc., 1964.

Martinez, Thomas M. "Advertising and Racism: "The Case of the Mexican-American," *El Grito,* Summer 1969, Volume II, Number 4.

McWilliams, Carey. *North from Mexico.* New York: Greenwood Press, 1948.

———. *The Mexicans in America.* New York: Teacher's College Press, 1968.

Rios, Francisco Armando. "The Mexican in Fact, Fiction, and Folklore," *El Grito,* Summer 1969, Volume II, Number 4.

Robinson, Cecil. *With the Ears of Strangers.* Tucson: University of Arizona Press, 1963.

Romano, Octavio Ignacio. "The Anthropology and Sociology of the Mexican-Americans: The Distortion of Mexican-American History," *El Grito,* Fall 1968, Volume II, Number 1.

Rosenthall, Robert, and Lenore Jacobson. *Pygmalion in the Classroom.* New York: Holt, Rinehart and Winston, Inc., 1968.

Steinfield, Melvin. *Cracks in the Melting Pot.* Beverly Hills, Calif.: Glencoe Press, 1970.

22. On Liberation: For Women, For All

MARLENE DIXON

Rise of Women's Liberation

The old women's movement burned itself out in the frantic decade of the 1920s. After a hundred years of struggle, women won a battle, only to lose the campaign: the vote was obtained, but the new millennium did not arrive. Women got the vote and achieved a measure of legal emancipation, but the real social and cultural barriers to full equality for women remained untouched.

For over thirty years the movement remained buried in its own ashes. Women were born and grew to maturity virtually ignorant of their own history of rebellion, aware only of a caricature of blue stockings and suffragettes. Even as increasing numbers of women were being driven into the labor force by the brutal conditions of the 1930s and by the massive drain of men into the military in the 1940s, the old ideal remained: a woman's place was in the home and behind her man. As the war ended and men returned to resume their jobs in factories and offices, women were forced back to the kitchen and nursery with a vengeance. This story has been repeated after each war and the reason is clear: women form a flexible, cheap labor pool that is essential to a capitalist system. When labor is scarce, they are forced onto the labor market. When labor is plentiful, they are forced out. Women and blacks have provided a reserve army of unemployed workers, benefiting capitalists and the stable male white working class alike. Yet the system imposes untold suffering on the victims—blacks and women—through low wages and chronic unemployment.

With the end of the war, the average age at marriage declined; the average size of families went up; and the suburban migration began in earnest. The political conservatism of the fifties was echoed in a social conservatism that stressed a Victorian ideal of the woman's life: a full womb and selfless devotion to husband and children.

As the bleak decade played itself out, however, three important social developments emerged that were to make a rebirth of the women's struggle inevitable. First, women came to make up more than a third of the labor force, the number of working women being twice the prewar figure. Yet the marked increase in female employment did nothing to better the position of women, who were more occupationally disadvantaged in the 1960s than they had been twenty-five years earlier. Rather than moving equally into all sectors of the occupational structure, they were being forced into the low-paying service, clerical and semi-skilled categories. In 1940, women had held 45 percent of all professional and technical positions; in 1967, they held only 37 percent. The proportion of women in service jobs meanwhile rose from 50 to 55 percent.

Second, the intoxicating wine of marriage and suburban life was turning sour; a generation of women woke up to find their children grown and a life (roughly thirty more productive years) of housework and bridge parties stretching out before them like a wasteland. For many younger women, the empty drudgery they saw in the suburban life was a sobering contradiction to adolescent dreams of romantic love and the fulfilling role of woman as wife and mother.

Third, a growing civil rights movement was sweeping thousands of young men and women into a moral crusade—a crusade that harsh political experience was to transmute into the New Left. The American Dream was riven and tattered in Mississippi and finally napalmed in Vietnam. Young Americans were drawn not to Levittown, but to Berkeley, Haight-Ashbury, and the East Village. Traditional political ideologies and cultural myths, sexual mores and sex roles with them, began to disintegrate in an explosion of rebellion and protest.

The three major groups that make up the new women's movement—working women, middle-class married women, and students—bring very different kinds of interests and objectives to women's liberation. Working women are most concerned with the economic issues of guaranteed employment, fair wages, job discrimination, and child care. Their most immediate oppression is rooted in industrial capitalism and felt directly through the vicissitudes of an exploitative labor market.

Middle-class women oppressed by the psychological mutilation and injustice of institutionalized segregation, discrimination, and imposed inferiority are most sensitive to the dehumanizing consequences of severely limited lives. Usually well educated and capable, these women are rebelling against being forced to trivialize their lives, to live vicariously through husbands and children.

Students, as unmarried, middle-class girls, have been most sensitized to the sexual exploitation of women. They have experienced the frustration of one-way relationships in which the girl is forced into a "wife" and companion role with none of the supposed benefits of marriage. Young women have increasingly rebelled not only against passivity and dependency in their relationships, but also against the notion that they must function as sexual objects, being defined in purely sexual rather than human terms, and being forced to package and sell themselves as commodities on the sex market.

Each group represents an independent aspect of the total institutionalized oppression of women. Yet, in varying degrees all women suffer from economic exploitation, from psychological deprivation, and from exploitive sexuality. Within women's liberation there is a growing understanding that the common oppression of women provides the basis for uniting to form a powerful and radical movement.

Racism and Male Supremacy

Clearly, for the liberation of women to become a reality, it is necessary to destroy the ideology of male supremacy that asserts the biological and social inferiority of women in order to justify massive institutionalized oppression.

The ideology of male chauvinism can only be understood when it is perceived as a form of racism, based on stereotypes drawn from a deep belief in the biological inferiority of women. The very stereotypes that express the society's belief in the biological inferiority of women are images used to justify oppression. The nature of women is depicted as dependent, incapable of reasoned thought, childlike in its simplicity and warmth, martyred in the role of mother, and mystical in the role of sexual partner.

It has taken over fifty years to discredit the scientific and social "proof" that once gave legitimacy to the myths of black racial inferiority. Today most people can see that the theory of the genetic inferiority of blacks is absurd. Yet few are shocked by the fact that scientists are still busy "proving" the biological inferiority of women.

Yet one of the obstacles to organizing women remains women's belief in their own inferiority. This dilemma is not a fortuitous one, for the entire society is geared to socialize women to believe in and adopt as immutable necessity their traditional and inferior role. From earliest training to the grave, women are constrained and propagandized. Spend an evening at the movies or watching television and you will see a grotesque figure called woman presented in a hundred variations upon the themes of "children, church, kitchen" or "the chick sex-pot." Such contradictions as these show how pervasive and deep-rooted is the cultural contempt for women, how difficult it is to imagine a woman as a serious human being, or conversely, how empty and degrading is the image of woman that floods the culture.

Countless studies have shown that black acceptance of white stereotypes leads to mutilated identity, to alienation, to rage and self-hatred. Human beings cannot bear in their own hearts the contradictions of those who hold them in contempt. The ideology of male supremacy creates self-contempt and psychic mutilation in women; it creates trained incapacities that put women at a disadvantage in all social relationships.

It is customary to shame those who would draw the parallel between women and blacks by a great show of concern over the suffering of black people. Yet this response itself reveals a refined combination of white middle-class guilt and male chauvinism, for it overlooks several essential facts. For example, the most oppressed group within the feminine population is made up of black women, many of whom take a dim view of the black male intellectual's adoption of white male attitudes of sexual superiority. Neither are those who make this pious objection to the racial parallel addressing themselves very adequately to the millions of white working-class women living at the poverty level, who are not likely to be moved by this middle-class, guilt-ridden oneupmanship while having to deal with the boss, the factory, or the welfare worker day after day. They are already dangerously resentful of the gains made by blacks, and much of their "racist backlash" stems from the fact that they have been forgotten in the push for social change. Emphasis on the real mechanisms of oppression—on the commonality of the process—is essential lest groups such as these, which should work in alliance, become divided against one another.

White middle-class males already struggling with the acknowledgment of their own racism do not relish an added burden of recognition: that to white guilt must soon be added "male." It is therefore understandable that they should refuse to see the harshness of the lives of most women—to face honestly the facts of massive institutionalized discrimination against women.

We must never forget that the root of the ideology of male superiority, female inferiority, and white racism is a system of white male supremacy. White male supremacy is part of the ideology of imperialism, first European, then American. The European powers stripped India, China, Africa, and the New World of their wealth in raw materials—in gold, slaves, in cheap labor. Such brutal forms of exploitation required justification, and that justification was found in the doctrines of white racial superiority and the supremacy of European and American "civilization" over the "heathen" civilizations of Africa, Asia, and Latin America. Even more, we must never forget that the doctrine of white supremacy included the *supremacy of white women* as well as of white men.

The rise of capitalism in the West was based upon the wealth looted from other civilizations at the point of a gun: imperialism was the root and branch of racism and genocide then as it is now. It is at the root of mass prostitution in Saigon, of the torture and murder of innocent Vietnamese and Indochinese women and children, of all the sufferings of war inflicted upon the innocent at home and in Indochina. White American women must understand their oppression in its true context, and that context *is* a brutal, antihuman system of total exploitation having its corporate headquarters in New York and its political headquarters in Washington, D.C. And white women must understand that they are part of the system, benefiting from the loot secured through genocide.

This is why we must clearly understand that male chauvinism and racism *are not the same thing.* They are alike in that they oppress people and justify systems of exploitation, but in no way does a white woman suffer the exploitation and brutalization of women who are marked by both stigmata: being female *and* nonwhite. It is only the racism of privileged white women, self-serving in their petty, personal interests, who can claim that they must serve their own interests first, that they suffer *as much* as black women or Indochinese women or any women who experience the cruelty of white racism or the ruthless genocide of American militarism.

The contradiction of racism distorts and contaminates every sector of American life, creeps into every white insurgent movement. Understanding their own oppression can and must help white women to confront and to repudiate their own racism, for otherwise there will be no freedom, there will be no liberation.

Marriage: Genesis of Women's Rebellion

The institution of marriage is the chief vehicle for the perpetuation of the oppression of women: it is through the role of wife that the subjugation of women is maintained. In a very real way the role of wife has been the genesis of women's rebellion throughout history.

Looking at marriage from a detached point of view, one may well ask why anyone gets married, much less women. One answer lies in the economics of women's position, for women are so occupationally limited that drudgery in the home is considered to be infinitely superior to drudgery in the factory. Secondly, women themselves have no independent social status. Indeed, there is no clearer index of the social worth of a woman in this society than the fact that she has none in her own right. A woman is first defined by the man to whom she is attached, but more particularly by the man she marries, and secondly by the children she bears and rears—hence the anxiety over sexual attractiveness, the frantic scramble for boyfriends and husbands. Having obtained and married a man, the race is then on to have children, in order that their attractiveness and accomplishments may add more social worth. In a woman, not having children is seen as an incapacity somewhat akin to impotence in a man.

Beneath all of the pressures of the sexual marketplace and the marital status game, however, there is a far more sinister organization of economic exploitation and psychological mutilation. The housewife role, usually defined in terms of the biological duty of a woman to reproduce and her "innate" suitability for a nurturant and companionship role, is actually crucial to industrial capitalism in an advanced state of technological development. In fact, the housewife (some 44 million women of all classes, ethnic groups, and races) provides, unpaid, absolutely essential services and labor. In turn, her assumption of all household duties makes it possible for the man to spend the majority of his time at his work place.

It is important to understand the social and economic exploitation of the married woman, since the real productivity of her labor is denied by the commonly held assumption that she is dependent on her husband, exchanging her keep for emotional and nurturant services. Household labor, including child care, constitutes a huge amount of socially necessary labor. Nevertheless, in a society based on commodity production, it is not usually considered even as 'real work' since it is outside of trade and the marketplace. In a society in which money determines value, women are a group who work outside the money economy. Their work is not worth money, is therefore valueless, is therefore not even real work. And women themselves, who do this valueless work, can hardly be expected to be worth as much as men, who work for money.

Women are essential to the economy not only as free labor, but also as consumers. The American system of capitalism depends for its survival on the consumption of vast amounts of socially wasteful goods, and a prime target for the unloading of this waste is the housewife. She is the purchasing agent for the family, but beyond that she is eager to buy because her own identity depends on her accomplishments as a consumer and her ability to satisfy the wants of her husband and children. This is not, of course, to say that she has any power in the economy. Although she spends the wealth, she does not own or control it—it simply passes through her hands.

In addition to their role as housewives and consumers, increasing numbers of women are taking outside employment. These women leave the home to join an exploited labor force, only to return at night to assume the double burden of housework on top of wage work—that is, they are forced to work at two full-time jobs. No man is required or expected to take on such a burden. The result: two workers from one household in the labor force with no cutback in essential female functions—three for the price of two, quite a bargain. Regardless of her status in the larger society, within the context of the family, the woman's relationship to the man is one of proletariat to bourgeoisie. One consequence of this class division in the family is to weaken the capacity of oppressed men and women to struggle together against it.

For third-world people within the United States, the oppressive nature of marriage is reflected negatively—for example, motherhood out of wedlock is punished, either through discriminatory welfare legislation or through thinly disguised and genocidal programs of enforced sterilization. This society punishes unmarried women even more than it punishes married women. As a result, many third-world and poor white women want help with their families and need a husband in the home. The destruction of families among poor people, as a result of economic exploitation and social oppression, results in the deprivation of every facet of life for poor women and children. White middle-class women, bound up with the psychological oppression of marriage, have often been blind to the extent of suffering—and the extent of the needs —that the deliberate destruction of the families of the poor has created. Unemployment and pauperization through welfare programs creates very different problems than does the experience of boredom in the suburbs.

In all classes and groups, the institution of marriage nonetheless functions to a greater or lesser degree to oppress women; the unity of women of different classes hinges upon our understanding of that common oppression. The nineteenth-century women's movement refused to deal with marriage and sexuality and chose instead to fight for the vote and to elevate the feminine mystique to a political ideology. That decision retarded the movement for decades. But 1969 is not 1889. For one thing, there now exist alternatives to marriage. The cultural revolution—experimentation with life-style, communal living, collective child rearing—have all come from the rebellion against dehumanized sexual relationships, against the notion of women as sexual commodities, against the hardship, alienation, and loneliness of American life.

Lessons must be learned from the failures of the earlier movement. The feminine mystique must not be mistaken for politics or legislative reform for winning human rights. Women are now at the bottom of their respective worlds and the basis exists for a common focus of struggle for women in American society. It remains for the movement to understand this, to avoid the mistakes of the past, to respond creatively to the possibilities of the present.

Economic Exploitation

Women's oppression, although rooted in the institution of marriage, does not stop at the kitchen or the bedroom door. Indeed, the economic exploitation of women in the work place is the most commonly recognized aspect of the oppression of women.

The rise of new agitation for the occupational equality of women also coincided with the reentry of the "lost generation"—the housewives of the 1950s—into the job market. Women from middle-class backgrounds, faced with an "empty nest" (children grown or in school) and a widowed or divorced rate of one-fourth to one-third of all marriages, returned to the work place in large numbers. But once there, they discovered that women, middle class or otherwise, are the last hired, the lowest paid, the least often promoted, and the first fired. Furthermore, women are more likely to suffer job discrimination on the basis of age, so the widowed and divorced suffer particularly, even though their economic need to work is often urgent. Age discrimination also means that the option of work after child rearing is limited. Even highly qualified older women find themselves forced into low-paid, unskilled, or semiskilled work—if they are lucky enough to find a job in the first place.

Most women who enter the labor force do not work for "pin money" or "self-fulfillment." Sixty-two percent of all women working in 1967 were doing so out of economic need (that is, were either alone or with husbands earning less than $5,000 a year). In 1963, 36 percent of American families had an income of less than $5,000 a year. Women from these families work because they must; they contribute 35 to 40 percent of the family's total income when working full time and 15 to 20 percent when working part time.

Despite their need, however, women have always represented the most exploited sector of the industrial labor force. Child and female labor were introduced during the early stages of industrial capitalism, at a time when most men were gainfully employed in crafts. As industrialization developed and craft jobs were eliminated, men entered the industrial labor force, driving women and children into the lowest categories of work and pay. Indeed, the position of women and children industrial workers was so pitiful and their wages so small that the craft unions refused to organize them. Even when women organized themselves and engaged in militant strikes and labor agitation—from the shoemakers of Lynn, Massachusetts, to the International Ladies' Garment Workers and their great strike of 1909—male unionists continued to ignore their needs. As a result of this male supremacy in the unions, women remain essentially unorganized, despite the fact that they are becoming an ever larger part of the labor force.

The trend is clearly toward increasing numbers of women entering the work force: women represented 55 percent of the growth of the total labor force in 1962, and the number of working women rose from 16.9 million in 1957 to 24 million in 1962. There is every indication that the number of women in the labor force will continue to grow as rapidly in the future.

Job discrimination against women exists in all sectors of work, even in occupations that are predominantly made up of women. This discrimination is reinforced in the field of education, where women are being short-changed at a time when the job market demands higher educational levels. In 1962, for example, while women constituted 53 percent of the graduating high school class, only 42 percent of the entering college class were women. Only one in three people who received a B.A. or M.A. in that year was a woman, and only one in ten who received a Ph.D. was a woman. These figures represent a decline in educational achievement for women since the 1930s, when women received two out of five of the B.A. and M.A. degrees given, and one out of seven of the Ph.Ds. While there has been a dramatic increase in the number of people, including women, who go to college, women have not kept pace with men in terms of educational achievement. Furthermore, women have lost ground in professional employment. In 1960 only 22 percent of the faculty and other professional staff at colleges and universities were women—down from 28 percent in 1949, 27 percent in 1930, 26 percent in 1920. 1960 does beat the 20 percent of 1919: "you've come a long way, baby"—right back to where you started! In other professional categories, 10 percent of all scientists are women, 7 percent of all physicians, 3 percent of all lawyers, and 1 percent of all engineers.

Even when women do obtain an education, in many cases it does them little good. Women, whatever their educational levels, are concentrated in the lower-paying occupations. The figures tell a story that most women know and few men will admit: most women are forced to work at clerical jobs, for which they are paid, on the average, $1,600 less per year than men doing the same work. Working-class women in the service and operative (semiskilled) categories, making up 30 percent of working women, are paid $1,900 less per year on the average than are men. Of all working women, only 13 percent are professionals (including low-pay and low-status work such as teaching, nursing, and social work), and they earn $2,600 less per year than do professional men. Household workers, the lowest category of all, are predominantly women (over 2 million) and predominantly black and third world, earning for their labor barely over $1,000 per year.

Beginnings: The New Consciousness

Not only are women forced onto the lowest rungs of the occupational ladder, they are in the lowest income levels as well. The most constant and bitter injustice experienced by all women is the income differential. While women might passively accept low-status jobs, limited opportunities for advancement, and discrimination in the factory, office, and university, they choke finally on the daily fact that the male worker next to them earns more and usually does less. In 1965, the median wage or salary income of year-round, full-time women workers was only 60 percent that of men, a 4 percent loss since 1955. Twenty-nine percent of working women earned less than $3,000 a year as compared with 11 percent of the men; 43 percent of the women earned from $3,000 to $5,000 a year as compared with 19 percent of the men; and 9 percent of the women earned $7,000 or more as compared with 43 percent of the men.

What most people do not know is that in certain respects all women suffer more than do nonwhite men and that black and third-world women suffer most of all.

Women, regardless of race, are more disadvantaged than are men, including nonwhite men. White women earn $2,600 less than white men and $1,500 less than nonwhite men. The brunt of the inequality is carried by 2.5 million nonwhite women, 94 percent of whom are black. They earn $3,800 less than white men, $1,900 less than nonwhite men, and $1,200 less than white women.

There is no more bitter paradox in the racism of this country than that the white man, articulating the male supremacy of the white male middle class, should provide the rationale for the oppression of black women by black men. Black women constitute the largest minority in the United States, and they are the most disadvantaged group in the labor force. The further oppression of black women will not liberate black men, for black women were never the oppressors of their men—that is a myth of the liberal white man. The oppression of black men comes from institutionalized racism and economic exploitation, from the world of the white man.

Consider the following facts and figures. The percentage of black working women has always been proportionately greater than that of white women. In 1900, 41 percent of black women were employed, as compared to 17 percent for white women. In 1963, the proportion of black women employed was still a fourth greater than that of whites. In 1960, 44 percent of black married women with children under six years were in the labor force, in contrast to 29 percent for white women. While job competition requires ever higher levels of education, the bulk of illiterate women are black. On the whole, black women—who often have the greatest need for employment—are the most discriminated against in terms of opportunity. Forced by an oppressive and racist society to carry unbelievably heavy economic and social burdens, black women stand at the bottom of that society, doubly marked by the caste signs of color and sex.

Faced with discrimination on the job—after being forced into the lower levels of the occupational structure—millions of women are inescapably presented with the fundamental contradictions in their unequal treatment and their massive exploitation. The rapid growth of women's liberation as a movement is related in part to the exploitation of working women in all occupational categories.

Conclusion

Male supremacy, marriage, and the structure of wage labor—each of these aspects of women's oppression and exploitation has been crucial to the resurgence of the women's struggle. It must be abundantly clear that revolutionary social change must occur before there can be significant improvement in the social position of *all* women.

The heart of the movement, as in all freedom movements, rests in women's knowledge, whether articulated or still only an illness without a name, that they are not inferior—not chicks or bunnies or quail or crows or bitches or ass or meat. Women hear the litany of their own dehumanization each day. Yet all the same, women know that they are not animals or sexual objects or commodities. They know their lives are mutilated, because they see within themselves a promise of creativity and personal integration. Feeling the contradiction between the essentially creative and self-actualizing human being within her and the cruel and degrading less-than-human role she is compelled to play, a woman begins to experience the internal violence that liberates the human spirit, to experience the justice of her own rebellion. This is the rage that impels women into a total commitment to women's liberation, a ferocity that stems from a denial of mutilation. It is a cry for life, a cry for the liberation of the spirit.

Yet, we must never forget that we women are not unique in our oppression, in our exploitation. Understanding ourselves should help us understand all others like us and not divide us from them. We must also remember that in one way white American women are unique, for they suffer least of all: their experience cannot approach the abysmal suffering of the third-world women or of third-world men, subject to American racism and imperialism. How does one understand rape; forced prostitution; torture; and mutilation; twisted, crippled children; deformed babies; a homeland laid waste; memories of perpetual war; perpetual oppression? It is not a question of guilt; it is a question of revolutionary struggle.

Epilogue 1969–1971

1969 was a year of explosive growth and measureless optimism for women's liberation. It was the year of sisterhood: "sisterhood is powerful!" "sisterhood is beautiful!" "sisterhood is unity!" The turning point for the women's struggle was 1969, the year in which the movement came up from underground by gaining recognition and legitimacy—recognition from the male-dominated white left and legitimacy as a protest "issue" in the larger society. The slogans of sisterhood reflected a joyful optimism, an overwhelming intuitive belief that *all* women could identify with each other, all women could struggle together —even lead—a vast movement or social transformation.

By 1971, the joyful optimism was increasingly being replaced by a sense of dismay and conflict in many women: "women's liberation is a nonstruggle movement"; "women's liberation is a racist movement"; "women's liberation is an apolitical movement"; "women's liberation is a class chauvinist movement"; "women's liberation is a liberal, middle-class movement." What did all of this mean? What had happened to the women's movement?

The United States of America had "happened" to women's liberation: all of the contradictions of a society torn by class and racial conflict, all of the contradictions of a society that is in fact based upon militarized state capitalism and institutionalized racism and class exploitation began to tear the women's movement apart. The apolitical simplicity of "sisterhood is unity" and "understand your own psychological oppression" was powerless to contend with or understand the internal, disruptive forces of the most exploitative, brutal, and complex oppressor nation in the history of Western imperialism —the United States of America.

The women's movement is no longer a struggling, tender shoot; it has become a mass movement; and women remain, often despite the movement, potentially a powerful, radical force. In the beginning, women were attacked from every quarter, most destructively from the left, for left politics became identified with male chauvinism. Originally, the attack from the left was corrupt, a ploy by radical men to keep women down. Now, however, the criticism does not come from the men, but from women within women's liberation. A movement that cannot learn from its past, that is too insecure and fearful to engage in self-criticism, that is too self-interested to be able to change its direction, too blind to see that all women are *not* sisters—that class exploitation and racism are fundamental to American society and exist *within* the women's movement—becomes a trap, not a means to liberation. In the brief critique that follows, I am correcting some of my own mistakes, for I too believed in sisterhood, I too believed that "common oppression provides the basis for uniting across class and race lines." In that belief I was wrong; this is what I have learned from the past year of the movement. There are many women and many groups within the women's struggle to which the following criticism does not apply, but there are still more who were, and still are, wrong.

Class Conflict

The mysticism of *sisterhood* disguised the reality that most women in women's liberation were white, young, and middle class, so that under all the radical rhetoric the movement's goals were reformist and its ideology was almost exclusively of middle-class female psychological oppression. The women's movement did not talk about *exploitation,* but about *oppression*—always in subjective terms. The women's movement did not talk about class struggle, nationalization of medicine, abolition of welfare, or the ultimate destruction of American imperialism. The needs of poor women, of working women, of black women were nowhere central to the demands or the rhetoric of women's liberation. The middle-class, reformist nature of the movement was not clearly and objectively revealed until the struggle over the equal rights amendment— an amendment that would have made *discrimination* unconstitutional but would not have included a single reference reference to exploitation, an amendment that would have benefited professional women at the expense of working-class women.

Fighting against *discrimination* is a middle-class, reformist goal—it says: let us *in* so that the privileges of our middle-class men can be extended to us middle-class women. Fighting against *exploitation* is revolutionary. To end exploitation, it is necessary to end "militarized state capitalism." To end class exploitation, it is necessary to abolish classes. To end racism, it is necessary to abolish white male supremacy, to abolish imperialism. White middle-class America, male and female, enjoys an affluence that is looted from half the world, that is stolen by means of poor white and black soldiers, that is turned into new cars and washing machines by workers, black and white, male and female. White middle-class America, *male and female,* enjoys incomes protected from inflation by means of the deliberate unemployment of workers, black and white, male and female, who suffer enforced pauperization so that the young girls of the middle class can go to the university and struggle for a women's center to give them a better education, the better to enjoy their class privileges, the better to explore the meaning of life and the adventures of a new, untrammeled sexuality. Genocide is committed against the people of Vietnam; war spreads to all the peoples of Indochina. So who cares? It's only a "penis war." It is of no concern to the young women of the middle class, who will never be soldiers, never be workers, never be on welfare, never suffer racism. The problem is *discrimination.* Women can only earn $10,000 a year teaching college while men earn $15,000 a year—that is the problem! "Sisterhood is unity! Don't criticize the movement! Don't make us feel guilty! Don't show us the blood on *our* hands—after all, we are oppressed too!"

Racism

The "black analogy" was originally used in women's liberation to help women through their understanding of their own oppression, to understand the oppression of others. By 1971 the "black analogy" has become a tool of white racism. The cries "we are oppressed too" and even more terrible "we are equally oppressed" permitted white middle-class women to dismiss the black struggle, to dismiss their complicity in a racist system, to dismiss criticisms of the movement from black women as motivated by the influence "the male chauvinism of black men" has upon them—ultimately to complete the cycle of white middle-class racism by reducing black and third-world people within the United States to invisibility. White middle-class women, bloated with their own pious claim to oppression, blind within their own racism, refused to see that black women were trying to teach them something when they spoke at conferences, saying: "I am black and a woman, but am I first black or first a woman? First I am black." Or "we fear the abortion program, it may be used against us." Or "we must destroy exploitation and racism *before* black women can be liberated—for what does it mean to us, black women, if you white women end discrimination? We are still black; we are still exploited; we are still destroyed and our children with us." All the white women could answer with was "black male chauvinism!" They remained completely blind to the fact that third-world people are a colony and a minority within the heart of the monster, that their survival depends upon resolution to the contradiction of male chauvinism and male supremacy that *does not* divide black women and black men into antagonistic factions.

Female Chauvinism

The purest expression of self-serving middle-class ideology is reflected in the blind hatred of men that makes no distinction between the system of white male supremacy and male chauvinism. Only very privileged women can in the security of their class status and class earning power create a little "manless Utopia" for themselves. They need only withdraw from the psychological discomfort of male chauvinism to create a new and different life for themselves —they are not faced, as a class, with the necessity to struggle against another class; they are not driven by exploitation and repression to understand that male chauvinism is reactionary but that it can also be defeated, so that men and women can resolve the contradiction between them, emerge stronger, and unite in mutual opposition to their real enemies—the generals, the corporate bosses, the corrupt politicians.

Liberal Guilt

Liberal guilt is worthless. Appealing to women who are completely devoted to their own self-serving class interests is equally useless. There is no mass movement in the United States that can avoid the contradictions of racism and class conflict, thus moralistic pleas are a waste of time. Nonetheless, women in the United States—and everywhere outside of the revolutionary world—are oppressed and exploited, suffer and die in silence. For the thousands and thousands of women who are poor, who are working class, who were born into the middle class but have turned away from it in disgust and revulsion, the women's movement, as a revolutionary struggle, remains their chief commitment and their only hope. Our challenge is to correct past mistakes, to learn what we must know to avoid future mistakes, to teach and to learn from each other. We *must* learn how to build, within the very heart of the monster, a revolutionary movement devoted to the liberation of all people *in practice.* Such a movement will not be self-serving, cannot be merely reformist. It must be political, must know history and economics, must understand that all revolutionary movements in the world today are interdependent. We can no longer be an island of affluence, blind to the lesson that what happens to women in Vietnam happens to us, that what happens to a black woman happens to us. The United States is not an empire that will stand for a thousand years, but is an oppressive monster that the peoples of the world will dismember and destroy before the world is all finished. We must choose which side we will be on—the path of revolution or the path of exploitation and genocide.

The women's movement is turning and twisting within its contradictions. Some women speed off into mysticism, claiming, but not explaining, how women by rejecting "male" politics and finding "female" politics effect world revolution—a world revolution in which the people's war in Vietnam plays no part, in which all previous world revolutions—Russian, Chinese, North Vietnamese, North Korean, Cuban—play no part. Still others seek escape in "sexual liberation," hoping to find, as does the youth movement, a personalized, individual salvation in a "life-style revolution" in which racism is dismissed as a problem of "black male chauvinism" and Vietnam is dismissed as a "penis war" of no concern to women. To be in the "vanguard," it is only necessary to love a woman sexually. Still others cling to the worn-out slogans of the early days, continuing with "consciousness raising" as weekly therapy and engaging in endless discussions of anti-elitism (an elite being anyone who does anything at all threatening to any woman in a small group) and "anti-elitist structure" in the organization of the women's center.

These tendencies reflect the other face of women's oppression, not anger or strength, but fearfulness, turning inward to avoid challenge, to avoid thinking, to avoid struggle, to avoid the large and frightening world of conflict and revolution, which cannot be contained within a small group or understood through the subjective oppression of a privileged woman. Women *are* mutilated, especially passive, nurturant middle-class women. They are made manipulative, dishonest, fearful, conservative, hypocritical, and self-serving. Celebrating women's weakness—elevating mutilation to a holy state of female grace—corrupts the movement into a reactionary and self-serving force.

Women are seen as absurd, and they blame the media. Women are criticized for being reactionary and racist. They howl "male defined," "male identified." Women are isolated from the liberation struggles of other people, and they scream that those movements are *male-dominated!* How many more excuses will be found until women have the strength to confront their mistakes and their failures? How many revolutions are we going to be called upon to make to assure rich and comforting interpersonal relationships and unhampered fucking for the people whose privilege is so great that they can afford to worry about their spirits instead of their bellies? How many more people are we going to help die in Indochina by howling that fighting against imperialism is "anti-woman" or a "penis war" or "dominated by men"? How long are we going to remain absurd because, in the eyes of the vast majority of peoples in the world, *we are absurd, self-seeking, blind,* and *ignorant!*

Beginnings: The New Consciousness

It is time, past time, to get our heads together, to listen to and learn from women who have made and are making revolutions, to study to fight, to fight to win, with strength and dignity and a proper respect for the suffering of others and a complete devotion to ending all oppression practiced against the majority of the peoples of the world, male and female, in the colonies of the monster and in the heart of the monster. Then, and only then, shall we know something of liberation.

Reprinted from the *Journal of Social Issues*, **23**, 3 (1967), 52–75.

23. The Liberated Generation: An Exploration of the Roots of Student Protest

RICHARD FLACKS

As all of us are by now aware, there has emerged, during the past five years, an increasingly self-conscious student movement in the United States. This movement began primarily as a response to the efforts by southern Negro students to break the barriers of legal segregation in public accommodations —scores of northern white students engaged in sympathy demonstrations and related activities as early as 1960. But as we all know, the scope of the student concern expanded rapidly to include such issues as nuclear testing and the arms race, attacks on civil liberties, the problems of the poor in urban slum ghettoes, democracy and educational quality in universities, the war in Vietnam, conscription.

This movement represents a social phenomenon of considerable significance. In the first place, it is having an important direct and indirect impact on the larger society. But secondly it is significant because it is a phenomenon which was unexpected—unexpected, in particular, by those social scientists who are professionally responsible for locating and understanding such phenomena. Because it is an unanticipated event, the attempt to understand and explain the sources of the student movement may lead to fresh interpretations of some important trends in our society.

Radicalism and the Young Intelligentsia

In one sense, the existence of a radical student movement should not be unexpected. After all, the young intelligentsia seem almost always to be in revolt. Yet if we examine the case a bit more closely I think we will find that movements of active disaffection among intellectuals and students tend to be concentrated at particular moments in history. Not every generation produces an organized oppositional movement.

In particular, students and young intellectuals seem to have become active agents of opposition and change under two sets of interrelated conditions:

When they have been marginal in the labor market because their numbers exceed the opportunities for employment commensurate with their abilities and training. This has most typically been the case in colonial or underdeveloped societies; it also seems to account, in part, for the radicalization of European Jewish intellectuals and American college-educated women at the turn of the century (Coser, 1965; Shils, 1960; Veblen, 1963).

When they found that the values with which they were closely connected by virtue of their upbringing no longer were appropriate to the developing social reality. This has been the case most typically at the point where traditional authority has broken down due to the impact of Westernization, industrialization, modernization. Under these conditions, the intellectuals, and particularly the youth, felt called upon to assert new values, new modes of legitimation, new styles of life. Although the case of breakdown of traditional authority is most typically the point at which youth movements have emerged, there seems, historically, to have been a second point in time—in Western Europe and the United States—when intellectuals were radicalized. This was, roughly, at the turn of the century, when values such as gentility, laissez faire, naive optimism, naive rationalism, and naive nationalism seemed increasingly inappropriate due to the impact of large scale industrial organization, intensifying class conflict, economic crisis and the emergence of total war. Variants of radicalism waxed and waned in their influence among American intellectuals and students during the first four decades of the twentieth century. (Aaron, 1965; Eisenstadt, 1956; Lasch, 1965).

If these conditions have historically been those which produced revolts among the young intelligentsia, then I think it is easy to understand why a relatively superficial observer would find the new wave of radicalism on the campus fairly mysterious.

In the first place, the current student generation can look forward, not to occupational insecurity or marginality, but to an unexampled opening up of opportunity for occupational advance in situations in which their skills will be maximally demanded and the prestige of their roles unprecedentedly high.

In the second place, there is no evident erosion of the legitimacy of established authority; we do not seem, at least on the surface, to be in a period of rapid disintegration of traditional values—at least no more so than a decade ago when sociologists were observing the *exhaustion* of opportunity for radical social movements in America (Bell, 1962; Lipset, 1960).

In fact, during the Fifties sociologists and social psychologists emphasized the decline in political commitment, particularly among the young, and the rise of a bland, security-oriented conformism throughout the population, but most particularly among college students. The variety of studies conducted then reported students as overwhelmingly unconcerned with value questions, highly complacent, status-oriented, privatized, uncommitted (Jacob, 1957; Golden, *et al,* 1960). Most of us interpreted this situation as one to be expected given the opportunities newly opened to educated youth, and given the emergence of liberal pluralism and affluence as the characteristic features of postwar

America. Several observers predicted an intensification of the pattern of middle class conformism, declining individualism, and growing "other-directedness" based on the changing styles of childrearing prevalent in the middle class. The democratic and "permissive" family would produce young men who knew how to cooperate in bureaucratic settings, but who lacked a strongly rooted ego-ideal and inner control (Miller and Swanson, 1958; Bronfenbrenner, 1961; Erikson, 1963). Although some observers reported that some students were searching for "meaning" and "self-expression," and others reported the existence of "subcultures" of alienation and bohemianism on some campuses (Keniston, 1965a; Trow, 1962; Newcomb and Flacks, 1963), not a single observer of the campus scene as late as 1959 anticipated the emergence of the organized disaffection, protest and activism which was to take shape early in the Sixties.

In short, the very occurrence of a student movement in the present American context is surprising because it seems to contradict our prior understanding of the determinants of disaffection among the young intelligentsia.

A Revolt of the Advantaged

The student movement is, I think, surprising for another set of reasons. These have to do with its social composition and the kinds of ideological themes which characterize it.

The current group of student activists is predominantly upper middle class, and frequently these students are of elite origins. This fact is evident as soon as one begins to learn the personal histories of activist leaders. Consider the following scene at a convention of Students for a Democratic Society a few years ago. Toward the end of several days of deliberation, someone decided that a quick way of raising funds for the organization would be to appeal to the several hundred students assembled at the convention to dig down deep into their pockets on the spot. To this end, one of the leadership, skilled at mimicry, stood on a chair, and in the style of a Southern Baptist preacher, appealed to the students to come forward, confess their sins and be saved by contributing to SDS. The students did come forward, and in each case the sin confessed was the social class or occupation of their father. "My father is the editor of a Hearst newspaper, I give $25!" "My father is Assistant Director of the _____ Bureau, I give $40." "My father is dean of a law school, here's $50!"

These impressions of the social composition of the student movement are supported and refined by more systematic sources of data. For example, when a random sample of students who participated in the anti-Selective Service sit-in at the University of Chicago Administration Building was compared with a sample composed of non-protesters and students hostile to the protests, the protesters disproportionately reported their social class to be "upper middle," their family incomes to be disproportionately high, their parents' education to be disproportionately advanced. In addition, the protesters' fathers' occupations were primarily upper professional (doctors, college faculty, law-yers) rather than business, white collar, or working class. These findings parallel those of other investigators (Braungart, 1966). Thus, the student movement represents the disaffection not of an underprivileged stratum of the student population but of *the most advantaged* sector of the students.

One hypothesis to explain disaffection among socially advantaged youth would suggest that, although such students come from advantaged back-grounds, their academic performance leads them to anticipate downward mobility or failure. Stinchcombe, for example, found high rates of quasi-delinquent rebelliousness among middle class high school youth with poor academic records (Stinchcombe, 1964). This hypothesis is not tenable with respect to college student protest, however. Our own data with respect to the anti-draft protest at Chicago indicate that the grade point average of the protesters averaged around B–B+ (with 75% of them reporting a B– or better average). This was slightly higher than the grade point average of our sample of nonprotesters. Other data from our own research indicate that student activists tend to be at the top of their high school class; in general, data from our own and other studies support the view that many activists are academi-cally superior, and that very few activists are recruited from among low academic achievers. Thus, in terms of *both* the status of their families of origins *and* their own scholastic performance, student protest movements are predominantly composed of students who have been born to high social advan-tage and who are in a position to experience the career and status opportunities of the society without significant limitations.

Themes of the Protest

The positive correlation between disaffection and status among college stu-dents suggested by these observations is, I think, made even more paradoxical when one examines closely the main value themes which characterize the student movement. I want to describe these in an impressionistic way here; a more systematic depiction awaits further analysis of our data.

Romanticism: There is a strong stress among many Movement participants on the quest for self-expression, often articulated in terms of leading a "free" life—i.e., one not bound by conventional restraints on feeling, experience, communication, expression. This is often coupled with aesthetic interests and a strong rejection of scientific and other highly rational pursuits. Students often express the classic romantic aspiration of "knowing" or "experiencing" "ev-erything."

Anti-authoritarianism: A strong antipathy toward arbitrary rule, central-ized decision-making, "manipulation." The anti-authoritarian sentiment is fundamental to the widespread campus protests during the past few years; in most cases, the protests were precipitated by an administrative act which was interpreted as arbitrary, and received impetus when college administrators continued to act unilaterally, coercively or secretively. Anti-authoritarianism is manifested further by the styles and internal processes within activist organizations; for example, both SDS and SNCC have attempted to decentralize their operations quite radically and members are strongly critical of leadership within the organization when it is too assertive.

Egalitarianism, populism: A belief that all men are capable of political participation, that political power should be widely dispersed, that the locus of value in society lies with the people and not elites. This is a stress on something more than equality of opportunity or equal legal treatment; the students stress instead the notion of "participatory democracy"—direct participation in the making of decisions by those affected by them. Two common slogans—"One man, one vote"; "Let the people decide."

Anti-dogmatism: A strong reaction against doctrinaire ideological interpretations of events. Many of the students are quite restless when presented with formulated models of the social order, and specific programs for social change. This underlies much of their antagonism to the varieties of "old left" politics, and is one meaning of the oft-quoted (if not seriously used) phrase: "You can't trust anyone over thirty."

Moral purity: A strong antipathy to self-interested behavior, particularly when overlaid by claims of disinterestedness. A major criticism of the society is that it is "hypocritical." Another meaning of the criticism of the older generation has to do with the perception that (a) the older generation "sold out" the values it espouses; (b) to assume conventional adult roles usually leads to increasing self-interestedness, hence selling-out, or "phoniness." A particularly important criticism students make of the university is that it fails to live up to its professed ideals; there is an expectation that the institution ought to be *moral*—that is, not compromise its official values for the sake of institutional survival or aggrandizement.

Community: A strong emphasis on a desire for "human" relationships, for a full expression of emotions, for the breaking down of interpersonal barriers and the refusal to accept conventional norms concerning interpersonal contact (e.g., norms respecting sex, status, race, age, etc.). A central positive theme in the campus revolts has been the expression of the desire for a campus "community," for the breaking down of aspects of impersonality on the campus, for more direct contact between students and faculty. There is a frequent counterposing of bureaucratic norms to communal norms; a testing of the former against the latter. Many of the students involved in slum projects have experimented with attempts to achieve a "kibbutz"-like community amongst themselves, entailing communal living and a strong stress on achieving intimacy and resolving tensions within the group.

Anti-institutionalism: A strong distrust of involvement with conventional institutional roles. This is most importantly expressed in the almost universal desire among the highly involved to avoid institutionalized careers. Our data suggest that few student activists look toward careers in the professions, the sciences, industry or politics. Many of the most committed expect to continue to work full-time in the "movement" or, alternatively, to become free-lance writers, artists, intellectuals. A high proportion are oriented toward academic careers—at least so far the academic career seems still to have a reputation among many student activists for permitting "freedom."

Several of these themes, it should be noted, are not unique to student activists. In particular, the value we have described as "romanticism"—a quest for self-expression—has been found by observers, for example Kenneth Keniston (1965b), to be a central feature of the ideology of "alienated" or "bohemian" students (see also Keniston's article in this issue). Perhaps more important, the disaffection of student activists with conventional careers, their low valuation of careers as important in their personal aspirations, their quest for careers outside the institutionalized sphere—these attitudes toward careers seem to be characteristic of other groups of students as well. It is certainly typical of youth involved in "bohemian" and aesthetic subcultures; it also characterizes students who volunteer for participation in such programs as the Peace Corps, Vista and other full-time commitments oriented toward service. In fact, it is our view that the dissatisfaction of socially advantaged youth with conventional career opportunities is a significant social trend, the most important single indicator of restlessness among sectors of the youth population. One expression of this restlessness is the student movement, but it is not the only one. One reason why it seems important to investigate the student movement in detail, despite the fact that it represents a small minority of the student population, is that it is a symptom of social and psychological strains experienced by a larger segment of the youth—strains not well understood or anticipated heretofore by social science.

If some of the themes listed above are not unique to student activists, several of them may characterize only a portion of the activist group itself. In particular, some of the more explicitly political values are likely to be articulated mainly by activists who are involved in radical organizations, particularly Students for a Democratic Society, and the Student Non-violent Coordinating Committee. This would be true particularly for such notions as "participatory democracy" and deep commitments to populist-like orientations. These orientations have been formulated within SDS and SNCC as these organizations have sought to develop a coherent strategy and a framework for establishing priorities. It is an empirical question whether students not directly involved in such organizations articulate similar attitudes. The impressions we have from a preliminary examination of our data suggest that they frequently do not. It is more likely that the student movement is very heterogeneous politically at this point. Most participants share a set of broad orientations, but differ greatly in the degree to which they are oriented toward ideology in general or to particular political positions. The degree of politicization of student activists is probably very much a function of the kinds of peer group and organizational relationships they have had; the underlying disaffection and tendency toward activism, however, is perhaps best understood as being based on more enduring, pre-established values, attitudes and needs.

Social-Psychological Roots of
Student Protest: Some Hypotheses

How, then, can we account for the emergence of an obviously dynamic and attractive radical movement among American students in this period? Why should this movement be particularly appealing to youth from upper-status, highly educated families? Why should such youth be particularly concerned with problems of authority, of vocation, of equality, of moral consistency? Why should students in the most advantaged sector of the youth population be disaffected with their own privilege?

It should be stressed that the privileged status of the student protesters and the themes they express in their protest are not *in themselves* unique or surprising. Student movements in developing nations—e.g., Russia, Japan and Latin America—typically recruit people of elite background; moreover, many of the themes of the "new left" are reminiscent of similar expressions in other student movements (Lipset, 1966). What is unexpected is that these should emerge in the American context at this time.

Earlier theoretical formulations about the social and psychological sources of strain for youth, for example the work of Parsons (1965), Eisenstadt (1956), and Erikson (1959), are important for understanding the emergence of self-conscious oppositional youth cultures and movements. At first glance, these theorists, who tend to see American youth as relatively well-integrated into the larger society, would seem to be unhelpful in providing a framework for explaining the emergence of a radical student movement at the present moment. Nevertheless, in developing our own hypotheses we have drawn freely on their work. What I want to do here is to sketch the notions which have guided our research; a more systematic and detailed exposition will be developed in future publications.

What we have done is to accept the main lines of the argument made by Parsons and Eisenstadt about the social functions of youth cultures and movements. The kernel of their argument is that self-conscious subcultures and movements among adolescents tend to develop when there is a sharp disjunction between the values and expectations embodied in the traditional families in a society and the values and expectations prevailing in the occupational sphere. The greater the disjunction, the more self-conscious and oppositional will be the youth culture (as for example in the situation of rapid transition from a traditional-ascriptive to a bureaucratic-achievement social system).

In modern industrial society, such a disjunction exists as a matter of course, since families are, by definition, particularistic, ascriptive, diffuse, and the occupational sphere is universalistic, impersonal, achievement-oriented, functionally specific. But Parsons, and many others, have suggested that over time the American middle class family has developed a structure and style which tends to articulate with the occupational sphere; thus, whatever youth culture does emerge in American society is likely to be fairly well-integrated with conventional values, not particularly self-conscious, not rebellious (Parsons, 1965).

The emergence of the student movement, and other expressions of estrangement among youth, leads us to ask whether, in fact, there may be families in the middle class which embody values and expectations which do *not* articulate with those prevailing in the occupational sphere, to look for previously unremarked incompatibilities between trends in the larger social system and trends in family life and early socialization.

The argument we have developed may be sketched as follows:

First, on the macro-structural level we assume that two related trends are of importance: one, the increasing rationalization of student life in high schools and universities, symbolized by the "multiversity," which entails a high degree of impersonality, competitiveness and an increasingly explicit and direct relationship between the university and corporate and governmental bureaucracies; two, the increasing unavailability of coherent careers independent of bureaucratic organizations.

Second, these trends converge, in time, with a particular trend in the development of the family; namely, the emergence of a pattern of familial relations, located most typically in upper middle class, professional homes, having the following elements:

(a) a strong emphasis on democratic, egalitarian interpersonal relations
(b) a high degree of permissiveness with respect to self-regulation
(c) an emphasis on values *other than achievement;* in particular, a stress on the intrinsic worth of living up to intellectual, aesthetic, political, or religious ideals.

Third, young people raised in this kind of family setting, contrary to the expectations of some observers, find it difficult to accommodate to institutional expectations requiring submissiveness to adult authority, respect for established status distinctions, a high degree of competition, and firm regulation of sexual and expressive impulses. They are likely to be particularly sensitized to acts of arbitrary authority, to unexamined expression of allegiance to conventional values, to instances of institutional practices which conflict with professed ideals. Further, the values embodied in their families are likely to be reinforced by other socializing experiences—for example, summer vacations at progressive children's camps, attendance at experimental private schools, growing up in a community with a high proportion of friends from similar backgrounds. Paralleling these experiences of positive reinforcement, there are likely to be experiences which reinforce a sense of estrangement from peers or conventional society. For instance, many of these young people experience a strong sense of being "different" or "isolated" in school; this sense of distance is often based on the relative uniqueness of their interests and values, their inability to accept conventional norms about appropriate sex-role behavior, and the like. An additional source of strain is generated when these young people perceive a fundamental discrepancy between the values espoused by their parents and the style of life actually practiced by them. This discrepancy is experienced as a feeling of "guilt" over "being middle class" and a perception of "hypocrisy" on the part of parents who express liberal or intellectual values while appearing to their children as acquisitive or self-interested.

Fourth, the incentives operative in the occupational sphere are of limited efficacy for these young people—achievement of status or material advantage is relatively ineffective for an individual who already has high status and affluence by virtue of his family origins. This means, on the one hand, that these students are less oriented toward occupational achievement; on the other hand, the operative sanctions within the school and the larger society are less effective in enforcing conformity.

It seems plausible that this is the first generation in which a substantial number of youth have both the impulse to free themselves from conventional status concerns *and can afford to do so.* In this sense they are a "liberated" generation; affluence has freed them, at least for a period of time, from some of the anxieties and preoccupations which have been the defining features of American middle class social character.

Fifth, the emergence of the student movement is to be understood in large part as a consequence of opportunities for prolonged interaction available in the university environment. The kinds of personality structures produced by the socializing experiences outlined above need not necessarily have generated a collective response. In fact, Kenneth Keniston's recently published work on alienated students at Harvard suggests that students with similar characteristics to those described here were identifiable on college campuses in the Fifties. But Keniston makes clear that his highly alienated subjects were rarely involved in extensive peer-relationships, and that few opportunities for collective expressions of alienation were then available. The result was that each of his subjects attempted to work out a value-system and a mode of operation on his own (Keniston, 1965b; and this issue).

What seems to have happened was that during the Fifties, there began to emerge an "alienated" student culture, as students with alienated predispositions became visible to each other and began to interact. There was some tendency for these students to identify with the "Beat" style and related forms of bohemianism. Since this involved a high degree of disaffiliation, "cool" non-commitment and social withdrawal, observers tended to interpret this subculture as but a variant of the prevailing privatism of the Fifties. However, a series of precipitating events, most particularly the southern student sit-ins, the revolutionary successes of students in Cuba, Korea and Turkey, and the suppression of student demonstrations against the House Un-American Activities Committee in San Francisco, suggested to groups of students that direct action was a plausible means for expressing their grievances. These first stirrings out of apathy were soon enmeshed in a variety of organizations and publicized in several student-organized underground journals—thus enabling the movement to grow and become increasingly institutionalized. The story of the emergence and growth of the movement cannot be developed here; my main point now is that many of its characteristics cannot be understood solely as consequences of the structural and personality variables outlined earlier—in addition, a full understanding of the dynamics of the movement requires a "collective behavior" perspective.

Sixth, organized expressions of youth disaffection are likely to be an increasingly visible and established feature of our society. In important ways, the "new radicalism" is *not* new, but rather a more widespread version of certain subcultural phenomena with a considerable history. During the late 19th and early 20th century a considerable number of young people began to move out of their provincial environments as a consequence of university education; many of these people gathered in such locales as Greenwich Village and created the first visible bohemian subculture in the United States. The Village bohemians and associated young intellectuals shared a common concern with radical politics and, influenced by Freud, Dewey, etc., with the reform of the process of socialization in America—i.e., a restructuring of family and educational institutions (Lash, 1965; Coser, 1965). Although many of the reforms advocated by this group were only partially realized in a formal sense, it seems to be the case that the values and style of life which they advocated have become strongly rooted in American life. This has occurred in at least two ways: first, the subcultures created by the early intellectuals took root, have grown and been emulated in various parts of the country. Second, many of the *ideas* of the early twentieth century intellectuals, particularly their critique of the bourgeois family and Victorian sensibility, spread rapidly; it now seems that an important defining characteristic of the college-educated mother is her willingness to adopt child-centered techniques of rearing, and of the college educated couple that they create a family which is democratic and egalitarian in style. In this way, the values that an earlier generation espoused in an abstract way have become embodied as *personality traits* in the new generation. The rootedness of the bohemian and quasi-bohemian subcultures, and the spread of their ideas with the rapid increase in the number of college graduates, suggests that there will be a steadily increasing number of families raising their children with considerable ambivalence about dominant values, incentives and expectations in the society. In this sense, the students who engage in protest or who participate in "alienated" styles of life are often not "converts" to a "deviant" adaptation, but people who have been socialized into a developing cultural tradition. Rising levels of affluence and education are drying up the traditional sources of alienation and radical politics; what we are now becoming aware of, however, is that this same situation is creating new sources of alienation and idealism, and new constituencies for radicalism.

The Youth and Social Change Project

These hypotheses have been the basis for two studies we have undertaken. Study One, begun in the Summer of 1965, involved extensive interviews with samples of student activists and nonactivists and their parents. Study Two, conducted in the Spring of 1966, involved interviews with samples of participants, nonparticipants and opponents of the tumultuous "anti-ranking" sit-in at the University of Chicago.

Study one—the socialization of student activists

For Study One, fifty students were selected from mailing lists of various peace, civil rights, and student movement organizations in the Chicago area. An additional fifty students, matched for sex, neighborhood of parents' residence, and type of college attended, were drawn from student directories of Chicago-area colleges. In each case, an attempt was made to interview both parents of the student respondent, as well as the student himself. We were able to interview both parents of 82 of the students; there were two cases in which no parents were available for the interview, in the remaining 16 cases, one parent was interviewed. The interviews with both students and parents averaged about three hours in length, were closely parallel in content, and covered such matters as: political attitudes and participation; attitudes toward the student movement and "youth"; "values," broadly defined; family life, child-rearing, family conflict and other aspects of socialization. Rating scales and "projective" questions were used to assess family members' perceptions of parent-child relationships.

It was clear to us that our sampling procedures were prone to a certain degree of error in the classification of students as "activists" and "nonactivists." Some students who appeared on mailing lists of activist organizations had no substantial involvement in the student movement, while some of our "control" students had a considerable history of such involvement. Thus the data to be reported here are based on an index of Activism constructed from interview responses to questions about participation in seven kinds of activity: attendance at rallies, picketing, canvassing, working on a project to help the disadvantaged, being jailed for civil disobedience, working full-time for a social action organization, serving as an officer in such organizations.

Study two—the "anti-ranking" sit-in

In May, 1966, about five hundred students sat-in at the Administration Building on the campus of the University at Chicago, barring the building to official use for two and a half days. The focal issue of protest, emulated on a number of other campuses in the succeeding days, was the demand by the students that the University not cooperate with the Selective Service System in supplying class standings for the purpose of assigning student deferments. The students who sat-in formed an organization called "Students Against the Rank" (SAR). During the sit-in another group of students, calling themselves "Students for a Free Choice" (SFC) circulated a petition opposing the sit-in and supporting the University Administration's view that each student had a right to submit (or withhold) his class standings—the University could not withhold the "rank" of students who requested it. This petition was signed by several hundred students.

Beginning about 10 days after the end of the sit-in, we undertook to interview three samples of students: a random sample of 65 supporters of SAR (the protesters); a random sample of 35 signers of the SFC petition (the anti-protesters); approximately 60 students who constituted the total population of two randomly selected floors in the student dormitories. Of about 160 students thus selected, 117 were finally either interviewed or returned mailed questionnaires. The interview schedule was based largely on items used in the original .study; it also included some additional items relevant to the sit-in and the "ranking" controversy.

Some preliminary findings

At this writing, our data analysis is at an early stage. In general, however, it is clear that the framework of hypotheses with which we began is substantially supported, and in interesting ways, refined, by the data. Our principle findings thus far include the following:[1]

Activists tend to come from upper status families. As indicated earlier, our study of the Chicago sit-in suggests that such actions attract students predominantly from upper-status backgrounds. When compared with students who did not sit-in, and with students who signed the anti-sit-in petition, the sit-in participants reported higher family incomes, higher levels of education for both fathers and mothers, and overwhelmingly perceived themselves to be "upper-middle class." One illustrative finding: in our dormitory sample, of 24 students reporting family incomes of above $15,000, half participated in the sit-in. Of 23 students reporting family incomes below $15,000, only two sat-in.

Certain kinds of occupations are particularly characteristic of the parents of sit-in participants. In particular, their fathers tend to be professionals (college faculty, lawyers, doctors) rather than businessmen, white collar employees or blue-collar workers. Moreover, somewhat unexpectedly, activists' mothers are likely to be employed, and are more likely to have "career" types of employment, than are the mothers of non-activists.

Also of significance, although not particularly surprising, is the fact that activists are more likely to be Jewish than are nonactivists. (For example, 45% of our SAR sample reported that they were Jewish; only about one-fourth of the non-participants were Jewish). Furthermore, a very high proportion of both Jewish and non-Jewish activists report no religious preference for themselves and their parents. Associated with the Jewish ethnicity of a large proportion of our activist samples is the fact the great majority of activists' grandparents were foreign born. Yet, despite this, data from Study One show that the grandparents of activists tended to be relatively highly educated as compared to the grandparents of non-activists. Most of the grandparents of non-activists had not completed high school, nearly half of the grandparents of activists had at least a high school education and fully one-fourth of their maternal grandmothers had attended college. These data suggest that relatively high status characterized the families of activists over several generations; this conclusion is supported by data showing that, unlike non-activist

---

[1]A more detailed report of the procedures and findings of these studies is available in Flacks (1966).

BEGINNINGS

grandfathers, the grandfathers of activists tended to have white collar, professional and entrepreneurial occupations rather than blue collar jobs.

In sum, our data suggest that, at least at major Northern colleges, students involved in protest activity are characteristically from families which are urban, highly educated, Jewish or irreligious, professional and affluent. It is perhaps particularly interesting that many of their mothers are uniquely well-educated and involved in careers, and that high status and education has characterized these families over at least two generations.

Activists are more "radical" than their parents; but activists' parents are decidedly more liberal than others of their status. The demographic data reported above suggests that activists come from high status families, but the occupational, religious and educational characteristics of these families are unique in several important ways. The distinctiveness of these families is especially clear when we examine data from Study One on the political attitudes of students and their parents. In this study, it should be remembered, activist and non-activist families were roughly equivalent in status, income and education because of our sampling procedures. Our data quite clearly demonstrate that the fathers of activists are disproportionately liberal. For example, whereas forty per cent of the nonactivists' fathers said that they were Republican, only thirteen per cent of the activists' fathers were Republicans. Only six per cent of nonactivists' fathers were willing to describe themselves as "highly liberal" or "socialist," whereas sixty per cent of the activists' fathers accepted such designations. Forty per cent of the non-activists' fathers described themselves as conservative; none of the activists' fathers endorsed that position.[2]

In general, differences in the political preferences of the students paralleled these parental differences. The non-activist sample is only slightly less conservative and Republican than their fathers; all of the activist students with Republican fathers report their own party preferences as either Democrat or independent. Thirty-two per cent of the activists regard themselves as "socialist" as compared with sixteen per cent of their fathers. In general, both nonactivists and their fathers are typically "moderate" in their politics; activists and their fathers tend to be at least "liberal," but a substantial proportion of the activists prefer a more "radical" designation.

A somewhat more detailed picture of comparative political positions emerges when we examine responses of students and their fathers to a series of 6-point scales on which respondents rated their attitudes on such issues as: US bombing of North Vietnam, US troops in the Dominican Republic, student participation in protest demonstrations, civil rights protests involving civil disobedience, Lyndon Johnson, Barry Goldwater, congressional investigations of "unAmerican activities," full socialization of all industries, socialization of the medical profession.

[2]For the purposes of this report, "activists" are those students who were in the top third on our Activism index; "nonactivists" are those students who were in the bottom third—this latter group reported virtually no participation in any activity associated with the student movement. The "activists," on the other hand, had taken part in at least one activity indicating high commitment to the movement (e.g. going to jail, working full-time, serving in a leadership capacity).

Table 1 presents data on activists and non-activists and their fathers with respect to these items. This table suggests, first, wide divergence between the two groups of fathers on most issues, with activist fathers typically critical of current policies. Although activists' fathers are overwhelmingly "liberal" in their responses, for the most part, activist students tend to endorse "left-wing" positions more strongly and consistently than do their fathers. The items showing strongest divergence between activists and their fathers are interesting. Whereas activists overwhelmingly endorse civil disobedience, nearly half of their fathers do not. Whereas fathers of both activists and non-activists tend to approve of Lyndon Johnson, activist students tend to disapprove of him. Whereas activists' fathers tend to disapprove of "full socialization of industry," this item is endorsed by the majority of activists (although fewer gave an extremely radical response on this item than any other); whereas the vast majority of activists approve of socialized medicine, the majority of their fathers do not. This table provides further support for the view that activists, though more "radical" than their fathers, come predominantly from very liberal homes. The attitudes of nonactivists and their fathers are conventional and supportive of current policies; there is a slight tendency on some items for nonactivist students to endorse more conservative positions than their fathers.

TABLE 1

STUDENTS' AND FATHERS' ATTITUDES ON CURRENT ISSUES

Issue	Activists		Nonactivists	
	Students	Fathers	Students	Fathers
Per cent who approve:				
Bombing of North Vietnam	9	27	73	80
American troops in Dominican Republic	6	33	65	50
Student participation in protest demonstrations	100	80	61	37
Civil disobedience in civil rights protests	97	57	28	23
Congressional investigations of "un-American activities"	3	7	73	57
Lyndon Johnson	35	77	81	83
Barry Goldwater	0	7	35	20
Full socialization of industry	62	23	5	10
Socialization of the medical profession	94	43	30	27
N	34	30	37	30

It seems fair to conclude, then, that most students who are involved in the movement (at least those one finds in a city like Chicago) are involved in neither "conversion" from nor "rebellion" against the political perspectives of their fathers. A more supportable view suggests that the great majority of these students are attempting to fulfill and renew the political traditions of their families. However, data from our research which have not yet been analyzed as of this writing, will permit a more systematic analysis of the political orientations of the two generations.

Activism is related to a complex of values, not ostensibly political, shared by both the students and their parents. Data which we have just begun to analyze suggest that the political perspectives which differentiate the families of activists from other families at the same socioeconomic level are part of a more general clustering of values and orientations. Our findings and impressions on this point may be briefly summarized by saying that, whereas nonactivists and their parents tend to express conventional orientations toward achievement, material success, sexual morality and religion, the activists and their parents tend to place greater stress on involvement in intellectual and esthetic pursuits, humanitarian concerns, opportunity for self-expression, and tend to de-emphasize or positively disvalue personal achievement, conventional morality and conventional religiosity.

When asked to rank order a list of "areas of life," nonactivist students and their parents typically indicate that marriage, career and religion are most important. Activists, on the other hand, typically rank these lower than the "world of ideas, art and music" and "work for national and international betterment"—and so, on the whole, do their parents (see also the relevant data presented by Trent and Craise in this issue).

When asked to indicate their vocational aspirations, nonactivist students are typically firmly decided on a career and typically mention orientations toward the professions, science and business. Activists, on the other hand, are very frequently undecided on a career; and most typically those who have decided mention college teaching, the arts or social work as aspirations.

These kinds of responses suggest, somewhat crudely, that student activists identify with life goals which are intellectual and "humanitarian" and that they reject conventional and "privatized" goals more frequently than do nonactivist students.

Four Value Patterns

More detailed analyses which we are just beginning to undertake support the view that the value-patterns expressed by activists are highly correlated with those of their parents. This analysis has involved the isolation of a number of value-patterns which emerged in the interview material, the development of systems of code categories related to each of these patterns, and the blind coding of all the interviews with respect to these categories. The kinds of data we are obtaining in this way may be illustrated by describing four of the value patterns we have observed:

Romanticism: esthetic and emotional sensitivity

This variable is defined as: "sensitivity to beauty and art—appreciation of painting, literature and music, creativity in art forms—concern with esthetic experience and the development of capacities for esthetic expression—concern with emotions deriving from perception of beauty—attachment of great significance to esthetic experience. More broadly, it can be conceived of as involving explicit concern with experience as such, with feeling and passion, with immediate and inner experience; a concern for the realm of feeling rather than the rational, technological or instrumental side of life; preference for the realm of experience as against that of activity, doing or achieving." Thirteen items were coded in these terms: for each item a score of zero signified no mention of "romanticist" concerns, a score of one signified that such a concern appeared. Table 2 indicates the relationship between "romanticism" and Activism. Very few Activists received scores on Romanticism which placed them as "low"; conversely, there were very few high "romantics" among the nonactivists.

TABLE 2

SCORES ON SELECTED VALUES BY ACTIVISM
(PERCENTAGES)

		Activists	*Nonactivists*
(a)	*Romanticism*		
	High	35	11
	Medium	47	49
	Low	18	40
(b)	*Intellectualism*		
	High	32	3
	Medium	65	57
	Low	3	40
(c)	*Humanitarianism*		
	High	35	0
	Medium	47	22
	Low	18	78
(d)	*Moralism*		
	High	6	54
	Medium	53	35
	Low	41	11
	N	34	37

Intellectualism

This variable is defined as: "Concern with ideas—desire to realize intellectual capacities—high valuation of intellectual creativities—appreciation of theory and knowledge—participation in intellectual activity (e.g., reading, studying, teaching, writing)—broad intellectual concerns." Ten items were scored for "intellectualism." Almost no Activists are low on this variable; almost no nonactivists received a high score.

Humanitarianism

This variable is defined as: "Concern with plight of others in society; desire to help others—value on compassion and sympathy—desire to alleviate suffering; value on egalitarianism in the sense of opposing privilege based on social and economic distinction; particular sensitivity to the deprived position of the disadvantaged." This variable was coded for ten items; an attempt was made to exclude from this index all items referring directly to participation in social action. As might be expected, "humanitarianism" is strongly related to Activism, as evidenced in Table 2.

Moralism and self control

This variable is defined as: "Concern about the importance of strictly controlling personal impulses—opposition to impulsive or spontaneous behavior—value on keeping tight control over emotions—adherence to conventional authority; adherence to conventional morality—a high degree of moralism about sex, drugs, alcohol, etc.—reliance on a set of external and inflexible rules to govern moral behavior; emphasis on importance of hard work; concern with determination, 'stick-to-itiveness'; antagonism toward idleness—value on diligence, entrepreneurship, task orientation, ambition." Twelve items were scored for this variable. As Table 2 suggests, "moralism" is also strongly related to Activism; very few Activists score high on this variable, while the majority of nonactivists are high scorers.

These values are strongly related to activism. They are also highly intercorrelated, and, most importantly, parent and student scores on these variables are strongly correlated.

These and other value patterns will be used as the basis for studying value transmission in families, generational similarities and differences and several other problems. Our data with respect to them provide further support for the view that the unconventionality of activists flows out of and is supported by their family traditions.

Activists' parents are more "permissive" than parents of nonactivists. We have just begun to get some findings bearing on our hypothesis that parents of Activists will tend to have been more "permissive" in their child-rearing practices than parents of equivalent status whose children are not oriented toward activism.

One measure of parental permissiveness we have been using is a series of rating scales completed by each member of the family. A series of seven-point bipolar scales was presented in a format similar to that of the "Semantic Differential". Students were asked to indicate "how my mother (father) treated me as a child" on such scales as "warm-cold"; "stern-mild"; "hard-soft"—10 scales in all. Each parent, using the same scales, rated "how my child thinks I treated him."

Table 3 presents data on how sons and daughters rated each of their parents on each of four scales: "mild-stern"; "soft-hard"; "lenient-severe"; and "easy-strict." In general, this table shows that Activist sons and daughters tend to rate their parents as "milder," "more lenient," and "less severe" than do nonactivists. Similar data were obtained using the parents' ratings of themselves.

TABLE 3

SONS AND DAUGHTERS RATINGS OF PARENTS BY ACTIVISM
(PERCENTAGES)

	Males		Females	
Trait of Parent	Hi Act	Lo Act	Hi Act	Lo Act
mild-stern				
per cent rating mother "mild"	63	44	59	47
per cent rating father "mild"	48	33	48	32
soft-hard				
per cent rating mother "soft"	69	61	60	57
per cent rating father "soft"	50	50	62	51
lenient-severe				
per cent rating mother "lenient"	94	61	66	63
per cent rating father "lenient"	60	44	47	42
easy-strict				
per cent rating mother "easy"	75	50	77	52
per cent rating father "easy"	69	44	47	37
N	23	24	27	26

A different measure of permissiveness is based on the parents' response to a series of "hypothetical situations." Parents were asked, for example, what they would do if their son (daughter) "decided to drop out of school and doesn't know what he really wants to do." Responses to this open-ended question were coded as indicating "high intervention" or "low intervention." Data for fathers on this item are reported in Table 4. Another hypothetical situation presented to the parents was that their child was living with a member of the opposite sex. Responses to this item were coded as "strongly intervene, mildly intervene, not intervene." Data for this item for fathers appears in Table 5. Both tables show that fathers of Activists report themselves to be much less interventionist than fathers of non-activists. Similar results were obtained with mothers, and for other hypothetical situations.

Clearly both types of measures just reported provide support for our hypothesis about the relationship between parental permissiveness and activism. We expect these relationships to be strengthened if "activism" is combined with certain of the value-patterns described earlier.

TABLE 4

FATHER'S INTERVENTION—"IF CHILD
DROPPED OUT OF SCHOOL"
(PERCENTAGES)

	Activism of Child	
Degree of Intervention	High	Low
Low	56	37
High	44	63
N	30	30

A Concluding Note

The data reported here constitute a small but representative sampling of the material we have collected in our studies of the student movement. In general, they provide support for the impressions and expectations we had when we undertook this work. Our view of the student movement as an expression of deep discontent felt by certain types of high status youth as they confront the incongruities between the values represented by the authority and occupational structure of the larger society and the values inculcated by their families and peer culture seems to fit well with the data we have obtained.

TABLE 5

FATHER'S INTERVENTION—"IF CHILD WERE
LIVING WITH MEMBER OF OPPOSITE SEX"
(PERCENTAGES)

	Activism of Child	
Degree of Intervention	High	Low
None	20	14
Mild	50	28
Strong	30	58
N	30	30

A variety of questions remain which, we hope, can be answered, at least in part, by further analyses of our data. Although it is clear that value differences between parents of activists and nonactivists are centrally relevant for understanding value, attitudinal and behavioral cleavages among types of students on the campus, it remains to be determined whether differences in family status, on the one hand, and childrearing practices, on the other, make an independent contribution to the variance. A second issue has to do with political ideology. First impressions of our data suggest that activists vary considerably with respect to their degree of politicization and their concern with ideological issues. The problem of isolating the key determinants of this variation is one we will be paying close attention to in further analysis of our interview material. Two factors are likely to be of importance here—first, the degree to which the student participates in radical student organizations; second, the political history of his parents.

At least two major issues are not confronted by the research we have been doing. First, we have not examined in any detail the role of campus conditions as a determinant of student discontent (see the introduction by Sampson and the article by Brown for a further discussion of these institutional factors.) The research reported here emphasizes family socialization and other antecedent experiences as determinants of student protest, and leads to the prediction that students experiencing other patterns of early socialization will be unlikely to be in revolt. This view needs to be counterbalanced by recalling instances of active student unrest on campuses where very few students are likely to have the backgrounds suggested here as critical. Is it possible that there are two components to the student protest movement—one generated to a great extent by early socialization; and second by grievances indigenous to the campus? At any rate, the inter-relationships between personal dispositions and campus conditions need further detailed elucidation.

A second set of questions unanswerable by our research has to do with the future—what lies ahead for the movement as a whole and for the individual young people who participate in it? One direction for the student movement is toward institutionalization as an expression of youth discontent. This outcome, very typical of student movements in many countries, would represent a narrowing of the movement's political and social impact, a way of functionally integrating it into an otherwise stable society. Individual participants would be expected to pass through the movement on their way to eventual absorption, often at an elite level, into the established institutional order. An alternative direction would be toward the development of a full-fledged political "left," with the student movement serving, at least initially, as a nucleus. The potential for this latter development is apparent in recent events. It was the student movement which catalyzed professors and other adults into protest with respect to the Vietnam war. Students for a Democratic Society, the main organizational expression of the student movement, has had, for several years, a program for "community organizing," in which students and ex-students work full-time at the mobilization of constituencies for independent radical political and social action. This SDS program began in poverty areas; it is now beginning to spread to "middle class" communities. These efforts, and others like them, from Berkeley to New Haven, became particularly visible during the 1966 congressional elections, as a wave of "new left" candidates emerged

across the country, often supported by large and sophisticated political organizations. Moreover, in addition to attempts at political organizations, SDS,
through its "Radical Education Project" has begun to seek the involvement
of faculty members, professionals and other intellectuals for a program of
research and education designed to lay the foundations for an intellectually
substantial and ideologically developed "new left."

At its convention in September, 1966, SDS approached, but did not finally
decide, the question of whether to continue to maintain its character as a
campus-based, student organization or to transform itself into a "Movement
for a Democratic Society." Characteristically, the young people there assembled amended the organization's constitution so that anyone regardless of
status or age could join, while simultaneously they affirmed the student character of the group by projecting a more vigorous program to organize uncommitted students.

The historical significance of the student movement of the Sixties remains
to be determined. Its impact on the campus and on the larger society has
already been substantial. It is clearly a product of deep discontent in certain
significant and rapidly growing segments of the youth population. Whether it
becomes an expression of generational discontent, or the forerunner of major
political realignments—or simply disintegrates—cannot really be predicted by
detached social scientists. The ultimate personal and political meaning of the
student movement remains a matter to be determined by those who are involved with it—as participants, as allies, as critics, as enemies.

References

Aaron, Daniel. *Writers on the left.* New York: Avon, 1965.
Bell, Daniel. *The end of ideology.* New York: The Free Press, 1962.
Braungart, R. G. Social stratification and political attitudes. Pennsylvania State Uni-
versity, 1966, (unpublished ms.).
Bronfenbrenner, U. The changing american child: A speculative analysis. *Merrill-
Palmer Quarterly,* 1961, **7,**73–**85.**
Cosel, Lewis. *Men of ideas.* New York: The Free Press, 1965.
Erikson, Erik. Identity and the life-cycle. *Psychological Issues,* 1959, **1,** 1–171.
Erikson, Erik. *Childhood and society.* New York: Norton, 1963, 306–325.
Eisenstadt, Shmuel N. *From generation to generation.* Glencoe: The Free Press, 1956.
Flacks, R. The liberated generation. University of Chicago, 1966. (mimeo)
Goldsen, Rose; Rosenberg, Moris; Williams, Robin; and Suchman, Edward. *What
college students think,* Princeton: Van Nostrand, 1969.
Jacob, Philip. *Changing values in college.* New York: Harper, 1957.
Keniston, Kenneth. *The uncommitted.* New York: Harcourt Brace, 1965a.
Keniston, Kenneth. Social change and youth in America. In E. Erikson (Ed.), *The
challenge of youth.* Garden City: Doubleday Anchor, 1965b.
Lasch, Christopher. *The new radicalism in America.* New York: Knopf, 1965.
Lipset, Seymour. *Political man, the social bases of politics.* Garden City: Doubleday
Anchor, 1960.

Lipset, Seymour. University students and politics in underdeveloped countries. *Comparative Education Review,* 1966, **10,** 320–349.

Lipset, Seymour and Altbach, P. Student politics and higher education in the United States. *Comparative Education Review,* 1966, **10,** 320–349.

Miller, Daniel and Swanson, G. E. *The changing american parent.* New York: Wiley, 1958.

Newcomb, Theodore and Flacks, R. *Deviant subcultures on a college campus.* US Office of Education, 1963.

Parsons, Talcott. Youth in the context of American society. In E. Erikson (Ed.), *The challenge of youth.* Garden City: Doubleday Anchor, 1965.

Shils, Edward. The intellectuals in the political development of new states. *World Politics,* 1969, **12,** 329–368.

Stinchcombe, Arthur. *Rebellion in a high school.* Chicago: Quadrangle, 1964.

Trow, Martin. Student cultures and administrative action. In Surtherland, R. *et al* (Eds.), *Personality factors on the college campus.* Austin: Hogg Foundation for Mental Health, 1962.

Veblen, Thorstein. The intellectual pre-eminence of Jews in modern Europe. In B. Rosenberg (Ed.), *Thorstein Veblen.* New York: Crowell, 1963.

24. Grow Old Along with Me! The Best Is Yet to Be

BERNICE L. NEUGARTEN

Most of us have a half-conscious and irrational fear that one day we will find ourselves old, as if suddenly we will fall off a cliff, and that what we *will be* then has little to do with what we *are* now. Recent research has shown, however, that nothing could be farther from the truth.

It would be a gross over-simplification, of course, to say that no changes occur in personality as people move from middle age through old age, just as it would be a distortion to say that life-styles always remain consistent. But within broad limits—and with no overwhelming biological accidents—the pattern of aging is predictable for the individual if we know his personality in middle age and how he has dealt with earlier life events.

Arc

Several years' research that I and other investigators have done at the University of Chicago has led us to conclude that aging should be seen as one part of the continuous life cycle. It is shaped by the individual's past—his childhood, adolescence and adulthood. Like earlier periods in life, aging brings new situations and new problems. It calls for new adaptations.

Middle age and old age are eventful periods, and grandparenthood, retirement, widowhood, illness, and the recognition of approaching death can be as dramatic as anything that happens earlier. In adapting to the biological changes that are going on inside and to the social changes that are going on outside, the aging person draws upon what he has been as well as what he is. How else shall we account for the fact that one person copes well, another poorly, with the succession of late-life events?

Nevertheless, most people see aging as alien to the self and tend to deny or repress the associated feelings of distaste and anxiety. We have an irrational fear of aging and, as a result, we maintain a psychological distance between ourselves and older persons.

This irrational fear has its basis in our stereotypical thinking about age groups. Stereotypes about the young, the middle-aged and the old influence our behavior in subtle ways. They affect our perceptions of appropriate and inappropriate behavior in ourselves and in other persons. They constrain our attitudes and our actions. They make it difficult to improve relationships among persons of various ages.

Animus

While the stereotyping of any age group is full of pitfalls, we are just now beginning to realize that stereotypes about aging and the aged create a particularly complex set of problems. In addition to making us fear aging, the stereotypes lead to a divisiveness in society at large that has been called ageism—that is, negative or hostile attitudes between age groups that lead to socially destructive competition. So long as we believe that old persons are poor, isolated, sick and unhappy (or, to the contrary, powerful, rigid and reactionary), we find the prospect of old age particularly unattractive. We can then separate ourselves comfortably from older persons and relegate them to inferior status.

Conflict between generations probably is a universal theme in history, but the intensity of the conflict and the focus of the hostility obviously fluctuate according to historical, social and economic factors. Some social scientists are alarmed that generational conflicts are increasing in the 1970s. Although the generation gap has been described mainly as a gap between the young and everybody else, it is entirely possible that conflicts will also appear in the other direction—that is, between the old and everybody else.

Anger toward the old may be on the rise. One of every 10 Americans is now 65 or older, and an industrialized society whose citizens live increasingly longer becomes in many ways a gerontocratic society. Older persons occupy an increasing proportion of power positions in judicial, legislative, economic and professional areas, and the young and the middle-aged often resent them. Older persons themselves are learning the politics of confrontation. The appeal to Senior Power and the recent growth of national organizations that act as advocates for older persons suggest that the conflict is being joined by those who might otherwise be its victims.

Stereotypes of the aged are difficult to dispel, largely because research on aging is a recent development in both the biological and the social sciences and research findings reach the public at a snail's pace. Many widely held but inaccurate images, inadvertently repeated through the mass media, come from social workers who serve the poor, the lonely and the isolated, and from physicians and psychiatrists who see the physically ill and the mentally ill. Thus we base many of our current stereotypes on a picture of the needy rather than on a picture of the typical older person.

Studies of large and representative samples of older persons are now appearing, however, and they go far toward exploding some of our outmoded images. For example, old persons do not become isolated and neglected by their families, although both generations prefer separate households. Old persons are not dumped into mental hospitals by cruel or indifferent children. They are not necessarily lonely or desolate if they live alone. Few of them ever show overt signs of mental deterioration or senility, and only a small proportion ever become mentally ill. For those who do, psychological and psychiatric treatment is by no means futile.

Retirement and widowhood do not lead to mental illness, nor does social isolation. Retirement is not necessarily bad: some men and women want to keep on working, but more and more choose to retire earlier and earlier. Increasing proportions of the population evidently value leisure more than they value work. Nor do retired persons sicken physically from idleness and feelings of worthlessness. Three fourths of the persons questioned in a recent national sample reported that they were satisfied or very satisfied with their lives since retirement. This is in line with earlier surveys. Most persons over 65 think of themselves as being in good health and they act accordingly, no matter what their physicians think.

Cut-Off

The belief that 65 is a useful marker of old age is another stereotype. It was historical accident that set 65 as the age of eligibility for Social-Security payments. The decision reflected the economic situation and the manpower needs of the country in the 1930s. Age 65 otherwise has no reality as a turning point in the life of the individual. Because people are beginning to retire at earlier ages, perhaps we should call 60 or 55 the beginning of old age. Or, on the other hand, because 65-year-olds are generally more youthful today than their fathers were, and because longevity is increasing, perhaps we should use 75 as the marker. (The 1970 U.S. census shows that in the last 10 years the number of persons aged 75 and over increased three times as fast as the number of those aged 65 to 74.)

But the most insidious stereotype of all, in many ways, puts the old (or, for that matter, the young or the middle-aged) into a distinct category or a distinct group. There is, in truth, no such thing as "the" young, or "the" old. People *do* differ; they also become increasingly different over time, as each person accumulates an idiosyncratic set of experiences and becomes committed to a unique set of people, things, interests and activities. One has only to recall, for instance, the range of differences among the members of one's high-school graduating class and then to see these persons at a class reunion 25 years later. They are much more varied as 40-year-olds than they were as 18-year-olds. In a society as complex as ours, with increasing social permissiveness for people to follow their own bents, a good case can be made that—despite the counter-pressures that create conformity—increased differentiation occurs over the life cycle.

To put the same point another way, calendar age or chronological age is a poor basis for grouping people who have attained biological maturity. Study after study of the happiness, intelligence, personality or health of adults has shown that age is a poor index of the differences between people.

Probe

Older persons are not a homogeneous group, then, no matter from what perspective we look at them. This fact has become particularly clear to our group at Chicago in carrying out a long line of studies of middle age and aging over the past 15 years: studies of personality, of adaptational patterns, of career lines, of age-norms, of attitudes and values across social-class and generational lines. The number of men and women who have participated now totals more than 2,000. We based each study in the series upon a relatively large sample of normal persons; none was a volunteer and all were living in one or another metropolitan community in the Midwest.

One study that illustrates the point about heterogeneity focused on persons aged 70 to 79. We were pursuing these questions: Would retired persons who stayed actively engaged in various family and community activities be happier than those who were relatively inactive? How would longstanding personality differences affect these relationships? To find out, we gathered various psychological test data and conducted home interviews repeatedly over a seven-year period. We made systematic assessments in three areas: personality, degree of satisfaction with life, and extent of social-role activity.

In the area of personality, we assessed each person on 45 dimensions. Then, by appropriate statistical methods, we derived four major personality types, which we called *integrated, defended, passive-dependent,* and *disintegrated.*

Points

Our life-satisfaction measure involved five components. We rated an individual high to the extent that he 1) took pleasure from the round of activities that constituted his everyday life—the person who enjoyed sitting at home watching television could rate as high as the one who enjoyed his job; 2) regarded his life as meaningful and accepted responsibility for what his life had been; 3) felt he had succeeded in achieving his major goals; 4) held a positive self-image; and 5) maintained optimistic attitudes and moods.

For role-activity, we rated both the extent and the intensity of activity (that is, the amount of time and energy invested and the emotional significance attached) in each of 11 social roles: parent, spouse, grandparent, kin-group member, worker, homemaker, citizen, friend, neighbor, club-and-association member, and church member. For example, with regard to the role of spouse, we rated a man low if he lived with his wife but shared few activities with her other than perfunctory routines such as eating his meals in her presence. A man who planned and carried out most of his day's activities in the company of his wife rated high. We summed the ratings in the 11 roles to obtain a role-activity score.

We also asked about an individual's activities in each role area when he had been age 60, then systematically assessed the differences that had developed as time passed. For this group as a whole, activity levels had decreased and members showed levels of social interaction that were lower than they were when they were 60. Yet the more dramatic finding was the great range of differences in terms of present activity patterns and life-styles. Using our various sets of data for each person, we found eight major patterns among the four major personality types that follow:

1. *Integrated.* The majority of these 70-year-olds remained integrated personalities—well-functioning persons with complex inner lives, intact cognitive abilities and competent egos. They accepted and maintained a comfortable degree of control over their impulses; they were flexible and open to new stimuli, mellow and mature. All were high in life satisfaction. At the same time, they differed among themselves with regard to role activity and therefore showed different patterns of aging.

One pattern we called the *reorganizers,* competent people who were engaged in a wide variety of activities. They were the optimum agers in some respects —at least in the American culture, which places a high value on continuing to be active. These persons substituted new activities for lost ones; when they retired from work, they gave time to community affairs or to the church or to other associations. They reorganized their patterns of activity. One such person was a retired schoolteacher who, at 75, was selling life insurance and making more money than ever. He held elective office in an association of retirees, attended concerts and the theater with his wife, and visited regularly with friends.

Another group of complex and well-integrated personalities we called the *focused* because they had become selective in their activities, devoting energy to the few roles that were important to them. One was an emeritus university professor who, at 75, was still teaching, but only those courses she wanted to teach. She had withdrawn from organizations that she felt were needlessly time-consuming; she felt free to accept or decline invitations at will. It was a relief to have her husband at home now, because he did things around the house that she had had to do earlier, but otherwise, he played a very secondary role in her life. She seldom saw her children and liked it that way. She was glad to be free of responsibility, and to invest all her energies in her work.

A third pattern we called the *disengaged.* These were also well-integrated personalities with high life satisfaction, but with low activity; they had moved away voluntarily from role commitments, not in response to external losses or physical deficits, but because of preference. These were self-directed, though not shallow, persons. They were interested in the world, but they were not imbedded in networks of social interaction. They had high feelings of self-regard, just as the first two groups did, but they had chosen the "rocking-chair" approach to old age—a calm, withdrawn, but contented pattern. One was a retired man who had dropped his club memberships, seldom saw his former work colleagues or friends, and welcomed the opportunity to lead a relaxed life at home, visiting with his children and grandchildren, gardening a little, and occasionally helping his wife around the house.

2. *Defended.* In the next major personality category were men and women whom we called "armored" or "defended." These were the striving, ambitious, and achievement-oriented persons who drove themselves hard. They had high defenses against anxiety and needed to maintain tight control over impulse life. This personality group provided two patterns of aging.

The *holding-on* pattern included the persons who said, "So long as you keep busy, you'll get along all right," or "I'll work until I drop." This group had medium to high life satisfaction because they managed to maintain relatively high levels of activity. One such woman had been an office worker all her life, had never married, and regarded herself as strong and tough. She said that when she was younger she was much too busy to feel lonely; now that she was retired, she kept busy as the historian and recording secretary for the local DAR. She had arteriosclerosis and had suffered a heart attack five years earlier, but she said that she did not let her illness get her down: "You can't slow down just because you happen to have some physical limitations."

The other group of defended personalities we called the *constricted.* These persons were busy defending themselves against aging; preoccupied with losses and deficits, they constricted their social interactions and shut out new experiences, fending off what they seemed to regard as imminent collapse. Given their personalities, their approach to the world worked fairly well, and they had medium or even high levels of satisfaction and contentment. Mr. B, for example, had worked out elaborate rituals for maintaining his health. He talked of little else. He and his wife spent hours shopping for just the right foods, and they made vegetable juices fresh every day. He took long drives into the country each week to bring back pure spring water. He was not much different now, he said, from when he was younger. All his life he had been cautious about himself, and even as a young man he "always thought twice before making any rash decisions."

3. *Passive dependent.* Among members of the passive-dependent group, there were also two patterns of aging.

The *succorance-seeking* were those persons with strong dependency needs who sought responsiveness from others. They showed medium levels of activity, for the most part, and medium satisfaction with life; they did fairly well so long as each had at least one or two other persons to lean on. One woman, for example, looked back to the time when her husband was alive because he always took such good care of her. Now she was diabetic and felt particularly helpless. But she said she counted on her son, who lived in the same city and visited her every day. He took her shopping on Saturdays, paid all her bills and saw to it that she took her medicine.

There were a small number of the *apathetic,* those in whom passivity was the most striking personality feature. They had few activities and very little interaction with others; they showed little interest in the world about them. Life was hard, they said, and there was never much that could be done about it, was there? One, for instance, was a woman who limited her activities entirely to meeting her physical needs and caring for her two cats. She seldom interacted even with her brother and sister-in-law, who lived on the floor above her, because, as she said, "They are old and sick, too, and don't go anywhere."

4. *Disintegrated.* Finally, there were a few whom we called the disintegrated or *disorganized,* persons who showed gross defects in psychological functions and deterioration in thought processes. They managed to maintain themselves in the community, either because of protective families or because of the forbearance of the people around them. Mr. G, for instance, was a paranoid, isolated man who lived in a run-down section of the city. He did a little janitorial work around the building in exchange for a room in the basement.

Others

These eight patterns do not exhaust the variations we found in this group of 70-year-olds, and the group itself did not include the full range. There are, of course, some persons in their 70s who are too ill to be interviewed, a small number who live in hospitals and homes for the aged, and a few who have moved to leisure communities in the South and Southwest.

But it is the variation rather than the similarity among 70-year-olds that is impressive. And the diversity is likely to become even greater in the future. At present, there is an over-representation of the foreign-born, the poorly educated and the poor among those who are 65 and over. In future decades, with better health, more education and more financial resources, older men and women will have greater freedom to choose life-styles that suit them.

Another point is equally important. The individuals we studied in such great detail over seven years seemed to show relatively consistent patterns of coping and adjustment. Although we had no systematic data gathered when these persons were young or middle-aged, we knew a great deal about their life histories and we had information from family members. The general picture was one of personality continuities over time.

Bridge

Looked at realistically, then, and with the stereotypes dispelled, aging is not a leveler of individual differences. For most people it brings no sudden and drastic transformation of personality. This being so, aging will not separate the individual's present from his future self. Just as every person changes as he grows up, he will continue to change as he grows old. But aging will not destroy the continuities between what he has been, what he is, and what he will be. Recognition of this fact should lessen the fear of growing old. At the social level, the knowledge that our stereotypes are ill-founded should make older persons seem less distant and less alien, and should help to bridge the psychological barriers between people of different ages.

25. The Forgotten American

PETER SCHRAG

There is hardly a language to describe him, or even a set of social statistics. Just names: racist-bigot-redneck-ethnic-Irish-Italian-Pole-Hunkie-Yahoo. The lower middle class. A blank. The man under whose hat lies the great American desert. Who watches the tube, plays the horses, and keeps the niggers out of his union and his neighborhood. Who might vote for Wallace (but didn't). Who cheers when the cops beat up on demonstrators. Who is free, white, and twenty-one, has a job, a home, a family, and is up to his eyeballs in credit. In the guise of the working class—or the American yeoman or John Smith—he was once the hero of the civics book, the man that Andrew Jackson called "the bone and sinew of the country." Now he is "the forgotten man," perhaps the most alienated person in America.

Nothing quite fits, except perhaps omission and semi-invisibility. America is supposed to be divided between affluence and poverty, between slums and suburbs. John Kenneth Galbraith begins the foreword to *The Affluent Society* with the phrase, "Since I sailed for Switzerland in the early summer of 1955 to begin work on this book . . ." But *between* slums and suburbs, between Scarsdale and Harlem, between Wellesley and Roxbury, between Shaker Heights and Hough, there are some eighty million people (depending on how you count them) who didn't sail for Switzerland in the summer of 1955, or at any other time, and who never expect to. Between slums and suburbs: South Boston and South San Francisco, Bell and Parma, Astoria and Bay Ridge, Newark, Cicero, Downey, Daly City, Charlestown, Flatbush. Union halls, American Legion posts, neighborhood bars and bowling leagues, the Ukrainian Club and the Holy Name. Main Street. To try to describe all this is like trying to describe America itself. If you look for it, you find it everywhere: the rows of frame houses overlooking the belching steel mills in Bethlehem, Pennsylvania, two-family brick houses in Canarsie (where the most common slogan, even in the middle of a political campaign, is "curb your dog"); the Fords and Chevies with a decal American flag on the rear window (usually a cut-out from the *Reader's Digest,* and displayed in counter-protest against peaceniks and "those bastards who carry Vietcong flags in demonstrations");

the bunting on the porch rail with the inscription, "Welcome Home, Pete." The gold star in the window.

When he was Under Secretary of Housing and Urban Development, Robert C. Wood tried a definition. It is not good, but it's the best we have:

> He is a white employed male . . . earning between $5,000 and $10,000. He works regularly, steadily, dependably, wearing a blue collar or white collar. Yet the frontiers of his career expectations have been fixed since he reached the age of thirty-five, when he found that he had too many obligations, too much family, and too few skills to match opportunities with aspirations.
>
> This definition of the "working American" involves almost 23-million American families.
>
> The working American lives in the gray area fringes of a central city or in a close-in or very far-out cheaper suburban subdivision of a large metropolitan area. He is likely to own a home and a car, especially as his income begins to rise. Of those earning between $6,000 and $7,500, 70 per cent own their own homes and 94 per cent drive their own cars.
>
> 94 per cent have no education beyond high school and 43 per cent have only completed the eighth grade.

He does all the right things, obeys the law, goes to church and insists—usually—that his kids get a better education than he had. But the right things don't seem to be paying off. While he is making more than he ever made—perhaps more than he'd ever dreamed—he's still struggling while a lot of others—"them" (on welfare, in demonstrations, in the ghettos) are getting most of the attention. "I'm working my ass off," a guy tells you on a stoop in South Boston. "My kid's don't have a place to swim, my parks are full of glass, and I'm supposed to bleed for a bunch of people on relief." In New York a man who drives a Post Office trailer truck at night (4:00 P.M. to midnight) and a cab during the day (7:00 A.M. to 2:00 P.M.), and who hustles radios for his Post Office buddies on the side, is ready, as he says, to "knock somebody's ass.""The colored guys work when they feel like it. Sometimes they show up and sometimes they don't. One guy tore up all the time cards. I'd like to see a white guy do that and get away with it."

What Counts

Nobody knows how many people in America moonlight (half of the eighteen million families in the $5,000 to $10,000 bracket have two or more wage earners) or how many have to hustle on the side. "I don't think anybody has a single job anymore," said Nicholas Kisburg, the research director for a Teamsters Union Council in New York. "All the cops are moonlighting, and the teachers; and there's a million guys who are hustling, guys with phony social-security numbers who are hiding part of what they make so they don't get kicked out of a housing project, or guys who work as guards at sports events and get free meals that they don't want to pay taxes on. Every one of them is cheating. They are underground people—*Untermenschen*. . . . We really have no systematic data on any of this. We have no ideas of the attitudes of the white worker. (We've been too busy studying the black worker.) And yet he's the source of most of the reaction in this country."

The reaction is directed at almost every visible target: at integration and welfare, taxes and sex education, at the rich and the poor, the foundations and students, at the "smart people in the suburbs." In New York State the legislature cuts the welfare budget; in Los Angeles, the voters reelect Yorty after a whispered racial campaign against the Negro favorite. In Minneapolis a police detective named Charles Stenvig, promising "to take the handcuffs off the police," is elected mayor by a margin stunning even to his supporters: in Massachusetts the voters mail tea bags to their representatives in protest against new taxes, and in state after state legislatures are passing bills to punish student demonstrators. ("We keep talking about permissiveness in training kids," said a Los Angeles labor official, "but we forget that these are our kids.")

And yet all these things are side manifestations of a malaise that lacks a language. Whatever law and order means, for example, to a man who feels his wife is unsafe on the street after dark or in the park at any time, or whose kids get shaken down in the school yard, it also means something like normality —the demand that everybody play it by the book, that cultural and social standards be somehow restored to their civics-book simplicity, that things shouldn't be as they are but as they were supposed to be. If there is a revolution in this country—a revolt in manners, standards of dress and obscenity, and, more importantly, in our official sense of what America is—there is also a counter-revolt. Sometimes it is inarticulate, and sometimes (perhaps most of the time) people are either too confused or apathetic—or simply too polite and too decent—to declare themselves. In Astoria, Queens, a white working-class district of New York, people who make $7,000 or $8,000 a year (sometimes in two jobs) call themselves affluent, even though the Bureau of Labor Statistics regards an income of less than $9,500 in New York inadequate to a moderate standard of living. And in a similar neighborhood in Brooklyn a truck driver who earns $151 a week tells you he's doing well, living in a two-story frame house separated by a narrow driveway from similar houses, thousands of them in block after block. This year, for the first time, he will go on a cruise—he and his wife and two other couples—two weeks in the Caribbean. He went to work after World War II ($57 a week) and he has lived in the same house for twenty years, accumulating two television sets, wall-to-wall carpeting in a small living room, and a basement that he recently remodeled into a recreation room with the help of two moonlighting firemen. "We get fairly good salaries, and this is a good neighborhood, one of the few good ones left. We have no smoked Irishmen around."

Stability is what counts, stability in job and home and neighborhood, stability in the church and in friends. At night you watch television and sometimes on a weekend you go to a nice place—maybe a downtown hotel—for dinner with another couple. (Or maybe your sister, or maybe bowling, or maybe, if you're defeated, a night at the track.) The wife has the necessary appliances, often still being paid off, and the money you save goes for your daughter's orthodontist, and later her wedding. The smoked Irishmen—the colored (no one says black; few even say Negro)—represent change and instability, kids who cause trouble in school, who get treatment that your kids never got, that you never got. ("Those fucking kids," they tell you in South Boston, "raising hell, and not one of 'em paying his own way. Their fucking mothers are all on welfare.") The black kids mean a change in the rules, a double standard in grades and discipline, and—vaguely—a challenge to all you believed right. Law and order is the stability and predictability of established ways. Law and order is equal treatment—in school, in jobs, in the courts—even if you're cheating a little yourself. The Forgotten Man is Jackson's man. He is the vestigial American democrat of 1840: "They all know that their success depends upon their own industry and economy and that they must not expect to become suddenly rich by the fruits of their toil." He is also Franklin Roosevelt's man—the man whose vote (or whose father's vote) sustained the New Deal.

There are other considerations, other styles, other problems. A postman in a Charlestown (Boston) housing project: eight children and a ninth on the way. Last year, by working overtime, his income went over $7,000. This year, because he reported it, the Housing Authority is raising his rent from $78 to $106 a month, a catastrophe for a family that pays $2.20 a day for milk, has never had a vacation, and for which an excursion is "going out for ice cream." "You try and save for something better; we hope to get out of here to someplace where the kids can play, where there's no broken glass, and then something always comes along that knocks you right back. It's like being at the bottom of the well waiting for a guy to throw you a rope." The description becomes almost Chaplinesque. Life is humble but not simple; terrors of insolent bureaucracies and contemptuous officials produce a demonology that loses little of its horror for being partly misunderstood. You want to get a sink fixed but don't want to offend the manager; want to get an eye operation that may (or may not) have been necessitated by a military injury five years earlier, "but the Veterans Administration says I signed away my benefits"; want to complain to someone about the teenagers who run around breaking windows and harassing women but get no response either from the management or the police. "You're afraid to complain because if they don't get you during the day they'll get you at night." Automobiles, windows, children, all become hostages to the vague terrors of everyday life; everything is vulnerable. Liabilities that began long ago cannot possibly be liquidated; "I never learned anything in that school except how to fight. I got tired of being caned by the teachers so at sixteen I quit and joined the Marines. I still don't know anything."

American culture? Wealth is visible, and so, now, is poverty. Both have become intimidating clichés. But the rest? A vast, complex, and disregarded world that was once—in belief, and in fact—the American middle: Greyhound and Trailways bus terminals in little cities at midnight, each of them with its neon lights and its cardboard hamburgers; acres of tarpaper beach bungalows in places like Revere and Rockaway; the hair curlers in the supermarket on Saturday, and the little girls in the communion dresses the next morning; pinball machines and the *Daily News,* the *Reader's Digest* and Ed Sullivan; houses with tiny front lawns (or even large ones) adorned with statues of the Virgin or of Sambo welcomin' de folks home; Clint Eastwood or Julie Andrews at the Palace; the trotting tracks and the dog tracks—Aurora Downs, Connaught Park, Roosevelt, Yonkers, Rockingham, and forty others—where gray men come not for sport and beauty, but to read numbers, to study the dope. (If you win you have figured something, have in a small way controlled your world, have surmounted your impotence, if you lose, bad luck, shit. "I'll break his goddamned head.") Baseball is not the national pastime; racing is. For every man who goes to a major-league baseball game there are four who go to the track and probably four more who go to the candy store or the barbershop to make their bets. (Total track attendance in 1965: 62 million plus another 10 million who went to the dogs.)

There are places, and styles, and attitudes. If there are neighborhoods of aspiration, suburban enclaves for the mobile young executives and the aspiring worker, there are also places of limited expectation and dead-end districts where mobility is finished. But even there you can often find, however vestigial, a sense of place, the roots of old ethnic loyalties, and a passionate, if often futile, battle against intrusion and change. "Everybody around here," you are told, "pays his own way." In this world the problems are not the ABM or air pollution (have they heard of Biafra?) or the international population crisis; the problem is to get your street cleaned, your garbage collected, to get your husband home from Vietnam alive; to negotiate installment payments and to keep the schools orderly. Ask anyone in Scarsdale or Winnetka about the schools and they'll tell you about new programs, or about how many are getting into Harvard, or about the teachers; ask in Oakland or the North Side of Chicago, and they'll tell you that they have (or haven't) had trouble. Somewhere in his gut the man in those communities knows that mobility and choice in this society are limited. He cannot imagine any major change for the better; but he can imagine change for the worse. And yet for a decade he is the one who has been asked to carry the burden of social reform, to integrate his schools and his neighborhood, has been asked by comfortable people to pay the social debts due to the poor and the black. In Boston, in San Francisco, in Chicago (not to mention Newark or Oakland) he has been telling the reformers to go to hell. The Jewish schoolteachers of New York and the Irish parents of Dorchester have asked the same question: "What the hell did Lindsay (or the Beacon Hill Establishment) ever do for us?"

The ambiguities and changes in American life that occupy discussions in university seminars and policy debates in Washington, and that form the backbone of contemporary popular sociology, become increasingly the conditions of trauma and frustration in the middle. Although the New Frontier and Great Society contained some programs for those not already on the rolls of social pathology—federal aid for higher education, for example—the public priorities and the rhetoric contained little. The emphasis, properly, was on the poor, on the inner cities (e.g., Negroes) and the unemployed. But in Chicago a widow with three children who earns $7,000 a year can't get them college loans because she makes too much; the money is reserved for people on relief. New schools are built in the ghetto but not in the white working-class neighborhoods where they are just as dilapidated. In Newark the head of a white vigilante group (now a city councilman) runs, among other things, on a platform opposing pro-Negro discrimination. "When pools are being built in the Central Ward—don't they think white kids have got frustration? The white can't get a job; we have to hire Negroes first." The middle class, said Congressman Roman Pucinski of Illinois, who represents a lot of it, "is in revolt. Everyone has been generous in supporting anti-poverty. Now the middle-class American is disqualified from most of the programs."

The frustrated middle. The liberal wisdom about welfare, ghettos, student revolt, and Vietnam has only a marginal place, if any, for the values and life of the working man. It flies in the face of most of what he was taught to cherish and respect; hard work, order, authority, self-reliance. He fought, either alone or through labor organizations, to establish the precincts he now considers his own. Union seniority, the civil-service bureaucracy, and the petty professionalism established by the merit system in the public schools became sinecures of particular ethnic groups or of those who have learned to negotiate and master the system. A man who worked all his life to accumulate the points and grades and paraphernalia to become an assistant school principal (no matter how silly the requirements) is not likely to relinquish his position with equanimity. Nor is a dock worker whose only estate is his longshoreman's card. The job, the points, the credits become property:

> Some men leave their sons money [wrote a union member to the *New York Times*], some large investments, some business connections, and some a profession. I have only one worthwhile thing to give: my trade. I hope to follow a centuries-old tradition and sponsor my sons for an apprenticeship. For this simple father's wish it is said that I discriminate against Negroes. Don't all of us discriminate? Which of us . . . will not choose a son over all others?

Suddenly the rules are changing—all the rules. If you protect your job for your own you may be called a bigot. At the same time it's perfectly acceptable to shout black power and to endorse it. What does it take to be a good American? *Give the black man a position because he is black, not because he necessarily works harder or does the job better.* What does it take to be a good American? Dress nicely, hold a job, be clean-cut, don't judge a man by the color of his skin or the country of his origin. What about the demands of Negroes, the long hair of the students, the dirty movies, the people who burn draft cards and American flags? Do you have to go out in the street with picket signs, do you have to burn the place down to get what you want? What does it take to be a good American? *This is a sick society, a racist society, we are fighting an immoral war.* ("I'm against the Vietnam war, too," says the truck driver in Brooklyn. "I see a good kid come home with half an arm and a leg in a brace up to here, and what's it all for? I was glad to see *my kid* flunk the Army physical. Still, somebody has to say no to these demonstrators and enforce the law.") What does it take to be a good American?

The conditions of trauma and frustration in the middle. What does it take to be a good American? Suddenly there are demands for Italian power and Polish power and Ukrainian power. In Cleveland the Poles demand a seat on the school board, and get it, and in Pittsburgh John Pankuch, the seventy-three-year-old president of the National Slovak Society, demands "action, plenty of it to make up for lost time." Black power is supposed to be nothing but emulation of the ways in which other ethnic groups made it. But have they made it? In Reardon's Bar on East Eighth Street in South Boston, where the workmen come for their fish-chowder lunch and for their rye and ginger, they still identify themselves as Galway men and Kilkenny men; in the newsstand in Astoria you can buy *Il Progresso, El Tiempo,* the *Staats-Zeitung,* the *Irish World,* plus papers in Greek, Hungarian, and Polish. At the parish of Our Lady of Mount Carmel the priests hear confession in English, Italian, and Spanish and nearby, the biggest attraction is not the stickball game, but the *bocce* court. Some of the poorest people in America are white, native, and have lived all of their lives in the same place as their fathers and grandfathers. The problems that were presumably solved in some distant past, in that prehistoric era before the textbooks were written—problems of assimilation, of upward mobility—now turn out to be very much unsolved. The melting pot and all: millions made it, millions moved to the affluent suburbs; several million—no one knows how many—did not. The median income in Irish South Boston is $5,100 a year but the community-action workers have a hard time convincing the local citizens that any white man who is not stupid or irresponsible can be poor. Pride still keeps them from applying for income supplements or Medicaid, but it does not keep them from resenting those who do. In Pittsburgh, where the members of Polish-American organizations earn an estimated $5,000 to $6,000 (and some fall below the poverty line), the Poverty Programs are nonetheless directed primarily to Negroes, and almost everywhere the thing called urban blacklash associates itself in some fashion with ethnic groups whose members have themselves only a precarious hold on the security of affluence. Almost everywhere in the old cities, tribal neighborhoods and their styles are under assault by masscult. The Italian grocery gives way to the supermarket, the ma-and-pa store and the walk-up are attacked by urban renewal. And almost everywhere, that assault tends to depersonalize and to alienate. It has always been this way, but with time the brave new world that replaces old patterns becomes increasingly bureaucratic, distant, and hard to control.

Yet beyond the problems of ethnic identity, beyond the problems of Poles and Irishmen left behind, there are others more pervasive and more dangerous.

272   BEGINNINGS

For every Greek or Hungarian there are a dozen American-Americans who are past ethnic consciousness and who are as alienated, as confused, and as angry as the rest. The obvious manifestations are the same everywhere—race, taxes, welfare, students—but the threat seems invariably more cultural and psychological than economic or social. What upset the police at the Chicago convention most was not so much the politics of the demonstrators as their manners and their hair. (The barbershops in their neighborhoods don't advertise Beatle Cuts but the Flat Top and the Chicago Box.) The affront comes from middle-class people—and their children—who had been cast in the role of social exemplars (and from those cast as unfortunates worthy of public charity) who offend all the things on which working class identity is built: "hippies [said a San Francisco longshoreman] who fart around the streets and don't work"; welfare recipients who strike and march for better treatment; "all those [said a California labor official] who challenge the precepts that these people live on." If ethnic groups are beginning to organize to get theirs, so are others: police and firemen ("The cop is the new nigger"); schoolteachers; lower-middle-class housewives fighting sex education and bussing; small property owners who have no ethnic communion but a passionate interest in lower taxes, more policemen, and stiffer penalties for criminals. In San Francisco the Teamsters, who had never been known for such interests before, recently demonstrated in support of the police and law enforcement and, on another occasion, joined a group called Mothers Support Neighborhood Schools at a school-board meeting to oppose—with their presence and later, apparently, with their fists—a proposal to integrate the schools through bussing. ("These people," someone said at the meeting, "do not look like mothers.")

Which is not to say that all is frustration and anger, that anybody is ready "to burn the country down." They are not even ready to elect standard model demagogues. "A lot of labor people who thought of voting for Wallace were ashamed of themselves when they realized what they were about to do," said Morris Iushewitz, an officer of New York's Central Labor Council. Because of a massive last-minute union campaign, and perhaps for other reasons, the blue-collar vote for Wallace fell far below the figures predicted by the early polls last fall. Any number of people, moreover, who are not doing well by any set of official statistics, who are earning well below the national mean ($8,000 a year), or who hold two jobs to stay above it, think of themselves as affluent, and often use that word. It is almost as if not to be affluent is to be un-American. People who can't use the word tend to be angry; people who come too close to those who can't become frightened. The definition of affluence is generally pinned to what comes in, not to the quality of life as it's lived. The $8,000 son of a man who never earned more than $4,500 may, for that reason alone, believe that he's "doing all right." If life is not all right, if he can't get his curbs fixed, or his streets patrolled, if the highways are crowded and the beaches polluted, if the schools are ineffectual he is still able to call himself affluent, feels, perhaps, a social compulsion to do so. His anger, if he is angry, is not that of the wage earner resenting management—and certainly not that of the socialist ideologue asking for redistribution of wealth—but that of the consumer, the taxpayer, and the family man. (Inflation and taxes are wiping out most of the wage gains made in labor contracts signed during the past three years.) Thus he will vote for a Louise Day Hicks in Boston who promises to hold the color line in the schools or for a Charles Stenvig calling for law enforcement in Minneapolis but reject a George Wallace who seems to threaten his pocketbook. The danger is that he will identify with the politics of the Birchers and other middle-class reactionaries (who often pretend to speak for him) even though his income and style of life are far removed from theirs; that taxes, for example, will be identified with welfare rather than war, and that he will blame his limited means on the small slice of the poor rather than the fat slice of the rich.

If you sit and talk to people like Marjorie Lemlow, who heads Mothers Support Neighborhood Schools in San Francisco, or Joe Owens, a house painter who is president of a community-action organization in Boston, you quickly discover that the roots of reaction and the roots of reform are often identical, and that the response to particular situations is more often contingent on the politics of the politicians and leaders who appear to care than on the conditions of life or the ideology of the victims. Mrs. Lemlow wants to return the schools to some virtuous past; she worries about disintegration of the family and she speaks vaguely about something that she can't bring herself to call a conspiracy against Americanism. She has been accused of leading a bunch of Birchers, and she sometimes talks Birch language. But whatever the form, her sense of things comes from a small-town vision of national virtues, and her unhappiness from the assaults of urban sophistication. It just so happens that a lot of reactionaries now sing that tune, and that the liberals are indifferent.

Joe Owens—probably because of his experience as a Head Start parent, and because of his association with an effective community-action program—talks a different language. He knows, somehow, that no simple past can be restored. In his world the villains are not conspirators but bureaucrats and politicians, and he is beginning to discover that in a struggle with officials the black man in the ghetto and the working man (black or white) have the same problems. "Every time you ask for something from the politicians they treat you like a beggar, like you ought to be grateful for what you have. They try to make you feel ashamed."

The imponderables are youth and tradition and change. The civics book and the institution it celebrates—however passe—still hold the world together. The revolt is in their name, not against them. And there is simple decency, the language and practice of the folksy cliché, the small town, the Boy Scout virtues, the neighborhood charity, the obligation to support the church, the rhetoric of open opportunity: "They can keep Wallace and they can keep Alabama. We didn't fight a dictator for four years so we could elect one over here." What happens when all that becomes Mickey Mouse? Is there an urban ethic to replace the values of the small town? Is there a coherent public philosophy, a consistent set of beliefs to replace family, home, and hard work? What happens when the hang-ups of upper-middle-class kids are in fashion and those of blue-collar kids are not? What happens when Doing Your Own Thing becomes not the slogan of the solitary deviant but the norm? Is it possible that as the institutions and beliefs of tradition are fashionably denigrated a blue-collar generation gap will open to the Right as well as to the Left? (There is statistical evidence, for example, that Wallace's greatest support within the unions came from people who are between twenty-one and twenty-nine, those, that is, who have the most tenuous association with the liberalism of labor.) Most are politically silent; although SDS has been trying to organize blue-collar high-school students, there are no Mario Savios or Mark Rudds—either of the Right or the Left—among them. At the same time the union leaders, some of them old hands from the Thirties, aren't sure that the kids are following them either. Who speaks for the son of the longshoreman or the Detroit auto worker? What happens if he doesn't get to college? What, indeed, happens when he does?

Vaguely but unmistakably the hopes that a youth-worshiping nation historically invested in its young are becoming threats. We have never been unequivocal about the symbolic patricide of Americanization and upward mobility, but if at one time mobility means rejection of older (or European) styles it was, at least, done in the name of America. Now the labels are blurred and the objectives indistinct. Just at the moment when a tradition-bound Italian father is persuaded that he should send his son to college—that education is the only future—the college blows up. At the moment when a parsimonious taxpayer begins to shell out for what he considers an extravagant state university system the students go on strike. Marijuana, sexual liberation, dress styles, draft resistance, even the rhetoric of change become monsters and demons in a world that appears to turn old virtues upside down. The paranoia that fastened on Communism twenty years ago (and sometimes still does) is increasingly directed to vague conspiracies undermining the schools, the family, order and discipline. "They're feeding the kids this generation-gap business," says a Chicago housewife who grinds out a campaign against sex education on a duplicating machine in her living room. "The kids are told to make their own decisions. They're all mixed up by situation ethics and open-ended questions. They're alienating children from their own parents." They? The churches, the schools, even the YMCA and the Girl Scouts, are implicated. But a major share of the villainy is now also attributed to "the social science centers," to the apostles of senstivity training, and to what one California lady, with some embarrassment, called "nude therapy." "People with sane minds are being altered by psychological methods." The current major campaign of the John Birch Society is not directed against Communists in government or the Supreme Court, but against sex education.

(There is, of course, also sympathy with the young, especially in poorer areas where kids have no place to play. "Everybody's got to have a hobby," a South Boston adolescent told a youth worker. "Ours is throwing rocks." If people will join reactionary organizations to protect their children, they will also support others: community-action agencies which help kids get jobs; Head Start parent groups, Boys Clubs. "Getting this place cleaned up" sometimes refers to a fear of young hoods; sometimes it points to the day when there is a park or a playground or when the existing park can be used. "I want to see them grow up to have a little fun.")

Beneath it all there is a more fundamental ambivalence, not only about the young, but about institutions—the schools, the churches, the Establishment— and about the future itself. In the major cities of the East (though perhaps not in the West) there is a sense that time is against you, that one is living "in one of the few decent neighborhoods left," that "if I can get $125 a week upstate (or downstate) I'll move." The institutions that were supposed to mediate social change and which, more than ever, are becoming priesthoods of information and conglomerates of social engineers, are increasingly suspect. To attack the Ford Foundation (as Wright Patman has done) is not only to fan the embers of historic populism against concentrations of wealth and power, but also to arouse those who feel that they are trapped by an alliance of upper-class Wasps and lower-class Negroes. If the foundations have done anything for the blue-collar worker he doesn't seem to be aware of it. At the same time the distrust of professional educators that characterizes the black militants is becoming increasingly prevalent among a minority of lower-middle-class whites who are beginning to discover that the schools aren't working for them either. ("Are all those new programs just a cover-up for failure?") And if the Catholic Church is under attack from its liberal members (on birth control, for example) it is also alienating the traditionalists who liked their minor saints (even if they didn't exist) and were perfectly content with the Latin Mass. For the alienated Catholic liberal there are other places to go; for the lower-middle-class parishioner in Chicago or Boston there are none.

Perhaps, in some measure, it has always been this way. Perhaps none of this is new. And perhaps it is also true that the American lower middle has never had it so good. And yet surely there is a difference, and that is that the common man has lost his visibility and, somehow, his claim on public attention. There are old liberals and socialists—men like Michael Harrington—who believe that a new alliance can be forged for progressive social action:

> From Marx to Mills, the Left has regarded the middle class as a stratum of hypocritical, vacillating rear-guarders. There was often sound reason for this contempt. But is it not possible that a new class is coming into being? It is not the old middle class of small property owners and entrepreneurs, nor the new middle class of managers. It is composed of scientists, technicians, teachers, and professionals in the public sector of the society. By education and work experience it is predisposed toward planning. It could be an ally of the poor and the organized workers—or their sophisticated enemy. In other words, an unprecedented social and political variable seems to be taking shape in America.
>
> The American worker, even when he waits on a table or holds open a door, is not servile; he does not carry himself like an inferior. The openness, frankness,

and democratic manner which Tocqueville described in the last century persists to this very day. They have been a source of rudeness, contemptuous ignorance, violence—and of a creative self-confidence among great masses of people. It was in this latter spirit that the CIO was organized and the black freedom movement marched.

There are recent indications that the white lower middle class is coming back on the roster of public priorities. Pucinski tells you that liberals in Congress are privately discussing the pressure from the middle class. There are proposals now to increase personal income-tax exemptions from $600 to $1,-000 (or $1,200) for each dependent, to protect all Americans with a national insurance system covering catastrophic medical expenses, and to put a floor under all incomes. Yet these things by themselves are insufficient. Nothing is sufficient without a national sense of restoration. What Pucinski means by the middle class has, in some measure, always been represented. A physician earning $75,000 a year is also a working man but he is hardly a victim of the welfare system. Nor, by and large, are the stockholders of the Standard Oil Company or U.S. Steel. The fact that American ideals have often been corrupted in the cause of self-aggrandizement does not make them any less important for the cause of social reform and justice." As a movement with the conviction that there is more to people than greed and fear," Harrington said, "the Left must . . . also speak in the name of the historic idealism of the United States."

The issue, finally, is not *the program* but the vision, the angle of view. A huge constituency may be coming up for grabs, and there is considerable evidence that its political mobility is more sensitive than anyone can imagine, that all the sociological determinants are not as significant as the simple facts of concern and leadership. When Robert Kennedy was killed last year [1969], thousands of working-class people who had expected to vote for him—if not hundreds of thousands—shifted their loyalties to Wallace. A man who can change from a progressive democrat into a bigot overnight deserves attention.

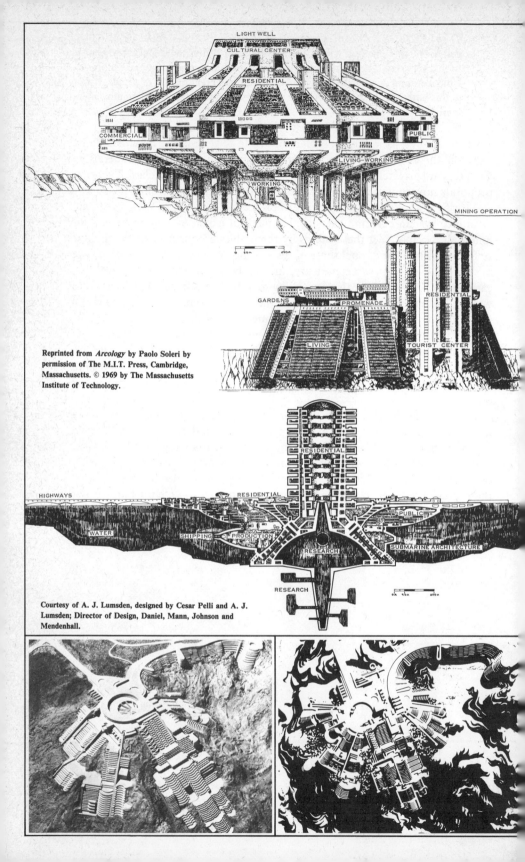

LIGHT WELL

CULTURAL CENTER

RESIDENTIAL

COMMERCIAL

PUBLIC

LIVING-WORKING

WORKING

MINING OPERATION

GARDENS

PROMENADE

RESIDENTIAL

LIVING

TOURIST CENTER

Reprinted from *Arcology* by Paolo Soleri by permission of The M.I.T. Press, Cambridge, Massachusetts. © 1969 by The Massachusetts Institute of Technology.

RESIDENTIAL

HIGHWAYS

RESIDENTIAL

PUBLIC

WATER

SHIPPING

PRODUCTION

RESEARCH

SUBMARINE ARCHITECTURE

RESEARCH

Courtesy of A. J. Lumsden, designed by Cesar Pelli and A. J. Lumsden; Director of Design, Daniel, Mann, Johnson and Mendenhall.

Beginnings: Communes and Cities

"Arthur Clarke ... foresees sweeping changes touched off by communications satellites. Cities, he thinks, may disappear. Their principal reason for being is to cluster people closer together where they can see and talk with each other, a process that is not always enjoyable. When an executive can instantly reach all his contacts, wherever they may be, by television he will have little reason for leaving home."

Time, May 14, 1965

"Cities, as we know them, are obsolete in respect to yesterday's function as a warehouse and trading post. Trying to rebuild cities to make them accommodate the new needs of World Man is like trying to reconstruct and improve a wrecked ship as it rests upon a surf-pounded reef. The great cities, like New York, Paris, London, Tokyo, will turn into universities as automation replaces the humans who function only as automatons."

R. Buckminster Fuller

"Man has evolved from such a simple open state. Modern complexity requires a corresponding degree of privacy. We can't turn back the clock; you must build an environment to reflect reality."

Paolo Soleri

26. Communes: The Alternative Life-Style

HERBERT A. OTTO*

Angelina is a tall, striking blonde in her mid-forties, with a husky voice and a motherly, forthright air about her. She had been a successful interior decorator in a well-known college town in Oregon. Following her divorce, Angelina decided to rent some of the extra bedrooms in her house to students.

"I was shocked seeing people dirty and with unwashed hair—until I got to know them better and saw their soul reflected in their eyes. They wanted country life and animals. They wanted to be creative and to be themselves. At that time, I was attending a Unitarian church. I talked to the minister about starting a commune. He said it wouldn't work."

Angelina felt she needed new ideas and viewpoints, and she went to the Esalen Institute at Big Sur, California. She stayed three months. "I could see so much, feel so much, I thought I was really called."

Upon returning to her business, which she had left in competent hands, Angelina decided to sell out and was able to do so at a favorable price. "I made up my mind I wanted the family feeling. At this point, it was like Providence when I heard about the hundred and fifty acres. The price was so reasonable, I thought there was something wrong with the place. But when I saw it—with the half-dozen springs, three streams, and the mixed timber—I knew this was the spot for a nature commune."

Angelina started the commune two-and-a-half years ago with a young couple she had met at Esalen. Today, there are thirty young people and eight children in the community. Twelve of this group are called "stable"; they have made a commitment to the commune. Median age within the commune is in the mid-twenties. Sixty-five per cent of the group are young men. There are many high school and college dropouts, but also a number of successful former businessmen and professionals, several teachers, and two engineers.

*Herbert A. Otto is chairman of the National Center for the Exploration of Human Potential, La Jolla, California. He is editor of the recently released *The Family in Search of a Future*. In researching this article, Dr. Otto visited thirty communes in various parts of the country.

This commune, with Angelina as its prime mover and guiding spirit, is just one of many such living arrangements that have mushroomed around the country. Over the past few years, the commune movement has grown at an unprecedented and explosive rate, and there is every indication that this is only the initial phase of a trend that is bound to have far-reaching implications for the function and structure of our contemporary society. Some traditional institutions are already beginning to feel the impact of this explosive growth.

The commune movement has passed far beyond its contemporary origins in hippie tribalism and can no longer be described as a movement for youth exclusively. There are a rapidly growing number of communes composed of persons in their mid-twenties to upper thirties. A source at the National Institute of Health has estimated that more than 3,000 urban communes are now in operation. This figure closely corresponds to a recent *New York Times* inquiry that uncovered 2,000 communes in thirty-four states.

Certain common viewpoints, almost a *Weltanschauung,* are shared by members of the contemporary commune movement. First, there is a deep respect and reverence for nature and the ecological system. There is a clear awareness that 70 per cent of the population lives on 1 per cent of the land and that this 1 per cent is severely polluted, depressingly ugly, and psychologically overcrowded. Commune members generally believe that a very small but influential minority with no respect for the ecological system or the beauty of nature exploits all of the land for its own gain. Surpassing the credo of conservationist organizations, most commune members stress the rehabilitation of *all* lands and the conservation of *all* natural resources for the benefit of *all* the people.

Anti-Establishment sentiment is widespread, as is the conviction that a change in social and institutional structures is needed to halt man's dehumanization and to give him an opportunity to develop his potential. Considerable divergence of opinion exists on how social change is to be brought about, but there is general agreement that the commune movement contributes to change by bringing man closer to himself and to his fellow man through love and understanding.

Communes widely accept the idea that life is meant to be fundamentally joyous and that this is of the essence in doing, and enjoying, what you want to do—"doing your thing." Work in this context becomes a form of joyous self-expression and self-realization. Many commune members believe that existence can be an almost continuous source of joyous affirmation. They usually trace the absence of authentic joy in contemporary society to the confining nature of many of our social institutions, the stifling of spontaneity, and the preponderance of game-playing and of devitalized artificial ways of relating socially.

A strong inner search for the meaning of one's own life, an openness and willingness to communicate and encounter, coupled with a compelling desire for personal growth and development, are hallmarks of the movement. A strong anti-materialistic emphasis prevails; it decries a consumption-oriented society. In many communes, what does not fit into a room becomes commune property. A considerable number of communes aim for this type of self-sufficiency through which they can exist independently of "the system."

There is a strong trend toward ownership of land and houses by communes. Leasing arrangements have not proved satisfactory; in too many instances, landlords have canceled leases when community pressures were exerted. The non-urban communes I have visited are strongly aware of ecological factors, and, because of this, members usually had consulted with local health authorities concerning the construction and placement of sanitary facilities. Among the urban communes, toilet and bath facilities were in most cases short of the demand.

Marked preferences for vegetarianism and for organically grown food are noticeable in the commune movement. Many individual members also experiment with different health diets. Roughly 40 percent of the communes I visited were vegetarian; 20 per cent served both vegetarian and non-vegetarian meals. The remainder served meat when available—usually two to six times a week. This third group, although not vegetarian by choice, liked their vegetarian meals and expressed very little craving for meat. Whenever possible, communes concentrate on growing and raising their own food. An estimated 60 per cent of the urban communes are now purchasing some or most of their supplies from health-food stores or similar sources.

Not surprisingly, the commune has become the repository of repressed man's erotic fantasy. I was continuously told that visitors who come not to learn and understand but to peek and ogle invariably ask two questions: "Who sleeps with whom?" And, "Do you have group sex?" There appears to be much fantasizing by outsiders about the sex life in communes.

Although there is considerable sexual permissiveness, I found a high degree of pairing with a strong tendency toward interpersonal commitment in a continuing relationship. Nudism is casual and accepted, as is the development of a healthy sensuality, and natural childbirth, preferably within the commune, is encouraged. Group sex involving the whole commune occurs quite rarely, although there may be sexual experimentation involving two or more couples or combinations.

The research team of Larry and Joan Constantine has studied multilateral (group) marriage for the past three years. They have written and published more studies in this area than other behavioral scientists, but have found only one commune practicing group marriage. Most likely, there are others. About two dozen independent families are known to be engaged in multilateral marriage, taking as their model Bob Rimmer's novel *Proposition 31,* which presents a case for group marriage. Many others prefer to keep their arrangement totally secret for fear of reprisals. According to an article by the Constantines, entitled "Personal Growth in Multiple Marriages," failure rate is better than one out of two, because "group marriage is a marathon that does not end —it takes a real commitment to genuine, substantial, and unrelenting personal growth to really make it function and work."

Interest in spiritual development is a dominant theme in most communes. Study of and acquaintance with Eastern and Western mystics and religious philosophies is widespread. Religiosity and denominationalism were seldom encountered. On the other hand, I was struck by the deep commitment to spiritual search of so many members in all the communes I visited. Many members were trying different forms of meditation, and books on Eastern religions and mysticism were prominent on shelves.

I find that although there is some overlapping of functions and categories, a member of distinct types of communes can be recognized and are found in operation.

• The Agricultural Subsistence Commune: The main thrust is to farm or till the soil (mostly organic farming) so that the land will provide most, if not all, needs and make the commune independent and self-supporting. Many of these communes cultivate such specialized crops as organically grown grain, vegetables, and other produce, which are then sold to health-food stores, health-food wholesalers, or supermarkets.

• The Nature Commune: Emphasis is on supporting the ecological system and on the enjoyment of nature. Buildings and gardening or farming plots are designed to fit into the landscape to preserve its natural beauty. Everyone "does his own thing," and economic support for subsistence usually comes from such varied sources as sale of produce and handicrafts, wages from part-time work, welfare support, etc.

• The Craft Commune: One or several crafts, such as weaving, pottery making, or carpentry (including construction or work on buildings outside the commune), occupy the interest of members. They often spend considerable blocks of time enjoying the exercise of their craft with the income contributed to the commune. Many of the craft communes sell directly to the consumer as a result of local, regional, or sometimes national advertisements and publicity. Profit margins vary since the vast majority of such communes do not subscribe to the amassing of profits as the primary aim of their enterprise. Included in this category are the multimedia communes that specialize in light shows, video tape, and filmmaking.

• The Spiritual/Mystical Commune: The ongoing spiritual development of members is recognized to be of primary importance. There may be adherence to a religious system, such as Buddhism, Sufism, or Zen, and a teacher or guru may be involved. Studies of various texts and mystical works, use of rituals, a number of forms of meditation (such as transcendental or Zen meditation), and spontaneous spiritual celebrations play key roles in the life of the commune. Several of these communes also describe themselves as Christian and have a strong spiritual, but not denominational, emphasis.

• The Denominational Commune: There is a religious emphasis with membership restricted to those of a particular denomination. Examples are the Episcopalian Order of St. Michael, in Crown Point, Indiana, and the Catholic Worker Farm, in Tivoli, New York.

• The Church-sponsored Commune: Such a commune may be originated or sponsored by a church. There is usually a religious emphasis, but denominationalism is not stressed.

• The Political Commune: Members subscribe to or share a common ideology. They may identify themselves as anarchists, socialists, pacifists, etc. Emphasis is on the communal living experience with others sharing the same viewpoint. This is seen as fostering the individuals' political development. The commune is rarely engaged in direct social action in opposition to the Establishment.

• The Political Action Commune: Members are committed and practicing political activists (or activists-in-training) for the purpose of changing the social system. Classes are conducted, strategy formulated and carried out. The commune may be identified with a minority cause or be interested in organizing an industry, community, or ghetto neighborhood. It often identifies itself by the single word "revolutionary."

• The Service Commune: The main goal is social service. Emphasis is on organizing communities, helping people to plan and carry out community projects, offering professional or case-aide services, etc. Some of these communes include members from the helping professions. There are several such communes in the Philadelphia and New York ghettos; another example is the Federation of Communities, which services several locations in the Appalachians.

• The Art Commune: Artists from different fields or the same field come together to share in the stimulating climate of communal artistic creativity. As compared with the craft commune, members of the art commune are often painters, sculptors, or poets, who usually sell their art works independently rather than collectively. There are poetry and street theater communes in Berkeley and San Francisco.

• The Teaching Commune: Emphasis is on training and developing people who are able both to live and to teach others according to a particular system of techniques and methods. Communes whose purpose or mainstay is to conduct a school or schools also fall into this category.

• The Group Marriage Commune: Although members may be given the freedom to join in the group marriage or not, the practice of group marriage plays an important and often central role in the life of the commune. All adults are considered to be parents of the members' children.

• The Homosexual Commune: Currently found in large urban areas, with admissions restricted to homophiles. The aim of these communes is to afford individuals who share a common way of life an opportunity to live and communicate together and to benefit from the economies of a communal living arrangement. Some of the communes subscribe to the principles of the homophile liberation movement. From a recent ad in *Kaliflower,* the bi-weekly information journal for communes in the San Francisco Bay Area: "OUR GAY COMMUNE HAS ROOM FOR TWO MORE. CALL AND RAP."

•The Growth-centered Commune: The main focus is on helping members to grow as persons, to actualize their potential. There are ongoing group sessions; sometimes professionals are asked to lead these. The commune continues to seek out new experiences and methods designed to develop the potentialities of its members.

• The Mobile, or Gypsy, Commune: This is a caravan, usually on the move. Cars, buses, and trucks provide both transportation and living quarters. Members usually include artists, a rock group, or a light-show staff. The mobile commune often obtains contributions from "happenings" or performances given in communities or on college campuses.

• The Street, or Neighborhood, Commune: Several of these communes often are on the same street or in the same neighborhood. Ownership of property is in the hands of commune members or friendly and sympathetic neighbors. Basically the idea is of a free enclave or free community. For example, in a recent *New York Times* article, Albert Solnit, chief of advance planning for California's Marin County, was reported at work "on a city of 20,000 for those who wish to live communally." Several neighborhood or city communes are in the planning stage, but none to my knowledge has as yet been established.

Among the major problems faced by all communes are those involving authority and structure. Ideally, there is no one telling anyone else what to do; directions are given by those best qualified to do a job. In practice, strong personalities in the communes assume responsibility for what happens, and there is a tendency toward the emergence of mother and father figures. There are, however, a clear awareness of this problem and continuing efforts toward resolution. At present, opposition to any form of structure, including organizational structure, is still so strong that communes have found it almost impossible to cooperate with each other in joint undertakings of a major nature. Interestingly enough, communes with transcendent or spiritual values are the most stable and have the highest survival quotient. It is my conclusion that the weekly or periodic meetings of all commune members, which are often run as encounter groups, have a limited effectiveness in the resolution of interpersonal problems and issues. Although trained encounter leaders may be present as facilitators, their effectiveness is often considerably curtailed due to their own deep involvement in the issues that are the subject of confrontation. One answer to this dilemma might be to bring in a trained facilitator or for communes to exchange facilitators.

It is difficult to determine to what extent narcotics represent a problem for communes precisely because their consumption is as casual, widespread, and accepted as is the downing of alcoholic beverages in the business community.

Marijuana and hashish are widely enjoyed, while use of such hard drugs as heroin is seldom encountered, especially in the non-urban communes. In a number of communes where drug use was extensive, I noticed a general air of lassitude and a lack of vitality. I also had the distinct impression that "dropping acid" (LSD) was on the decline; among commune members there seemed to be a general awareness of the danger of "speed," or methedrine. A number of communes are totally opposed to the use of narcotics, especially those with members who were former drug addicts. In most communes the subject of drugs periodically comes up for discussion so that changes in the viewpoint of the commune flow from the experience of the members. Similarly, problems of sexual possessiveness and jealousy appear to be less critical and are also handled by open group discussion. I noticed a tendency toward the maintenance of traditional sex roles, with the women doing the cooking and sewing, the men cutting lumber, etc. Upon questioning this, I repeatedly received the same answer: "Everyone does what they enjoy doing."

Another major problem in most communes is overcrowding and the consequent lack of privacy and alone-time. Rarely does a member enjoy the opportunity of having a room to himself for any length of time. The common practice is to walk off into the woods or fields, but this is an inadequate substitute for real privacy.

Community relations remains a major and critical problem since many communes are "hassled" by authorities or are located amid unfriendly neighbors. As one member described it, the emotional climate in a hassled commune is "full of not so good vibes—you don't know what they will try next, and you keep looking over your shoulder. That takes energy." Today's commune members generally have a clear awareness of the importance of establishing good community relations.

Many of the communes that have got under way this past year or are now being organized are beginning on a sound financial basis. This trend appears to be related to the strong influx of people in their mid-twenties, early or mid-thirties, and beyond. These individuals have financial reserves or savings and are, for the most part, successful professionals and businessmen with families.

One example is the Morehouse Commune, which now consists of thirteen houses in the San Francisco Bay Area, two in Hawaii, and another in Los Angeles; total assets are in excess of $2-million. Morehouse was founded a year and half ago by Victor Baranco, a former attorney who is now head of the Institute of Human Abilities, in Oakland, California. There are several categories of membership or involvement in this commune. Members who belong to "the family" give all their assets to the commune, which then "takes care of them," although family members are expected to continue to make a productive contribution within their chosen fields. All income from family members goes into a general fund, but if a family member wishes to withdraw, his assets are returned, including a standard rate of interest for their having been used. Each Morehouse commune in effect makes its own arrangements with members, who may be paid a salary or placed on an allowance system. All communes have a house manager, who assigns tasks or work on a rotating basis. In some Morehouse communes, certain categories of members pay in a fixed monthly sum (as much as $200) toward expenses.

About a third of the Morehouse couples are married and have children. According to one member, "There is no pressure to be married or unmarried. Nobody cares who lives with whom." Morehouse is a teaching commune built around a philosophy and way of life often described by group members as "responsible hedonism." The commune trains its own teachers and offers a considerable number of courses, such as Basic Sensuality, Advanced Sensuality, and Basic Communication.

The aim and credo of this group are taken from a description of the Institute of Human Abilities published in the commune journal *Aquarius:* "We offer the tools of deliberate living; we offer the techniques of successful communication on any level. We offer the knowledge of the human body and its sensual potential. And we offer love to a world that holds love to be suspect."

The rapid growth of the Morehouse communes is by no means an isolated example. A minister in Los Angeles founded a social-service and action-type commune that within a year grew to seven houses. Other instances can be cited. An unprecedented number of people want to join communes. In all but a few instances I was asked to conceal the name and location of the commune to make identification impossible. "We don't know what to do with all the people who come knocking on our door now," I was told repeatedly. In every commune, I heard of people who had recently left either to start a new commune or to join in the founding of one.

There is considerable mobility in communes, which is symptomatic of an endemic wanderlust and search. If people have to leave for any reason, once they have been exposed to communal living, they tend to return. They like the deep involvement with others in a climate of freedom, openness, and commitment. This feeling of belonging has been described as both "a new tribalism" and "a new sense of brotherhood." One young woman with whom I spoke had this to say about her commune experience: "When a white man walks into a room full of other whites, he doesn't feel he is among brothers like the black man does. In the communes, we are now beginning to feel that man has many brothers. . . . There is a new sense of honesty. You can say things to each other and share things like you never could in the family. I never had so much love in my whole life—not even in my own family." She also indicated, however, that commune living is highly intense and possibly not for everyone: "In the commune, there is nothing you can hide. Some people can't take it. They get sick or they leave."

Alvin Toffler in his recent book *Future Shock* notes that "most of today's 'intentional communities' reveal a powerful preference for the past, . . . but society as a whole would be better served by utopian experiments based on super- rather than pre-industrial forms. . . . In short, we can use utopianism as a tool rather than as an escape, if we base our experiments on the technology and society of tomorrow rather than of the past."

Although Toffler's observation is relevant, we must recognize that the commune movement, as with most other movements, is passing through certain developmental stages. At this stage, there is little readiness for communes to define themselves as laboratories for the exploration of alternative models that might benefit the society of the future. Disenchantment with and opposition to science and technology are other impediments to the adoption of the laboratory concept. With today's communes, faith in the future of mankind appears to be at too low an ebb to produce any sustained interest in what Toffler calls "scientific future-sensing and the techniques of scientific futurism."

Although David Cooper, a colleague and disciple of British psychiatrist Ronald Laing, has sounded a death knell in his new book *The Death of the Family,* I believe we are far from writing the epitaph. The traditional nuclear family will continue, although its form, to some extent, may change; in the years to come, possibly as high as 20 per cent of the population will explore alternative models of social living.

It would be a mistake to characterize the commune movement as a collection of dropouts who are content to exist like lilies in the field. A considerable number of successful people from all walks of life are now involved; they have merely shifted their sphere of interest and the nature of their creative contribution. We are dealing with a massive awakening of the awareness that life holds multiple options other than going from school to job to retirement. The commune movement has opened a new and wide range of alternative life-styles and offers another frontier to those who have the courage for adventure. It is the test tube for the growth of a new type of social relatedness, for the development of an organization having a structure that appears, disappears, and reappears as it chooses and as it is needed. Communes may well serve as a laboratory for the study of the processes involved in the regeneration of our social institutions. They have become the symbol of man's new freedom to explore alternative life-styles and to develop deep and fulfilling human relationships through the rebirth and extension of our capacity for familial togetherness.

"Where are the parents of these kids? Many of them come from well-to-do homes. Why am I so alone in this?"

The nature commune that Angelina started two years ago has a reputation as one of the oldest and best run among the eight communes located within a twenty-five-mile radius of a small town in southern Oregon. This is a hilly farm and lumber region where in winter it sometimes rains for weeks on end, after which the appearance of the sun is greeted with festivity.

I had arranged to first meet Angelina at a local coffee shop one afternoon. She was wearing a colorful dress, which, she explained, she had designed and sewn herself. She also explained that the couple she had met at Esalen and with whom she had founded the commune had since left. And that among the thirty-eight members presently living in the commune there are five individuals with exceptional skills as plumbers, mechanics, electricians, and carpenters. A stonemason is also in residence. Financial support of the commune derives from a number of sources, including member contributions, with Angelina—as owner of the property—playing a major role. Of the dozen members considered "stable," Angelina also explained: "They all have to split every once in a while, but they feel it's their home." We talked for about an hour over coffee, and then Angelina invited me to come to the commune for supper.

Located fifteen miles from town on a blacktop road, the commune is flanked by well-kept small farms. An elaborately carved and painted sign close to the road announces "The Good Earth Commune." Immediately behind the sign is an improvised parking field. It was filled with about two dozen cars and trucks and a bus, which obviously served as living quarters. Some of the cars had thick layers of dust and either were abandoned or had not been used for a long time. As we drove past, five boys and two girls, all deeply suntanned, were gathered around a pickup truck and were talking leisurely while watching two of their number work on the motor. They seemed like high school or college kids on a summer vacation.

Over a slight rise, hidden from the road and surrounded by old oak trees, stands the barn. This was the only building on the property when Angelina bought it and it now serves as the main gathering place of the commune. The interior of the barn has been rebuilt and there is a large kitchen with a long, well-scrubbed wooden table; this area also serves as the dining room. Next to this room is a communal quarter, with an improvised fireplace in the center of the dirt floor and barrels and pieces of logs or wooden blocks to sit on. Further construction is under way, but a well-stocked library can be reached by climbing a ladder. In the middle of the library's floor squats an old-fashioned woodburning iron stove. There are pillows scattered around to sit on and a few old easy chairs that show signs of having been repaired with care.

Hal, who is one of the four left from the original group of fifteen that started the commune with Angelina, volunteered to act as guide. He is a slender, blond-haired man in his middle or upper twenties; he was dressed in clean, faded bluejeans, sandals, and a multi-hued shirt he had dyed himself. He was also wearing an ankh suspended from a deceptively crude-looking, handmade brass chain around his neck. A dropout from a social science doctoral program at Yale, Hal has a habit of carefully forming his sentences. While dusk drew near, we walked together along paths through the wooded hillsides. More than a dozen single-room buildings had been so neatly fitted into the landscape that they are hard to distinguish from their surroundings. Each is different and has been constructed by the people who live in it from materials found on the land—old lumber and odds and ends. Some are built into the hillside and overlook the valley, and each structure is totally isolated, with no other neighbor visible. Only the sounds of birds could be heard; it was very peaceful.

Hal and I looked into several houses whose owners were away on trips. Most of these houses had one room dominated by a fireplace or an iron stove. There were mattresses on the floor, and chairs for the most part were improvised from lumber or were hand-hewn from logs. Navajo rugs and colorful madras cloth and prints from India provided decorative touches. Everything appeared neat and clean, and I was reminded of the outdoor shower and washing facilities near the barn, which we had investigated earlier and which had been shown with much pride.

On a different path back to the barn, we passed a tepee and a tent. A good-sized, intensively cultivated garden grows next to the barn; it furnishes the commune with most of the vegetables needed. Two nude girls with beautiful uniform tans were busy weeding. Hal explained that those who want to, go nude whenever they feel like it. As we passed the garden, we noticed Angelina walking along another path trying to join us. Although we slowed our pace so she could catch up with us, she had difficulty doing so, because out of nowhere would appear members who engaged her in intense conversations.

As we strolled on, I noticed several other people hovering in the background waiting. I asked Hal if Angelina functioned as guru or leader and if she were directing the course of the commune. He was emphatic—as were several others to whom I put the same question later—that Angelina is not in charge: "We all decide what we want to do."

Earlier, both Angelina and two of the other older members of the commune had made almost identical remarks: "We have lots of ideas and very little energy." Hal felt the reason was: "There is a lot of grass around and people drop acid." Although he did add, philosophically, "Everybody is into his own thing—each person is free to follow his own needs and interests. No one is forced to do anything. Everyone knows what needs to be done, and finally it gets done."

The commune has meetings once a week "to discuss everything that bothers us." There are seldom any major problems. Hal felt that the commune's only significant problem was the lack of energy. Other neighboring communes have functional disputes, hostile neighbors, suffer from lack of food and shelter, or are unable to pay their taxes. The Good Earth Commune's relations with neighbors are friendly. As Angelina had put it at the coffee shop, "We live a very honest life." She had related a story of how one of the commune members had stolen a pump from a lumber company. This was discussed at one of the weekly meetings, and although the commune has definite strong feelings about lumber companies, the pump was returned.

During the weekly meetings, the group discusses what projects have priority; those members who want to, then volunteer for a particular project. To feed the commune, there is a kitchen list. Two members are chosen daily to provide the food and help prepare it. Farmers bring fruits and vegetables, which they barter for home-baked bread.

Eventually, Angelina caught up with us and led the way to her house. The second largest building on the grounds, it is almost circular in shape; members of the commune built it for her of field stones, hand-hewn timber, and used lumber. The large bedroom in the two-room dwelling has a fireplace and a double bed; placed here and there are many healthy-looking green plants in pots and on stands. An antique desk, a chest of drawers, a candelabra, and antique paintings and prints add richness to the room. The combination kitchen-living room was filled with young people reading, talking quietly, or playing the guitar and singing. Here also is the only phone in the commune. A young blonde girl was talking to her father. I could overhear snatches of her conversation: "No, Dad, I don't need any money. Just send me the plane ticket to Santa Barbara and I'll see you there at the house." Later, Angelina casually mentioned that the seventeen-year-old daughter of a two-star general is at the commune with the consent of her father. (She was not the girl using the telephone.)

The clanging of an old school bell called us to the barn for supper. Everyone formed a huge circle around the dinner table on which candles and kerosene lamps flickered. The room slowly grew quiet as the children scampered to their places in the circle. We all held hands. There was a long moment of silent communion, with heads bowed and eyes closed. The only sound was a dog barking in the distance. With no word spoken, the circle was broken. Conversation resumed, and we served ourselves buffet-style. The vegetarian meal consisted of a pea soup spiced with garden herbs; a combination entree of brown rice with onions, green peppers, and squash; a mixed green salad; freshly baked bread; and, for desert, bran muffins with nuts and dried fruit. Following supper, a fire was lighted in the large unfinished room next door and there was chanting, singing, and dancing.

As the evening progressed, Angelina told me that she would like to meet a warm, loving, sensitive type of man, maybe a minister—someone who knows how to counsel and work with young people. She said, "I haven't had a vacation for two years. I want to live in my house and get uninvolved. I want to travel. Older people point their finger at the commune instead of helping. I want some people with money to get involved. Where are the parents of these kids? Many of them come from well-to-do homes. Why am I so alone in this?"

As I prepared to leave, a phone call came from another commune asking for advice. Going out the door, I could hear Angelina's husky voice as she offered sympathy and suggestions. She was obviously very much involved and perhaps not really as alone as she thought.

"Triton City: A Prototype Floating Community" by Buckminster Fuller. A paper prepared for The President's Task Force on Suburban Problems.

27. Triton City: A Prototype Floating Community

BUCKMINSTER FULLER

Suppose you could choose from all possible alternatives exactly where you wanted to live? Where would that be? In one of the new, luxurious, downtown high-rise apartment buildings? In one of the fashionable suburbs, exurbs, or new towns? Or in a renovated town house in a rediscovered center-city residential neighborhood?

Many of the fortunate who can afford freedom of choice and who have tried one or two of these possibilities are turning to yet another, one which combines the advantages of urban and suburban living, but without most of the drawbacks of each. This is waterfront living in the central city.

Over 80 percent of our major metropolitan areas—those with a metropolitan population of more than one million persons—are situated on or near large bodies of water: the two oceans, the Great Lakes, or continental rivers. This is not surprising since they grew at a time when waterborne shipping and transportation were essential to the success of new settlements. The potential for waterside development then exists in a variety of American cities: the very large ones like Boston, Chicago, Cleveland, Detroit, Los Angeles, New Orleans, New York, Philadelphia, and any number of smaller cities which border on water.

Today, partly in conjunction with the general concern with urban renewal, but also as a function of heightened interest in water sites, a number of major cities have begun large-scale programs to redevelop their hitherto badly neglected waterfronts. Most notable for this planning are the eastern seaboard cities of Baltimore, Boston, New York, and Philadelphia. What has occurred in connection with this trend is a rebirth of interest in land on and near the shoreline. Outmoded unused wharfs, piers, and docks are being reclaimed for use as commercial and recreational sites; warehouses are being converted to luxury apartments. In some cities the most promising area is just that waterfront which a few years ago had been one of the worst problems, and waterside residence is becoming as prestigious as suburban estate housing. Just as the garden suburb was the prevalent notion of the post-war years, the idea of the waterfront community may well be the focal point for the 1970's and 1980's.

But, however desirable they are for cities and for the people who live in them, waterfront communities will not develop spontaneously. The existing supply of urban waterfront properties is severely limited, the structures very old, and renovation and remodeling extremely expensive; consequently, rents are prohibitively high. As a result, people with lower and middle incomes are left with only two choices: stay in the city under unpleasant conditions of dirt, overcrowding, and dilapidation or move out and incur a daily round of commuting ranging anywhere from one to three hours.

It is in this context that investigation is being made of the technical and economic feasibility of developing the water areas of major cities by floating entirely new communities on the water adjacent to the urban core. Since most of our metropolitan areas grew up around port facilities, they possess the necessary deep and sheltered water close to shore. In most cases, the available water depth is sufficient to float an average load of twenty stories above the water surface. This means that if some sections of the floating structures were lower than twenty stories, others could be still higher.

Findings of this study indicate that it is definitively possible and practicable to provide waterfront living for large numbers of city dwellers on floating communities at the shores of our major cities. What does this mean to the average metropolitan area resident? It means that he could have an attractive, reasonably priced apartment which is not only close to the heart of the city but also offers the glamorous view, the open vista, the light, sun, and cool, fresh breezes of the waterfront. It means that he could combine the healthy and unfettered feeling of living in the suburbs with the conveniences of, and rapid access to, the downtown area. It means that he could save hours of commuting time and, better yet, could have immediately available recreational and cultural facilities to serve his increased leisure.

Certainly the concept is an exciting one. How can it be translated into reality? Actually, the technology necessary to build a floating city is already in existence. We have been building super liners for many years that accommodate populations of the size of entire towns (The S. S. *United States*, for example, carries 3000 persons, including crew and passengers). Super tankers are now being constructed which weigh over 200,000 tons dead weight (The 5000 person neighborhoods will weigh 150,000 tons). Floating platforms for oil derricks and oceanographic experiments have long been in successful operation—some in conditions of unprotected water which do not trouble our city sites. The individual techniques are there and have proven themselves. It is in the combination of these methods that the essence of the technological breakthrough lies. This alliance of technologies will yield lower construction costs as well as the economies derived from large-scale implementation and a systematic approach to the entire service network of the community.

The basic unit of Triton City is a neighborhood sized community which will accommodate 3500 to 6500 people. This unit, averaging 5000 residents, is the size required to support an elementary school, a small supermarket, and local convenience stores and services. There are two kinds of neighborhood modules designed for the city. One is composed of a string of four to six small platforms, each holding about 1000 people; the other is a larger, triangular-shaped platform which will be of higher density and have capacity for as many as 6500. Three to six of these neighborhoods, with a population of 15,000 to 30,000, will form a town. At this point, an additional platform including a high school, more commercial, recreational and civic facilities, and possibly some light industry, will be added.

Given this system of aggregation of separate modules, flexible arrangements of total communities up to 100,000 persons can either grow gradually, starting with a cluster of two or three neighborhoods, or be built up with great rapidity. When the community has reached the level of three to seven towns (90,000 to 125,000 population), it becomes a full-scale city and incorporates a city center module containing governmental offices, medical facilities, a shopping center, and some form of special city-based activity like a community college or specialized industry.

Should the requirements alter after the city has been established, units can be added to or subtracted from the total as change or growth may dictate, and not cause disruption of the entire fabric. Cities interested in the Triton City adjunct, but unsure of how well it will work for their particular problems, can develop the facilities incrementally, without having to make a greater expenditure than is actually warranted at any given point in time. Additionally, the modular concept of physical organization will allow each city to develop its own floating configurations in accord with its individual needs and the dimensions of its water basin (e.g., in one case, the floating city might be a line of platforms stretched along the shoreline of the city, while in another, the configuration could be a tight cluster which comes close to the shore at only one or two places).

One of the important attributes of Triton City is that it offers "the best of two worlds": the dynamic quality of life in a milieu of urban high density and the immediately adjacent open space which is traditionally the province of suburban and rural areas. It has been observed that a minimum of two hundred dwelling units to the acre are required for a healthy, energized urban neighborhood. The proposed density for the floating communities is approximately three hundred dwelling units per acre. This is about the same as Brooklyn's Brooklyn Heights and Boston's North End, both urban neighborhoods of recognized vitality and cohesiveness. It has also been demonstrated that very high densities are tolerable in proportion to the amount of adjunct open space and support facilities; and the floating platforms are, of course, surrounded by open space—water for boating, swimming, and other recreation—and floating playfields and parks fitted in between neighborhood modules. Also, since the community is intended as a city complement, it will have all the existing urban amenities, including entertainment and educational and cultural activities, to draw upon as well.

The high density of population will economically support swift, efficient public mass transportation between the community and the city core. While there is automobile access to and from the floating platforms and parking for residents' cars, it is anticipated that movement from platform to platform (i.e., from one neighborhood to another) would be a walkable distance or accomplished by public transit. In order to discourage automobile congestion in the floating city, there will be little provision for transient parking. All wheeled vehicles will be restricted to a single level in the city complex, which is segregated from pedestrian areas. At this level will be truck loading and unloading facilities, transit stations, and ramp access to parking garages. It is probable that the transit system will be rubber tired and will circulate on the same roadbed as automobiles, buses and trucks. However, possible use of a system such as the Westinghouse sky bus is being considered.

Because the megastructure constitutes a neighborhood entity, some new departures in aesthetics and safety can be realized. All parking is underground, so that one major contemporary eyesore, the parking lot, is removed from view. Since wheeled vehicles are not permitted above the entrance level, the streets will be safe for pedestrians. Every neighborhood child can walk to school—and in no danger of being run over. As another precaution, the elevators and stairs, which are housed in vertical towers, will have glazed sides, so that everyone inside is visible at all times. The installation of vertical circulation facilities in three centrally located towers also means that they can be surveyed from one vantage point and that they will be intensively used, thus dually insuring the safety of residents. Moreover, there are no dangerous alleyways and no hidden access to any dwelling, as all doors are directly on the streets, which are side, straight, and easily patrolled.

The dwelling units all have frontage directly on the water, and the exterior faces slope slightly backward so that apartments on the higher levels look on the garden terraces of those below rather than clifflike, straight down to the water. Apartments on the upper levels give magnificent views while those on the lower levels offer an equally fascinating closeness to the water.

The front doors of the dwelling units open onto broad (about 18 feet wide) "streets in the air" that are solely for pedestrian use and very much resemble the promenade decks of ocean liners. These streets are connected by bridges to the schools, shops, and other community facilities, which are in the interior portion of the megastructure. At the higher levels, the apartment units surround and enclose the village square, a public space open to the sky. The many roof levels of the structure are terraced and landscaped for various kinds of recreation. Some contain tennis courts; others provide nursery or play areas; still others are small parks for walking, sitting or reading.

This arrangement of residential, institutional, commercial, and recreational facilities creates a new kind of townscape. In contrast to the ordinary concept of the town as horizontally developed, Triton City operates on the basis of both horizontal and vertical correspondences and accesses. High-rise apartments and office buildings demonstrate the principle of vertical organization; but there, of course, only one or two uses are involved, and all others remain on the horizontal plane. The Triton City megastructure organizes residential and commercial space vertically, but the commonly ground-oriented community facilities and services are available on all levels.

This volumetric organization of city functions allows for other human amenities beyond the operational requirements. Since there is no separation, either horizontally or vertically, of diverse facilities, a wealth of spatial variations can naturally be achieved within the megastructure. It is this constantly shifting pattern of use and the concomitant interplay of spaces which makes the most successful parts of our existing cities so exciting, for not only is the diversity interesting, but it also keeps the scale of activity appropriate to the human being. Thus, the community areas of Triton City, the interiors which are designed for human passage and leisure, will be engaging and will tend to encourage people to pass through, to stop and linger, and to participate in the activities.

Because the environment is inviting spatially, functionally, and in terms of safety, people can experience the pleasure of walking in urban spaces which is now limited to so few areas, such as Beacon Hill in Boston. Nor need this enjoyment be restricted to the inside of the community. Since they will be so close to the mainland, residents and visitors can walk to and from their floating city. This is one of the most attractive aspects of urban living to many of the people who choose to reside in the hearts of our major cities. And to be able to walk not only to and from work, but also to beaches, boating, and other leisure recreation increases the desirability of the floating city by yet another order of magnitude.

The siting of the city on water gives a unique opportunity for circumventing some of the constraints which currently limit full use by the construction industry of the potential of production technology. With the sea as highway, an entire neighborhood unit can be built in another location—such as a shipyard or dry dock—and then towed to its site in one piece. By employing a large, existing construction facility of this kind, the economies of shop fabrication can be brought to bear on the construction problems which are traditionally soluble only at the final site location—a process which is always more expensive.

Both structurally and organizationally, it is most sensible to provide relatively small (in terms of city sizes), discrete platforms—roughly the size, though not necessarily the same proportions, of large liners and tankers. Such platforms will be up to four acres in area and house as many as 5000 people. In this way, the structural elements are kept to sizes which can be reasonably handled by existing shipyard facilities, and movement of the platforms into place is easily accomplished. Larger town and city complexes can then be made by linking these platforms at the final location.

Maximum structural efficiency will also be effected by considering the platform and its superstructures—those portions of the buildings rising above the platform—as a complete framework (or in technical terminology, a megastructure). At the same time that this offers the best structural solution, it also makes possible the most flexible distribution of spatial uses: the requirements for large, open spaces are met, and needs for smaller spaces can be readily accommodated by light weight structures filling in the larger ones. The infilling components (apartments, classrooms, stores, offices) are factory produced as complete, finished units before they are fitted within the frame. This prefabrication of elements is a means of approaching the efficiency of the automobile industry in assembly line production and of achieving similar economies. Additionally, it will be possible to make subsequent changes by removing outmoded units and replacing them with new ones without disturbing the overall disposition of the city.

A whole neighborhood can be treated as a single building functionally and all mechanical services, including water, sewerage and waste, power, and heating and air conditioning, centrally provided. This has two advantages, the first that no duplication of costly central plant equipment for individual units is required, and the second that distribution of services is much more efficient. Also, as density of use gets higher, efficiency increases, so that the cost per person for services and utilities goes down. Use of the interior zone of the megastructure allows for a much more closely controlled environment than would be feasible in a usual sort of development—for temperature and humidity as well as for access and circulation. Moreover, the economies of centralized services mean that air conditioning of private dwellings, automatic trash and garbage disposal, and adequate lighting of corridors, streets, and other public areas are simple inclusions. (These are frequently not found, even in "luxury" apartments and developments, except as costly extras!)

Steel or concrete for building floating platforms is presently available at competitive prices and has been adequately tested to assure economy and safety. There are examples of concrete boats which have been in service for over forty years with no signs of weakening, leakage, or undue corrosion or fouling to the hull. In addition to ordinary and special steel alloys for the hulls, newer protective coatings for steel have proven durable in water applications.

Just as the depth of draft and "attitude" in the water are controlled in ships and submarines, floating platforms can be stabilized by pumping water or air through the flotation to compensate for changes in loading and for wind and wave effects. The platform can be made stable enough so that no more movement would be experienced than on an ocean liner in harbor.

Accurate cost comparisons of floating communities to orthodox developments on land are difficult to make because it is almost impossible to obtain any single complete, consistent, and accurate set of cost figures for existing communities and developments. Cost analyses for such developments are never done on the basis of total implementation, so that available figures are usually incomplete, inconclusive, and sometimes misleading. However, initial estimates indicate that the per person costs for the floating communities are less than the per person expense for conventional developments (considerably less when the extra amenities of the floating platform solution are added to the costs of usual suburban type developments) and comparable urban renewal projects in large cities.

But perhaps the most significant advantages of Triton City lie within the social context of the possibilities it can offer. Because of the economies inherent in the planning and construction of the community, the costs can be low enough for anybody to have the chance to live on the water. For the first time in our society, the pleasures of waterside living would be open to everyone and not just to the rich or "privileged" classes. Moreover, the standards of living would be higher than they are in almost all other kinds of residential development, with generous spatial allotments, convenient access, and clean, fresh, conditioned air circulated throughout all the living spaces. And importantly, the public areas, with adequate lighting and intensive use, would be far safer than our downtown streets at night (crime rates having been shown to be related directly to darkness and the absence of people on the streets). Since it is so close to the existing city and will economically support a rapid transit system, the community can enjoy both the benefits of urban living and access (five or ten minutes to the downtown area) and also the pleasant qualities of a seaside vacation home, with its fresh salt air, swimming, boating, etc. There is even the opportunity for marinas to be included in each neighborhood; both as private docks and as public marinas for rental of boats to visitors or permanent residents.

The idea of living in a spacious, clean apartment right on the water, yet immediately convenient to shops and schools, within minutes of downtown and at reasonable cost, is unquestionably an attractive one. There are a great many people who would be interested in this kind of opportunity for its own sake. Others, who ordinarily would wish to live in the suburbs for proximity to recreation and open space, could enjoy these and the added benefit of being close to place of employment, with a resultant increase in leisure time brought about by elimination of commutation between suburb and city. Those who already live in the city, and certainly those who govern it, will welcome the introduction of new, dynamic, effective means of urban revitalization.

28. In the Image of Man

DAVID BUTLER

The students clustered around Paolo Soleri have to strain to hear him. His voice never rises much above a whisper, and even after 20 years in this country the accent of his native Italy thickens it. Periodically, light planes pass through the desert sky; motorcycles putter off to town on the road just beyond the low dunes; ceramic and metal bells clunk and gong with the wind. But no one's attention wanders.

"There are two gas stations, a restaurant and a bar, and that's about it," Soleri says, describing Cordes Junction, a little settlement that sits like a bewildered prospector just off a winding superhighway 60 miles north of Phoenix. "The people are conservative. They are the children of the old-timers, the real old-timers. I beg you, if you must smoke pot, don't talk about it in the village."

Tomorrow these high school and college students—and dropouts—will begin six weeks of labor at a construction site off a dirt road winding away from Cordes Junction, a privilege for which each of them has paid $340. For now, they are bivouacked here at the very edge of the town of Paradise Valley, which is contiguous with the suburban sprawl of Scottsdale, itself part of the low sprawl of Phoenix. They sit cross-legged and half clothed on the broad shoulder of a raised, free-form swimming pool under a concrete canopy that weighs 20 tons but looks light as tortoise shell. The pool is one of a dozen cast-concrete structures, ranging in complexity from band-shell-like apses to finished houses, that Soleri and earlier disciples have set into this narrow patch of desert since 1956. Collectively, the buildings are called Cosanti, which translates as "against things," or "antimaterialism." The megastructure for 3000 people that the youngsters think they are going to work on up north tomorrow is called Arcosanti. The most important of Soleri's many activities takes place a few yards away, in the drafting room connected to the conventional ranch house in which he lives. There, day by day, he fills the pages of the seventh of a series of sketchbooks where all his ideas take their first form. These remind everyone who sees them of Da Vinci's notebooks, and if the schemes in them are half as important as Soleri thinks they are, the comparison will be appropriate.

Following the admonition about marijuana and a few words on the permanent workers at Arcosanti—a first-day-at-camp briefing—Soleri asks for questions. In response to an early one, he sketches in the history of Phoenix as he knows it: how the construction of the Roosevelt Dam on the Salt River in 1911 was followed by a wave of people coming to the area for health reasons, which triggered a general tourist influx. The dam also created a farming area, but the developing city is eating up the farmland around it. "If you fly over the city," Soleri says, "you see that this area of arable land—which is not very vast—is being taken over by suburbia. The farmers can make more money selling to land developers than growing crops."

The houses that only recently have reached what was an isolated tract when Soleri and his wife came to camp on it 15 years ago are high-priced stylizations of ranch bunkhouses and Spanish villas, and they surround a metropolis the commercial sections of which would have made Da Vinci bug-eyed by their ugliness. Thanks in part to a campaign led by Barry Goldwater, some of the rough diminutive mountains that Phoenix is built against have been saved from development, but their preservation is nearly the only intelligent thing the people of the valley have done for the appearance of their surroundings. One almost never sees Phoenix except from the woolly interior of an air-conditioned car, and then as a grid of broad bare avenues lined with auto agencies, stores, gas stations and branch banks, most of them set off in their own parking lots and heralded by startling signs. The city has little more of the feel of the Southwest to it than U.S. Route 1 in Saugus, Massachusetts.

A student asks what the arcologies—Soleri's compact, single-structure cities—have to do with the problems of existing cities.

"Well, we know what the kind of developments that we are building *now* do," he says. "They gulp land. They isolate people from one another, from the institutions of the city and from nature. They impose an ecological burden that is absolutely staggering. To keep things moving in a city, we are required to pay enormous costs. First, we are required to buy a car every two or three years and to maintain it, feed it, store it. Beyond that there are all the cycles that are initiated and never closed. We are paying by having the skies gray, the rivers going to pieces. Even the oceans are starting to be polluted. An endless waste of price tags. The creatures that are supposed to be served by this physical environment become less and less sane, because they see themselves as prisoners, physically even, of their condition. Beyond that, they see themselves as having jobs that are worse then having no jobs: They work to produce pollution."

The student interrupts: "What I meant were the problems of the city core, which are problems of congestion. . . ."

"No," Soleri says. "They are not problems of congestion, they are problems of *dereliction*. When something goes derelict, you have also congestion. But it's the fact that we never cared about the public aspect of the city. And if you ignore the public aspect of the city, you may as well ignore the city, because the city is made up of what is common among the people. If the streets are abandoned, if the courtyards are abandoned, if the schools are abandoned—all the institutions that have somehow to do with the communal patrimony—then naturally you have the problems of cities. But congestion is just a consequence of physical and mental bankruptcy."

Soleri is perched on an upcropping of concrete that makes a stool, and wears a sleeveless T-shirt, a greenish-yellow stretch bathing suit with a diamondback pattern in the waistband, dark-green anklets and black-and-white sneakers. His ears peak close to his head and his eyes in the sun are black houndstooth checks. His bare slender legs are long-muscled like a frog's and he clasps one knee like a resting dancer. Often many seconds pass before anyone asks a question. Through these pauses, he doesn't fidget at all. He looks at the students with a faint smile, as if trying to guess which will think himself ready to open his mouth.

Someone had asked earlier about ESP; there is a remark now about the beauties of the Eastern mind and the proposition is put forward that the world would be better off if America had been left to the Indians. Soleri says he thinks ESP is a low level of communication. He identifies himself as very much a Westerner ("I agree with Teilhard de Chardin that in order to be really Christian today, you must embrace technology"). And he resists the sentimentalization of the Indian. Yet with each question he is patient and careful, apparently resolved to believe that every student is intelligent, even in the face of the undergraduate fantasies and infatuations of the hour.

A girl tells Soleri that both her mother and her history teacher were appalled at the prospect of living in arcologies; the teacher had met her enthusiasm with the stories about what overcrowding does to rats, an argument Soleri has evidently heard before.

"Your history teacher wasn't being very historical," Soleri says softly. "History is basically culture. You give me a society of rats that has any culture at all and I will eat them all. The rat society is a social system of some sort and human society is a cultural system. It's a quantum jump. To relate the two is shallow and very dangerous. It might well be that we as humans need exactly the sort of conditions the rat cannot stand. In other words, as cultural creatures, we have to crowd.

"Now I'm not suggesting that we shrink living spaces—though I have suggested that we could shrink *people* to a certain degree. Giantism is certainly not the best route for any species to take. But my idea is mainly a matter of taking away the dead spaces. And there are so *many* dead spaces. The largest set of them, of course, is everything that is given to the car. If you took all the roads and parking lots out of the city, it would immediately shrink to half its size."

"I think in the case of my mother," the girl says, "and with a lot of us, the reaction against arcologies is because the only experience most of us have had with very dense housing is slums, the ghetto."

"Again," Soleri says, "the ghetto is a corruption—a degeneration—of the city. If you take the worst of any phenomenon, you can condemn the phenomenon. I don't know what the background of your mother is, but if she had lived in a successful city—and I'm thinking of a European city—then possibly her outlook would be different. To take a person who was born in the country and who goes into the city only occasionally and then finds things that are displeasing, and to teach this person that the city is possibly a *great* phenomenon is just about impossible. Things of that nature have to be experienced."

He is asked which cities he considers successful. "Until the Second World War, at least, there were many towns and cities in Europe that you could call successful, in the sense that the people living in those cities really were part of a cultural and social system that was giving them something of substance. I would call the city where I was born—Torino, fifty years ago—very successful."

What was, at least in memory, the integrated, substantive cultural and social life of Turin, Italy, was set in a compact grid of streets and parks and plazas on the left bank of the Po, facing cultivated hills in one direction and the peaks of the Alps in the other. From the time he was five, Soleri was taken to the mountains for weekend hikes, leaving him, he says, with a love for wilderness and for heights. At 18, offered only a course in architecture and one in civil engineering, he chose art over technology. With interruptions for 22 months of service with the Italian army engineers and periods of work for his family and for tuition, Soleri was 26 when he finally got his doctorate from the Turin Polytechnical Institute. But the degree was with highest honors and shortly after receiving it he was accepted as an apprentice by Frank Lloyd Wright. He joined the master at Taliesin West—the complex of low-lined studios, living quarters and geometric gardens set like flagstones into the McDowell Mountains ten miles north of Scottsdale.

The differences between Cosanti and Taliesin today obscure their similarities. Like Soleri in his first years in Paradise Valley, Wright spent his first winter at Taliesin, in the Thirties, camping out. Wright thought of his students as apprentices to the master, and the 30 young architects who pay $2500 a year today to work at Taliesin are the establishment counterparts of Soleri's motlier crews. The two studios even share the problems of blight: While affluent suburbia slowly surrounds Cosanti, the very reason for being of the Taliesin site—the view to the south, toward Cosanti—was marred in 1963 by a procession of high-tension wires marching across the hillside. (Wright was unable to interest his neighbors in a joint venture to put the lines underground.)

But the spirit of radical innovation assuredly resides today at Cosanti, not at Taliesin. The major commission of the prosperous architectural firm Wright left behind is for a palace and a vacation home for the sister of the shah of Iran. And if it can get its hands on the land around Taliesin, it plans to dot the hills with a resort hotel, a motor inn and golf courses.

After a year and a half at Taliesin, it became evident that Soleri was not constituted to work on someone else's designs; he left Wright in 1949 and camped out with a fellow ex-apprentice on nearby Camelback Mountain.

Eventually they were tracked down there by Mrs. Leonora Woods, a Pittsburgh socialite looking for someone to design a desert home for her at less than Taliesin prices. The house they built achieved national recognition for its roof —a glass dome with an opaque panel that rotates with the sun. And before it was finished, Soleri married Mrs. Woods's daughter, Colly, who looks more like a pretty clubwoman from someplace like Winnetka, Illinois, than the wife of an underfunded Italian genius.

Following the birth of his second daughter, Soleri returned to Italy, where he thought he might open his own studio. That hope failed to materialize, but during his stay there he won his first major commission—for a ceramics factory on the Amalfi Coast. With an open, dramatic interior and an exterior of inverted cones that reflect and blend with the cliffs they hug, the building is regarded as an unusually successful experiment.

Since his return to the United States in 1954, Soleri has built only one structure—a theater for the Institute of American Indian Arts in Santa Fe— besides the uncommissioned structures at Cosanti. He supported himself for years on the income from the sale of ceramic wind bells, the molds for which were holes that he dug with his hands in the desert silt. Today, conventionally cast bronze and aluminum bells have been added to the trade and a younger brother imported from Italy supervises all the casting. And much of Soleri's income, which he channels through the Cosanti Foundation, comes from his lecture tours. Yet he still spends evenings carving Styrofoam forms for the cast arms from which clusters of the bells are hung, and still himself etches the strong designs into the molds that give them their character.

Most of the buildings at Cosanti were as primitively cast as the bells. First Soleri and his apprentices would bulldoze the earth into a low mound. Then they'd cut ridges in it for reinforcing rods and pour concrete over it. Sometimes paint would be spread over the dirt and the concrete would pick up a dull, deeply embedded coloring. When the concrete had hardened, the piled dirt and a few feet of the desert floor were excavated. The resulting structures are exquisitely adapted to their site—providing shade in the summer, when the sun is high, and gathering the warmth of the low winter sun—and the wind bells are among the finest crafted objects in the country. But neither the buildings nor the bells have much to do with the growing international interest in Soleri. That derives from his vision of the universe and man's place in it, and especially from the structures and philosophy of arcology—the word blends architecture and ecology—which, he's convinced, is crucial to the next step in the cultural evolution of the species.

Soleri's thought begins with the Scholastic truth that in the progression from matter to vegetal and then animal life, and finally to the human brain, there is an increase not only in complexity but in compactness. He argues that compactness is the essence of life—"life is in the thick of things"—and that evolution tends toward density, away from dispersion. "In its evolution from matter to mind," Soleri writes, "the real has been submitted to numerous phases of miniaturization so as to fit more things into smaller spaces in shorter times. This process, from haphazardness and dislocation to coordination and fitness, has been mandatory because each successive form of reality carried in itself a greater degree of complexity. Any higher organism contains more performances than a chunk of the unlimited universe light-years thick, and it ticks on a time clock immensely swifter. This miniaturization process may well be one of the fundamental rules of evolution.

"Now that the inquietude of man is turned to the construction of the superorganism, which society is, a new phase of miniaturization is imperative. Arcology is a step toward it." In other words, the philosophy that Soleri calls arcology, and the buildings that that philosophy demands, buildings which he also calls arcologies, are nothing less than a necessary next step in the development of society. For a time in the late Fifties, Soleri turned to the idea of harnessing the energy of the sun in individual reflector-generators on the roofs of spread-out individual dwellings. But he soon decided that the pattern of the broadleaf, while efficient for photosynthesis, is grossly inefficient as a pattern for almost everything else, and especially for the settlements of men. Flatness gobbles land and greenness. Because people and goods have to be moved great distances in the two dimensions of the horizontal city, transportation networks squander energy. More importantly, the flatness debilitates and suppresses the individual. Once a man is positioned within a square mile of suburbia, he's effectively cut off from nature. Only experiences that can be transmitted electronically aren't hindered by dispersion. All the other contacts that enrich life —nights at the theater, visits to museums, face-to-face encounters with family, friends and strangers—are made so difficult by the spread-out city that we cut them out and surrender ourselves to what the electricity will deliver.

The arcologies that Soleri sees as the sane alternative to today's cities and suburbs are three-dimensional megastructures, usually several hundred stories high and proportionally broad at the base. They look like aircraft carriers, or dams, or gargantuan crystals, and correspond not to plants but to animals. Like the higher organisms, cities can in fact ingest and store concentrated energy from many sources, and the tasks performed in cities are of a complexity and delicacy analogous, Soleri says, to those performed by the organs of the body—specifically, the human body. Thus, the city in the image of man, which is the title of Soleri's first book.

The arcologies would, undeniably, offer great environmental and economic savings. Most of the cost of transporting goods would disappear. All the systems of the megastructures—including the centralized industrial complexes most would have—would be closed, the waste of one process filtering usefully through another. Cars would be used only to get from one arcology to another or to explore the surrounding wilderness. Every institution of learning in the city would be closer—for everyone—than most schools are now for their own students. Medical personnel would walk to house calls the way they make rounds in hospitals. Man would live on the skin of the arcology, facing in one direction a city any part of which he could reach in 15 or 20 minutes by elevator, moving sidewalk or his own locomotion, and in the other the face of nature, marred only by a few access highways and rail systems and, in the distance, the homes of those who choose to live apart.

This is the bare outline of the argument as it leads to arcologies, but no summary can do justice to the richness of the full Soleri intellectual construction. *Arcology: The City in the Image of Man,* which flops open to a width of four feet, includes not only drawings of the arcologies but page after page of diagrams that give graphic shape to a unified metaphysical vision. In one, Fate, which is described as "entropic, statistical, granular, indifferent, static, rational, structural, torpid, automatic and amorphous," is contrasted with "joyful, conscious, harmonious, superstructural, superrational, dynamic, compassionate, pervasive, willful and complex Destiny." In another, a vector labeled "the aesthetocompassionate metamorphosis" soars out of a black puddle representing "anguish reduced to a nonshrinkable residual." Except for someone willing to steep himself in Soleri's thought, this is shorthand theorizing and virtually inaccessible—but great fun nevertheless. All the writing is alternately obscure and powerful, sometimes in consecutive sentences: "It is the naked mind and the desensitized body that find an obsolescent environment to their liking," he writes in his second book, *The Sketchbooks of Paolo Soleri.* But then: "They indeed are alike, both sensing the presence of a dark chasm of senselessness only one step ahead of themselves, as if man's Fall reflected itself endlessly on the sloping bastions of a deterministic and indifferent universe."

There is much rage in the texts, and it is always well turned: "The atomistic nature of suburbia plays the sweetest song to the production madness of 'free' enterprise. Nothing is indeed sweeter than raping nature and getting dollar bills in return, with its concomitant exhilarating power. Forests are transformed into cheap lumber, then cheaper shelters, from wilderness to slums in a matter of half a generation."

And the impersonality of big government is as contemptible to him as the excesses of unbridled free enterprise: "As the city cannot be speculative, so it cannot be a handout by 'authority.' The handout never cares. It is indifferent, just another aspect of the speculative exercise. Any care it may have had at its origin has been lost in bureaucratic meanders and their parasitic agents. Care is a first-person undertaking. The care of the citizen is the sap of the city. But one can care only for that which one loves. Lovableness is the key to a living city. A lovely city is not an accident, as a lovely person is not an accident."

The question, of course, is whether the arcologies would constitute cities of love or a new architecture of fascism. "As architecture," critic Thomas Albright has written, "Soleri's designs seem reactionary rather than revolutionary in concept, attempting to impose a rationale on the ugliest, most irrational features of urban life—high density, plastic sterility, overcentralization—and freezing them in inflexible monuments whose cost would tend to make them permanent features of the landscape, as impervious to change as dinosaurs. . . . His models look like Platonic or Euclidean ideal forms into which human needs have been arbitrarily poured, edited and redefined—ideal forms for one man's notion of an ideal society."

A couple of ideas are wrong in this: High density isn't an ugly aspect of urban life, it's the rough essence of it. And if Soleri's principles are correct, society would *want* the arcologies to be permanent—that is, if we've retained at all the ability to plan projects intended to last beyond our lifetimes. The men who built Notre Dame didn't worry about permanently scarring the landscape of Paris; and it's hardly a defect in Soleri's vision that young people have adjusted to the thought of living in temporary inflatables in the woods.

But Albright's assertion that Soleri seems to ignore human needs is justified. "Social, ethical, political and aesthetic implications are left out," Soleri writes in *The City in the Image of Man,* "as they are valid and final only if and when physical conditions are realistically organized." The students at the swimming pool wanted to know both how the arcologies would change the people who lived in them and what sort of government Soleri envisioned for them. He answered neither question lucidly, beyond saying that he expects the arcologies to produce surprising and positive changes in people—"they would inspire you rather than frustrate you"—and that no one would be coerced to live in them. When asked directly if he thought the compact city would lend itself to totalitarian control, he did somewhat better, noting that Papa Doc Duvalier had been able to control spread-out, low-technology settlements very well. The systems of an arcology would obviously lend themselves to computerization, but "having the computer take care of the red and green lights is not an imposition on the freedom of man." The smoothly operating systems will, in fact, liberate people, Soleri claims: "If you don't want to take that escalator, you move to the next one. You have more options. There's more fluidity, more choice. And the basic choice is that you can get from one place to another, which is not the choice you have now."

All this is more vague and evasive than it need be. Soleri in fact knows the kinds of changes he expects the arcologies both to produce and to reflect, but they have to be deduced from widely separated, sometimes dense, passages in the two books. "Perhaps a metamorphosis of the protogilded encasement for an asphyxiating society may mean the uncovering of a different set of values, better aligned with the basic tenderness of the human constitution," he writes in *The City in the Image of Man.* The search is for "an urban society seeking to contain the robotization of man." Flesh is tender, and "the burgeoning monster flower of automation must be handled with great care lest we become robots." Ultimately, the goal is the creation of "aesthetocompassionate man" and an "aesthetocompassionate society," the coined superword hiding the baldness of the real goal: that we rearrange our surroundings in a way that will give us not only more artists but more artists in a just society.

Out of their philosophical context, the models of the arcologies simply scare most people. When the unholy scale of the things was explained to a seven-year-old girl at the Chicago stop of the major Soleri exhibition that's been touring this country and Canada for the past three years, she burst into tears. The models look, people say, like sets for a big-budget production of *1984.*

Soleri will have an easier time convincing the world that his structures are the crucial next step in man's amplification of his humanity as the bright young designers in residence at Cosanti do more details of interior spaces for Arcosanti, something that they got down to in earnest this past winter. Clearly, Soleri will approve only those designs that possess the cavelike warmth and vaulted spaciousness of the buildings at Cosanti. Dimensions for the living units in a typical arcology are usually given as 20 feet high by 40 feet wide by 60 feet deep—"enough room," as writer Richard Register has observed, "to build two floors, move in earth and start a good-sized garden."

Most important, as such details come off the drawing boards, we'll finally get a look at Soleri's ideas for the public places in his arcologies. Cities' open areas—Rio's Copacabana, the Boston Public Gardens, the Champs Elysées in Paris—give them whatever character they have, and the corresponding parts of the arcologies promise to be wondrous. Imagine a ride on a curving, 30-story escalator suspended or cantilevered into the center of an arcology: rising in minutes through a commercial center, then a terraced layer of playing fields, theaters and auditoriums, now a zoo, above it the city senate—all of them festooned with footbridges and elevators and hung in great shafts of light. For the more fantastic cities, the setting would determine the spirit of the place: The arcology called Stonebow is intended to span a canyon, where the successive geological, fossil and floral layers would "remind man of the miracle of life emerging and perpetuating itself in endless ways." Soleri's Arcoindian cities would be cut into great gashes in cliff faces; life would take place in a vast amphitheater facing the desert or the sea under a broad semidome of sky. Novanoah I is intended to float free on the seas, harvesting them in the pursuit of "an all-new and fantastic culture, adding new folds to the human condition."

But what if there's a power failure—or an earthquake or an enemy attack? And won't the arcologies be noisy as Bedlam? Certainly with each miniaturization they would become more vulnerable to breakdown from failed generators, from acts of God—and of the Kremlin or Peking, if one's thinking runs that way. But presumably they'd be built away from earth faults (and in fact would be more stable than slender high-rises). Because they'd be planned from scratch, they'd have at least as much fire resistance and backup power capability as Manhattan has. And they'd be roughly as susceptible to attack as Manhattan is—indeed, as any city is.

All the larger arcologies include plans for airstrips or landing pads on their peripheries, and—the noise of the planes aside—it seems obvious that the guts and workings of the structures would make them hum, as high-rise buildings do. Soleri has confidence that existing and expectable technology can guarantee silence in the private and even the public places of the megabuildings: He refers to the arcaded shopping centers of the Phoenix area as examples of successful sound engineering. These enclosed, colonnaded malls are eerily quiet even when milling with people—"almost too quiet," Soleri says, "for the Latin temperament."

But if noise can be shut out, people can't, and this is the heart of the matter. The actual density in the arcologies is somewhat lower than first appearances suggest, but clearly the essence of the arcological idea is a commitment to living in close, continuous contact with others. It may call for a greater change than any of us is capable of or will ever want to attempt. The first use of real wealth today is the purchase of privacy—in the form of a 30-acre farm in exurbia or a roomy penthouse fortified against strangers by location, guards and remote-control television. If a man who lives in an apartment at the top of Chicago's towering, multipurpose John Hancock Center wants to work at midnight in his office 20 floors below, he rides down to the lobby, like a Bantu shows a pass to a guard, and then boards another elevator for the ride up to the office. He does so willingly, knowing that the procedure keeps the real Bantus from his sanctuaries.

If we delight in the company of our own children and tolerate the presence of our parents, we surely don't surround ourselves with other people's children, other people's old folks. But Soleri remembers Turin, where all the citizens were "part of a cultural and social system that was giving them something of substance." He writes: "The playground [in today's city] is the act of condescending to playfulness in a habitat where grimness, ugliness and danger are endemic and offer the last measure of unconcern in an adult world gone sour. The playground is segregative. The absence of children in the so-called respectable public places is disheartening. The child has reason to become irresponsible and destructive, caged, as he is, away from the 'other world.' Arcology is an 'environmental toy.' As a miniaturized universe it offers unending elements for surprise and stimulation. There will not be fenced-in playgrounds. The whole city is the place where the child is acting out the learning process, one aspect of which is play."

And on old people: "One of the ravages of 'mobility,' or at least directly accountable to it, is the institutionalized ghetto for the elderly. Following the generalized scattering of things and thoughts, the family has broken down into four main fragments: the young, the parents, the grandparents and the anonymous relative. Aging being common to all (the lucky ones), all will have a taste of the tragic segregation of the aged; the insurance company and social security will not do, lest man become or remain marketable goods. The implications of 'arcological life' are the most favorable for reintegration of the different age groups and thus for the knitting of family strands."

Soleri's intention, then, is nothing less than the destruction of the alienation we feel not only from the underclasses in our cities but from our parents and acquaintances. The project may be hopeless. It may even be undesirable. (One can at least entertain the idea that we should all become more isolated, more mute.) But if life is truly in the thick of things—if contact with others, and the care for them that follows contact, is the stuff of life—then arcology, if only as an experiment, is desirable. And the way Arcosanti is taking shape suggests that, at least on a small scale, the undertaking may be feasible.

Three days after he met with the apprentices at the swimming pool—this still at the beginning of last summer, Arcosanti's first full building season— Soleri joined them at the site. It's in ranching country, high desert halfway between Phoenix and Flagstaff. When Arcosanti is built, it will straddle a modest-sized mesa that looks down onto a plain traversed by the gulch of the Agua Fria River. You come over the lip of the mesa to get to the work camp below it, at the edge of the riverbank, and the sight is quintessentially Western: The earth is suede gray, mottled with chaparral and cacti. Ash and cotton-woods stand along the banks of the branch, their tops hugely round and kelly green in the sunlight, forest green in the broad angled shadow of the butte.

"It's going to be right on the edge of that mesa," a goofy, insurrectionary staffer named Jerry O'Shaughnessey said, "and it'll look down into this valley, so everyone can sit up there and get stoned and say how beautiful it is." He paused, grinned. "We can all look at the cracks in the cement."

"Why will the cement crack?"

"Because everything Soleri does has cracks in it. It's his touch. It's the Italian touch."

One of the girls from the new group had discovered she couldn't make it without her boyfriend and headed back to the East Coast, but the rest were flushed with sunburns and work. The mesa itself had been surveyed and there'd been some surface excavation, but last summer the main construction was to be at the workers' camp, which won't be attached to the main structure. The kids had been pouring and smoothing concrete in modular slabs that were lifted and fitted together to make cubes with big circular holes in the walls; some of them slept in the cubes, some in a long wooden dormitory. When Arcosanti is built, this area might become a playground. Already someone had hung a 40-foot Tarzan's rope from one of the tall cottonwoods overhanging the gully.

On his arrival, Soleri ran into a problem: A volunteer had spent the morning laying out a 20' x 60' vegetable garden in a plot at the edge of the riverbank. On close inspection, Soleri determined that the land sloped in the direction of the tilled rows, although the tilt was nearly impossible to see, less than a couple of degrees. Soleri insisted that the rows be laid out in the other direction, to follow what amounted to an imagined contour of the land, despite the young man's protest that with the intensive French horticulture he'd planned for the garden, even a visible contour wouldn't matter. Soleri would have none of it, for the first time in four days exhibiting an unbending willfulness.

He seemed more himself later in the day, when he led his manual laborers on a trek up the river bed. He'd bought 860 acres of this land from a rancher, with a lease on an additional 3200 acres, and wanted to show the heart of it to his apprentices. The banks of the gulch the Agua Fria has cut rise 30 feet and the trees add another 30 or 40 feet to that. The group walked along the shaded, spacious tunnel of the bottom. (Soleri had hoped to use this river silt as the base for Arcosanti's concrete, but experimentation finally convinced him that he'd have to import standard sand—part of the explanation for O'Shaugh-nessey's cracks.) Early in the walk, he bent to show the youngsters the water cress that grows in the stream and suggested that one of them come down every day to gather it for their kitchen. Farther along, he stopped to let the straggle catch up with him and pointed above his head to the spot where Arcosanti will rise. He stopped again to indicate the general location of the ranch buildings —which he urged the apprentices not to approach. "They're very nice people," he said. "But they don't like to be bothered."

There was an archetypal fat boy in the group: *Lord of the Flies'* Piggy grown older, pudgier and more nearsighted. In several places, the stream broadened and swung close to a bank, so the file had to leap it or clamber a few feet up the steep, crumbly bank. Heads turned to see if the quiet misfit bringing up the rear would be able to make the jump. Nobody was actively helping him yet—this was only the fourth day they'd been together and his forlorn, stoic expression discouraged it. But heads did turn, concern for him was in the air, and a girl trailed with him—not aligned with him, her expression said, but just as obviously there, ready for him if he fell.

The field trip reached its destination at a stand of smooth boulders near the head of the property. The group climbed onto the broadest rock in the midafternoon sun for another question-and-answer session, this one preceded by a loving, rambling dissertation by Soleri on the land they'd just explored. He told them of the antelope he'd seen on it, insisted on the value of the French Charolais cattle that graze it, apologized for the fact that the rancher has to set poison out for coyotes. He said that he wants to keep the canyon untouched but in fact envisions a service road and pathways cutting through it and suggested that eventually he might want to carve sculpture in the rocky walls. His eyes lit when he described finding the site after years of casual looking in the general area: "It has everything—water, accessibility, power. And variety to the land: We have both a top and a bottom, and shade and rock formations. You can really play with it quite a bit."

The first question was from O'Shaughnessey, who last summer was vaguely in charge of integrating the summer workshop groups into the program designed by Soleri and his few permanent staff members: He asked where you catch the bus out. Soleri went along with the laughter and at the same time got across the information that the road connecting Phoenix and Flagstaff was less than a mile away and that a bus stopped at Cordes Junction.

In the course of a discussion about the milk that the camp cook bought from a nearby private school, a girl got Soleri's attention and asked, "Why don't we buy a cow?"

"Yes, why don't you?" Soleri said. A boy volunteered to go out and round up some cows and Soleri said, "Well, you better talk to them first, because they may not know about milk."

More than half this group had come from schools in New York. "I wouldn't know the milking cows from the nonmilking ones," the boy said.

"Well, the first thing to know," Soleri said, "is that it doesn't come from the horns."

Most of the serious questions were about money. After two days of pouring concrete, the young workers had suddenly become obsessed with the discovery that the project they were working on was underfinanced. The foundation is strained to the bottom of its resources by the purchase of the land. Soleri got a used crane for $7500 last year, and there are several salaries to be paid. After the land is paid for, he told them, they might be able to hire a professional who really knows concrete, or a carpenter. He talked about the possibility of getting retired craftsmen to help. But the kids were thinking in terms of major infusions of cash and wondered out loud why the project hadn't gotten support from the big foundations, business or the Government.

Soleri explained that he has no fund raiser because he doesn't have the funds to pay for one. He talked with some bitterness about the developers—there was a group from Dallas that he remembers especially well—that come, and look, and come back and look again, and say they're going to commission or support a major undertaking and then are never heard from again. Finally, he said: "We built Earth House, the first building in Cosanti, in 1956. Every summer since then, production has doubled. The choice was not to build Arcosanti at all or to build it the way we are building it. I could wait until all the millions are flying in or we can go to work now."

Less than five miles away, a Phoenix developer is putting up a patch of conventional second homes, which Soleri is delighted to have so close to Arcosanti as a measure of the value of his vision. He also thinks the current work at Arcosanti will present the Federal Government with an urban alternative in which the experimental stage has already been completed. But he treated the youngsters' continued insistence on the desirability of a few bulldozers romantically and imperiously. "You shouldn't worry so much about how it will be built," he said. "When they wanted to build a great monastery four hundred years ago, they didn't have machines. They did it with the love and skills of the laborers."

Meanwhile, down in Houston, plans were proceeding for something called the Houston Center, ground for which was broken in January 1972. The center will cover 74 acres in the heart of the city with office towers, hotels, stores and apartment buildings. One guess at the final cost of the project to its developers is one and a half billion dollars. William L. Pereira Associates, the Los Angeles firm that planned it, has separated pedestrian and vehicular traffic, and its low-rise elements suggest an Aztec city. But the 15 towers—slabs and cylinders —that soar out of the life below are vertical filing cabinets. Among the best of the new towns being planned for the desert outside Phoenix is one called Fountain Hills, the principal attraction of which is a plume of white water shooting almost 100 feet higher into the sky than the top of the Great Pyramid of Cheops. Sitting on the boulders with Soleri and his wife and the mix of lost youngsters and tough, accomplished ones he attracts, with thoughts of the other projects in mind—the cautiousness of the designs, the hedged wordings in the hundreds of contracts involved, the spirit in which the laborers work —cynicism about Soleri's naïveté began to seem cheap. If some of the billions of dollars that will be spent on urban experiments in this country in the next couple of decades doesn't flow to Soleri, it will mean that the system determining who gets cash for major undertakings in this society is failing. Funding Soleri surely won't be easy—no matter who does it, there'll be a furious tension between the sponsor and the artist, who hasn't had to answer to anyone but himself through most of his working life. Soleri and Colly will keep the fat kid on the project in one capacity or another, and it's hard to imagine a sponsor standing for that expense. But for all the reasons that can be symbolized by the fact that he *will* keep the fat kid with him, it's time for Soleri's coherent vision to meet the test that adequate financing would provide.

The group had been on the rock for 45 minutes now, and O'Shaughnessey made another joke about the availability of the bus. There was some confusion about which company made the run, and Soleri leaned over as if to touch his ear to the ground: "To tell the difference between a Trailways and a Greyhound," he said, "that takes a real Indian."

Soleri was one of the last off the boulders as the session broke up, and he called down to a clutch of youngsters, urging them to leave the river bottom but not to cross the grounds near the ranch buildings. They couldn't understand him—in part because of his accent, in part because he knew east from west and they didn't—and one boy in particular kept asking if he was supposed to stay to the left or the right. Finally, Colly said, "He doesn't understand a word you said, Paolo," and Soleri thought he recognized the missing key: "Yes, well," he said, turning to beam down at the boy, who looked like Prince Valiant, "Stay to the east, *man.*"

Not the least of the paradoxes about Soleri is the fact of his dependence on the anti-authoritarian, usually anti-city counterculture. The kids not only come and pay him to work for him each summer, they return to school, many of them, and proselytize for his ideas in situations where, increasingly, what the students want to study is what will damned well be taught. In return, Soleri gives them a chance to pick up some construction skills for the cost of approximately three weeks of conventional school and a communal experience in the service of an idea, whether or not they understand the implications of that idea. "I don't know exactly why I'm here," said a young man who had just dropped out of his third year in engineering at George Washington University. "I'm certainly not going to see anything of any dimensions built. But it seems like a good cause, and there aren't that many good causes around."

For all of Soleri's pretensions to Wrightian masterfulness, the atmosphere at both of his work sites is loose and long-haired. Very early in the morning, especially on weekends, when Soleri is most likely to be working alone, the loudspeakers at Cosanti carry a variety of classical music. Later in the day, that gives way to The Rolling Stones, or Steve Stills, or the album of the month. One night last spring, in one of the earth houses the apprentices had camped in, a pot of spaghetti cooking on the stove and Tom Rush on a portable KLH and the indigo sky in low arched windows made a mood you could drown in.

And Arcosanti is a cross between a summer camp in God's country and a commune, complete last summer with a boy who saluted the sunset upside down, standing on his head for half an hour.

Most important, the experience includes face-to-face contact with the kind of master-teacher we only occasionally produce. Before the walk up the canyon, Soleri sat the group down at the two long tables where they were to eat for the next six weeks and spelled out a few more operating rules. A gentle landlord, he asked that they not paint the concrete but encouraged them to do any other decorating they wished with the inside walls of their cubes. "After a while," he said, "the abandoned, the careless, gets on everybody's nerves. So you might have a wild idea. Fine. But demonstrate that that wild idea is cared for—that you are really interested in doing it, and are not going to abandon it."

Soleri is an innocent. He doesn't know how to approach the foundations for grants, or clients for commissions. His ideas are wilder than the countryside he's adopted and the fantasies of the youngsters he attracts. But he cares for them with a passion, and they assuredly will not be abandoned.

Through the rest of last summer and, with smaller crews, on through the winter, he accomplished much more at Arcosanti than a skeptical visitor had thought possible. Except for finishing touches, the work camp is now complete. It includes a spacious octagonal meetinghouse, a geodesic dome that has been used as a carpentry shop and this summer will be converted into a dormitory, and its final complement of 24 cubes. More important, the first small pieces of Arcosanti itself have been set into the mesa. By this fall, the structure will house a concrete casting plant, a ceramics workshop and a foundry, as well as a few living areas and possibly a swimming pool. (It's desert, after all, and Soleri wants to build without air conditioning.) He no longer talks about hiring more professionals: There are five architects and an engineer on the salaried staff, and he feels that he's developing a steady supply of competent craftsmen in the workshops.

Standing in Arcosanti's rough concrete foundation, on the edge of the empty Arizona sky, the visitor this spring remembered the walk back to the camp from the boulders. Then it was Soleri who lagged. He stopped to scoop up a sheet of heavy plastic that had blown down into the gulch from the camp—and filled the other hand with bunch after bunch of water cress. The visitor realized for the first time that, if it takes 20 years, Arcosanti will be built, with or without the foundations. And even if the millions do start flowing in, Soleri will continue to police and harvest the Agua Fria, teaching a generation that there are things to be built, and ways to build them, that will outlast even the concrete dream.

Beginnings: Planning

For, you see, so many out-of-the-way things had happened lately, that Alice began to think very few things indeed were really impossible.

LEWIS CARROLL

ANGELA: Planning doesn't usually go in an Introduction to Sociology textbook, but I think it's a subject that should be looked into. The environmentalists are telling us that planning is going to have to go into effect, and that we'll have to look at the way that everything interacts with everything else.

DICK: I agree, it's an interesting topic, but don't you think it's a little far from sociology?

ANGELA: Oh, no, that's just the point. The three areas of planning I wanted in this section were the planning of architecture, the impact of technology, and of people's behavior. Now, the thing with architecture or design is that certain types of environments will be conducive to certain types of interactions. When I teach, for instance, I notice that the way the chairs are arranged in the classroom has a big influence on the way the class goes.

RICH: The thing that bothers me about planning is that it can keep us from making big changes to improve social conditions. The people who don't want society to change—although they say they're trying to stop society from "falling apart"—those are the people who have the biggest vested interest in keeping society running the way it is; you know, the corporate elite. And they'll probably control planning.

SCOTT: You mean they wouldn't allow this planning of social change?

RICH: We can read about planning a factory in such a way that all the workers are happy work better, and therefore produce more, and few of us will ever question the basic assumption that workers should be manipulated like that so they will increase the profits of the company.

ANGELA: What about when you start planning people's behavior?

RICH: It's the same thing. It sounds fine to say you're going to control behavior so that all the bad traits are taken out, but who decides what "bad" behavior is? Not people like you and me.

DICK: I see what you're saying, that "planning" and "control" are opposite faces of the same coin, right?

RICH: Exactly.

DICK: And that the people who determine what type of social planning to initiate are also going to determine what types of controls are involved.

RICH: And whose interests those controls protect. Designers and planners are capable of designing a lot of different things, but what they *will* design is what they are *paid* to design, and a company won't pay someone to come up with a plan that ends the company. The System will only pay for planning that ensures the perpetuation of that System.

ANGELA: You know, Dick, it's as you just said about opposite faces of the same coin. The possibilities that Rich is talking about are frightening, and yet there are many things that could be done through social planning to make this country a better place in which to live. There's potential for a lot of peril and a lot of promise in this topic.

From *The Black Seventies* by Floyd D. Barbur (ed.). Reprinted by permission of Porter Sargent, Publisher.

29. Design and Reality in the 70's

JAMES A. CHAFFERS

Architecture is not a virtuoso effort undertaken for the aesthetic gratification of a particular designer, but rather a social responsibility undertaken to enhance the quality of human life.

GROPIUS

As an architect, I am concerned primarily with and about the physical environment of man. As a black American, I share a greater concern and a common lot with the continuing struggle of black people in our quest for liberty and equality.

In this era of black consciousness, there are those who will grasp and accept the full meaning of this statement. I can only assume that when it is recognized that a growing majority of black people (far exceeding the population of most nations) is now concentrated in the heart of our major urban centers, locked into racial enclaves devised and maintained to exploit and oppressively restrict the life-chances and choices of black people, that the irrelevancy of defensive attitudes will become apparent. Further, the whole subject of "rebuilding our cities" takes on an added dimension when one considers that the extreme conditions of deterioration in our existing urban environments are most evident within these black enclaves; reflected not only in terms of physical blight, but (far more importantly) in social and human decay as well.

With regard to the struggle of black people, the hour has long since passed for "pimping" and "game playing," and now requires that we reassess our position, critically analyze our strategies and goals, and move forward from there.

With one lone exception, this will not be a recitation of the "facts" of poverty and discrimination evident within the central cores of our nation's urban centers. The growing economic disparity and deplorable conditions of physical blight that characterize the concrete realities of life for the masses of black

Beginnings: Planning 317

inhabitants, relative to a dominant white society, have been more than documented elsewhere. Further, most reports (including National Commission findings), from which many statistics and "poverty facts" are derived, emphasize the attitudes and feelings that provided the content for an extremely powerful form of racism, rather than the system of *privilege* and *control* that is inherent in our society's economic structure and which goes more to the heart of the matter.

Starting from the basic premise that physical change is inseparable from a broader community environment, the bulk of my research thus far has been an effort to gain a greater understanding of some of the basic social, economic, and political forces currently active within the urban central core. This ongoing analysis, of necessity, also includes other relevant forces that originate outside this boundary.

Working (sometimes daily) within this context, two points have become increasingly clear. First, the general march of the black movement in the United States, whose history is rooted in the legacy of a black slave system, is steadily gaining momentum. Somewhere within the last fifteen years (according to persons with more age and wisdom than I) it has made a fundamental shift from a struggle for Rights to what is clearly now a struggle for Power. Secondly, because of the worn and deteriorated conditions of the central urban environment and a resulting proliferation of physical rebuilding schemes, a "strategy on housing" may well govern all other strategies among and affecting black people as they move to accomplish other more definable objectives.

In attempting to gauge the broader dimension and deeper meanings of prevailing political issues and attitudes, I found very quickly that I had to address myself to a phenomenon that was not readily comprehensible, or even easily defined. It was only later that I uncovered a relatively short statement of written material that amazingly expresses, almost precisely, the kind of common spirit that I have encountered; one which has (seemingly) infused all aspects of political decision-making within an ever-increasing number of black neighborhoods.

Speaking at Hearings before the Subcommittee On Housing and Urban Affairs of the Committee On Banking and Currency, United States Senate, Milton Kotler spoke of the political interest expressed by a new power in the black communities. As he stated:

> This power is the power of all classes and groups within black communities; common to all, and thus the power of community. Since the interest which this community power seeks is of common value to all groups, it cannot be met by fulfilling the special interest of any one group in that community. Nor is the political interest held in common and expressed in a unity of power in the black community the sum of the interests of particular groups and classes within the community. This additive notion of community does not hold. Were government to meet every special interest of each group in a community—liberal relief for welfare mothers, jobs for the unemployed, business loans for black merchants,

better houses for those poorly housed, et cetera—a common interest would still stand unmet: not patronage, but liberty.[1]

Stated in another way, black people are increasingly realizing the ethnic basis and power-oriented nature of American politics; and, of necessity and for reasons of survival, are developing an identity as a group and are beginning to look upon themselves as a power structure among other power structures. The irreversible thrust of this political activity, which is both a national and social struggle, is necessarily aimed at altering the distribution of power and the related dynamics of social change and political reform in our society.

These aims are revolutionary in the sense that: 1) the reallocation of resources in American society necessary to transform the economic and social status of black people is of enormous magnitude; 2) the social system, in part designed to limit black participation in society, will have to be reformed; and 3) the reallocation of national resources and the reform of the social system will have to be executed during a period of rapid and accelerating urbanization (and related technological change) and rising domestic racial tension.[2]

If only to underscore the nature and exercise of power in America, others might also add (and I am inclined to agree), that most workable visions for fundamental and far-reaching changes in the life-chances and -choices of black ghetto residents, and, by necessity, in the overall social and political organization of our cities will come about (short of revolution) only by a complex bargaining process within political mechanisms that sort out and deal with conflicting group interests.[3]

However, I am personally pessimistic about any meaningful resolution of our crisis through this quasi-democratic procedure, mainly because the whole question of racial conflict brings with it basic limits and constraints on the bargaining process. Clearly, one of the most serious of these constraints is profound and widespread ignorance, much of which is self-imposed. I would tend to think that for most Americans, more or less educated, the enslavement of black people for 200 years, their economic and social plight since the Civil War, and the further dehumanizing, destructive impact of life in an involuntary ghetto has little meaning or relevance.

But be that as it may, the reality and continuing existence of massive slum ghetto systems in our nation's urban regions reflect, in a very real sense, the status quo of economic and political power distribution in the American social structure; and it is within this context of unequal resources that most black leaders will have to operate (at least at this juncture) as they address themselves to the unanswered question of how to amass the kind of power necessary to bring about significant advances and revolutionary changes in the life opportunities of the mass of black Americans.

[1] Kotler, Milton. Institute for Policy Studies, "Hearings before the Subcommittee On Housing And Urban Affairs of the Committee On Banking And Currency, United States Senate, Ninetieth Congress, First Session on Proposed Housing Legislation for 1967" (Washington, D.C. Government Printing Office, 1967).
[2] Schuchter, Arnold. *White Power/Black Freedom* (Boston: Beacon Press, 1968), p. 12.
[3] *Ibid.,* p. 6.

Lest there be any doubt, this critical mass must include those in the most pressing need of rapid development, who also represent the fastest growing section of the black community These are the black (youth) street force, the ADC mothers, welfare recipients, domestic servants, unskilled laborers, etc., who must be given an opportunity to exercise initiative, to make important and meaningful decisions, and for higher education, if the black community is to be developed.[4]

Implicit in any on-going struggle or movement in quest of long range goals, is the formulation and planned accomplishment of a continuing series of short-range objectives. There is a constantly evolving set of priorities, resulting partly from varying and shifting philosophical reasonings of how best to proceed, and in part from major external influences that have the potential for drastically altering even a loosely defined course of action.

Externalities from the development and eventual implementation of "mass production housing systems," primarily aimed (as a result of mounting social and political pressures) at providing much faster constructed housing shelters at significantly lower cost than presently possible, could be of this magnitude. For it has been proven time and again, that given the increasingly systematic nature of operation and response inherent in a highly industrialized society (system) such as ours, the introduction of a major developmental change in a previously underdeveloped area of our economy, will create repercussions throughout all its parts.

Recognizing that the urban core is made up primarily of black families and individuals of low income who occupy a large and growing number of substandard dwelling units, the pressures will be understandably great from all quarters to have massive numbers of such units built for their consumption; even at the risk of sub-optimizing the need for more houses in the overall priorities of the black movement.

The particular significance that this has for whatever strategy black leadership develops or has already developed with regard to housing, should be rather obvious.

In an effort to bring about "lowest cost housing," most of our funding, research, and attention thus far is being directed at ways and means of depressing the construction and operating costs of the physical structure. To this end, the implementation of a new "industrialized" building technology which would make possible the production of high volumes of housing shelters through a combination of larger standardized building components and mass production techniques (along with substantially improved means and methods of financing), is seen as imperative in order to bring housing within the means of lower income groups.

In my judgment, the decision to seek this basically technical solution is a crucial point, with the end result being that the stress will invariably be on the house as an end in itself; viewed, in the main, as an impersonal product to be

[4]Boggs, James. "The Myth and Irrationality of Black Capitalism." Paper delivered at the National Black Economic Development Conference, Detroit, Michigan, April 25, 1969, p. 5.

measured at the point of consumption. Granted, for some this may be all that is necessary, but the thrust of this whole discussion is that, that portion of the overall black population is a small (and conceivably dwindling) minority, relative to the swelling mass. And in effect, as it stands now, we are really talking about the beginning of yet another cog in this nation's gigantic productive apparatus; where undue emphasis on material success and the "sanctity of private enterprise" (in great part, the causes of *black underdevelopment*) have always taken primacy over human values whenever and wherever conflict has arisen, in pursuit of profit.

It would seem that there has been very little thought, if any, given to a relating of this planned physical change to political and social development in areas of our urban centers where such needs are clearly evident.

This is not to say that the process of physical renewal of the environment offers the total panacea for our urban ills, but, if past and recent history is, in any way, an accurate indicator of what we may expect in the future, then housing programs will be major determinants of any significant shifts in economic and population flows (and resulting political muscle); two of the basic ingredients necessary for the development of a (potentially) better-quality environment. Moreover, it is no secret that "the present day political, economic, and bureaucratic dilemma that the cities of America, and their slum and ghetto-dwellers find themselves trapped in, is due, in part, to public (and private) default on its responsibilities to ensure decent housing.[5] Finally, when one considers the order of magnitude of housing construction that we have set as a concrete goal to attain, its importance to all aspects of future urban growth and development can hardly be overstated.

Given the current state of political activity within black communities, which says, in effect, that any program that merely aims at providing houses (as if that function can be abstracted from their political life) will have no meaning, it is important to realize that there are other approaches to "lowest cost housing" to be considered. Basically, and very briefly, these are:

Economic approach—adjusting certain economic factors to aid the consumer's basic ability to pay;

Performance Design approach—maximization of general benefits from various investment levels;

Social approach—reflect the special needs of particular consumers in the design requirement for housing.

Development Process approach—coordinate the process which generates residential environment for maximum efficiency and cost savings; and

Operational approach—successful application to the "real world" of research output from all forementioned approaches to the problem of housing costs.[6]

---

[5]Schuchter, *op. cit.,* p. 125.
[6]Collins, Terry. "taken from a flow diagram of a Low-cost Housing Study, conducted by the Institute for Applied Technology" (Washington, D.C. Government Printing Office, 1968).

When this wider range of approaches is considered, a number of extremely pertinent questions are raised. Is it possible for employment-derived consumer income to be improved so that the gap between housing costs and the consumer's capacity to pay is eliminated? What are the considerations, steps, and relationships that *should* influence the design of housing? How can knowledge of these considerations, steps, and relationships be structured and organized to influence the design in a fully effective and coordinated fashion? What is the clearest, most direct, and complete statement that can be made about performance concepts to be used in the design of housing? What are the elements of such a concept? "Housing for low-income people" may not be the same thing as "lowest cost housing." What special characteristics then, if any, should "housing" for low-income people have? The cost of housing may lay not simply in the way the physical product is organized, but in the way the *process* that produces it is organized. Approaching the housing problem this way, what cost-savings can be realized? Is research available which organizes the relationship between user requirements, activity configurations, and the housing design process?

In light of the obvious merit of all the approaches mentioned earlier, it is probably safe to say that a "technical solution" is being sought partly because of our existing technological resources (with accompanying lobbyist and pressure groups) and ability to operate comfortably and effectively within this sphere; and in part because of our apparent lack of any meaningful quantitative or qualitative data necessary to deal with this problem from other points of view.

> For technology to apply to the real need of people seeking housing, their requirements must be understood. Yet, appropriate studies of activity patterns which may be stated as user needs have not been made, and are not available to be plugged into the housing design and development process. Consequently, it is difficult to specify exactly what it is (beyond the minimum physical requirements) that should be developed in order to provide appropriate housing for any group; particularly for persons of low or moderate income.
>
> The performance criteria for building programs today relate, by and large, to patterns of life assumed appropriate or acceptable for people who can independently afford "good" housing, and fail to allow for more complex living patterns among persons of lower income.[7]

It has also been noted that the scale at which we work is increasing in both size and speed, and opportunities for our cities to grow and evolve gradually, with sympathetic response to the community, have given way to large-scale programs that are attempting to "design" qualities that previously developed through evolution.[8]

[7]"Report of The National Commission on Urban Problems to the Congress and to the President of the United States" (Washington, D.C. Government Printing Office, 1969), p. 499.
[8]*Ibid.,* p. 499.

Significantly, in a classic understatement, a National Urban Commission concluded that, "we must develop systematic procedures for determining the evolving needs of people."[9]

Again, Kotler speaks more to the point when he says:

> Programs do not succeed by their goals alone, nor by their ingenious mechanism or colossal allocations. They must have a structure of operation that is natural and in compatibility with the aspirations of the people these programs intend to serve.
>
> No technical ingenuity can make up for the "defect of principle," and no enlargement of goal can compensate for unnaturalness of the program operation.[10]

More specifically, programs intended to serve the needs of black people in America must do so in the course of the ongoing black political struggle; any program (housing or whatever) that undercuts the legitimate political aspirations of black people is inevitably doomed to failure.

Given the almost total rule of black communities by outside forces, we must begin to understand that the current revolt of black people, by sheer necessity, will have to be pushed beyond the average white or black man's tolerance for change, and repeated change, and repeated change.

I am under no illusions about "liberty and justice for all" in our society, but I do possess a certain degree of residual hope. And if there is, in fact, a growing and true concern for improving the quality of our urban environment, as expressed by our Presidents, our National Congress, and others less powerful, but equally important, then it is perhaps reasonable to assume that there are those (with resources) who both understand and accept the need for a fundamental reordering of our priorities and processes in urban rebuilding, and who are willing to pursue the development of housing production systems that are compatible with urban realities.

I recognize that this is an omnibus task with a vast range of varying elements and variables to be defined and developed. A great deal of attention, however, must be paid to the emerging (and potentially critical) interrelationships between the aspirations and evolving goals of black people in quest of fundamental change and the "process of mass housing design."

It is my hope that out of such investigation will come clearer directions for the development of a structured means by which the performance requirements of each of these two major forces could be co-ordinated (and conceivably interlocked at some future point) for mutual gain and benefit.

Resources

Abrams, Charles. *Forbidden Neighbors* (New York: Harper & Row, 1954).
Bellush and Hausknecht. *Urban Renewal: People, Politics and Planning* (New York: Doubleday & Company, 1967).

[9]*Ibid.,* p. 499.
[10]Kotler, *op. cit.*

Boggs, James. *Manifesto for a Black Revolutionary Party* (Philadelphia: Pace setters Publishers, 1969).

Chinitz, Benjamin. *City and Suburb: The Economics of Metropolitan Growth* (Englewood Cliffs, N.J.: Prentice-Hall, 1966).

Ewald, William R., Jr. *Environment for Man* (Bloomington & London: Indiana University Press, 1968).

Gamson, William. *Power and Discontent* (Homewood, Ill.: Dorsey Press, 1968.)

Handlin, Oscar. *Fire-Bell in the Night* (Boston: Little, Brown & Company, 1964).

Kain, John. "The Distribution and Movement of Jobs and Industry." Chamber of Commerce of the United States (Washington, D.C., 1967).

Keniston, Kenneth. *The Uncommitted* (New York: Harcourt, Brace & World, Inc., 1968).

Lundberg, Ferdinand. *The Rich and the Super-Rich* (New York: Lyle Stuart, Inc., 1968).

Meier, Richard. *A Communications Theory of Urban Growth* (Cambridge, Mass.: MIT Press, 1962).

Ray, Paul. "A Political Profile of Lansing, Michigan." (M.E.T.R.O. Internal Report No. 11, mimeo).

Schuchter, Arnold. *White Power/Black Freedom* (Boston: Beacon Press, 1968).

Building The American City. "Report of The National Commission on Urban Problems to the Congress and to the President of the United States" (Washington, D.C. Government Printing Office, 1969).

30. Behavioral Research and Environmental Programming

ROBERT SOMMER

To a greater extent than perhaps any other nation, we Americans have become an "indoor" people. A large portion of our lives—working, sleeping, playing—is spent in buildings: buildings over whose design and construction we have little or no control; buildings whose physical and economic distribution are only remotely conditioned by our needs; buildings whose effect upon our health and happiness is only obscurely understood.

J.M. FITCH, *American Building*

As a psychologist in the design fields, I write articles on hospital design for hospital administrators, on outdoor study spaces for landscape designers, on classroom seating for teachers and principals, and so on. I am less interested in the specific substance of my results, since I lack the time, facilities, and commitment to do a really extensive study of any single setting, than in demonstrating the relevance of behavior research to practitioners. The goal is to stimulate individuals in the field to undertake this research themselves. When someone comes into a situation, does research, and then leaves, barely a ripple of change appears. It is better to get the people involved in the situation to conduct the research themselves, even if the research is of inferior quality. This is one lesson of the Peace Corps experience. Although it is easier for the corpsmen to build a well or a school themselves than to get the local people to do it, if they do it themselves and leave, the situation would revert to the *status quo* quickly. Not until practitioners in the design fields and space managers become concerned with how their buildings affect people are we going to have some meaningful changes taking place. When a designer or user participates in evaluation research, the situation is no longer one of an outsider coming in, telling him in a foreign language how to run his business, and leaving on the next plane.

An occupational hazard of environmental consulting is that the client receives the impression that all problems can be solved by pushing through a wall or rearranging the chairs. Things just are not that simple. Any change in the physical or organizational structure of a hospital, office, or household will require some rearrangement of other items, but there is no guarantee that any single change will produce the desired results. Frequently it is the fact of change itself that is important—shaking things up or "making it hot for them," to use Terry Southern's phrase.

More than anything else, the interest shown by management in environmental change conveys to others that experiment and innovation are encouraged and will be supported. Such changes within an organization tend to be infectious. Department heads feel that they cannot sit still when others are experimenting with new procedures and programs. A new car on the block creates some dissatisfaction among neighbors on all sides. When one man redecorates his office, others will follow. So much is written about the deterioration of environment, that we tend to overlook people's desires for beauty and harmony. A single renovation or beautification program accomplishes more by creating an awareness of the possibilities of change than as a statistical increment of beauty in a desolate or ugly world.

The contributions of social scientists to design fields are going to change over the years. Right now they will be most useful in teaching designers how to evaluate existing structures and in participating in such evaluations as a member of a research team. This means going out into windowless schools and offices, low income housing projects, and adventure playgrounds to see how the people are using the facilities and what they think of them. This will provide a good body of case studies of individual design solutions. If there is great consistency in the way that people react to certain design features or a larger architectural element, some generalization may be possible.

Considered from the standpoint of a single building, evaluation research is not very practical since the findings will come too late to be of use to the clients. However if we are dealing with a building system that will expand and change over time, then this criticism becomes invalid. A 300-bed hospital may not be constructed all at one time but rather in three increments of 100 beds each. This will make it possible to include the results from behavioral studies of the first wing into the planning and design of the second and third wings. Such a procedure was followed by Wheeler in his collaboration with an architectural firm designing college dormitories for several Indiana campuses. From the study of the first unit they derived information that modified the plans for the subsequent dormitories. The first dormitory lounge was a large open area, the usual sort of status space that impresses parents and visitors but provides limited privacy for the residents. In the second residence hall a two-level plan reduced complaints substantially. The formal lounge was divided into four areas by means of a central chimney; activity areas were located on a mezzanine.[1]

[1]Lawrence Wheeler, *Behavioral Research for Architectural Planning and Design* (Terre Haute, Indiana: Ewing Miller, Associates, 1967).

Where circumstances permit, the research team can conduct experiments within the setting. In view of the amount of money involved in large-scale renovation, these will probably be rather modest ventures. Time will also be a limitation since a structure or area should be observed over a period of years rather than weeks. In terms of priorities, it would seem that collecting the observational and survey data from existing settings would have the greatest immediate payoff.

Given our present state of ignorance, I have serious misgivings about social scientists becoming involved in the actual design of buildings. When an architect comes to me with plans for a conference room or college dormitory, I can only make the wildest guesses as to how these are going to work in practice —unless of course they are so obvious that any observer could make the same predictions. I have no special competence in predicting how customers will react to an open-plan bank or a round auditorium. All I can say is: "If you are interested in knowing about open-plan banks, build one and let me observe it, or hire me to visit open-plan banks and a few closed-plan structures for comparison purposes." Even when I advise about a building type I know well —college dormitories—I feel compelled to preface it this way: "Although we found these opinions held at 20 dormitories in California, your situation in Salt Lake City or Toronto may be different, so borrow carefully from our findings."

I feel that at this point in time, social scientists can be most useful in evaluating existing structures. It is premature to involve them in the design process unless they have had prior experience with a building type or will have sufficient time to acquire relevant data. It would be regrettable if social scientists were brought into architectural firms as status symbols, for their great potential contribution as data gatherers will be lost if they become merely sources of ancedote, myth, and analogy.

The need for translating scientific findings into a form usable by practitioners exists in almost every field. Few engineers can read physics journals and few medical men can read journals of biochemistry. It would be a waste of time for architects to keep abreast of journals in psychology or sociology; few social scientists are able to do this either. The one relevant article in a hundred would have an ambiguous title: "The Effects of Proximity on Clique Structure," or "Luminosity and Color Perception." Furthermore, the practical implications of relevant findings are not always apparent. It has been shown that there are more friendships in dormitories with common washrooms than in those with private washrooms, but what does this mean to an architect who wants to design for privacy as well as for friendliness? For almost every item in a building program there is the qualification that too much of a good thing is undesirable.

The delay in using social science data in the design fields is a product of several factors. There is, for one thing, the reluctance of designers to replace their reliance on intuition, artistry, and perceptual values such as harmony, integrity, and cohesion with the jargon of a new group of self-proclaimed experts. The coalescing of individuals and professions with diverse training, viewpoint, and perceptual style requires the time for each group to become accustomed to each other and this can only occur in a nonthreatening situation. Case studies of design solutions such as buildings or parks cannot be undertaken with an attitude of finding out what is wrong with the place. This is particularly true when it comes to publishing the results of such studies. Fortunately there is some precedent in biomedical research where case studies are published without the names of the individuals. A physician describes twenty cases of sleeping sickness, the first is a woman age 54 with two children, the second a man age 38, unmarried, and so on; a public health team describes the locale of its study as "A small Kansas town of 1500 people, primarily a marketing and commercial center for the surrounding agriculture area." Community surveys typically employ pseudonyms (Middletown or Prairieville) or a general statement about "three suburban communities on the east coast." Economists and others studying business organizations do not identify a company by name in published articles. Many precedents exist for evaluating schools, office buildings, and housing projects without mentioning the individuals or companies involved and thus avoiding *ad hominem* arguments or the creation of a form of negative awards system.

Also needed is a middleman who is acquainted with the design fields as well as with the social sciences to translate relevant behavioral data into terms meaningful to designers. Thomas Seabrook advocates the category of planner-sociologist in the city planning field.[2] Such a person would translate behavioral theories and facts into the range of tolerance with which the physical planner can cope. Seabrook asks of what relevance is it to know that poorer families are less mobile, more neighborhood oriented; and depend to a greater degree on their neighbors for psychological support? If one can penetrate the jargon, these data are more interesting than helpful to planners. Someone has to tease out their design implications by asking the right questions. Does the shortage of money mean that the children and parents will spend more time in the park? Does the increased leisure of the upper middle class mean a greater need for outdoor recreational spaces? Do older people and retired individuals have special needs for benches, shaded areas, and access to restroom facilities that are not included in standard park designs?

The behavioral scientist differs from the subject-matter specialist in that he is an expert on methods for obtaining information and may know little, at least at the outset, about particular settings. Let us consider the design of a library for a NASA academy. It would be desirable for the planning board to bring in a library consultant, probably a trained librarian interested and experienced in library construction, someone who is knowledgeable about the history of the field, present developments, and where things are heading. The money invested in experienced library consultants will be returned many times over in the improved efficiency of the building and actual cost savings on specific items.

[2]Thomas G. Seabrook, "The Role of the Sociologist in the Planning Professions," *Habitat* (March-April 1965), pp. 20–24.

However, the needs of a particular agency in a specific situation are unique, so it would be hazardous to rely solely on subject-matter knowledge in designing for specific clients. What are the special needs of NASA people? What provisions can be made for storing classified materials so they can be retrieved easily? An architect can learn much from visiting libraries at West Point and the Air Force Academy as well as from talking with librarians at regional NASA sites. To tie all this material together as well as to obtain information on the specific work habits and needs of NASA personnel may take more time and effort than the architect is willing to invest. It would be wasteful to use library consultants as data gatherers, people who go out and interview NASA personnel at various sites, although this practice has been followed. A more reasonable procedure would involve delegating the task of learning the opinions and work habits of the building's prospective residents to some person trained in the social sciences. He would introduce a different perspective, the viewpoint of someone who has assisted with environmental programming in a variety of settings. Called in by NASA, he may know nothing about military librarianship—his last job might have been with a community redevelopment agency trying to unslum a salvageable district and, before that, with a state agency drawing up specifications for playgrounds. This work has taught him how to find the needs of clients and express them in such a way that they are meaningful to designers. It is the architect who translates the building program into sketches and the sketches into a three-dimensional form, but it is the behavioral scientist who feeds information into the system about the needs of the specific people involved, just as the subject-matter expert feeds in information about like buildings elsewhere and new developments in the field.

Designers need concepts that are relevant to both physical form and human behavior. Much of architecture affects people from beyond the focus of awareness. People are not sure what it is about a building or room that affects them, nor are they able to express how they feel in different surroundings. Norbitt Mintz interviewed a large number of students in three sorts of rooms—one very attractive with modern decor, the second a room of average appearance, and the third an ugly room resembling a janitor's closet in a sad state of disrepair with an exposed light bulb, torn shade, and a tin can serving as a receptacle for cigarette ashes. When he questioned the students afterwards, he found that only 29 per cent mentioned anything about the appearance of the rooms, 46 per cent mentioned that something seemed wrong in the experiment but could not say what it was, and 25 per cent reported that the experiment was "fine."[3]

Not only do people have difficulty expressing what they feel about architecture, but most of their reactions to a division of space is on an emotional rather than a rational level. This is especially true in regard to the division of space within a house rather than the shell or enclosure. Architects rely on language even though it is apparent that words may mean different things to an architect

[3]Norbitt Mintz, "Effects of Aesthetic Surroundings," *Journal of Psychology,* XLI (1956), 459–66.

than to a client. The way an architect uses the word "cell" to describe an office may disturb a corporation executive who associates the term with prisons.

In their studies of highway experience, Appleyard and his associates believed that their first task was to develop techniques for recording, analyzing, and communicating the visual and kinesthetic sequences of highway travel. Without such techniques, it is difficult to express or refine design alternatives short of building full-scale roads. Sensing the inadequacies of photographic recording for detailed analysis of visual experience, they have developed an intriguing system analogous to the music notations used by composers in which the road becomes a spatial and kinesthetic rhythmic experience—a symphony.[4] Recently there have been attempts to develop techniques for studying the subjective connotations of structures as well as their objective dimensions. One such technique is the semantic differential developed by Charles Osgood at the University of Illinois in which concepts are rated along various scales, good to bad, strong to weak, active to passive, and so forth.[5] The same object may have vastly different connotations to different people— a hammer is a toy to a child and a tool to his father; a slum neighborhood can mean security and warmth to a child growing up there and a social problem to a city planner. One study was aimed specifically at exploring how architects use the concept of space. Architects speak of "interesting spaces" and "vital spaces," but laymen use the term to refer to a void or absence of something. Architecture students saw space as more valuable, active, and more potent than did the liberal arts students.[6] Such techniques can help us to clarify and to understand people's reactions to their surroundings. Most present architectural criticism has been written by highly literate and sensitive individuals who visit buildings for short periods and whose reactions may be unrepresentative of the building's inhabitants. Another solution is to increase the sensitivity and correct the visual and emotional blindness of people so that they can present their needs and feelings in a form that others can understand and appreciate. This may require considerable effort, and the task is being made more difficult by electronic technology, which leaves little room for human experience and meaningful social intercourse.

Methods for Gathering Data

Laboratory experiments have generally yielded discouraging results when it comes to evaluating environmental effects on human performance. There are extremes of heat, cold, and humidity that have an obvious effect on behavior, but these are rarely the concern of designers interested in the normal range of sensory stimulation. Edward Thorndike conducted an elaborate series of tests

[4]Donald Appleyard, Kevin Lynch, and J. R. Myer, *The View from the Road* (Cambridge, Mass.: M.I.T. Press, 1964).
[5]Charles E. Osgood, G. Suci, and P. Tannenbaum, *The Measurement of Meaning* (Urbana: University of Illinois Press, 1957).
[6]Robert Sommer, "The Significance of Space," *AIA Journal* (May 1965), pp. 63–65.

for the New York State Commission on Ventilation on the efficiency of student performance under various conditions of temperature, humidity, and air movement. The tasks included laboratory exercises in naming colors and canceling digits as well as school exercises in arithmetic, English composition, and typing. Environmental conditions ranged from those that, at the time, were considered optimal (68 degrees, 50 per cent relative humidity, and 45 feet per person per minute of outside air) to those that were regarded as very unfavorable (86 degrees, 80 per cent relative humidity, and no circulation or change of air). The authors concluded:

> With the forms of work and lengths of period used, we find that when an individual is urged to do his best he does as much, and does it as well, and improves as rapidly in a hot, humid, sterile, and stagnant air condition as in an optimum condition. . . . We find further that when an individual is given work to do that is of no interest or value to him and is deprived even of the means of telling how well he does it, and is in other ways tempted to relax standards and do work of poor quality, he still shows no inferiority in the quality of the product. . . . Finally we find that when an individual is left to his own choice as to whether he shall do mental work or read stories, rest, talk, or sleep, he does as much work per hour when the temperature is 75 degrees as when it is 68 degrees.[7]

Productivity in the laboratory tends to remain constant regardless of environment. When conditions are unfavorable, the subject works harder to compensate for his handicaps. Many effects of a noxious environment are insidious and reveal themselves over the long run rather than immediately. On the other hand, it is true that symphonies have been created in basements, inventions made in garages, and masterpieces painted in unheated garrets. Whether these heroes are able to triumph because of the challenge of adversity or in spite of it is only part of the answer. We must also know how the vast majority of ordinary mortals perform in different environments. I can read a novel (but not a technical book) with the phonograph playing, but someone else will react differently.

If a ten-year-old child in New York can survive the crowding, noise, crime, and litter, it is unlikely that rearranging the chairs in his classroom will have a significant effect on how much he learns if he wants to. A small desk or obnoxious roommate in a college dormitory is not going to lower a student's grades if he can go elsewhere to study. It will change his behavior, increasing the amount of study outside the room, but this is not a "hard performance variable" like grade point average. In the classroom experiments discussed in Chapter 7, the escape behaviors could be attributed to room environment, but there was no difference in class grades between the sections. At Rensselaer Polytechnic Institute an experimental classroom has been developed whose

---

[7]Edward L. Thorndike, W. A. McCall, and J. C. Chapman, "Ventilation in Relation to Mental Work," *Teachers College Contributions to Education,* LXXVIII (1916), 82.

lighting, colored surfaces, seating types, and projection display surfaces can all be altered systematically. After several years of research, the authors admit that the question "How well does this environment perform in supporting learning?" has not been answered.[8]

Let me pose a conundrum that I think will elucidate some of the important but hidden issues in the criterion problem.

> We have two chairs in a classroom, Type A and Type B, and whenever a student is given a choice, he sits in Type A. The result is that Type A chairs are occupied first and Type B remain empty when there are surplus chairs in the room. However, when there are only as many chairs as there are pupils, or students must sit in assigned places without regard to chair type, we find no difference in examination scores between students sitting in A and B chairs.

What does this mean? Does the lack of difference in examination scores mean that a school board can purchase either chair or the cheaper of the two in good conscience, that is, with the realization that the amount of learning taking place will be unaffected by their decision? I do not accept this view, and I will try to explain why. For one thing, it overlooks the totalitarian nature of institutional experience. If a house builder constructs two models, A and B, and nobody buys B, the question of whether he builds both A and B is academic. In the free market situation, he does not build anything that people will not buy. However, a school, library, or hospital board, corporation committee, or any other institutional client does not have to worry about the vagaries of the market place. If they construct small classrooms, two-man offices, and four-bed hospital rooms, they will be used and, in terms of performance criteria, probably will be just as effective as single rooms or three-man rooms. Institutional arrangements place people in situations they would not otherwise choose. We can cut the Gordian knot by making the realization of individual choice and satisfaction as values in their own right. If people say they like something or show by their behavior that they prefer it, this should be a value fed into the design process even though it cannot be proven that this makes a difference on a profit-and-loss statement or an academic record. Many performance criteria deal with only a single aspect of a multigoal organization. The encouragement of academic achievement is one objective of a good classroom teacher, but she also strives for personal growth, maturity, and self-direction on the part of her pupils. I am not saying that performance criteria such as profit-and-loss, days-in-hospital, or grades should be discarded. When a measure fits only a single dimension of a situation, the solution is not to reject all measurement, but to develop measures for the other aspects. Single item evaluation tends to encourage *criterion-directed performance,* which neglects important but unmeasured aspects of program success.

[8]A. Green, "Architectural Research and the Learning Environment" (Paper presented at the Second National Conference on Architectural Psychology, Park City, Utah, 1966).

In a changing world it seems reasonable to establish *variety* and *flexibility* as important goals in a building program. I do not propose substituting them for harmony, unity, balance, rhythm, excitement, or the other traditional design values. Both variety and flexibility inherently increase the range of individual choice. A necessary corollary of these two values is that we must establish institutional arrangements—rules, procedures, and personnel practices—that enable individuals to exploit the variety and possibilities for flexibility in their environment. By *variety* I mean a multiplicity of settings and spaces a person can select to suit his individual needs. On my campus there is a policy regarding dormitory construction that no new residence hall complex should be identical with an existing one. The goal is to increase the range of choices available to students at the beginning of the term. The same principle can be applied to other design elements; rather than installing benches of one kind or size in parks and recreation areas, it is preferable to vary one's purchases and arrangements. *Flexibility* is expressed in such terms as multipurpose, multiuse, and convertible spaces. With rapidly changing technology and the inability to predict institutional practices even five years ahead, its importance seems obvious. It is closely tied in with *personalization* since it permits a man to adapt a setting to his unique needs.

The Hawthorne Myth

Perhaps the least understood and most maligned study in the history of the social sciences was the research into worker productivity conducted at Western Electric Company. Many people have heard of the *Hawthorne effect* or the way that production rose as working conditions improved.[9] However, when some of the changes were reversed, production continued to rise. This has been interpreted to mean that environment did not make any difference, it was all a placebo effect—like getting a reaction to a sugar pill. However, what the Western Electric study showed conclusively was that environment did make a difference. Almost every change in environmental conditions had its effect on the workers and, often, on their production. The study also demonstrated that there is no simple relationship between single environmental elements and complex human behavior. The effects of environmental changes are mediated by individual needs and group processes. The worker does not react to improved lighting or a coffee break as the rat does to the lever in his cage that brings him a food pellet. In an atmosphere of trust and understanding, he accepts environmental changes as indications that management is interested in his welfare. In an atmosphere of distrust and hostility, he wonders how management hopes to exploit him by changing his working conditions; he looks upon environmental programming as manipulation. Behavior produced by a sugar pill is just as real and observable as behavior

[9]F. J. Roethlisberger and W. J. Dickson, *Management and the Worker* (Cambridge, Mass.: Harvard University Press, 1939).

produced by amphetamine. Just as some people are made sleepy by pep pills and the magnitude of their reaction is influenced by the presence or absence of other people, so changes in man's internal environment are not simple conditioned reflexes in which A automatically produces B.

Studies of schools, hospitals, prisons, and slums have shown that it is nearly impossible to isolate the specific factors responsible for a given outcome. Neither can we tell precisely why one city can support a major league team and another cannot, or why Topeka, Kansas, became a world-renowned center of psychiatry, but Wichita, which is a much larger city, did not, or why one town can pass a large school bond issue that is defeated in an adjacent city. There is no single factor that can explain any of these phenomena. Frequently it appears that the reason is connected with the town's self-image as a sports capital or a cultural center or a good business town. The citizens then support the programs that fit the town's image. San Franciscans believe themselves to be cosmopolitan and are therefore willing to tolerate toplessness and gay bars; the citizens of Green Bay accept with joy or resignation the annual fall football madness. An image that is believed becomes a self-fulfilling prophecy. The image of a city as a bad business town can doom that city, and the stereotype of a neighborhood as good or bad will raise or lower real estate values. Any attempt to trace the origin of these beliefs will produce a score of causal agents, major as well as minor. The mechanisms involved in this process are similar to the Hawthorne effect. People who are concerned with solutions to particular problems are less concerned with how something works than the fact that it works. A recent review of programs for geriatric patients includes these comments: "... whether by a Hawthorne effect or by the specific action of the milieu program on the staff or patients, most of these programs have succeeded in raising the functioning level of their recipients in a measurable manner,"[10] and "Almost any type of facility works with older brain-damaged patients. The main thing is stimulation from the environment and, of course, a radical change in attitude on the part of personnel."

The methods of the biological sciences, particularly animal biology and ecology, which rely heavily upon observation and field experimentation over long periods, seem more applicable to the design fields than the single variable laboratory experiments characteristic of physics and chemistry. A designer would profit more from training in the techniques of systematic observation than in the empty rituals included under the category of experimental design. It is extremely difficult if not impossible to execute a rigorous experiment that deals with important relationships under natural conditions. Experiments in the field are replete with unanticipated variables and *post hoc* explanations. It is unlikely that the use of laboratory models in teaching students will increase the number of field experiments or improve their quality, since the techniques necessary to undertake a good field study differ radically from those of a laboratory. For one thing the field investigator must be extremely sensitive

[10]M. Powell Lawton, "Planning a Building for the Mentally Impaired Aged," mimeo., 1965.

BEGINNINGS

to the structure of the environment, the important processes that are taking place, the people with whom he works, the administrative procedures that must be followed. In the classroom evaluation studies described earlier, the administrative arrangements took more time and effort than the research itself. A study in a public school requires the permission of individual teachers, the school principal and his assistants, the local school board, the county superintendent of schools and his assistants, as well as the approval and cooperation of students and parents. If any single step is omitted and some key person is not consulted, the affair can turn into a debacle. A recent article describes a study that had been cleared with all the important names on the official school hierarchy, but the investigator forgot to contact several assistants to key people (one was out of town during the orientation session, and the other was away on a two-year leave), and, to the investigator's dismay, these assistants were the ones responsible for interpreting headquarters' policy to individual schools. Field studies are not for the soft-hearted or the administratively ignorant, they are far more complex from the standpoint of human relationships and sensitivity to social structure than laboratory studies. Occasionally an investigator finds a situation where a high-ranking official in a large operation becomes interested in behavioral studies and gives them his enthusiastic support. This was the case in the studies by Wells of the new office building of the Cooperative Insurance Company in Manchester.[11] It would have been impossible to undertake individual interviews and systematic observational studies without management's full cooperation. One cannot undertake creative environmental experimentation without the support and interest of those who are administratively responsible for the environment.

None of these methods can be applied arbitrarily. One has to learn when, where, and how to gain information. This requires a feeling for the nature of the setting and the people in it. One does not use a printed questionnaire with migrant workers, geriatric patients, or ghetto children. On the other hand, the questionnaire is a most efficient and appropriate tool for college students accustomed to written examinations and who may indeed be troubled by a personal interview that requires direct confrontation with an older person— a novel experience for many of them! With children I would choose direct observation in situations where many options are available, supplemented by interviews (both individual and group) after the observations had continued for some time. With migrant workers the use of participant observation would seem appropriate provided the researcher spoke the workers' language. Thus far we have said little about participant observation where the observer shares the daily lives of the people under study, observing things that happen, listening to what is said, and questioning people over some length of time. The method produces data that are often strikingly different from those obtained through interview or casual observation methods. A designer or some member

[11]Brian W. P. Wells, "The Psycho-Social Influence of Building Environment," *Building Science,* I (1965), 153–65.

of his staff might live in a migrant workers' camp or accompany hospital attendants through their daily routine for a few days. As an insider he sees, hears, smells, and feels things to which the general public or infrequent visitors are not privy. Spending time in a setting allows him to gain the confidence and learn the private language of the participants. He is able to question people about matters that he has observed directly (the toilet facilities in the camp or the temperature in the building on an extremely hot day) rather than employ abstract questions about heating, lighting, and ventilation. Becker and Geer believe that participant observation is most useful when a situation or institution is in a state of change. Living and working in the situation will assist the researcher in distinquishing between reactions to the present situation, memories of the past, and hopes for the future.[12]

The expense of building mock-ups and the need to evaluate building systems before they are opened to the public has created an interest in various simulation techniques ranging from wide-screen photography in assessing reactions to the cityscape to hypnosis. Aaronson has been using hypnotic induction to learn the effects of color and sound on mood, the way a person behaves when the world is lacking in depth, or when he is four feet tall. All these conditions exert a powerful influence on the way a person perceives and behaves. When the hypnotic suggestion was made to a subject that he had diminished in size, he responded by seeing everything as if it were twice as far away as usual. Events and objects took on a dreamlike character and things seemed to be moving faster than they were. He became withdrawn and apathetic and felt isolated, sleepy, and without interest. When the hypnotic set of his diminished size was removed, he felt pleased and seemed normal except for his feeling that everything looked smaller. He described the world as toylike and was much impressed with how much prettier and daintier everybody and everything looked.[13]

There is no single best method—questionnaire, interview, simulation, or experiment—for studying man's adaptations to his environment. One chooses methods to suit the problem and the people and not vice versa. These methods are generally complementary rather than mutually exclusive. One would not only interview office workers and managers, he might also work alongside them at a desk for a few weeks, observe who drinks coffee with whom and to which desk people go when they want to borrow things, and he might also examine various artifacts such as interoffice mail envelopes, which would show communication patterns within the office.

There are important ethical questions about the user's role and participation in environmental experimentation. The whole matter of experimentation with human subjects is receiving long-needed critical attention from medical and

---

[12]Howard S. Becker and Blanche Geer, "Participant Observation and Interviewing: A Comparison," *Human Organization,* XVI (1957), 28–32.
[13]Bernard S. Aaronson, "Lilliput and Brobdignag—Self and World," *American Journal of Clinical Hypnosis,* X (1968), 160–66.

behavioral researchers as well as lawyers and legislators. The need for strict surveillance in cases involving radiation hazards and pesticides is clear enough. The situation becomes murky in cases of sonic booms and crowded beaches, annoyances rather than dangers. Most of the building evaluation work discussed in preceding chapters did not involve serious risks to anyone's health or livelihood. However, one can still imagine a lawsuit brought by a parent who maintained that his son failed in school because he had been placed in a six-man dormitory room to fit an experimental plan devised by college authorities to evaluate the effects of room size upon study habits. To determine the justification of his complaint, one would have to know whether the student or his parents had protested his being assigned to a six-man room, whether there was a decline in his school work that seemed related to his study situation, and whether the college authorities had made some attempt to ensure that participants in the study would not suffer as a result of the room assignments. I do not feel it is immoral to assign students to facilities that are presently being used on hundreds of campuses in order to learn how they work in practice. On the contrary, it seems immoral to build and use dormitories without making some systematic attempt to evaluate their effectiveness.

Administrative practices and informal understandings within an organization imprint themselves upon people until they accept them without question. The evidence from perceptual experiments is consistent in finding that familiarity does not breed contempt, but rather increased liking. This can be seen as an adaptive reaction in the human organism to permit it to adjust to a multitude of conditions. Not only will people adapt to crowding, noise, and traffic in the city, they will find it difficult to live in any other environment. Zajonc and Harrison have studied the connection between exposure and preference. In one study people were shown a series of photographs of faces—some faces were exposed once, some twice, some ten times, some 25 times. Afterwards it was found that the more a face had been shown to a person, the more he liked it. The same result was obtained when Chinese characters were used as stimuli. The more a Chinese character was exposed, the more likely did people feel that it stood for an attractive word or something they would like.[14]

Studies like this can tell us something about the dynamics of habituation and environmental preference. There are many other perceptual experiments dealing with illusions[15] and the effects of human needs on perception[16] that are relevant to spatial behavior. However it is important that architects guard themselves against *perceptual reductionism.* This attitude has all the weak-

[14]Robert B. Zajonc, "The Attitudinal Effects of Mere Exposure," *Journal of Personality and Social Psychology,* monograph supplement, IX (1968), 1–27. Also see A. A. Harrison, "Response Competition and Attitude Change as a Function of Repeated Stimulus Exposure" (Ph.D. thesis, University of Michigan, 1967).

[15]A. Ames, "Visual Perception and the Rotating Trapezoidal Window," *Psychological Monographs,* No. 324 (1951).

[16]Charles M. Solley and Gardner Murphy, *Development of the Perceptual World* (New York: Basic Books, Inc., Publishers, 1960).

nesses of the biological reductionism of Ardrey[17] and others who see in man's spatial behavior the clear expression of instinctual drives. On a technical level, the distinction here is one of analogy and homology. Behavior that is similar in appearance between species may be triggered by entirely different mechanisms. A person's behavior is affected by how he perceives the world as well as his biological makeup but both are overlaid and shaped through learning. Environmental adaptations are too complex and multidetermined to be reduced either to instincts or perceptual laws.

Finally we come to the question of applying the results of these studies. Any building must meet the diverse needs of occupants whose interests frequently conflict. A wife's need for cooking space will compete with TV space and play area for the children. A public building that serves numerous client groups will have an even larger number of competing demands made upon it. One cannot design a college dormitory solely for individual privacy since this is also the students' main social area. A store must serve the needs of shoppers, clerks, and store detectives. Some engineers and scientists have tried to sidestep this problem by substituting harmony, coherence, or efficiency as the ultimate criterion of a design solution. A recent review states:

> Man is the most unreliable part of the man-machine-environment complex with which the system engineer deals. For the time being, he is tolerated in the system because he is either cheaper or has some skill which no machine has. Eventually he will be displaced by a more reliable component. This will not be so bad so long as some people remain in the system, but at last the day will come when even the system engineer will be replaced by a superior robot designer. At that stage, society will have developed a set of design values to replace the more old-fashioned and inefficient human values.[18]

One can design a system in which machines work efficiently to serve other machines, prisons that serve the short-term interests of people outside, and universities that serve the needs of researchers rather than students. One outcome is as feasible as any other. A design problem is a value problem: whose interests are to be served.

It is difficult for the ordinary citizen to get a handle on the larger environmental problems of pollution, pesticides, and congestion where the causes are complex, relationships between cause and effect obscure, effects insidious, and cures expensive. Most of the time we are spectators at a grand tragedy wondering if we can last through the final act. The minor spaces around us, our bedrooms, offices, schools, and streets bring problems of another, more manageable magnitude. A man's office can be a stimulating, esthetically pleasing, and highly personal place, or it can be a cold, impersonal, and bureaucratic area that belongs to the company through its surrogates, the custodians. A conference room can bring people together or it can prevent them from hearing

[17]Robert Ardrey, *The Territorial Imperative* (New York: Atheneum Publishers, 1966).
[18]Luigi Petrullo, review of *The New Utopians*, in *Contemporary Psychology*, XII (1967), 165.

and seeing one another, diminish their interest in the proceedings, and create cliques. Privacy for Americans is mainly a matter of visual protection against other people, but open plan housing is moving in the opposite direction. The bank manager may tell a customer that they cannot be overheard as they talk in the center of a large office, but the customer will not feel comfortable, nor will the manager believe that the space is really his unless he can personalize it in some way. The myth of infinite plasticity must be discarded in the design of minor spaces, too. The price paid in adapting to uncongenial environments may be difficult to estimate in money, sickness, inefficiency, and turnover, but it is too high if we can design congenial environments for the same money or less. There is a lesson to be learned when executives put calendars and charts on the backs of glass doors, college students choose old barracks over modern dormitories, and Sylvia Ashton-Warner, the talented teacher of Maori children, prefers her dilapidated prefab to the elegant glass castle where the teachers are concerned with proper coathooks and preventing the chairs from scraping the new floor. People like spaces they can call their own and make over; they reject an alien environment that is built according to detailed square footage allocations for a standard model of impersonal humanity in the most durable and antiseptic condition. The man of tomorrow whose capacity to respond to the environment is reduced, may be excused from this lesson, but we are not.

The situation in the agricultural fields is instructive. Engineers and agricultural economists believe that if the production of a crop cannot be mechanized, the crop will eventually disappear. Since ordinary tomatoes cannot withstand the rough treatment of mechanical harvesting in which the fruit is shaken from the vine and placed in large bins, a new breed of tomato has been developed. It has a tough skin, and the fruit ripens at the same time so a machine can make a single run through a field. Experiments are underway to give a cube shape so it can be stored easily. "Tomatoes" are being harvested mechanically but they are a different fruit from the ones we have known. "Man" of the future, barring a nuclear holocaust, will adapt to hydrocarbons in the air, detergents in the water, crime in the streets, and crowded recreational areas. Good design becomes a meaningless tautology if we consider that man will be reshaped to fit whatever environment he creates. The long-range question is not so much what sort of environment we want, but what sort of man we want.

31. Proxemics in a Cross-Cultural Context: Germans, English, and French

EDWARD T. HALL

The Germans, the English, the Americans, and the French share significant portions of each other's cultures, but at many points their cultures clash. Consequently, the misunderstandings that arise are all the more serious because sophisticated Americans and Europeans take pride in correctly interpreting each other's behavior. Cultural differences which are out of awareness are, as a consequence, usually chalked up to ineptness, boorishness, or lack of interest on the part of the other person.

The Germans

Whenever people from different countries come into repeated contact they begin to generalize about each other's behavior. The Germans and the German Swiss are no exception. Most of the intellectual and professional people I have talked to from these two countries eventually get around to commenting on American use of time and space. Both the Germans and the German Swiss have made consistent observations about how Americans structure time very tightly and are sticklers for schedules. They also note that Americans don't leave any free time for themselves (a point which has been made by Sebastian de Grazia in *Of Time, Work, and Leisure*).

Since neither the Germans nor the Swiss (particularly the German Swiss) could be regarded as completely casual about time, I have made it a point to question them further about their view of the American approach to time. They will say that Europeans will schedule fewer events in the same time than Americans do and they usually add that Europeans feel less "pressed" for time than Americans. Certainly, Europeans allow more time for virtually everything involving important human relationships. Many of my European subjects observed that in Europe human relationships are important whereas in the United States the schedule is important. Several of my subjects then took the next logical step and connected the handling of time with attitudes toward space, which Americans treat with incredible casualness. According to European standards, Americans use space in a wasteful way and seldom plan adequately for public needs. In fact, it would seem that Americans feel that people have no needs associated with space at all. By overemphasizing the schedule Americans tend to underemphasize individual space needs. I should mention at this point that all Europeans are not this perceptive. Many of them go no further than to say that in the United States they themselves feel pressured by time and they often complain that our cities lack variety. Nevertheless, given these observations made by Europeans one would expect that the Germans would be more upset by violations of spatial mores than the Americans.

Germans and intrusions

I shall never forget my first experience with German proxemic patterns, which occurred when I was an undergraduate. My manners, my status, and my ego were attacked and crushed by a German in an instance where thirty years' residence in this country and an excellent command of English had not attenuated German definitions of what constitutes an intrusion. In order to understand the various issues that were at stake, it is necessary to refer back to two basic American patterns that are taken for granted in this country and which Americans therefore tend to treat as universal.

First, in the United States there is a commonly accepted, invisible boundary around any two or three people in conversation which separates them from others. Distance alone serves to isolate any such group and to endow it with a protective wall of privacy. Normally, voices are kept low to avoid intruding on others and if voices are heard, people will act as though they had not heard. In this way, privacy is granted whether it is actually present or not. The second pattern is somewhat more subtle and has to do with the exact point at which a person is experienced as actually having crossed a boundary and entered a room. Talking through a screen door while standing outside a house is not considered by most Americans as being inside the house or room in any sense of the word. If one is standing on the threshold holding the door open and talking to someone inside, it is still defined informally and experienced as being *outside.* If one is in an office building and just "pokes his head in the door" of an office he's still outside the office. Just holding on to the doorjamb when one's body is inside the room still means a person has one foot "on base" as it were so that he is not quite inside the other fellow's territory. None of these American spatial definitions is valid in northern Germany. In every instance where the American would consider himself *outside* he has already entered the German's territory and by definition would become involved with him. The following experience brought the conflict between these two patterns into focus.

It was a warm spring day of the type one finds only in the high, clean, clear air of Colorado, the kind of day that makes you glad you are alive. I was standing on the doorstep of a converted carriage house talking to a young woman who lived in an apartment upstairs. The first floor had been made into an artist's studio. The arrangement, however, was peculiar because the same entrance served both tenants. The occupants of the apartment used a small entryway and walked along one wall of the studio to reach the stairs to the apartment. You might say that they had an "easement" through the artist's territory. As I stood talking on the doorstep, I glanced to the left and noticed that some fifty to sixty feet away, inside the studio, the Prussian artist and two of his friends were also in conversation. He was facing so that if he glanced to one side he could just see me. I had noted his presence, but not wanting to appear presumptuous or to interrupt his conversation, I unconsciously applied the American rule and assumed that the two activities—my quiet conversation and his conversation—were not involved with each other. As I was soon to learn, this was a mistake, because in less time than it takes to tell, the artist had detached himself from his friends, crossed the intervening space, pushed my friend aside, and with eyes flashing, started shouting at me. By what right had I entered his studio without greeting him? Who had given me permission?

I felt bullied and humiliated, and even after almost thirty years, I can still feel my anger. Later study has given me greater understanding of the German pattern and I have learned that in the German's eyes I really had been intolerably rude. I was already "inside" the building and I intruded when I could *see* inside. For the German, there is no such thing as being inside the room without being inside the zone of intrusion, particularly if one looks at the other party, no matter how far away.

Recently, I obtained an independent check on how Germans feel about visual intrusion while investigating what people look at when they are in intimate, personal, social, and public situations. In the course of my research, I instructed subjects to photograph separately both a man and a woman in each of the above contexts. One of my assistants, who also happened to be German, photographed his subjects out of focus at public distance because, as he said, "You are not really supposed to look at other people at public distances *because it's intruding.*" This may explain the informal custom behind the German laws against photographing strangers in public without their permission.

The "private sphere"

Germans sense their own space as an extension of the ego. One sees a clue to this feeling in the term "Lebensraum," which is impossible to translate because it summarizes so much. Hitler used it as an effective psychological lever to move the Germans to conquest.

In contrast to the Arab, as we shall see later, the German's ego is extraordinarily exposed, and he will go to almost any length to preserve his "private sphere." This was observed during World War II when American soldiers were offered opportunities to observe German prisoners under a variety of circumstances. In one instance in the Midwest, German P.W.s were housed four to a small hut. As soon as materials were available, each prisoner built a partition so that he could have *his own space.* In a less favorable setting in Germany when the *Wehrmacht* was collapsing, it was necessary to use open stockades because German prisoners were arriving faster than they could be accommodated. In this situation each soldier who could find the materials built his own tiny dwelling unit, sometimes no larger than a foxhole. It puzzled the Americans that the Germans did not pool their efforts and their scarce materials to create a larger, more efficient space, particularly in view of the very cold spring nights. Since that time I have observed frequent instances of the use of architectural extensions of this need to screen the ego. German houses with balconies are arranged so that there is visual privacy. Yards tend to be well fenced; but fenced or not, they are sacred.

The American view that space should be shared is particularly troublesome to the German. I cannot document the account of the early days of World War II occupation when Berlin was in ruins but the following situation was reported by an observer and it has the nightmarish quality that is often associated with inadvertent cross-cultural blunders. In Berlin at that time the housing shortage was indescribably acute. To provide relief, occupation authorities in the American zone ordered those Berliners who still had kitchens and baths intact to share them with their neighbors. The order finally had to be rescinded when the already overstressed Germans started killing each other over the shared facilities.

Public and private buildings in Germany often have double doors for sound-proofing, as do many hotel rooms. In addition, the door is taken very seriously by Germans. Those Germans who come to America feel that our doors are flimsy and light. The meanings of the open door and the closed door are quite different in the two countries. In offices, Americans keep doors open; Germans keep doors closed. In Germany, the closed door does not mean that the man behind it wants to be alone or undisturbed, or that he is doing something he doesn't want someone else to see. It's simply that Germans think that open doors are sloppy and disorderly. To close the door preserves the integrity of the room and provides a protective boundary between people. Otherwise, they get too involved with each other. One of my German subjects commented, "If our family hadn't had doors, we would have had to change our way of life. Without doors we would have had many, many more fights. . . . When you can't talk, you retreat behind a door. . . . If there hadn't been doors, I would always have been within reach of my mother."

Whenever a German warms up to the subject of American enclosed space, he can be counted on to comment on the noise that is transmitted through walls and doors. To many Germans, our doors epitomize American life. They are thin and cheap; they seldom fit; and they lack the substantial quality of German doors. When they close they don't sound and feel solid. The click of the lock is indistinct, it rattles and indeed it may even be absent.

The open-door policy of American business and the closed-door patterns of German business culture cause clashes in the branches and subsidiaries of

American firms in Germany. The point seems to be quite simple, yet failure to grasp it has caused considerable friction and misunderstanding between American and German managers overseas. I was once called in to advise a firm that has operations all over the world. One of the first questions asked was, "How do you get the Germans to keep their doors open?" In this company the open doors were making the Germans feel exposed and gave the whole operation an unusually relaxed and unbusinesslike air. Closed doors, on the other hand, gave the Americans the feeling that there was a conspiratorial air about the place and that they were being left out. The point is that whether the door is open or shut, it is not going to mean the same thing in the two countries.

Order in space

The orderliness and hierarchical quality of German culture are communicated in their handling of space. Germans want to know where they stand and object strenuously to people crashing queues or people who "get out of line" or who do not obey signs such as "Keep out," "Authorized personnel only," and the like. Some of the German attitudes toward ourselves are traceable to our informal attitudes toward boundaries and to authority in general.

However, German anxiety due to American violations of order is nothing compared to that engendered in Germans by the Poles, who see no harm in a little disorder. To them lines and queues stand for regimentation and blind authority. I once saw a Pole crash a cafeteria line just "to stir up those sheep."

Germans get very technical about intrusion distance, as I mentioned earlier. When I once asked my students to describe the distance at which a third party would intrude on two people who were talking, there were no answers from the Americans. Each student knew that he could tell when he was being intruded on but he couldn't define intrusion or tell how he knew when it had occurred. However, a German and an Italian who had worked in Germany were both members of my class and they answered without any hesitation. Both stated that a third party would intrude on two people if he came within seven feet!

Many Americans feel that Germans are overly rigid in their behavior, unbending and formal. Some of this impression is created by differences in the handling of chairs while seated. The American doesn't seem to mind if people hitch their chairs up to adjust the distance to the situation—those that do mind would not think of saying anything, for to comment on the manners of others would be impolite. In Germany, however, it is a violation of the mores to change the position of your chair. An added deterrent for those who don't know better is the weight of most German furniture. Even the great architect Mies van der Rohe, who often rebelled against German tradition in his buildings, made his handsome chairs so heavy that anyone but a strong man would have difficulty in adjusting his seating position. To a German, light furniture is anathema, not only because it seems flimsy but because people move it and thereby destroy the order of things, including intrusions on the "private sphere." In one instance reported to me, a German newspaper editor who had moved to the United States had his visitor's chair bolted to the floor "at the proper distance" because he couldn't tolerate the American habit of adjusting the chair to the situation.

The English

It has been said that the English and the Americans are two great people separated by one language. The differences for which language gets blamed may not be due so much to words as to communications on other levels beginning with English intonation (which sounds affected to many Americans) and continuing to ego-linked ways of handling time, space, and materials. If there ever were two cultures in which differences of the proxemic details are marked it is in the educated (public school) English and the middle-class Americans. One of the basic reasons for this wide disparity is that in the United States we use space as a way of classifying people and activities, whereas in England it is the social system that determines who you are. In the United States, your address is an important cue to status (this applies not only to one's home but to the business address as well). The Joneses from Brooklyn and Miami are not as "in" as the Joneses from Newport and Palm Beach. Greenwich and Cape Cod are worlds apart from Newark and Miami. Businesses located on Madison and Park avenues have more tone than those on Seventh and Eighth avenues. A corner office is more prestigious than one next to the elevator or at the end of a long hall. The Englishman, however, is born and brought up in a social system. He is still Lord—no matter where you find him, even if it is behind the counter in a fishmonger's stall. In addition to class distinctions, there are differences between the English and ourselves in how space is allotted.

The middle-class American growing up in the United States feels he has a right to have his own room, or at least part of a room. My American subjects, when asked to draw an ideal room or office, invariably drew it for themselves and no one else. When asked to draw their present room or office, they drew only their own part of a shared room and then drew a line down the middle. Both male and female subjects identified the kitchen and the master bedroom as belonging to the mother or the wife, whereas Father's territory was a study or den, if one was available; otherwise, it was "the shop," "the basement," or sometimes only a workbench or the garage. American women who want to be alone can go to the bedroom and close the door. The closed door is the sign meaning "Do not disturb" or "I'm angry." An American is available if his door is open at home or at his office. He is expected not to shut himself off but to maintain himself in a state of constant readiness to answer the demands of others. Closed doors are for conferences, private conversations, and business, work that requires concentration, study, resting, sleeping, dressing, and sex.

The middle- and upper-class Englishman, on the other hand, is brought up in a nursery shared with brothers and sisters. The oldest occupies a room by himself which he vacates when he leaves for boarding school, possibly even at the age of nine or ten. The difference between a room of one's own and early conditioning to shared space, while seeming inconsequential, has an important effect on the Englishman's attitude toward his own space. He may never have a permanent "room of his own" and seldom expects one or feels he is entitled to one. Even Members of Parliament have no offices and often conduct their business on the terrace overlooking the Thames. As a consequence, the English are puzzled by the American need for a secure place in which to work, an office. Americans working in England may become annoyed if they are not provided with what they consider appropriate enclosed work space. In regard to the need for walls as a screen for the ego, this places the Americans somewhere between the Germans and the English.

The contrasting English and American patterns have some remarkable inplications, particularly if we assume that man, like other animals, has a built-in need to shut himself off from others from time to time. An English student in one of my seminars typified what happens when hidden patterns clash. He was quite obviously experiencing strain in his relationships with Americans. Nothing seemed to go right and it was quite clear from his remarks that we did not know how to behave. An analysis of his complaints showed that a major source of irritation was that no American seemed to be able to pick up the subtle clues that there were times when he didn't want his thoughts intruded on. As he stated it, "I'm walking around the apartment and it seems that whenever I want to be alone my roommate starts talking to me. Pretty soon he's asking 'What's the matter?' and wants to know if I'm angry. By then I am angry and say something."

It took some time but finally we were able to identify most of the contrasting features of the American and British problems that were in conflict in this case. When the American wants to be alone he goes into a room and shuts the door —he depends on architectural features for screening. For an American to refuse to talk to someone else present in the same room, to give them the "silent treatment," is the ultimate form of rejection and a sure sign of great displeasure. The English, on the other hand, lacking rooms of their own since childhood, never developed the practice of using space as a refuge from others. They have in effect internalized a set of barriers, which they erect and which others are supposed to recognize. Therefore, the more the Englishman shuts himself off when he is with an American the more likely the American is to break in to assure himself that all is well. Tension lasts until the two get to know each other. The important point is that the spatial and architectural needs of each are not the same at all.

Using the telephone

English internalized privacy mechanisms and the American privacy screen result in very different customs regarding the telephone. There is no wall or door against the telephone. Since it is impossible to tell from the ring who is on the other end of the line, or how urgent his business is, people feel compelled to answer the phone. As one would anticipate, the English when they feel the need to be with their thoughts treat the phone as an intrusion by someone who doesn't know any better. Since it is impossible to tell how preoccupied the other party will be they hesitate to use the phone; instead, they write notes. To phone is to be "pushy" and rude. A letter or telegram may be slower, but it is much less disrupting. Phones are for actual business and emergencies.

I used this system myself for several years when I lived in Santa Fe, New Mexico, during the depression. I dispensed with a phone because it cost money. Besides, I cherished the quiet of my tiny mountainside retreat and didn't want to be disturbed. This idiosyncrasy on my part produced a shocked reaction in others. People really didn't know what to do with me. You could see the consternation on their faces when, in answer to the question, "How do I get in touch with you?" I would reply, "Write me a post card. I come to the post office every day."

Having provided most of our middle-class citizens with private rooms and escape from the city to the suburbs, we have then proceeded to penetrate their most private spaces in their home with a most public device, the telephone. Anyone can reach us at any time. We are, in fact, so available that elaborate devices have to be devised so that busy people can function. The greatest skill and tact must be exercised in the message-screening process so that others will not be offended. So far our technology has not kept up with the needs of people to be alone with either their families or their thoughts. The problem stems from the fact that it is impossible to tell from the phone's ring who is calling and how urgent his business is. Some people have unlisted phones but then that makes it hard on friends who come to town who want to get in touch with them. The government solution is to have special phones for important people (traditionally red). The red line bypasses secretaries, coffee breaks, busy signals, and teen-agers, and is connected to White House, State Department, and Pentagon switchboards.

Neighbors

Americans living in England are remarkably consistent in their reactions to the English. Most of them are hurt and puzzled because they were brought up on American neighboring patterns and don't interpret the English ones correctly. In England propinquity means nothing. The fact that you live next door to a family does not entitle you to visit, borrow from, or socialize with them, or your children to play with theirs. Accurate figures on the number of Americans who adjust well to the English are difficult to obtain. The basic attitude of the English toward the Americans is tinged by our ex-colonial status. This attitude is much more in awareness and therefore more likely to be expressed than the unspoken right of the Englishman to maintain his privacy against the world. To the best of my knowledge, those who have tried to relate to the English purely on the basis of propinquity seldom if ever succeed. They may get to know and even like their neighbors, but it won't be because they live next door, because English relationships are patterned not according to space but according to social status.

Whose room is the bedroom?

In upper middle-class English homes, it is the man, not the woman, who has the privacy of the bedroom, presumably as protection from children who haven't yet internalized the English patterns of privacy. The man, not the woman, has a dressing room; the man also has a study which affords privacy. The Englishman is fastidious about his clothes and expects to spend a great deal of time and attention in their purchase. In contrast, English women approach the buying of clothes in a manner reminiscent of the American male.

Talking loud and soft

Proper spacing between people is maintained in many ways. Loudness of the voice is one of the mechanisms which also varies from culture to culture. In England and in Europe generally, Americans are continually accused of loud talking, which is a function of two forms of vocal control: (a) loudness, and (b) modulation for direction. Americans increase the volume as a function of distance, using several levels (whisper, normal voice, loud shout, etc.). In many situations, the more gregarious Americans do not care if they can be overheard. In fact, it is part of their openness showing that we have nothing to hide. The English do care, for to get along without private offices and not intrude they have developed skills in beaming the voice toward the person they are talking to, carefully adjusting it so that it just barely overrides the background noise and distance. For the English to be overheard is to intrude on others, a failure in manners and a sign of socially inferior behavior. However, because of the way they modulate their voices the English in an American setting may sound and look conspiratorial to Americans, which can result in their being branded as troublemakers.

Eye behavior

A study of eye behavior reveals some interesting contrasts between the two cultures. Englishmen in this country have trouble not only when they want to be alone and shut themselves off but also when they want to interact. They never know for sure whether an American is listening. We, on the other hand, are equally unsure as to whether the English have understood us. Many of these ambiguities in communication center on differences in the use of the eyes. The Englishman is taught to pay strict attention, to listen carefully, which he must do if he is polite and there are not protective walls to screen out sound. He doesn't bob his head or grunt to let you know he understands. He blinks his eyes to let you know that he has heard you. Americans, on the other hand, are taught not to stare. We look the other person straight in the eye without wavering only when we want to be particularly certain that we are getting through to him.

The gaze of the American directed toward his conversational partner often wanders from one eye to the other and even leaves the face for long periods. Proper English listening behavior includes immobilization of the eyes at social distance, so that whichever eye one looks at gives the appearance of looking straight at you. In order to accomplish this feat, the Englishman must be eight or more feet away. He is too close when the 12-degree horizontal span of the macula won't permit a steady gaze. At less than eight feet, one *must* look at either one eye or the other.

The French

The French who live south and east of Paris belong generally to that complex of cultures which border the Mediterranean. Members of this group pack together more closely than do northern Europeans, English, and Americans. Mediterranean use of space can be seen in the crowded trains, buses, automobiles, sidewalk cafés, and in the homes of the people. The exceptions are, of course, in the châteaus and villas of the rich. Crowded living normally means high sensory involvement. Evidence of French emphasis on the senses appears not only in the way the French eat, entertain, talk, write, crowd together in cafés, but can even be seen in the way they make their maps. These maps are extraordinarily well thought out and so designed that the traveler can find the most detailed information. One can tell from using these maps that the French employ all their senses. These maps make it possible for you to get around and they also tell you where you can enjoy a view; where you'll find picturesque drives, and, in some instances, places to rest, refresh yourself, take a walk, and even eat a pleasant meal. They inform the traveler which senses he can expect to use and at what points in his journey.

Home and family

One possible reason why the French love the outdoors is the rather crowded conditions under which many of them live. The French entertain at restaurants and cafés. The home is for the family and the outdoors for recreation and socializing. Yet all the homes I have visited, as well as everything I have been able to learn about French homes, indicate that they are often quite crowded. The working class and the petite bourgeoisie are particularly crowded, which means that the French are sensually much involved with each other. The lay-out of their offices, homes, towns, cities, and countryside is such as to keep them involved.

In interpersonal encounters this involvement runs high; when a Frenchman talks to you, he really looks at you and there is no mistaking this fact. On the streets of Paris he looks at the woman he sees very directly. American women returning to their own country after living in France often go through a period of sensory deprivation. Several have told me that because they have grown accustomed to being looked at, the American habit of *not* looking makes them feel as if they didn't exist.

Not only are the French sensually involved with each other, they have become accustomed to what are to us greatly stepped-up sensory inputs. The French automobile is designed in response to French needs. Its small size used to be attributed to a lower standard of living and higher costs of materials; and while there can be no doubt but that cost is a factor, it would be naïve to assume that it was the major factor. The automobile is just as much an expression of the culture as is the language and, therefore, has its characteristic niche in the cultural biotope. Changes in the car will reflect and be reflected in changes elsewhere. If the French drove American cars, they would be forced to give up many ways of dealing with space which they hold quite dear. The traffic along the Champs-Elysées and around the Arc de Triomphe is a cross between the New Jersey Turnpike on a sunny Sunday afternoon and the Indianapolis Speedway. With American-size autos, it would be mass suicide. Even the occasional "compact" American cars in the stream of Parisian traffic look like sharks among minnows. In the United States the same cars look normal because everything else is in scale. In the foreign setting where they stand out, Detroit iron can be seen for what it is. The American behemoths give bulk to the ego and prevent overlapping of personal spheres inside the car so that each passenger is only marginally involved with the others. I do not mean by this that all Americans are alike and have been forced into the Detroit mold. But since Detroit won't produce what is wanted, many Americans prefer the smaller, more maneuverable European cars which fit their personalities and needs more closely. Nevertheless, if one simply looks at the styles of the French cars, one sees greater emphasis on individuality than in the United States. Compare the Peugeot, the Citroen, the Renault and the Dauphine and the little 2 C.V. shoebox. It would take years and years of style changes to produce such differences in the United States.

French use of open spaces

Because total space needs must be maintained in balance, the urban French have learned to make the most of the parks and the outdoors. To them, the city is something from which to derive satisfaction and so are the people in it. Reasonably clean air, sidewalks up to seventy feet wide, automobiles that will not dwarf humans as they pass on the boulevards make it possible to have outdoor cafés and open areas where people congregate and enjoy each other. Since the French savor and participate in the city itself—its varied sights, sounds, and smells; its wide sidewalks and avenues and parks—the need for insulating space in the automobile may be somewhat less than it is in the United States where humans are dwarfed by skyscrapers and the products of Detroit, visually assaulted by filth and rubbish, and poisoned by smog and carbon dioxide.

The star and the grid

There are two major European systems for patterning space. One of these, "the radiating star" which occurs in France and Spain, is sociopetal. The other, the "grid," originated in Asia Minor, adopted by the Romans and carried to England at the time of Caesar, is sociofugal. The French-Spanish system connects all points and functions. In the French subway system, different lines repeatedly come together at places of interest like the Place de la Concorde, the Opéra, and the Madeleine. The grid system separates activities by stringing them out. Both systems have advantages, but a person familiar with one has difficulty using the other.

For example, a mistake in direction in the radiating center-point system becomes more serious the farther one travels. Any error, therefore, is roughly equivalent to taking off in the wrong direction. In the grid system, baseline errors are over the 90-degree or the 180-degree variety and are usually obvious enough to make themselves felt even by those with a poor sense of direction. If you are traveling in the right direction, even though you are one or two blocks off your course, the error is easily rectified at any time. Nevertheless, there are certain inherent advantages in the center-point system. Once one learns to use it, it is easier for example to locate objects or events in space by naming a point on a line. Thus it is possible, even in strange territory, to tell someone to meet you at the 50 KM mark on National Route 20 south of Paris; that is all the information he needs. In contrast, the grid system of co-ordinates involves at least two lines and a point to locate something in space (often many more lines and points, depending on how many turns one has to make). In the star system, it is also possible to integrate a number of different activities in centers in less space than with the grid system. Thus, residential, shopping, marketing, commercial, and recreation areas can both meet and be reached from central points.

It is incredible how many facets of French life the radiating star pattern touches. It is almost as though the whole culture were set up on a model in which power, influence, and control flowed in and out from a series of interlocking centers. There are sixteen major highways running into Paris, twelve into Caen (near Omaha Beach), twelve into Amiens, eleven for Le Mans, and ten for Rennes. Even the figures don't begin to convey the picture of what this arrangement really means, for France is a series of radiating networks that build up into larger and larger centers. Each small center has its own channel, as it were, to the next higher level. As a general rule, the roads between centers do not go through other towns, because each town is connected to others by its own roads. This is in contrast to the American pattern of stringing small towns out like beads on a necklace along the routes that connect principal centers.

In *The Silent Language* I have described how the man in charge of a French office can often be found in the middle—with his minions placed like satellites on strings radiating outward from him. I once had occasion to deal with such a "central figure" when the French member of a team of scientists under my direction wanted a raise because his desk was in the middle! Even De Gaulle bases his international policy on France's central location. There are those, of course, who will say that the fact that the French school system also follows a highly centralized pattern couldn't possibly have any relationship to the layout of offices, subway systems, road networks, and, in fact, the entire nation, but I could not agree with them. Long experience with different patterns of culture has taught me that the basic threads tend to be woven throughout the entire fabric of a society.

The reason for the review of the three European cultures to which the middle class of the United States is most closely linked (historically and culturally) is as much as anything else a means of providing contrast to highlight some of our own implicit patterns. In this review it was shown that different use of the senses leads to very different needs regarding space no matter on what level one cares to consider it. Everything from an office to a town or city will reflect the sense modalities of its builders and occupants. In considering solutions to problems such as urban renewal and city sinks it is essential to know how the populations involved perceive space and how they use their senses. The next chapter deals with people whose spatial worlds are quite different from our own, and from whom we can learn more about ourselves.

From *Technology and Man's Future* (reprinted from Report R-6, IFF, September 1969), pp. 5–22. Reprinted by permission of Institute for the Future, Menlo Park, Calif.

32. Forecasts of Some Technological and Scientific Developments and Their Societal Consequences

THEODORE J. GORDON AND ROBERT H. AMENT

Scientific and technological developments have profoundly altered man's institutions, his life styles, and his aspirations in the last several generations. What is striking about this transformation is not that it has occurred, but rather that it has occurred without preparation. For the consequences have been pervasive, and many of them, favorable and unfavorable alike, have left today's policy makers and policy advisors seriously behind the course of events, with the result that by the time their efforts have been translated into programs for action they have become infeasible or simply irrelevant. Long-range forecasting of scientific and technological developments can provide some of the information decision makers need to accommodate the long lead-times separating the evaluation of opportunities from the implementation of specific plans. The technological Delphi study reported in this article was undertaken to help provide such information.

The immediate objectives of the study were:
—To generate a list of important prospective events and developments in the physical and biological disciplines;
—To determine, using the judgment of experts, when these events and developments might take place;
—To ascertain what societal changes are likely to accompany these scientific and technological innovations;
—To determine whether the anticipated societal consequences appeared likely to be beneficial or detrimental to society as a whole;
—To determine whether intervention in the processes producing these consequences seemed feasible, and if so, through what means; and
—To test the use of the Delphi method for attaining reasonable consensus among groups of experts in dealing with questions of social change, values, and science policy.

The Delphi Technique

Most decision makers utilize expert advice in forming their judgment. Where the question being examined is so complex and involves such obscure inter-relationships that no single person could be expected to be expert in the many disciplines required, the traditional approach to the answer is to seek a consensus among experts through open discussion or a conference. However, joint committee activity often introduces certain undesirable psychological factors, "such as specious persuasion, unwillingness to abandon publicly expressed opinions, and the bandwagon effect of majority opinion."[1]

The Delphi technique, which was used in this study, makes it possible to avoid some of these difficulties because the experts involved exchange their opinions anonymously and through an intermediary, who controls the feedback of opinion in subsequent rounds of the inquiry. It has been found in previous studies of this type that the Delphi process—involving anonymity, iteration, and controlled feedback—tends to produce a converging group consensus.

In a typical Delphi investigation, the participants are sent a series of questionnaires through the mail. In the first, they might be asked to provide their judgment as to likely dates of occurrence of a group of events and developments. The collated responses normally reveal a spread of opinions; these data are presented to the respondents in the second questionnaire. In this round, the respondents are given the opportunity to revise their estimates in light of the group response, and those participants whose estimates have fallen earlier or later than those of the majority are asked to provide reasons for their positions. These reasons, along with the new estimates of the group as a whole, are collated and fed back to the respondents on the third questionnaire, and they are again asked to reassess their earlier estimates in view of the new group response and reasons provided for early and late dates.

The Delphi method has proven useful for long-range forecasting of expected technological and societal developments. Several corporations and government agencies have conducted future-oriented Delphi studies concerned with such subjects as political alliances,[2] technological potentials,[3] war prevention techniques,[4] economic indices,[5] and medical developments.[6] Results generally have been satisfactory; that is, in many cases a reasonable consensus seems

[1]N. C. Dalkey and O. Helmer, "An Experimental Application of the Delphi Method to the Use of Experts," *Management Science,* vol. 9, no. 3 (April 1963).

[2]Joseph Matino, *An Experiment with the Delphi Procedure for Long-Range Forecasting* (Washington, D.C.: Office of Scientific Research, US Air Force, 1967), AFOSR Document 670175.

[3]Harper Q. North and Donald L. Pyke, *A Probe of TRW's Future, The Next 20 Years,* a TRW proprietary document, 1966.

[4]See, for example, T. J. Gordon and O. Helmer, *Report on a Long-Range Forecasting Study,* The Rand Corporation, Paper P–2982 (September 1964).

[5]Robert M. Campbell, "Methodological Study of the Utilization of Experts in Business Forecasting," Ph.D. thesis, University of California, Los Angeles, September, 1966.

[6]Alan Sheldon, Laboratory of Community Psychiatry, Boston, 1969.

to have been achieved and the potential developments described provided a basis for subsequent planning, action, and analysis.

Even though this technique has been used with some success, however, it should not be interpreted as a device that produces "truth about the future." The Delphi method is designed to produce consensus judgments in inexact fields; it would be a mistake to consider such judgments as complete or precise descriptions about the future.

The future will contain events that are totally unanticipated today; perhaps this is the only thing that can be said about the future with absolute certainty. Furthermore, all techniques of forecasting that rely on judgment and opinion (rather than on the more rigid laws of causality of the natural sciences) depend on the imagination and technical adequacy of the forecasters. Nevertheless, forecasting the future seems to be a worthwhile enterprise despite the certainty of the unexpected and despite the limitations imposed by relying on human judgment, however well informed. Forecasts, even hazy forecasts, based on careful judgment can provide a seemingly coherent structure for testing alternative contemplated actions, for warning that certain other actions may be needed or should be avoided, and for defining the scope of reasonable expectations in a world where expectations sometimes seem unbounded.

Outline of the Study

As in all Delphi studies, the value of the results depends largely on the excellence and cooperation of the participants. Since this study dealt with scientific and technological events and their implications for society, the experimenters invited respondents who had, in the aggregate, skills which included the following:

Aerospace technology	History of science
Agriculture	Industrialization
Bacteriology	Manufacturing
Biochemistry	Mathematics
Brain physiology	Microbiology
Computer sciences	Molecular biology
Cytogenetics	Natural resources
Electron physics	Pediatrics
Engineering	Philosophy
Finance	Psychiatry
Genetics	Public administration
Gerontology	Science journalism
	Transportation

Four questionnaires were used in this study. The first presented a list of forty technological developments selected by the experimenters and asked that the respondents estimate the dates at which the item had, in their judgment, a 10 percent, a 50 percent, and a 90 percent chance of occurrence. The respondents were also asked to suggest additional scientific and technical developments which they believed might have significant social impact and to indicate how familiar they felt they were with each item. The responses to this questionnaire were collated. In all, forty-three additional items were suggested by the respondents and added to the study.

The new items were presented to the respondents in Questionnaire 2, along with a request that they provide estimates of the dates by which they judged the items to have a 10 percent, a 50 percent, and a 90 percent probability of occurence. A second part of this questionnaire asked the respondent to list what they considered to be socially important consequences likely to result from all of the technological and scientific events. The questionnaire suggested that the respondents consider a full spectrum of consequences—technological, demographic, political, personal, social.

Questionnaires 3 and 4 further refined the results of the study by informing respondents of items upon which agreement had been reached and asking them to reconsider their responses on other items, as well as (in certain cases) to state the reasons for their opinions. Questionnaire 4 also asked respondents to suggest specific policy strategies that might be used to intervene in the consequences of the events being discussed.

Forecasts and Consequences

The full range of results obtained from this study tells a fascinating story. Unfortunately, we are unable to present complete tabulations in the limited space afforded by the context of this article.[7] In the next section, these tabulations are used to delineate a series of scenarios, describing possible technological futures. Here, to give the reader a feeling for the type of findings upon which the scenarios were based, we present a number of sample tabulations. Some examples of the forecasts of the time of occurrence of events discussed by the panelists are presented in Figure 1. The polygons are used to depict the final range of opinions generated by the group. The high point on the bar indicates the median date at which the panelists judged there was a 50 percent chance the event would occur. The shorter legs of the polygon define the limits of the upper and lower quartiles, and the bar itself the interquartile range.

For each item in these figures, the asterisk denotes the median date of occurrence forecasted by the subset of respondents who rated themselves "expert" or "generally familiar" with the event in question.

The respondents also developed an extensive list of prospective consequences which they felt might be expected as a result of the forecasted technological and scientific developments. Each of these consequences was judged as to its likelihood of being a result of the event and, assuming it should occur, whether it was favorable or unfavorable.

The list of consequences for those items shown in Figure 1 is given in Figure 2; the polygons again indicate the interquartile range of the responses.

[7]See the report from which this article was condensed for a full presentation of the results.

Figure 1. Potential Physical and Biological Developments

	1969	1971	1975	1985	2000	2025	LATER	NEVER	DEVELOPMENT
									Establishment of a central data storage facility (or several regional facilities) with wide public access (perhaps in the home) for general or specialized information retrieval, primarily in the area of library, medical, and legal data.
									Feasibility of limited weather control in the sense of predictably affecting regional weather at acceptable cost.
									Human clone—the nucleus of an ovum is removed and replaced by somatic cell, allowing development in a host mother of an identical twin of the person supplying the somatic cell.
									Control of the behavior of some people in society by radio stimulation of the brain.

Beginnings: Planning   357

Figure 2. Consequences of Forecasted Events: Their Likelihood and Impact

NEW AUTOMATION AND COMMUNICATION TECHNIQUES		HOW LIKELY IS IT THAT THE RESULT WILL BE A CONSEQUENCE OF THE DEVELOPMENT?				WHAT WILL THE EFFECT OF THE CONSEQUENCE BE?				
IF THESE DEVELOPMENTS WERE TO OCCUR,	THEY MIGHT RESULT IN:	VIRTUALLY CERTAIN	PROBABLE	POSSIBLE	ALMOST IMPOSSIBLE	VERY FAVORABLE	FAVORABLE	LITTLE OR NO IMPORTANCE	DETRIMENTAL	VERY DETRIMENTAL
Establishment of a central data storage facility (or several regional or disciplinary facilities) with wide public access (perhaps in the home) for general or specialized information retrieval primarily in the areas of library, medical and legal data.	Use of home terminals for education; transformation of the home into a part-time school; growing competition between traditional teaching profession and advocates of programmed instruction.									
	Information storage becoming a salable service, resulting in widespread revision to business practices.									
	Improvement in social science research.									
	Individual citizens becoming proficient in law and medicine, through easy availability of the relevant data in the home.									

Figure 2 (continued)

NEW AUTOMATION AND COMMUNICATION TECHNIQUES (con't)		HOW LIKELY IS IT THAT THE RESULT WILL BE A CONSEQUENCE OF THE DEVELOPMENT?				WHAT WILL THE EFFECT OF THE CONSEQUENCE BE?				
IF THESE DEVELOPMENTS WERE TO OCCUR,	THEY MIGHT RESULT IN:	VIRTUALLY CERTAIN	PROBABLE	POSSIBLE	ALMOST IMPOSSIBLE	VERY FAVORABLE	FAVORABLE	LITTLE OR NO IMPORTANCE	DETRIMENTAL	VERY DETRIMENTAL
	The rise of new methods of computer-aided crime.									
	Information overload; the problem will be to select from the available plethora of information that which is important and relevant to the individual.									
	Great revolutions in library sciences, including greatly improved methods of searching for particular subjects.									
	Invasion of privacy (assuming data associated with individual people can be retrieved).									

Figure 2 (continued)

NEW METHODS OF MODIFYING THE ENVIRONMENT		HOW LIKELY IS IT THAT THE RESULT WILL BE A CONSEQUENCE OF THE DEVELOPMENT?				WHAT WILL THE EFFECT OF THE CONSEQUENCE BE?				
IF THESE DEVELOPMENTS WERE TO OCCUR,	THEY MIGHT RESULT IN:	VIRTUALLY CERTAIN	PROBABLE	POSSIBLE	ALMOST IMPOSSIBLE	VERY FAVORABLE	FAVORABLE	LITTLE OR NO IMPORTANCE	DETRIMENTAL	VERY DETRIMENTAL
Feasibility of limited weather control in the sense of predictably affecting regional weather at acceptable cost.	Great improvements in agricultural efficiency by creating rain on demand, avoidance of floods, and minimizing the number of clouds over farms during sunlight hours."		(distribution)				(distribution)			
	Disruption in ecological balance leading to extinction of some plant and animal species.		(distribution)						(distribution)	
	Weather being used as a military or economic weapon.			(distribution)					(distribution)	
	Great increase in the number of civil suits alleging damage caused by weather manipulation.	(distribution)							(distribution)	
	Emergence of a new power elite: "the weather makers."		(distribution)						(distribution)	

Figure 2 (continued)

NEW REPRODUCTIVE TECHNIQUES		HOW LIKELY IS IT THAT THE RESULT WILL BE A CONSEQUENCE OF THE DEVELOPMENT?				WHAT WILL THE EFFECT OF THE CONSEQUENCE BE?				
IF THESE DEVELOPMENTS WERE TO OCCUR,	THEY MIGHT RESULT IN:	VIRTUALLY CERTAIN	PROBABLE	POSSIBLE	ALMOST IMPOSSIBLE	VERY FAVORABLE	FAVORABLE	LITTLE OR NO IMPORTANCE	DETRIMENTAL	VERY DETRIMENTAL
Human Clone—the nucleus of an ovum is removed and replaced by somatic cells, allowing development in a host mother of an identical twin of the person supplying the somatic cell.	A replication of essential or great men, resulting in a kind of immortality.									
	Creation of a super race, an effective way to preserve and distribute good genotypes.									
	New animal breeding practices.									

Figure 2 (continued)

NEW BEHAVIOR MANIPULATION TECHNIQUES		HOW LIKELY IS IT THAT THE RESULT WILL BE A CONSEQUENCE OF THE DEVELOPMENT?				WHAT WILL THE EFFECT OF THE CONSEQUENCE BE?				
IF THESE DEVELOPMENTS WERE TO OCCUR,	THEY MIGHT RESULT IN:	VIRTUALLY CERTAIN	PROBABLE	POSSIBLE	ALMOST IMPOSSIBLE	VERY FAVORABLE	FAVORABLE	LITTLE OR NO IMPORTANCE	DETRIMENTAL	VERY DETRIMENTAL
Control of the behavior of some people in society by radio stimulation of the brain.	Decisive tool for control of abnormal (including criminal) behavior.									
	A substitution for penal institutions.									
	Development of protective and jamming systems.									
	Stimulation of socially useful responses, such as the wish to work.									
	Use in medicine as a form of sedation.									

Scenarios

The forecasts of events and their consequences can be used to form a number of scenarios which may be useful in a variety of long-range planning contexts. The scenarios presented here were written using group median dates as a basis for sorting the events into the various time intervals described; the important consequences of these events were then included.

The Technological World of 1985. Solution of the foreign-body rejection problem will have greatly improved the process of organ transplantation, to meet the need for natural transplantable organs, "parts" banks will be operating. Competition for organs will have encouraged black markets, although the importance of these markets will have been diminished by legislative regulation of transplantations within the hospital-physician community and by the development of artificial organs, including, for example, implantable artificial hearts with power sources capable of lasting five years. Research will be continuing into the use of tissue-compatible animals to provide yet another source of organs. This activity will have changed the emphasis in medicine from repair to replacement, a development accompanied by the rise of new industries, technologies, and classes of medical personnel.

Several other biological technologies will have significantly affected the world of 1985. Contraceptive drugs will have been developed which will lower fertility rates, being mass-administered as aerosols or as additions to water supplies or staples (as iodine is added to table salt). Societal acceptance of this practice will result from extensive public education about the consequences of overpopulation. But this development will have led to the possibility of a new form of warfare: surreptitious contraception. Research and development projects will have been implemented to create an anticontraceptive pill and detection system. The drug will form only one more addition to the arsenal of biological and chemical weapons.

There will have been an enormous increase in information-handling machines and in the complexities and pervasiveness of their operations. The importance of skilled programmers will have been enhanced. Central data storage facilities with wide public access will have been established and will provide library, medical, and legal data. Privacy will have been challenged by the large data banks, and new methods of computer-aided crime will have come on the scene. New computer and automation uses will include automated language translation capable of coping with idiomatic syntactical complexities and sophisticated teaching machines which will utilize adaptive programs responding not only to the students' answers but also to certain physiological responses, such as extreme tensions.

Perhaps most startling will be new opportunities and innovations in human reproduction. Nonsurgical techniques permitting the choice of the sex of offspring (with 90-percent certainty) will have been demonstrated, and chromosome typing will be used to discover human abnormalities within weeks of conception. There will be concern about the very detrimental effects of fads for sexes, and regulation of the sex ratio may take the form of legislation or financial incentives to those parents who help to maintain a socially desirable sex equilibrium.

Immunizing agents will have been developed to protect against most bacterial and viral diseases. Inexpensive nonnarcotic drugs for producing specific personality changes, such as euphoria, antiaggression, and increased attention, will be available to the public, and these will have led to improvements in mental therapy, education, and criminal control.

A primitive form of artificial life will have been created and protein usable for food will have been produced, spawning new industries and offering the hopeful prospect of specialized diet additives for protein-deficient populations. Conventional agriculture will be augmented by the advent of large-scale desalination plants which may, through their method of distribution, be instruments of international power politics.

Various high-speed transportation systems—such as VTOL-STOL, 200 mph trains, ground-effects machines—will be in wide use, but air traffic control problems and transit congestion in major urban city centers will still exist. Automobile engines, fuels, and accessories will have been produced that will permit operation of vehicles without harmful exhaust. While these devices will have eased the problems of air pollution, traffic congestion will still be with us.

A manned space station of relatively long duration will be orbiting the earth. It will have brought advances in meteorology, cartography, geology, resources mapping, astronomy, geophysics, and military intelligence. Satellite-derived weather forecasting will allow regular and reliable forecasts fourteen days in advance for areas as small as 100 square miles.

The Technological World of 2000. Between 1985 and 2000, biological research and development will have led to many results, including the development of new methods of behavior control, new reproductive techniques, and advances in medical technology. Apparently the threat of starvation will have lent impetus to the development of several new food-producing techniques. There is some fear that these techniques will offer only a short-term reprieve in the onset of world starvation, that the catastrophe of large-scale starvation will yet occur, since these advances will remove some incentives to the limiting of family size. To minimize this threat, some governments will have enacted legislation designed to limit family size; others may have used or encouraged the use of antifertility drugs. World food production will have been expanded through the development of techniques which bring 50 per cent more arable acreage under cultivation. Microbial systems converting petroleum to protein will contribute significantly to world food supplies, and ocean fish farming and aquaculture will also be in extensive use. Population pressures will demand all the food the world can produce.

New methods of behavior control which stem from biological research will have included (1) the development and use of LSD-like drugs to heighten perception and learning speed of retardates, (2) knowledge of how to stimulate cognitive growth to a maximum ability in preschool children, (3) brain surgery or psychochemicals for modifying the behavior of criminals, and (4) radio stimulation of the brains of some people in society. These forms of control will have been accompanied by break-throughs concerning our understanding of human behavior and motivation, including knowledge of the significance of dreams and REM (rapid-eye-movement) sleep in human cognitive development.

New reproductive techniques also will have been developed by 2000. For example, human ova will have been fertilized *in vitro* with subsequent implantation into a surrogate mother. The therapeutic uses of this technique will have allowed some mothers to bear children without their former fear of undesirable gene combinations resulting. Human beings will have been successfully cloned, and the technique will be used routinely for the breeding of other animals, especially in cattle farming.

The nations of the world will be using the oceans not only as a major source of food, as mentioned earlier, but also as a source of minerals through mining of the ocean floor. This may have led to extension of national sovereignties farther into the oceans and "claim staking" with concomitant political tensions. International treaties, modeled after 1959 Antarctica Treaty, will probably have been used to permit more orderly exploitation of the oceans.

An essential feature of man's growing control over his environment will be the relative ease with which he can create ecological catastrophe. His intrusions into the oceans and the advent of weather control, for example, will be subjected not only to political scrutiny but to ecological judgment as well. This new conscience will lead finally to very strong pressure to control the most threatening of all ecological problems: population expansion in the presence of inadequate food. Legislation, tax incentives, propaganda, and sterilization, as well as abortions in certain cases, will be in intensive use. Many aspects of scientific and technological development will be directed toward coping with problems that stem from the world's increasing population levels. For example, waste disposal will have become even more of a problem by the year 2000, necessitating innovations in the use of self-destroying material. Equally important will be the institution of new types of legislation and incentives which encourage the avoidance of pollution and the creation of a favorable environment.

Several other breakthroughs in physical technologies will have occurred between 1985 and 2000. Complex programmable and self-adaptive robots capable of performing many chores will have found use in the households of advanced countries. With such devices available, discretionary time will also have increased and with it the demand for educational and recreational services. Computers will have been built that will comprehend standard IQ tests and score above 150. On-the-spot communication will be increasingly available to the citizens of most advanced countries; individual, portable two-way communication devices will be in use, much to the consternation of teenagers required to "call in" on dates and to regulatory authorities required to allocate and control frequencies.

Beginnings: Planning

A permanent base will have been established on the moon. Its life support systems will be capable of sustaining ten men indefinitely. This base will provide the earth's most important radio and astronomical observatory. A radio observatory designed primarily to search for extraterrestrial life will have been constructed. Planetary exploration, primarily unmanned, will be continuing.

The Technological World of 2025. The biological research begun in the last decades of the twentieth century will have continued into the twenty-first, yielding new techniques of control and understanding of human development and behavior. A range of new human reproductive techniques will exist, including extrauterine development (as a result of the successful simulation of the placenta) and parthenogenesis. Of course, the choice of sex of one's offspring and human cloning, both demonstrated earlier, will have come into wider use. All of these techniques will have raised serious threats to conventional family structuring and many other social institutions that we currently take for granted.

Of particular importance to biomedicine early in the next century will be the capability of modifying genes through molecular engineering to overcome some human hereditary defects. This development will have stemmed from better understanding of the processes of differentiation and development and will provide the ability to control certain human phenotypes. Furthermore, skill in genetic engineering and deeper understanding of the genetic processes may have provided the capability to repair the central nervous system through regeneration of individual neurons; perhaps it will have been possible also to stimulate the growth of new organs and limbs in human beings.

This development will probably lead to intense discussion about which diseases should or should not be controlled. The arguments may involve the possibility of producing specialized classes, such as menials and supermen, and will probably consider the danger that a division between socioeconomic classes and, perhaps, between developed and less-developed nations will grow, depending on who has the technological capability and required financing to construct molecular engineering centers. Of course, the application of these techniques to food production will have proven beneficial to the world. The spectacular genetic breakthroughs expected earlier will have been matched by our growing control over the aging process; life expectancy at birth may have been extended chemically by fifty years, with a commensurate increase in vigor. New drugs will also have been used for raising the intelligence of some human beings and for the purpose of producing specific changes in personal characteristics, such as alterations in attitudes and life styles. This new capability of determining the effects of drugs will have resulted from the development of a theoretical pharmacological discipline and, thus, the prior analytic prediction of the medical effects of drugs.

The impact of these kinds of changes on social structure will have been immense. Some of the developments might be used to reward special groups, such as high ranking officials. Scientists might organize to prevent these capabilities from being used adversely. Less-developed nations might demand being made part of the technological present.

In the first part of the twenty-first century, research into the means of directly stimulating the cortex may have led to demonstration of man-machine symbiosis in which certain men (perhaps with implanted electrodes or other, less repugnant devices) will extend their intelligence by being connected to a computer. This development might have the effect of multiplying human intelligence manyfold.

Significant amounts of electrical power will have been transmitted by wireless means; superconductors operating in the range of 20-30°K, or even room temperature will have been demonstrated. Use of these new materials and processes will have resulted in the development of new families of vehicles and devices; room-temperature superconductors for example, could be used to make cars that float over magnetic highways. These techniques will permit cheaper electricity to be produced and, with it, the development of new techniques for refrigeration, communication, and transportation, amounting to a new dimension of control by man over his world. It is possible that research into the composition of matter will lead to the ability to produce any element from subatomic particles. If such a capability should be attained, rare earth elements could be produced in whatever quantities needed, and alloys and materials virtually unknown today would come into wide use.

Taken from: MITRE Corporation (Martin V. Jones), *A Technology Assessment Methodology (Some Basic Propositions)*, MTR 6009, Volume 1, page 79. Reproduced by permission.

33. Selected Impacts of the Automobile (1895 to present).

MARTIN V. JONES

The automobile has had an enormous and pervasive influence on human life. Author Jones prepared the following list merely to suggest a few of the ways that the automobile has changed our lives.

The automobile has had an enormous and pervasive influence on human life. Author Jones prepared the following list merely to suggest a few of the ways that the automobile has changed our lives.

Values
Geographic mobility.
Expansion of personal freedom.
Prestige and material status derived from automobile ownership.
Overevaluation of automobile as an extension of the self—an identity machine.
Privacy—insulates from both environment and human contact.
Consideration of automobile ownership as an essential part of normal living (household goods).
Development of automobile cultists (group identification symbolized by type of automobile owned).

Environment
Noise pollution.
Automobile junkyards.
Roadside litter.
Land usage for highways—takes away from recreation, housing, etc.
Land erosion from highway construction.
Water pollution (oil in streams from road run-off).
Unsightly billboards.
Air pollution—lead, asbestos, hydrogen chloride, carbon monoxide, oxides of nitrogen, oxides of sulfur.

Economic
Mainstay and prime mover of American economy in 20th century.
Large number of the jobs directly related to automobile industry (one out of every six).
Automobile industry the lifeblood of many other major industries.
Rise of small businesses such as service stations and tourist accommodations.
Suburban real estate boom.
Drastic decline of horse, carriage, and wagon businesses.
Depletion of fuel reserves.
Stimulus to exploration for and drilling of new oil fields and development of new refining techniques, resulting in cheaper and more sophisticated methods.
Increased expenditures for road expansion and improvement.
Increased Federal, state, and local revenues through automobile and gasoline sales taxes.
Decline of railroads (both passengers and freight).

Social
Changes in patterns of courtship, socialization and training of children, work habits, use of leisure time, and family patterns.
Created broad American middle class and reduced class differences.
Created new class of semiskilled industrial workers.
Substitution of automobile for mass transit.
Ready conversion of the heavy industrial capability of automobile factories during World War II to make weapons.
Many impacts on crime.
Increased tourism.
Changes in education through bussing (consolidated school versus "one room country schoolhouse").
Medical care and other emergency services more rapidly available.
Traffic congestion.
Annual loss of life from automobile accidents about 60,000.
Increased incidence of respiratory ailments, heart disease, and cancer.
Older, poorer neighborhood displacement through urban freeway construction.

Demography
Population movement to suburbs.
Shifts in geographic sites of principal U.S. manufacturers.
Displacement of agricultural workers from rural to urban areas.
Movement of business and industry to suburbs.
Increased geographic mobility.

Institutional
Automotive labor union activity set many precedents.
Decentralized, multidivisional structure of the modern industrial corporation evident throughout the auto industry.
Modern management techniques.
Consumer installment credit.
Unparalleled standard of living.
Emergence of U.S. as foremost commercial and military power in world.
Expansion of field of insurance.
Rise of entrepreneurship.
Basis for an oligopolistic model for other sectors of the economy.
Federal regulation of interstate highways and commerce as a pattern for other fields.
Highway lobby—its powerful influence.

34. A Technology of Behavior

B. F. SKINNER

In trying to solve the terrifying problems that face us in the world today, we naturally turn to the things we do best. We play from strength, and our strength is science and technology. To contain a population explosion we look for better methods of birth control. Threatened by a nuclear holocaust, we build bigger deterrent forces and anti-ballistic-missile systems. We try to stave off world famine with new foods and better ways of growing them. Improved sanitation and medicine will, we hope, control disease, better housing and transportation will solve the problems of the ghettos, and new ways of reducing or disposing of waste will stop the pollution of the environment. We can point to remarkable achievements in all these fields, and it is not surprising that we should try to extend them. But things grow steadily worse, and it is disheartening to find that technology itself is increasingly at fault. Sanitation and medicine have made the problems of population more acute, war has acquired a new horror with the invention of nuclear weapons, and the affluent pursuit of happiness is largely responsible for pollution. As Darlington has said, "Every new source from which man has increased his power on the earth has been used to diminish the prospects of his successors. All his progress has been made at the expense of damage to his environment which he cannot repair and could not foresee."

Whether or not he could have foreseen the damage, man must repair it or all is lost. And he can do so if he will recognize the nature of the difficulty. The application of the physical and biological sciences alone will not solve our problems because the solutions lie in another field. Better contraceptives will control population only if people use them. New weapons may offset new defenses and vice versa, but a nuclear holocaust can be prevented only if the conditions under which nations make war can be changed. New methods of agriculture and medicine will not help if they are not practiced, and housing is a matter not only of buildings and cities but of how people live. Overcrowding can be corrected only by inducing people not to crowd, and the environment will continue to deteriorate until polluting practices are abandoned.

In short, we need to make vast changes in human behavior, and we cannot make them with the help of nothing more than physics or biology, no matter how hard we try. (And there are other problems, such as the breakdown of our educational system and the disaffection and revolt of the young, to which physical and biological technologies are so obviously irrelevant that they have never been applied.) It is not enough to "use technology with a deeper understanding of human issues," or to "dedicate technology to man's spiritual needs," or to "encourage technologists to look at human problems." Such expressions imply that where human behavior begins, technology stops, and that we must carry on, as we have in the past, with what we have learned from personal experience or from those collections of personal experiences called history, or with the distillations of experience to be found in folk wisdom and practical rules of thumb. These have been available for centuries, and all we have to show for them is the state of the world today.

What we need is a technology of behavior. We could solve our problems quickly enough if we could adjust the growth of the world's population as precisely as we adjust the course of a spaceship, or improve agriculture and industry with some of the confidence with which we accelerate high-energy particles, or move toward a peaceful world with something like the steady progress with which physics has approached absolute zero (even though both remain presumably out of reach). But a behavioral technology comparable in power and precision to physical and biological technology is lacking, and those who do not find the very possibility ridiculous are more likely to be frightened by it than reassured. That is how far we are from "understanding human issues" in the sense in which physics and biology understand their fields, and how far we are from preventing the catastrophe toward which the world seems to be inexorably moving.

Twenty-five hundred years ago it might have been said that man understood himself as well as any other part of his world. Today he is the thing he understands least. Physics and biology have come a long way, but there has been no comparable development of anything like a science of human behavior. Greek physics and biology are now of historical interest only (no modern physicist or biologist would turn to Aristotle for help), but the dialogues of Plato are still assigned to students and cited as if they threw light on human behavior. Aristotle could not have understood a page of modern physics or biology, but Socrates and his friends would have little trouble in following most current discussions of human affairs. And as to technology, we have made immense strides in controlling the physical and biological worlds, but our practices in government, education, and much of economics, though adapted to very different conditions, have not greatly improved.

We can scarcely explain this by saying that the Greeks knew all there was to know about human behavior. Certainly they knew more than they knew about the physical world, but it was still not much. Moreover, their way of thinking about human behavior must have had some fatal flaw. Whereas Greek physics and biology, no matter how crude, led eventually to modern science, Greek theories of human behavior led nowhere. If they are with us today, it is not because they possessed some kind of eternal verity, but because they did not contain the seeds of anything better.

It can always be argued that human behavior is a particularly difficult field. It is, and we are especially likely to think so just because we are so inept in dealing with it. But modern physics and biology successfully treat subjects that are certainly no simpler than many aspects of human behavior. The difference is that the instruments and methods they use are of commensurate complexity. The fact that equally powerful instruments and methods are not available in the field of human behavior is not an explanation; it is only part of the puzzle. Was putting a man on the moon actually easier than improving education in our public schools? Or than constructing better kinds of living space for everyone? Or than making it possible for everyone to be gainfully employed and, as a result, to enjoy a higher standard of living? The choice was not a matter of priorities, for no one could have said that it was more important to get to the moon. The exciting thing about getting to the moon was its feasibility. Science and technology had reached the point at which, with one great push, the thing could be done. There is no comparable excitement about the problems posed by human behavior. We are not close to solutions.

It is easy to conclude that there must be something about human behavior which makes a scientific analysis, and hence an effective technology, impossible, but we have not by any means exhausted the possibilities. There is a sense in which it can be said that the methods of science have scarcely yet been applied to human behavior. We have used the instruments of science; we have counted and measured and compared; but something essential to scientific practice is missing in almost all current discussions of human behavior. It has to do with our treatment of the causes of behavior. (The term "cause" is no longer common in sophisticated scientific writing, but it will serve well enough here.)

Man's first experience with causes probably came from his own behavior: things moved because he moved them. If other things moved, it was because someone else was moving them, and if the mover could not be seen, it was because he was invisible. The Greek gods served in this way as the causes of physical phenomena. They were usually outside the things they moved, but they might enter into and "possess" them. Physics and biology soon abandoned explanations of this sort and turned to more useful kinds of causes, but the step has not been decisively taken in the field of human behavior. Intelligent people no longer believe that men are possessed by demons (although the exorcism of devils is occasionally practiced, and the daimonic has reappeared in the writings of psychotherapists), but human behavior is still commonly attributed to indwelling agents. A juvenile delinquent is said, for example, to be suffering from a disturbed personality. There would be no point in saying it if the personality were not somehow distinct from the body which has got itself into trouble. The distinction is clear when one body is said to contain several personalities which control it in different ways at different times. Psychoanalysts have identified three of these personalities—the ego, superego, and id—and interactions among them are said to be responsible for the behavior of the man in whom they dwell.

Beginnings: Planning

Although physics soon stopped personifying things in this way, it continued for a long time to speak as if they had wills, impulses, feelings, purposes, and other fragmentary attributes of an indwelling agent. According to Butterfield, Aristotle argued that a falling body accelerated because it grew more jubilant as it found itself nearer home, and later authorities supposed that a projectile was carried forward by an impetus, sometimes called an "impetuosity." All this was eventually abandoned, and to good effect, but the behavioral sciences still appeal to comparable internal states. No one is surprised to hear it said that a person carrying good news walks more rapidly because he feels jubilant, or acts carelessly because of his impetuosity, or holds stubbornly to a course of action through sheer force of will. Careless references to purpose are still to be found in both physics and biology, but good practice has no place for them; yet almost everyone attributes human behavior to intentions, purposes, aims, and goals. It it is still possible to ask whether a machine can show purpose, the question implies, significantly, that if it can it will more closely resemble a man.

Physics and biology moved farther away from personified causes when they began to attribute the behavior of things to essences, qualities, or natures. To the medieval alchemist, for example, some of the properties of a substance might be due to the mercurial essence, and substances were compared in what might have been called a "chemistry of individual differences." Newton complained of the practice in his contemporaries: "To tell us that every species of thing is endowed with an occult specific quality by which it acts and produces manifest effects is to tell us nothing." (Occult qualities were examples of the hypotheses Newton rejected when he said "Hypotheses non fingo," though he was not quite as good as his word.) Biology continued for a long time to appeal to the *nature* of living things, and it did not wholly abandon vital forces until the twentieth century. Behavior, however, is still attributed to human nature, and there is an extensive "psychology of individual differences" in which people are compared and described in terms of traits of character, capacities, and abilities.

Almost everyone who is concerned with human affairs—as political scientist, philosopher, man of letters, economist, psychologist, linguist, sociologist, theologian, anthropologist, educator, or psychotherapist—continues to talk about human behavior in this prescientific way. Every issue of a daily paper, every magazine, every professional journal, every book with any bearing whatsoever on human behavior will supply examples. We are told that to control the number of people in the world we need to change *attitudes* toward children, overcome *pride* in size of family or in sexual potency, build some *sense of responsibility* toward offspring, and reduce the role played by a large family in allaying *concern* for old age. To work for peace we must deal with the *will to power* or the *paranoid delusions* of leaders; we must remember that wars begin in the *minds* of men, that there is something suicidal in man—a *death instinct* perhaps—which leads to war, and that man is aggressive by *nature.* To solve the problems of the poor we must inspire *self-respect,* encourage *initiative,* and reduce *frustration.* To allay the disaffection of the young we must provide a *sense of purpose* and reduce feelings of *alienation* or *hopelessness.* Realizing that we have no effective means of doing any of this, we ourselves may experience a *crisis of belief* or a *loss of confidence,* which can be corrected only by returning to a *faith in man's inner capacities.* This is staple fare. Almost no one questions it. Yet there is nothing like it in modern physics or most of biology, and that fact may well explain why a science and a technology of behavior have been so long delayed.

It is usually supposed that the "behavioristic" objection to ideas, feelings, traits of character, will, and so on concerns the stuff of which they are said to be made. Certain stubborn questions about the nature of mind have, of course, been debated for more than twenty-five hundred years and still go unanswered. How, for example, can the mind move the body? As late as 1965 Karl Popper could put the question this way: "What we want is to understand how such nonphysical things as *purposes, deliberations, plans, decisions, theories, tensions,* and *values* can play a part in bringing about physical changes in the physical world." And, of course, we also want to know where these non-physical things come from. To that question the Greeks had a simple answer: from the gods. As Dodds has pointed out, the Greeks believed that if a man behaved foolishly, it was because a hostile god had planted $\alpha\tau\eta$ (infatuation) in his breast. A friendly god might give a warrior an extra amount of $\mu\epsilon\gamma\sigma$, with the help of which he would fight brilliantly. Aristotle thought there was something divine in thought, and Zeno held that the intellect *was* God.

We cannot take that line today, and the commonest alternative is to appeal to antecedent physical events. A person's genetic endowment, a product of the evolution of the species, is said to explain part of the workings of his mind and his personal history the rest. For example, because of (physical) competition during the course of evolution people now have (nonphysical) feelings of aggression which lead to (physical) acts of hostility. Or, the (physcial) punishment a small child receives when he engages in sex play produces (nonphysical) feelings of anxiety which interfere with his (physical) sexual behavior as an adult. The nonphysical stage obviously bridges long periods of time: aggression reaches back into millions of years of evolutionary history, and anxiety acquired when one is a child survives into old age.

The problem of getting from one kind of stuff to another could be avoided if everything were either mental or physical, and both these possibilities have been considered. Some philosophers have tried to stay within the world of the mind, arguing that only immediate experience is real, and experimental psychology began as an attempt to discover the mental laws which governed interactions among mental elements. Contemporary "intrapsychic" theories of psychotherapy tell us how one feeling leads to another (how frustration breeds aggression, for example), how feelings interact, and how feelings which have been put out of mind fight their way back in. The complementary line that the mental stage is really physical was taken, curiously enough, by Freud, who believed that physiology would eventually explain the workings of the mental apparatus. In a similar vein, many physiological psychologists continue to talk freely about states of mind, feelings, and so on, in the belief that it is only a matter of time before we shall understand their physical nature.

The dimensions of the world of mind and the transition from one world to another do raise embarrassing problems, but it is usually possible to ignore them, and this may be good strategy, for the important objection to mentalism is of a very different sort. The world of the mind steals the show. Behavior is not recognized as a subject in its own right. In psychotherapy, for example, the disturbing things a person does or says are almost always regarded merely as symptoms, and compared with the fascinating dramas which are staged in the depths of the mind, behavior itself seems superficial indeed. In linguistics and literary criticism what a man says is almost always treated as the expression of ideas or feelings. In political science, theology, and economics, behavior is usually regarded as the material from which one infers attitudes, intentions, needs, and so on. For more than twenty-five hundred years close attention has been paid to mental life, but only recently has any effort been made to study human behavior as something more than a mere by-product.

The conditions of which behavior is a function are also neglected. The mental explanation brings curiosity to an end. We see the effect in casual discourse. If we ask someone, "Why did you go to the theater?" and he says, "Because I felt like going," we are apt to take his reply as a kind of explanation. It would be much more to the point to know what has happened when he has gone to the theater in the past, what he heard or read about the play he went to see, and what other things in his past or present environments might have induced him to go (as opposed to doing something else), but we accept "I felt like going" as a sort of summary of all this and are not likely to ask for details.

The professional psychologist often stops at the same point. A long time ago William James corrected a prevailing view of the relation between feelings and action by asserting, for example, that we do not run away because we are afraid but are afraid because we run away. In other words, what we feel when we feel afraid is our behavior—the very behavior which in the traditional view expresses the feeling and is explained by it. But how many of those who have considered James's argument have noted that no antecedent event has in fact been pointed out? Neither "because" should be taken seriously. No explanation has been given as to why we run away *and* feel afraid.

Whether we regard ourselves as explaining feelings or the behavior said to be caused by feelings, we give very little attention to antecedent circumstances. The psychotherapist learns about the early life of his patient almost exclusively from the patient's memories, which are known to be unreliable, and he may even argue that what is important is not what actually happened but what the patient remembers. In the psychoanalytic literature there must be at least a hundred references to felt anxiety for every reference to a punishing episode to which anxiety might be traced. We even seem to prefer antecedent histories which are clearly out of reach. There is a good deal of current interest, for example, in what must have happened during the evolution of the species to explain human behavior, and we seem to speak with special confidence just because what actually happened can only be inferred.

Unable to understand how or why the person we see behaves as he does, we attribute his behavior to a person we cannot see, whose behavior we cannot explain either but about whom we are not inclined to ask questions. We probably adopt this strategy not so much because of any lack of interest or power but because of a longstanding conviction that for much of human behavior there *are* no relevant antecedents. The function of the inner man is to provide an explanation which will not be explained in turn. Explanation stops with him. He is not a mediator between past history and current behavior, he is a *center* from which behavior emanates. He initiates, originates, and creates, and in doing so he remains, as he was for the Greeks, divine. We say that he is autonomous—and, so far as a science of behavior is concerned, that means miraculous.

The position is, of course, vulnerable. Autonomous man serves to explain only the things we are not yet able to explain in other ways. His existence depends upon our ignorance, and he naturally loses status as we come to know more about behavior. The task of a scientific analysis is to explain how the behavior of a person as a physical system is related to the conditions under which the human species evolved and the conditions under which the individual lives. Unless there is indeed some capricious or creative intervention, these events must be related, and no intervention is in fact needed. The contingencies of survival responsible for man's genetic endowment would produce tendencies to *act* aggressively, not feelings of aggression. The punishment of sexual behavior changes sexual *behavior,* and any feelings which may arise are at best by-products. Our age is not suffering from anxiety but from the accidents, crimes, wars, and other dangerous and painful things to which people are so often exposed. Young people drop out of school, refuse to get jobs, and associate only with others of their own age not because they feel alienated but because of defective social environments in homes, schools, factories, and elsewhere.

We can follow the path taken by physics and biology by turning directly to the relation between behavior and the environment and neglecting supposed mediating states of mind. Physics did not advance by looking more closely at the jubilance of a falling body, or biology by looking at the nature of vital spirits, and we do not need to try to discover what personalities, states of mind, feelings, traits of character, plans, purposes, intentions, or the other perquisites of autonomous man really are in order to get on with a scientific analysis of behavior.

There are reasons why it has taken us so long to reach this point. The things studied by physics and biology do not behave very much like people, and it eventually seems rather ridiculous to speak of the jubilance of a falling body or the impetuosity of a projectile; but people do behave like people, and the outer man whose behavior is to be explained could be very much like the inner man whose behavior is said to explain it. The inner man has been created in the image of the outer.

A more important reason is that the inner man seems at times to be directly observed. We must infer the jubilance of a falling body, but can we not *feel* our own jubilance? We do, indeed, feel things inside our own skin, but we do not feel the things which have been invented to explain behavior. The possessed man does not feel the possessing *demon* and may even deny that one exists. The juvenile delinquent does not feel his *disturbed personality.* The intelligent man does not feel his *intelligence* or the introvert his *introversion.* (In fact, these dimensions of mind or character are said to be observable only through complex statistical procedures.) The speaker does not feel the *grammatical rules* he is said to apply in composing sentences, and men spoke grammatically for thousands of years before anyone knew there were rules. The respondent to a questionnaire does not feel the *attitudes* or *opinions* which lead him to check items in particular ways. We do feel certain states of our bodies associated with behavior, but as Freud pointed out, we behave in the same way when we do not feel them; they are by-products and not to be mistaken for causes.

There is a much more important reason why we have been so slow in discarding mentalistic explanations: it has been hard to find alternatives. Presumably we must look for them in the external environment, but the role of the environment is by no means clear. The history of the theory of evolution illustrates the problem. Before the nineteenth century, the environment was thought of simply as a passive setting in which many different kinds of organisms were born, reproduced themselves, and died. No one saw that the environment was responsible for the fact that there *were* many different kinds (and that fact, significantly enough, was attributed to a creative Mind). The trouble was that the environment acts in an inconspicuous way: it does not push or pull, it *selects.* For thousands of years in the history of human thought the process of natural selection went unseen in spite of its extraordinary importance. When it was eventually discovered, it became, of course, the key to evolutionary theory.

The effect of the environment on behavior remained obscure for an even longer time. We can see what organisms do to the world around them, as they take from it what they need and ward off its dangers, but it is much harder to see what the world does to them. It was Descartes who first suggested that the environment might play an active role in the determination of behavior, and he was apparently able to do so only because he was given a strong hint. He knew about certain automata in the Royal Gardens of France which were operated hydraulically by concealed valves. As Descartes described it, people

376   BEGINNINGS

entering the gardens "necessarily tread on certain tiles or plates, which are so disposed that if they approach a bathing Diana, they cause her to hide in the rosebushes, and if they try to follow her, they cause a Neptune to come forward to meet them, threatening them with his trident." The figures were entertaining just because they behaved like people, and it appeared, therefore, that something very much like human behavior could be explained mechanically. Descartes took the hint: living organisms might move for similar reasons. (He excluded the human organism, presumably to avoid religious controversy.)

The triggering action of the environment came to be called a "stimulus"— the Latin for goad—and the effect on an organism a "response," and together they were said to compose a "reflex." Reflexes were first demonstrated in small decapitated animals, such as salamanders, and it is significant that the principle was challenged throughout the nineteenth century because it seemed to deny the existence of an autonomous agent—the "soul of the spinal cord"— to which movement of a decapitated body had been attributed. When Pavlov showed how new reflexes could be built up through conditioning, a full-fledged stimulus-response psychology was born, in which all behavior was regarded as reactions to stimuli. One writer put it this way: "We are prodded or lashed through life." The stimulus-response model was never very convincing, however, and it did not solve the basic problem, because something like an inner man had to be invented to convert a stimulus into a response. Information theory ran into the same problem when an inner "processer" had to be invented to convert input into output.

The effect of an eliciting stimulus is relatively easy to see, and it is not surprising that Descartes' hypothesis held a dominant position in behavior theory for a long time, but it was a false scent from which a scientific analysis is only now recovering. The environment not only prods or lashes, it *selects.* Its role is similar to that in natural selection, though on a very different time scale, and was overlooked for the same reason. It is now clear that we must take into account what the environment does to an organism not only before but after it responds. Behavior is shaped and maintained by its consequences. Once this fact is recognized, we can formulate the interaction between organism and environment in a much more comprehensive way.

There are two important results. One concerns the basic analysis. Behavior which operates upon the environment to produce consequences ("operant" behavior) can be studied by arranging environments in which specific consequences are contingent upon it. The contingencies under investigation have become steadily more complex, and one by one they are taking over the explanatory functions previously assigned to personalities, states of mind, feelings, traits of character, purposes, and intentions. The second result is practical: the environment can be manipulated. It is true that man's genetic endowment can be changed only very slowly, but changes in the environment of the individual have quick and dramatic effects. A technology of operant behavior is, as we shall see, already well advanced, and it may prove to be commensurate with our problems.

That possibility raises another problem, however, which must be solved if we are to take advantage of our gains. We have moved forward by dispossessing autonomous man, but he has not departed gracefully. He is conducting a sort of rear-guard action in which, unfortunately, he can marshal formidable support. He is still an important figure in political science, law, religion, economics, anthropology, sociology, psychotherapy, philosophy, ethics, history, education, child care, linguistics, architecture, city planning, and family life. These fields have their specialists, and every specialist has a theory, and in almost every theory the autonomy of the individual is unquestioned. The inner man is not seriously threatened by data obtained through casual observation or from studies of the structure of behavior, and many of these fields deal only with groups of people, where statistical or actuarial data impose few restraints upon the individual. The result is a tremendous weight of traditional "knowledge," which must be corrected or displaced by a scientific analysis.

Two features of autonomous man are particularly troublesome. In the traditional view, a person is free. He is autonomous in the sense that his behavior is uncaused. He can therefore be held responsible for what he does and justly punished if he offends. That view, together with its associated practices, must be re-examined when a scientific analysis reveals unsuspected controlling relations between behavior and environment. A certain amount of external control can be tolerated. Theologians have accepted the fact that man must be predestined to do what an omniscient God knows he will do, and the Greek dramatist took inexorable fate as his favorite theme. Soothsayers and astrologers often claim to predict what men will do, and they have always been in demand. Biographers and historians have searched for "influences" in the lives of individuals and peoples. Folk wisdom and the insights of essayists like Montaigne and Bacon imply some kind of predictability in human conduct, and the statistical and actuarial evidences of the social sciences point in the same direction.

Autonomous man survives in the face of all this because he is the happy exception. Theologians have reconciled predestination with free will, and the Greek audience, moved by the portrayal of an inescapable destiny, walked out of the theater free men. The course of history has been turned by the death of a leader or a storm at sea, as a life has been changed by a teacher or a love affair, but these things do not happen to everyone, and they do not affect everyone in the same way. Some historians have made a virtue of the unpredictability of history. Actuarial evidence is easily ignored; we read that hundreds of people will be killed in traffic accidents on a holiday weekend and take to the road as if personally exempt. Very little behavioral science raises "the specter of predictable man." On the contrary, many anthropologists, sociologists, and psychologists have used their expert knowledge to prove that man is free, purposeful, and responsible. Freud was a determinist—on faith, if not on the evidence—but many Freudians have no hesitation in assuring their patients that they are free to choose among different courses of action and are in the long run the architects of their own destinies.

This escape route is slowly closed as new evidences of the predictability of human behavior are discovered. Personal exemption from a complete determinism is revoked as a scientific analysis progresses, particularly in accounting for the behavior of the individual. Jospeh Wood Krutch has acknowledged the actuarial facts while insisting on personal freedom: "We can predict with a considerable degree of accuracy how many people will go to the seashore on a day when the temperature reaches a certain point, even how many will jump off a bridge . . . although I am not, nor are you, compelled to do either." But he can scarcely mean that those who go to the seashore do not go for good reason, or that circumstances in the life of a suicide do not have some bearing on the fact that he jumps off a bridge. The distinction is tenable only so long as a word like "compel" suggests a particularly conspicuous and forcible mode of control. A scientific analysis naturally moves in the direction of clarifying all kinds of controlling relations.

By questioning the control exercised by autonomous man and demonstrating the control exercised by the environment, a science of behavior also seems to question dignity or worth. A person is responsible for his behavior, not only in the sense that he may be justly blamed or punished when he behaves badly, but also in the sense that he is to be given credit and admired for his achievements. A scientific analysis shifts the credit as well as the blame to the environment, and traditional practices can then no longer be justified. These are sweeping changes, and those who are committed to traditional theories and practices naturally resist them.

There is a third source of trouble. As the emphasis shifts to the environment, the individual seems to be exposed to a new kind of danger. Who is to construct the controlling environment and to what end? Autonomous man presumably controls himself in accordance with a built-in set of values; he works for what he finds good. But what will the putative controller find good, and will it be good for those he controls? Answers to questions of this sort are said, of course, to call for value judgments.

Freedom, dignity, and value are major issues, and unfortunately they become more crucial as the power of a technology of behavior becomes more nearly commensurate with the problems to be solved. The very change which has brought some hope of a solution is responsible for a growing opposition to the kind of solution proposed. This conflict is itself a problem in human behavior and may be approached as such. A science of behavior is by no means as far advanced as physics or biology, but it has an advantage in that it may throw some light on its own difficulties. Science *is* human behavior, and so is the opposition to science. What has happened in man's struggle for freedom and dignity, and what problems arise when scientific knowledge begins to be relevant in that struggle? Answers to these questions may help to clear the way for the technology we so badly need.

In what follows, these issues are discussed "from a scientific point of view," but this does not mean that the reader will need to know the details of a scientific analysis of behavior. A mere interpretation will suffice. The nature of such an interpretation is, however, easily misunderstood. We often talk about things we cannot observe or measure with the precision demanded by a scientific analysis, and in doing so there is much to be gained from using terms and principles which have been worked out under more precise conditions. The sea at dusk glows with a strange light, frost forms on the window-pane in an unusual pattern, and the soup fails to thicken on the stove, and specialists tell us why. We can, of course, challenge them: they do not have "the facts," and what they say cannot be "proved," but they are nevertheless more likely to be right than those who lack an experimental background, and they alone can tell us how to move on to a more precise study if it seems worthwhile.

An experimental analysis of behavior offers similar advantages. When we have observed behavioral processes under controlled conditions, we can more easily spot them in the world at large. We can identify significant features of behavior and of the environment and are therefore able to neglect insignificant ones, no matter how fascinating they may be. We can reject traditional explanations if they have been tried and found wanting in an experimental analysis and then press forward in our inquiry with unallayed curiosity. The instances of behavior cited in what follows are not offered as "proof" of the interpretation. The proof is to be found in the basic analysis. The principles used in interpreting the instances have a plausibility which would be lacking in principles drawn entirely from casual observation.

The text will often seem inconsistent. English, like all languages, is full of prescientific terms which usually suffice for purposes of casual discourse. No one looks askance at the astronomer when he says that the sun rises or that the stars come out at night, for it would be ridiculous to insist that he should always say that the sun appears over the horizon as the earth turns or that the stars become visible as the atmosphere ceases to refract sunlight. All we ask is that he can give a more precise translation if one is needed. The English language contains many more expressions referring to human behavior than to other aspects of the world, and technical alternatives are much less familiar. The use of casual expressions is therefore much more likely to be challenged. It may seem inconsistent to ask the reader to "keep a point in mind" when he has been told that mind is an explanatory fiction, or to "consider the idea of freedom" if an idea is simply an imagined precursor of behavior, or to speak of "reassuring those who fear a science of behavior" when all that is meant is changing their behavior with respect to such a science. The book could have been written for a technical reader without expressions of that sort, but the issues are important to the nonspecialist and need to be discussed in a nontechnical fashion. No doubt many of the mentalistic expressions imbedded in the English language cannot be as rigorously translated as "sunrise," but acceptable translations are not out of reach.

Almost all our major problems involve human behavior, and they cannot be solved by physical and biological technology alone. What is needed is a technology of behavior, but we have been slow to develop the science from which such a technology might be drawn. One difficulty is that almost all of what is called behavioral science continues to trace behavior to states of mind, feelings, traits of character, human nature, and so on. Physics and biology once followed similar practices and advanced only when they discarded them. The behavioral sciences have been slow to change partly because the explanatory entities often seem to be directly observed and partly because other kinds of explanations have been hard to find. The environment is obviously important, but its role has remained obscure. It does not push or pull, it *selects,* and this function is difficult to discover and analyze. The role of natural selection in evolution was formulated only a little more than a hundred years ago, and the selective role of the environment in shaping and maintaining the behavior of the individual is only beginning to be recognized and studied. As the interaction between organism and environment has come to be understood, however, effects once assigned to states of mind, feelings, and traits are beginning to be traced to accessible conditions, and a technology of behavior may therefore become available. It will not solve our problems, however, until it replaces traditional prescientific views, and these are strongly entrenched. Freedom and dignity illustrate the difficulty. They are the possessions of the autonomous man of traditional theory, and they are essential to practices in which a person is held responsible for his conduct and given credit for his achievements. A scientific analysis shifts both the responsibility and the achievement to the environment. It also raises questions concerning "values." Who will use a technology and to what ends? Until these issues are resolved, a technology of behavior will continue to be rejected, and with it possibly the only way to solve our problems.

Beginnings: Global Consciousness

FRED: You know, some people in your class really didn't go for this global stuff.

ANGELA: I didn't know that.

FRED: Yeah, some of these kids are only nineteen years old and their minds are already made up. They just don't see the relevance of talking about Protean man. It just doesn't make any sense; it seems too far out.

MOLLY: Sometimes I really like spacey ideas like McLuhan has, and other times I need something more concrete, something that relates to my life more directly.

FRED: Maybe you ought to cut out a few of the articles in this section.

ANGELA: You mean, just dump the section?

FRED: No, just tone it down a little.

ANGELA: But these ideas are influential today. I mean, these are fairly big ideas.

FRED: Maybe that's what I'm trying to say. You have to let them grow on you, or you grow on them. I guess you're becoming globalized overnight when you read this stuff.

35. The Onset of the Technetronic Age

ZBIGNIEW BRZEZINSKI

The impact of science and technology on man and his society, especially in the more advanced countries of the world, is becoming the major source of contemporary change. Recent years have seen a proliferation of exciting and challenging literature on the future. In the United States, in Western Europe, and, to a lesser degree, in Japan and in the Soviet Union, a number of systematic, scholarly efforts have been made to project, predict, and grasp what the future holds for us.

The transformation that is now taking place, especially in America, is already creating a society increasingly unlike its industrial predecessor. The post-industrial society is becoming a "technetronic" society:* a society that is shaped culturally, psychologically, socially, and economically by the impact of technology and electronics—particularly in the area of computers and communications. The industrial process is no longer the principal determinant of social change, altering the mores, the social structure, and the values of society. In the industrial society technical knowledge was applied primarily to one specific end: the acceleration and improvement of production techniques. Social consequences were a later by-product of this paramount concern. In the technetronic society scientific and technical knowledge, in addition to enhancing production capabilities, quickly spills over to affect almost all aspects of life directly. Accordingly, both the growing capacity for the instant calculation of the most complex interactions and the increasing availability of biochemical means of human control augment the potential scope of consciously chosen direction, and thereby also the pressures to direct, to choose, and to change.

Reliance on these new techniques of calculation and communication enhances the social importance of human intelligence and the immediate relevance of learning. The need to integrate social change is heightened by the increased ability to decipher the patterns of change; this in turn increases the

---

*The term "post-industrial" is used by Daniel Bell, who has done much of the pioneering thinking on the subject. However, I prefer to use the neologism "technetronic," because it conveys more directly the character of the principal impulses for change in our time. Similarly, the term "industrial" described what otherwise could have been called the "post-agricultural" age.

significance of basic assumptions concerning the nature of man and the desirability of one or another form of social organization. Science thereby intensifies rather than diminishes the relevance of values, but it demands that they be cast in terms that go beyond the more crude ideologies of the industrial age. (This theme is developed further in Part II.)

New Social Patterns

For Norbert Wiener, "the locus of an earlier industrial revolution before the main industrial revolution" is to be found in the fifteenth-century research pertaining to navigation (the nautical compass), as well as in the development of gunpowder and printing. Today the functional equivalent of navigation is the thrust into space, which requires a rapid computing capacity beyond the means of the human brain; the equivalent of gunpowder is modern nuclear physics, and that of printing is television and long-range instant communications. The consequence of this new technetronic revolution is the progressive emergence of a society that increasingly differs from the industrial one in a variety of economic, political, and social aspects. The following examples may be briefly cited to summarize some of the contrasts:

(1) In an industrial society the mode of production shifts from agriculture to industry, with the use of human and animal muscle supplanted by machine operation. In the technetronic society industrial employment yields to services, with automation and cybernetics replacing the operation of machines by individuals.

(2) Problems of employment and unemployment—to say nothing of the prior urbanization of the post-rural labor force—dominate the relationship between employers, labor, and the market in the industrial society, and the assurance of minimum welfare to the new industrial masses is a source of major concern. In the emerging new society questions relating to the obsolescence of skills, security, vacations, leisure, and profit sharing dominate the relationship, and the psychic well-being of millions of relatively secure but potentially aimless lower-middle-class blue-collar workers becomes a growing problem.

(3) Breaking down traditional barriers to education, and thus creating the basic point of departure for social advancement, is a major goal of social reformers in the industrial society. Education, available for limited and specific periods of time, is initially concerned with overcoming illiteracy and subsequently with technical training, based largely on written, sequential reasoning. In the technetronic society not only is education universal but advanced training is available to almost all who have the basic talents, and there is far greater emphasis on quality selection. The essential problem is to discover the most effective techniques for the rational exploitation of social talent. The latest communication and calculating techniques are employed in this task. The educational process becomes a lengthier one and is increasingly reliant on audio-visual aids. In addition, the flow of new knowledge necessitates more and more frequent refresher studies.

(4) In the industrial society social leadership shifts from the traditional rural-aristocratic to an urban-plutocratic elite. Newly acquired wealth is its foundation, and intense competition the outlet—as well as the stimulus—for its energy. In the technetronic society plutocratic pre-eminence is challenged by the political leadership, which is itself increasingly permeated by individuals possessing special skills and intellectual talents. Knowledge becomes a tool of power and the effective mobilization of talent an important way to acquire power.

(5) The university in an industrial society—in contrast to the situation in medieval times—is an aloof ivory tower, the repository of irrelevant, even if respected, wisdom, and for a brief time the fountainhead for budding members of the established social elite. In the technetronic society the university becomes an intensely involved "think tank," the source of much sustained political planning and social innovation.

(6) The turmoil inherent in the shift from a rigidly traditional rural society to an urban one engenders an inclination to seek total answers to social dilemmas, thus causing ideologies to thrive in the industrializing society. (The American exception to this rule was due to the absence of a feudal tradition, a point well developed by Louis Hartz.) In the industrial age literacy makes for static interrelated conceptual thinking, congenial to ideological systems. In the technetronic society audio-visual communications prompt more changeable, disparate views of reality, not compressible into formal systems, even as the requirements of science and the new computative techniques place a premium on mathematical logic and systematic reasoning. The resulting tension is felt most acutely by scientists, with the consequence that some seek to confine reason to science while expressing their emotions through politics. Moreover, the increasing ability to reduce social conflicts to quantifiable and measurable dimensions reinforces the trend toward a more pragmatic approach to social problems, while it simultaneously stimulates new concerns with preserving "humane" values.

(7) In the industrial society, as the hitherto passive masses become active there are intense political conflicts over such matters as disenfranchisement and the right to vote. The issue of political participation is a crucial one. In the technetronic age the question is increasingly one of ensuring real participation in decisions that seem too complex and too far removed from the average citizen. Political alienation becomes a problem. Similarly, the issue of political equality of the sexes gives way to a struggle for the sexual equality of women. In the industrial society woman—the operator of machines—ceases to be physically inferior to the male, a consideration of some importance in rural life, and begins to demand her political rights. In the emerging technetronic society automation threatens both males and females, intellectual talent is computable, the "pill" encourages sexual equality, and women begin to claim complete equality.

(8) The newly enfranchised masses are organized in the industrial society by trade unions and political parties and unified by relatively simple and

somewhat ideological programs. Moreover, political attitudes are influenced by appeals to nationalist sentiments, communicated through the massive increase of newspapers employing, naturally, the readers' national language. In the technetronic society the trend seems to be toward aggregating the individual support of millions of unorganized citizens, who are easily within the reach of magnetic and attractive personalities, and effectively exploiting the latest communication techniques to manipulate emotions and control reason. Reliance on television—and hence the tendency to replace language with imagery, which is international rather than national, and to include war coverage or scenes of hunger in places as distant as, for example, India—creates a somewhat more cosmopolitan, though highly impressionistic, involvement in global affairs.

(9) Economic power in the early phase of industrialization tends to be personalized, by either great entrepreneurs like Henry Ford or bureaucratic industrial officials like Kaganovich, or Minc (in Stalinist Poland). The tendency toward depersonalization of economic power is stimulated in the next stage by the appearance of a highly complex interdependence between governmental institutions (including the military), scientific establishments, and industrial organizations. As economic power becomes inseparably linked with political power, it becomes more invisible and the sense of individual futility increases.

(10) In an industrial society the acquisition of goods and the accumulation of personal wealth become forms of social attainment for an unprecedentedly large number of people. In the technetronic society the adaptation of science to humane ends and a growing concern with the quality of life become both possible and increasingly a moral imperative for a large number of citizens, especially the young.

Eventually, these changes and many others, including some that more directly affect the personality and quality of the human being himself, will make the technetronic society as different from the industrial as the industrial was from the agrarian.* And just as the shift from an agrarian economy and feudal politics toward an industrial society and political systems based on the individual's emotional identification with the nation-state gave rise to contemporary international politics, so the appearance of the technetronic society reflects the onset of a new relationship between man and his expanded global reality.

*Bell defines the "five dimensions of the post-industrial society" as involving the following: (1) The creation of a service economy. (2) The pre-eminence of the professional and technical class. (3) The centrality of *theoretical knowledge* as the source of innovation and policy formulation in the society. (4) The possibility of self-sustaining technological growth. (5) The creation of a new "intellectual technology." (Daniel Bell, "The Measurement of Knowledge and Technology," in *Indicators of Social Change,* Eleanor Sheldon and Wilbert Moore, eds., New York, 1968, pp. 152-53.)

36. Protean Man

ROBERT JAY LIFTON

In the course of studying young (and not so young) Chinese, Japanese, and Americans, I have become convinced that contemporary psychological patterns are creating a new kind of man—a "protean man."

I found that many East Asians I interviewed had experienced an extraordinary number of beliefs and emotional involvements, each of which they could readily abandon in favor of another. Observations I have been able to make in America have also led me to the conviction that a very general process is taking place. I do not mean to suggest that everybody is becoming the same, or that a totally new "world-self" is taking shape. But I am convinced that a new psychological style is emerging everywhere.

As illustration of this protean pattern, I would like to recount the remarkable history of one young Japanese whom I interviewed in Tokyo and Kyoto from 1960 to 1962. Though I mention him as an extreme example, there were many others who in various ways resembled him. This young man was 25 when I first spoke with him.

As the youngest son in a professional family, he was brought up to be a proper middle-class Japanese boy. But when he was evacuated to the country from the age of eight to eleven during and after the war, his contacts with farmers' and fishermen's sons created in him a lasting attraction to the life and the tastes of the "common man." He was at that time a fiery young patriot who was convinced of the sacredness of Japan's cause, revered her fighting men (especially his oldest brother, a naval pilot saved from a *kamikaze* death only by the war's end), accepted without question the historical myth of the Emperor's divine descent, and "hated the Americans." Japan's surrender came as a great shock and left him temporarily confused in his beliefs, though he felt curious about rather than hostile toward American soldiers. He soon became an eager young exponent of democracy, caught up in the "democracy boom" which then swept Japan and which seemed to most youngsters to promise "freedom" and moral certainty.

During junior high school and high school he was an all-round leader, excelling in his studies, prominent in student government and in social and athletic activities. Yet he also became an outspoken critic of society at large (on the basis of Marxist ideas current in Japanese intellectual circles) and of fellow students for their narrow careerism.

He was an English-speaking student, having concentrated since childhood on learning English, stimulated by his growing interest in America and by the size, wealth, and seemingly relaxed manner of individual Americans he had met and observed. Therefore, when he found himself unaccountably developing what he called a "kind of neurosis" in which he completely lost interest in everything he was doing, he decided to seek a change in mood and took advantage of an opportunity to become an exchange student for one year at an American high school.

During that year he became a convert to many aspects of American life, and was so moved by the direction and example of his American "father" (a Protestant minister and courageous defender of civil rights during McCarthyite controversies) that he made a sudden, emotional decision to be baptized as a Christian. He returned to Japan reluctantly, and there found himself looked upon as something of an oddity—one friend told him he "smelled like butter" (a traditional Japanese phrase for Westerners). Eager to regain acceptance, he re-immersed himself in Japanese experience—sitting on tatami, indulging in quiet, melancholy moods, drinking tea, and so on.

Yet he did not reintegrate himself to Japanese student life quickly enough to organize himself for the desperate all-out struggle to pass the entrance examination for Tokyo University. He failed in his first attempt and thereby became a *ronin* (in feudal days, a *samurai* without a master, now a student without a university) for one year, before passing the examination on his second attempt. Once admitted to the university, he found little to interest him and rarely attended classes until—through the influence of a Marxist professor and bright fellow students in an economics seminar—he became an enthusiastic *Zengakuren* activist. His embrace of the *Zengakuren* ideal of "pure communism" and his participation in student demonstrations and planning sessions gave him a sense of comradeship and fulfillment beyond any he had previously known. But when offered a position of leadership during his third year at the university, he decided that his character was not suited for "the life of a revolutionary" and that the best path for him was a conventional life of economic and social success within the existing society.

He left the *Zengakuren* and drifted into a life of dissipation, devoting his major energies to heavy drinking, marathon *mahjong* games, and affairs with bar girls. But when the time came, he had no difficulty in gaining employment with one of Japan's mammoth business organizations (and one of the *bêtes noires* of his Marxist days) and embarking upon the life of a young executive or *sarariman* (salaried man). In fact he did so with eagerness, careful preparation, and relief, but at the same time had fantasies and dreams of kicking over the traces, sometimes violently, and embarking upon a world tour (largely Hollywood-inspired) of exotic and sophisticated pleasure-seeking.

There are, of course, important differences between the protean life styles of this young man and his American counterparts—differences which have to do with cultural emphases and which contribute to what is generally called national character. But such is the intensity of the shared aspects of historical experience that contemporary Chinese, Japanese, and American self-process turn out to have striking points of convergence.

I use the term "self-process" rather than "character" or "personality" in order to convey the idea of flux and change. Erik Erikson's concept of identity has, among other things, been an effort to get away from the principle of fixity and permanence. My stress is even more specifically on the idea of flow. For it is quite possible that even the image of personal identity, insofar as it suggests inner stability and sameness, is derived from a vision of a traditional culture in which man's relationship to his institutions and symbols are still relatively intact—which is hardly the case today.

While stemming from the interplay of several factors, this new protean self-process is, I am convinced, shaped in large measure by the increasingly important part played in human behavior by those cultural traits related to modern (and particularly contemporary) historical forces. Two historical developments in particular have special importance for creating protean man.

The first is the worldwide sense of what I have called *historical* (or *psychohistorical*) *dislocation*. We are experiencing a break in the sense of connection which men have long felt with the vital and nourishing symbols of their cultural tradition—symbols revolving around family, idea systems, religions, and the life cycle in general. Today we perceive these traditional symbols as irrelevant, burdensome, or inactivating, and yet we cannot avoid carrying them within us or having our self-process profoundly affected by them.

The second large historical tendency is the *flooding of imagery* produced by the extraordinary flow of postmodern cultural influences over the mass communication networks, which readily cross local and national boundaries. Each individual is touched by everything, but at the same time he is overwhelmed by superficial messages and undigested cultural elements, by headlines and endless partial alternatives in every sphere of life. These alternatives, moreover, are universally and simultaneously shared—if not as courses of action, at least in the form of significant inner imagery.

In Greek mythology Proteus was able to change his shape with relative ease —from wild boar to lion to dragon to fire to flood. But what he found difficult, and would not do unless seized and chained, was to commit himself to a single form, the form most his own, and carry out his function of prophecy. We can say the same of protean man, but we must keep in mind his possibilities as well as his difficulties.

The protean style of self-process is characterized by an interminable series of experiments and explorations—some shallow, some profound—each of which may be readily abandoned in favor of still new psychological quests. The pattern in many ways resembles what Erikson has called "identity diffusion" or "identity confusion," and the impaired psychological functioning which those terms suggest can be very much present. But I would stress that the protean style is by no means pathological as such, and in fact may well be one of the central adaptive patterns of our day. It extends to all areas of human experience—to sexual as well as political behavior, to the holding and promulgating of ideas, and to the general organization of lives.

To illustrate the expression of the protean style in America and Europe, I would like to draw first from my psychotherapeutic work with patients and then from some observations on contemporary Western literature and art.

One patient of mine, a gifted young teacher, spoke of himself this way: "I have an extraordinary number of masks I can put on or take off. The question is: is there, or should there be, one face which should be authentic? I'm not sure that there is one for me. I cannot imagine a single act that I could not commit." He went on to compare himself to an actor on the stage who performs with a "certain kind of polymorphous versatility." And he asked: "Which is the real person, so far as an actor is concerned? Is he more real when performing on stage—or when he is at home? I tend to think that for people who have these many, many masks, there is no home."

My patient was by no means a happy man, but neither was he incapacitated. And although we can see the strain with which he carries his "polymorphous versatility," it could also be said that, as a teacher and a thinker, and in some ways as a man, it served him well.

In contemporary American literature, Saul Bellow is notable for creating protean men. In *The Adventures of Augie March,* one of his earlier novels, we meet a picaresque hero with an exceptional talent for adapting himself to divergent social worlds. Augie himself says: "I touched all sides, and nobody knew where I belonged. I had no good idea of that myself." A perceptive young English critic, Tony Tanner, describes Bellow's more recent protean hero, Herzog, as "a representative of modern intelligence, swamped with ideas, metaphysics, and values, and surrounded by messy facts. He labors to cope with them all."

A distinguished French literary spokesman for the protean style—in his life and in his work—is of course Jean-Paul Sartre. I believe it is precisely because of these protean traits that Sartre strikes us as such an embodiment of twentieth-century man. An American critic, Theodore Solotaroff, characterizes Sartre as "constantly on the go, hurrying from point to point, subject to subject; fiercely intentional, his thought occupies, fills, and distends its material as he endeavors to lose and find himself in his encounters with other lives, disciplines, books, and situations."

This image of repeated, autonomously willed death and rebirth of the self, so central to the protean style, is associated psychoanalytically with the theme of fatherlessness. Sartre writes:

> "There is no good father, that's the rule. Don't lay the blame on men but on the bond of paternity, which is rotten. To beget children, nothing better; *to have them,* what iniquity! Had my father lived, he would have lain on me at full length

and would have crushed me. . . . I move from shore to shore, alone and hating those invisible begetters who bestraddle their sons all their life long. I left behind me a young man who did not have time to be my father and who could now be my son. Was it a good thing or bad? I don't know. But I readily subscribed to the verdict of an eminent psychoanalyst: I have no Superego.

We note Sartre's image of interchangeability of father and son, of "a young man who did not have time to be my father and who could now be my son" —which in a literal sense refers to the age at which his father died, but symbolically suggests an extension of the protean style to intimate family relationships.

What has actually disappeared—in Sartre and in protean man generally— is not susceptibility to guilt, but rather the classic superego, the internalization of clearly defined criteria of right and wrong transmitted within a particular culture by parents to their children. Protean man requires freedom from that kind of superego—he requires a symbolic fatherlessness—in order to carry out his explorations. But rather than being free of guilt, his guilt merely takes on a different form.

In the visual arts, one of the most important postwar movements has been aptly named "action painting" to convey its stress upon process rather than fixed completion. And kinetic art, a more recent and related movement in sculpture, goes further. According to Jean Tinguely, one of its leading practitioners, "artists are putting themselves in rhythm with their time, especially with permanent and perpetual movement." I have frequently heard artists, themselves considered radical innovators, complain bitterly of a turnover in art movements so rapid as to discourage holding still long enough to develop a particular style.

John Cage, the composer, is an extreme exponent of the protean style, both in his music and in his sense of all of us as listeners. He concluded a recent letter to the *Village Voice* with the sentence: "Nowadays, everything happens at once and our souls are conveniently electronic, omniattentive." The comment is McLuhan-like, but I wish to stress particularly the idea of omniattention—the sense of contemporary man as having the capacity to receive and take in everything. In attending, as in being, nothing is off limits.

To be sure, one also observes a tendency which seems to be precisely the opposite of the protean style. I refer to the straight-and-narrow specialization in psychological as well as in intellectual life, a closing off and reluctance to let in any "extraneous" influences. But I would emphasize that where this kind of constricted or "one-dimensional" self-process exists, it is essentially reactive and compensatory. Continuous psychological work is required to fend off protean influences which are always abroad.

Just as protean man can readily experiment with and alter elements of his self, he can also embrace, modify, let go of, and reembrace idea systems and ideologies, all with an ease that stands in sharp contrast to the inner struggle we have in the past associated with such shifts. Until relatively recently, no more than one major ideological switch was likely to occur in a lifetime, and that one would be long remembered as a significant individual turning point, accompanied by profound soul-searching and conflict. But today it is not unusual to encounter several such shifts, accomplished relatively painlessly, within a year or even a month; and among many groups, the rarity is a man who has gone through life holding firmly to a single ideological vision.

While protean man is incapable of an unquestioning allegiance to the large ideologies and utopian thought of the nineteenth and early twentieth centuries, one does encounter in him a strong ideological hunger. He is starved for ideas and feelings that give coherence to his world. But here too his leaning is toward new combinations. While he is by no means without yearning for the absolute, he finds fragmentary images more acceptable than the complete ideologies of the past. And these images, although limited and often fleeting, can have great influence upon his psychological life. Thus political and religious movements, as they confront protean man, are likely to experience less difficulty convincing him to alter previous convictions than they do providing him with a set of beliefs which can command his allegiance for more than a brief experimental interlude.

Underlying his flux in emotions and beliefs is a profound inner sense of absurdity which most often finds expression in a tone of mockery. The feeling of absurdity, of course, has a considerable modern tradition, and has been discussed by writers like Camus as a function of man's spiritual homelessness and inability to find meaning in traditional belief systems. But absurdity and mockery have taken much more extreme form in the post-World War II world, and have in fact become a prominent part of a universal life style.

In American life, absurdity and mockery are everywhere. Perhaps their most vivid expression can be found in such areas as pop art and the more general burgeoning of "pop culture." Important here is the complex stance of the pop artist toward the objects he depicts. On the one hand he embraces the materials of the everyday world, celebrates and even exalts them—boldly asserting his creative return to representational art (in active rebellion against the previously reigning nonobjective school), and his psychological return to the "real world" of *things.* On the other hand, everything he touches he mocks. "Thingness" is pressed to the point of caricature. He is indeed artistically reborn as he moves freely among the physical and symbolic materials of his environment, but mockery is his birth certificate and his passport.

A similar spirit seems to pervade literature and social action alike. What is best termed a "literature of mockery" has come to dominate fiction and other forms of writing on an international scale. Günter Grass's *The Tin Drum* comes to mind as probably the greatest single example of this literature—a work, I believe, which will eventually be appreciated as much as a general evocation of contemporary man as of the particular German experience with Nazism. In this country the divergent group of novelists known as "black humorists" also fit into the general category—related as they are to a trend in the American literary consciousness which R. W. B. Lewis has called a "new kind of ironic literary form and disturbing vision, the joining of the dark thread of apocalypse with the nervous detonations of satiric laughter." For it is precisely death itself, and particularly threats of the contemporary apocalypse, that protean man ultimately mocks.

The relationship of mockery to political action has been less apparent but is, I would claim, equally significant. There have been signs of craving for mockery in major American expressions of protest such as the Negro movement and the opposition to the war in Vietnam. In the former a certain chord can be struck by the comedian Dick Gregory, and in the latter by the use of satirical skits and parodies, which revives the flagging attentions of protestors becoming gradually bored with the repetition of their "straight" slogans and goals. And on an international scale, I would say that during the past decade, Russian intellectual life has been enriched by a leavening spirit of mockery— against which the Chinese leaders are now, in the extremes of their Cultural Revolution, fighting a vigorous but ultimately losing battle.

Closely related to the sense of absurdity and the spirit of mockery is another characteristic of protean man which I will call "suspicion of counterfeit nurturance." I first began to think of the concept several years ago while working with survivors of the atomic bomb in Hiroshima. In psychological terms, the core problem here is severe conflict over dependency. I found that these survivors both felt themselves in need of special help, and resented whatever help was offered them because they equated it with weakness and inferiority.

Considering the matter more generally, I find this equating of aid or nurturance with a threat to autonomy a major theme of contemporary life. The breakdown of traditional institutions leads to increased dependency needs, and protean man seeks out replacements wherever he can find them. The large organizations to which he turns (government, business, academies, etc.), and which contemporary society more and more holds out as substitutes for traditional institutions, present a threat to his autonomy in one way; and the intense individual relationships in which he seeks to anchor himself threaten him in another. Both are likely, therefore, to be perceived as counterfeit. The obverse of this tendency, however, is an extending sensitivity to the unauthentic, which may be just beginning to exert its general creative force on man's behalf.

Technology (and technique in general), together with science, have special significance for protean man. Technical achievement of any kind can be strongly embraced to combat inner tendencies toward diffusion, and transcend feelings of absurdity and conflicts over counterfeit nurturance. The image of science itself, however, as the ultimate power behind technology and, to a considerable extent, behind contemporary thought in general, becomes much more difficult to cope with. Only in certain underdeveloped countries can one find, in relatively pure form, those expectations of scientific-utopian deliverance from all human want and conflict which are characteristic of eighteenth- and nineteenth-century Western thought. Protean man retains much of this utopian imagery, but he finds it increasingly undermined by massive disillusionment. More and more he calls forth the other side of the God-devil polarity generally applied to science and sees it as a purveyor of total destructiveness. This kind of profound ambivalence creates for him the most extreme psychic paradox: the very force he still feels to be his liberator from the heavy burdens of past irrationality also threatens him with absolute annihilation, even extinction. But this paradox may well be—in fact, I believe, already has been—the source of imaginative efforts to achieve new relationships between science and man, and indeed, new visions of science itself.

I suggested before that protean man was not free of guilt. Indeed he suffers considerably from it, but often without awareness of what is causing his suffering. For his is a form of hidden guilt: a vague but persistent kind of self-condemnation related to an awareness that he has no outlet for his loyalties and no symbolic structure for his achievements. This is the guilt of social breakdown, and it includes various forms of historical and racial guilt experienced by whole nations and peoples, both the privileged and the abused. Rather than a clear feeling of evil or sinfulness, it takes the form of a nagging sense of unworthiness, all the more troublesome for a lack of clear origin.

Vague constellations of anxiety and resentment are particularly tied in with the suspicion of counterfeit nurturance. Often feeling himself uncared for, even abandoned, protean man responds with diffuse fear and anger. But he can neither find a good cause for the former, nor a consistent target for the latter. He nevertheless cultivates his anger because he finds it more serviceable than anxiety—and because there are plenty of targets of one kind or another beckoning. His difficulty is that focused indignation is as hard for him to sustain as any single identification or conviction.

Involved in all of these patterns is a profound internal struggle with the idea of change itself. For here too protean man finds himself ambivalent in the extreme. He is intensely attracted to the idea of making all things, including himself, totally new. But he is equally drawn to the image of a mythical past of perfect harmony and prescientific wholeness. Amidst the extraordinarily rapid change surrounding his own life, nostalgia is pervasive, and can be one of his most explosive and dangerous emotions. This longing for a "Golden Age" not only sets the tone for the restorationism of the politically Rightist antagonists of history: the still-extant emperor-worshipping assassins in Japan, the Colons in France, and the John Birchites and Ku Klux Klanners in this country. It also, in more disguised form, energizes that totalistic transformationism of the Left which courts violence, and is even willing to risk nuclear violence, in a similarly elusive quest.

Central to all that I have been discussing are radical impairments to the symbolism of transition within the life cycle—the *rites de passages* surrounding birth, entry into adulthood, marriage, and death. Whatever rites remain seem shallow, inappropriate, fragmentary. Protean man cannot take them seriously, and he often seeks to improvise new ones with whatever contemporary materials he has available, including cars and drugs.

Perhaps the most crucial impairment here is that of symbolic immortality —of the universal need for imagery of connection predating and extending beyond the individual life span, whether the idiom of this symbolism is biological (living through children and grandchildren), theological (through a life after death), natural (*in* nature itself which outlasts all), or creative (through what man makes and does). This sense of immortality is a fundamental component of ordinary psychic life, and it is now being profoundly threatened; by simple historical velocity and, of particular importance to protean man, by the existence of nuclear weapons which, even without being used, call into question all modes of immortality. (Who can be certain of living on through children or grandchildren, through teachings or kindnesses?)

Protean man is left with two paths to symbolic immortality which he tries to cultivate, sometimes pleasurably and sometimes desperately. One is the natural mode we have mentioned. His attraction to nature and concern at its desecration has to do with an unarticulated sense that, in whatever holocaust, at least nature will endure—though such are the dimensions of our present weapons that he cannot be absolutely certain even of this.

His second path is that of "experiential transcendance"—of seeking a sense of immortality as mystics always have, through psychic experience of such intensity that time and death are, in effect, eliminated. This, I believe, is the larger meaning of the "drug revolution," of protean man's hunger for chemical aids to expanded consciousness. Indeed, all revolutions may be thought of, at bottom, as innovations in the struggle for immortality.

It is evident that young adults individually, and youth movements collectively, express most vividly the psychological themes of protean man. However, although it is true that these themes make contact with what we sometimes call the psychology of adolescence, we err badly if we overlook their expression in all age groups and dismiss them as mere adolescent phenomena. On the contrary, protean man's affinity for the young—his being metaphorically and psychologically so young in spirit—has to do with this never-ceasing quest for imagery of rebirth. He seeks such imagery from all sources: from ideas, techniques, religious and political systems, mass movements, and drugs; or from special individuals whom he sees as possessing that problematic gift of his namesake, the gift of prophecy.

The dangers inherent in this quest seem hardly to require emphasis. What perhaps needs most to be kept in mind is the general principle that renewal on a large scale is impossible to achieve without forays into danger, destruction, and negativity. The principle of "death and rebirth" is as valid historically as it is mythologically. However misguided many of his forays may be, protean man also carries with him an extraordinary range of possibility for man's betterment, or more important, for his survival.

From *The Futurist,* April 1972; reprinted by permission of The World Future Society, P.O. Box 30369, Bethesda Branch, Washington, D.C. 20014.

37. The Future of Man: Optimism vs. Pessimism

BURNHAM P. BECKWITH AND DENNIS L. MEADOWS

Computer simulations of world trends suggest that mankind is moving into a mounting crisis as the world's rapidly growing population and industrialization exhaust natural resources and pollute the environment.

These pessimistic conclusions concerning man's future, reported in the August 1971 issue of *THE FUTURIST,* represented a challenge to futurists with a more optimistic view of man's future.

In the following article, Burnham P. Beckwith, author of *The Next 500 Years,* picks up the challenge. Beckwith himself has forecasted continued gradual economic and social progress in the world, and feels that the MIT group's work has given him no reason to change his hopeful predictions. Beckwith believes that the results of the MIT group's study are "entirely the result of their false or dubious assumptions."

Professor Dennis L. Meadows, director of the computer simulation project, reviewed Beckwith's criticisms and prepared a response.

Beckwith: The Predicament of Man? A Reply

The August 1971 issue of *THE FUTURIST* contained three articles on the application of the computerized systems-dynamics method developed by MIT Professor Jay Forrester to the prediction of major long-run social trends. The first article, by a Forrester associate, Professor Dennis L. Meadows, was entitled "The Predicament of Mankind," and the second, "The Disturbing Implications of *World Dynamics,*" a summary by Jon D. Roland of Forrester's new book, also dealt with this predicament. Their new use of computers was discussed by Hazel Henderson in "Computers at the Crossroad."

The first two articles stated some alarming implications derived from analysis of their computer models, *World 2* and *World 3.* These include Meadows' novel and surprising claim that, "There is a strong probability that the western nations will witness a marked decline in their own national standard of living

Beginnings: Global Consciousness 397

within the next three or four decades" and Forrester's conclusion that there may be "a population dieback within 50 years" in which "the developed countries may suffer more than the underdeveloped countries." (I have read Forrester's book and I believe that Roland's summary of it is comprehensive and reliable.)

The extremist implications of the Forrester-Meadows study are in striking contrast to the often stated extremist prediction that automation will soon throw millions of men out of work and/or require a radical and continuing reduction in the hours of labor. The MIT professors imply that even with automation, full employment, and a 60-hour week men would soon be unable to produce enough to prevent mass starvation in the most automated economies. One group of prophets predicts a coming age of plenty and ridicules "the economics of scarcity" as hopelessly conservative. The other suggests that the traditional economics of scarcity is too improvident and wasteful to prevent universal famine and want. *THE FUTURIST* has presented both points of view. The truth probably lies about half way between these extremist positions, but nearer the prediction of abundance than that of world famine.

In my own book, *The Next 500 Years,* I predicted continued gradual economic and social progress in all advanced countries and in the world as a whole. Nothing in these articles has made me want to change my predictions.

Computers can produce any desired result

The use of computer models to predict the future has one basic fault that was ignored or grossly minimized in the August issue of *THE FUTURIST*. Such a method of analysis begs all the vital issues. It resembles the use of a deductive syllogism. I quote one of the best known:

All men are mortal.
Plato is a man.
Plato is mortal.

The conclusion, "Plato is mortal," is clearly implicit in the major premise, "All men are mortal." Now computers use a form of deductive logic. The data fed into them perform the same function as the premises of a deductive syllogism, and they imply the computer results. Thus one can obtain any results one desires by varying the data input. Forrester and Meadows illustrated this principle repeatedly by varying their computer inputs and securing widely differing results.

Since the conclusions derived from computer analysis of world models depend entirely upon the data input, Forrester and Meadows should have devoted most of their effort to justifying their choice of data, and Roland should have stressed the vital importance of such justification, but none of them did so. Meadows referred vaguely to "cooperation with professionals outside our university, in economics, demography . . . and so forth," but this is a very weak justification for dubious assumptions which imply that mankind faces a global catastrophe. He offered no other justification.

I have no quarrel with the use of computers or computer models to analyze social problems or social trends. But I wish to emphasize the fact that the results of such analysis depend entirely upon the data and instructions given to the computer. In her article, "Computers at the Crossroads," Hazel Henderson discussed the Forrester-Meadows use of computers without calling attention to this vital fact.

She also asserted that, "One of the greatest contributions of Meadows' project . . . is that it may dispel some of the dangerous myths and expectations of 'abundance' and 'progress.' As Meadows reported to me, 'There is no utopia; we may have to content ourselves with the proposition that this period . . . may be in fact the golden age.' " Unfortunately, she failed to add that this "greatest contribution" is merely the result of arbitrary premises put into a computer as data and instructions.

Assumptions in world model are mostly false or dubious

In his summary of Forrester's *World Dynamics,* Roland stated seven assumptions of Forrester's computer model, *World 2,* but noted no effort to justify them. Perhaps they are supposed to be obviously true, but to me most of them seem to be false or dubious.

The first assumption is that, "Crowding, pollution, and a high standard of living decrease the birth rate, and food increases it." But additional food has not increased the birth rate in western countries during the past 150 years, and it is very unlikely to do so in most countries in the future. Furthermore, I doubt that increased crowding and pollution have yet decreased birth rates in any country.

The fourth assumption is that, "The rate of capital investment increases with increased material standard of living." But in the United States the rate of investment to GNP has fallen rather than risen during the past 100 years, a period of great economic progress. And this rate is now much higher in relatively poor Japan and Russia than in the United States.

The fifth assumption is that, "Capital investment increases pollution, which in turn reduces food production." I do not believe that any such effect on world food output has ever been reported. And further heavy capital investment is badly needed to reduce pollution and increase food output.

The chief defect in this list of assumptions is that it fails to mention the most important ones, those chiefly responsible for the frightening conclusions of Forrester's study. For instance, he assumed that (1) future technological progress will not prevent a sharp rise in raw material costs, and/or (2) such progress will not provide ample supplies of cheap food, and/or (3) mankind will not sufficiently limit pollution, and/or (4) they will not limit population growth enough to permit a continued rise in real incomes per capita. I believe that all four of these crucial unstated assumptions are mistaken. Let us consider them individually.

Substitutes can be used
for scarce materials

Although the richest mineral deposits have been steadily used up during the past 200 years, the growing scarcity of irreplaceable raw materials has not increased material costs. The steady advance of technology has enabled men to discover many rich new deposits and to use ever poorer ores. Furthermore, men have learned how to substitute new or cheaper materials for scarce older materials—aluminum for copper, oil for coal, nickel for silver, etc. There is no good reason to assume that technological progress will fail to develop adequate new and cheaper substitutes for nearly all scarce natural materials.

Moreover, we can radically reduce the demand for most scarce irreplaceable minerals by redesigning consumers' goods and changing some social habits. For instance, the substitution of mass urban passenger transport for private car use in Europe and America would sharply reduce per capita consumption of steel, lead, chrome, and other metals. Redesigning private cars so that they would last twice as long, and standardizing them for decades so that all good parts in junked cars could be used to repair new cars would also sharply reduce metal consumption. Inducing or requiring most urban workers to walk or ride bicycles to work would not only conserve scarce raw materials but would improve their health. Many such conservation measures are available and will be adopted whenever raw material shortages threaten to slow down or stop economic progress in advanced countries.

Food production will
continue to grow

The assumption that technological progress will not assure ample supplies of cheap food in advanced countries is equally unjustified. The revolution in farm methods which began over 300 years ago and accelerated during the last 50 is almost certain to continue far into the future. Scientific research in food production is not going to stop tomorrow. Rather it will continue to grow. Within a generation or two it may yield methods of producing cheap synthetic foods which solve man's basic food problem for all time.

The assumption that men will allow pollution to grow enough to stop economic progress is also unjustified. During the last 50 years nearly all advanced countries have taken increasingly effective steps to check pollution. Air pollution in most old cities in advanced states is less serious today than it was a century ago, when coal soot, smoke, dust, and animal odors were much more apparent than they are today. And water supplies are much less polluted by disease germs than they once were. If pollution does become a serious threat to health and economic progress, as Forrester and Meadows predict, scientists and engineers will devote far more attention to pollution control. The long record of their past successes warrants the prediction that they will be able to keep pollution under control.

The assumption that men will not limit population growth enough to assure continuous social progress is perhaps the most plausible of the crucial unstated assumptions noted above. Some backward countries may indeed fail to restrict their population growth soon enough to prevent recurrent famine. But advanced countries have already reduced their population growth enough to permit continuous economic progress. And famines in Asia will have no significant effect on such progress in advanced countries. Furthermore, nearly all undeveloped nations will learn to practice adequate birth control during the next century.

Imminent decline of West
is questioned

I have been arguing that the results of the Forrester-Meadows study are entirely the result of their false or dubious assumptions. In his summary of *World Dynamics* Roland noted that the *World 2* model used by Forrester could be improved by changing some of its assumptions concerning substitution of materials, the growth of pollution, the nature of capital investment, and the advance of technology. But this concession comes after a statement of the major conclusions of the study, and there is no discussion of how such new assumptions would affect the conclusions. My contention is that desirable changes in these assumptions would reverse the conclusions on all new and controversial points, most notably on the imminent decline of the West. Moreover, I do not think that the statement of unsound and alarming conclusions can be justified by explaining afterwards that the method by which they were reached could be improved.

Did quality of life
rise during Depression?

One of the most curious features of the Forrester-Meadows study is that all their charts show that the "quality of life" rose steadily throughout the Great Depression and World War II but fell throughout the very prosperous period from 1950 to 1970 when real wages rose over 50% in advanced countries and most other factors affecting the quality of life also improved. For instance, health indices improved throughout the world during these two decades.

Another questionable point is the treatment of capital accumulation. Meadows claims that population growth rates will soon decline and that this will result in "a much slower rate of capital accumulation." But later he notes that, "The primary determinant of the fraction of output reinvested is the output per capita. Now any reduction in the birth rate tends to raise output per capita and increase saving. Other factors remaining the same, parents with two children can save more than parents with three or more children. Thus every decline in the rate of population growth should increase the rate of capital accumulation, and all additional capital can be used to reduce pollution and conserve scarce resources.

Roland stated eight major "implications for policy" which Forrester derived from his computer analysis of *World 2.* The first begins as follows: "Industrialization *may* be a more fundamental disturbing force in world ecology than is population." The term *may* is very vague. Does Forrester mean that there is one chance in a hundred that his claim is true, or only such a chance that it is not true? And is such a vague conclusion the result of computer analysis or of intuition?

Six of the other seven major conclusions of his study include the term *may,* and are therefore subject to the same criticism.

If we substitute *is* or *will* for *may* in these conclusions, they become much clearer, but they are still subject to criticism. The more plausible merely repeat theories which have long been accepted by most social scientists. Recognition of the dangers of rapid population growth goes back to Malthus, and these dangers have received wide recognition in recent years. The possible results of the growing scarcity of natural resources have also been discussed by many writers. Forrester's only novel or unorthodox conclusions are that men "may" not be able to solve the problems created by population growth, resource depletion, and pollution, and that rich nations "may" suffer more than poor nations as a result of this failure. I have explained above why both of these conclusions are unsound if they are meant to be predictions. Of course, almost anything "may" happen!

Was pessimistic conclusion sought?

One of Forrester's eight "implications for policy" deserves further comment:

4. *Exhortations and programs directed at population control may be inherently self-defeating. If population control begins to result . . . in higher per capita food supply and material standards of living, these very improvements may relax the pressures and generate forces to trigger a resurgence of population growth.*

This reasoning reveals a strong desire to arrive at a pessimistic conclusion. It can be used against almost any desirable social reform. For instance, more effective crime prevention would reduce crime, and therefore the demand for crime prevention, which would reduce funds available for crime prevention and permit a resurgence of crime. Can such a conclusion be based on computer analysis?

Dennis Meadows did not use the vague term *may* in stating his six "preliminary conclusions from the world simulation," but his conclusions are subject to most of my other comments on Forrester's "implications." The valid conclusions are old stuff, and the novel or unorthodox ones (numbers 3 and 6)— which predict the "marked decline" of the western nations and a "traumatic decline in population"—are probably invalid. Yet immediately after stating these dubious conclusions he asserted that, "No one we have talked with has offered any scientifically based disagreement with the above conclusions."

Apparently 10,000 years of social progress is not scientific evidence that such progress is likely to continue. And the unsupported claim that men will not be able to solve their social problems is more scientific than the claim, based on long experience, that they probably will solve these problems!

Advanced nations will
suffer less during "dieback"

The Forrester-Meadows thesis that advanced countries will suffer more than backward countries in the coming world "population dieback" is based in part upon the fact that undeveloped countries use much less scarce natural resources per capita, and in part upon the claim that advanced countries have more highly organized, integrated, and specialized economies. But it is precisely their greater organization, integration, and specialization which have in the past and will in the future enable advanced countries to solve their economic and social problems. And the fact that per capita resource use is relatively high in advanced states permits them to reduce such use sharply without any famine or serious hardship.

Population growth may well cause temporary economic stagnation and recurrent famine in some backward countries, but these misfortunes will have very little effect on advanced nations. Famine in Asia has occurred repeatedly without slowing economic progress in Europe or America. The West is not dependent upon Middle or East Asia for any essential raw materials or fuels. Petroleum comes from North Africa and the Near East, not from those countries most likely to suffer famine. And any shortage of mineral resources will injure backward countries much more than advanced countries because the latter can afford to pay much higher prices for scarce raw materials.

American imports total less than 5% of our GNP, and most of them are goods which could easily be produced in North America. Substitutes are available for the others. And in some good years our real GNP rises by 5%. A steady rise in the cost of imports would lead to ever-increasing substitution of domestic products for imported raw materials. The result would be only a slight decrease in our GNP growth rate.

The Forrester-Meadows study deals with a global model and predicts overall global conditions. But conditions vary so greatly from country to country that conclusions based on global analysis do not apply to any of them. The authors implicitly concede this when they explain that the coming population dieback will be much worse in advanced than in backward countries. Unfortunately, they err in making this prediction. The opposite prediction is far more likely. But both predictions imply that global analysis is of little value in analyzing social trends in advanced countries.

In conclusion, I would concede that all efforts to convince people of the great benefits of birth control, pollution limitation, and resource conservation deserve praise. Forrester and Meadows may have made these benefits more apparent to some readers. But they have begged the most controversial questions they discussed, and have arrived at unduly pessimistic conclusions based entirely on arbitrary and pessimistic assumptions. The use of a computer cannot validate conclusions based upon false or dubious assumptions.

Meadows: Response

Beckwith raises several important issues which can best be addressed in the context of historical perspective on the project which Professor Jay Forrester and I have conducted for the Club of Rome.

In preparation for a Club of Rome Executive Committee meeting at M.I.T. in July, 1970, Forrester constructed a preliminary theory of long-term interaction among five important processes: economic development; population growth; pollution generation; resource depletion; and food production. The study was not intended to be based on exhaustive, empirical research, but rather to serve as a summary of what Forrester had learned about that particular global system in the course of 12 years' research into the behavior of social systems. His model was extensively analyzed through computer simulation and was reported in a book entitled *World Dynamics.*

On the basis of that report, the Club of Rome decided to support at M.I.T. a research effort designed to test, revise, extend, and validate a model related to Forrester's. I took responsibility for that effort and assembled a research team of ten scientists and students from five countries. The lead article in the August 1971 issue of *THE FUTURIST* was based on my team's work with the second model. While the two models differ in many respects, the five basic conclusions they suggest are the same:

1. There are many factors which will prevent our global society from sustaining its current rates of population and economic growth for many more decades.

2. Our society's most probable mode of accommodation to finite limits is through overshoot and collapse.

3. The delays inherent in our social and ecological systems virtually ensure collapse if we continue to seek change only in response to crises which have already been realized.

4. Policies enacted now are already determining the timing and mode of the shift from exponential growth to global equilibrium.

5. A new and desirable phase of social development is possible, which would leave man in a viable and sustainable balance with his finite environment.

Computer offers advantages

With that brief background let me discuss several specific points raised by Beckwith. What Beckwith takes as a shortcoming of the computer—namely that it can only trace the implications of the assumptions it is fed in explicit terms—is an extreme advantage. In using computer models we are forced to make very precise the assumptions upon which our statements are based. Only that precision makes it possible for different individuals with expertise in relevant disciplines to evaluate the model assumptions. This testing of assumptions can be done in a way which is impossible with the verbal statements presented in most books of futurology.

It is true that if the initial assumptions are in error the conclusions will also be in error. Of course, this is also true for the verbal assumptions in books such as Beckwith's *The Next 500 Years.* An important advantage of mathematical models is that the process of computer simulation analysis is error-free. Thus, we are free to focus on the assumptions in a way which is never possible when a model is being intuitively analyzed. How often have we seen a discussion in which two people agree on their underlying assumptions, but disagree on the implications of those assumptions as they are traced intuitively? Verbal analyses are highly prone to error whenever more than a few relationships are involved. Mathematical models in no way limit the number or complexity of assumptions which may be studied. Any relationship which may be stated verbally can also be expressed mathematically. It gains no accuracy in the process, but does at least become unambiguous and thus much easier to test.

Neither Forrester in his study, nor my group in ours, has been seeking to predict the future. Our goal, rather, is to understand the basic behavior modes in the global system, to examine the basic determinants of growth, equilibrium, and decay, and to understand which policies shift the tendency of the system towards those modes of behavior most in consonance with society's long-term objectives. To perceive that a system tends to accommodate itself to a fixed limit by over-shooting and collapsing rather than by moving smoothly into equilibrium, is a far cry from making a precise prediction. We assign very little value to the precise values and the timing of turning points that are generated in alternative simulation runs. It is only the basic behavior of the parameters as they interact which can have any significance at this point.

"Quality of Life" Index is dropped

World 3, the model produced by my group over this past year, has no Quality of Life Index. The cover page and several photographs in the journal were taken from Forrester's book. Suffice it here to say that no study of the sort we have undertaken can determine the relative desirability of alternative futures. It can merely attempt to understand the future implications of alternative policies. Forrester's Quality of Life Index is a non-linear function of several variables important to most people's quality of life: food; crowding; pollution; and material standard of living. The index does serve as a gross measure of the desirability of the system represented by any particular configuration of parameter values. However, Forrester has never suggested that it defines a function which would be accepted by all people as a statement of their individual preferences. For those reasons, it has been dropped from my own study.

I think Beckwith would recognize that the globe is essentially a closed system and that material growth must eventually stop. His predilection for examining history should also have revealed that in the past, when growth in some region exceeded a particular limit, the typical response was to overshoot the limit and collapse. Famine, plague, and resource depletion have been evident in the fall of many empires. We should not automatically assume some as-yet-undiscovered factor will release our society from the life cycle which has characterized all societies in the past.

"Technological optimists" overlook certain facts

The data and a precise statement of the assumptions underlying our computer model will be available this spring in a technical report entitled, *The Dynamics of Global Equilibrium*. It is important to note that the five basic conclusions listed above are relatively insensitive to the individual assumptions in the model. Beckwith's criticisms of what he understands to be model assumptions can only be evaluated in the context of the full model description. However, several comments may be usefully made here. Beckwith is a technological optimist, one who believes that our considerable ability to design new devices can solve any problem. Technological optimists overlook two facts—

1. Most of the great social problems are not subject to technical solution.
2. The long delays inherent in our socio-economic system may mean that it is too late to solve a problem after it is perceived.

Let me illustrate each point very simply. The general quality of nutrition in the U.S. now is lower than it was in 1940. Several million people are physically starving today in the United States even though Beckwith says, "The assumption that technological process will not assume ample supplies of cheap food in advanced countries is equally unjustified."

Even if we were to curtail DDT production immediately, the level of DDT in marine animals would continue to rise for about 11 years. It would remain above its current level for 25 years. There is no practical technical means for avoiding that delay. If we wait until marine life is seriously affected by pollutants before finding technical solutions, it may be too late. The inevitable 25 years of DDT levels above those which prompted action could eliminate much marine life.

This second point also addresses Beckwith's reservations about the pollution relationships of the model. His counter example, air pollution, belongs to a special class of pollutants—those with high decay rates.

Many additional examples could be given to illustrate each of the two statements above. Together they suggest Beckwith's faith in technological progress is unfounded.

Rich countries cannot escape problems of poor countries

Beckwith also assumes that the industrialized nations can isolate themselves from the difficulties of the poor countries. He mentions that "famine in Asia has occurred repeatedly without slowing economic progress in Europe or America." In fact the last major famine was probably in 1934 when we were substantially less reliant on those poorer countries for our natural resources. The U.S. must import today at least a portion of 27 of the 36 raw materials on which our economy is dependent. Our dependence on overseas supplies is supposed to increase markedly over the next thirty years. How independent is our "economic progress" from the oil-rich countries in the Middle East?

We have always viewed the analysis of global trends as merely a prelude to simulation studies of long-term national perspectives. The world is not homogeneous. While no nation or region can experience population and economic growth indefinitely, the mode of accommodation to the limits on growth will certainly vary from one region to another. To understand the options realistically open to national governments we have begun a series of cooperative efforts with scientific personnel in several countries. That phase of our work will engage my team for at least the next several years.

Our models are very imperfect—though I believe them to be better bases for evaluating long term global policies than any others currently available. Nevertheless I will close by stressing not the importance of these particular models, but the potential of this approach to social problems. Our work continues. I hope that three or four years from now we may have evolved in our understanding to the point where these initial models seem very naive. I personally doubt, however, that we will uncover anything which leads us to reverse our basic conclusions. At least when the work is pursued in this way, it puts our assumptions and analytical methods on a basis which does subject them to constructive criticism and informed discussion. In contrast, a statement like Beckwith's, "Nearly all underdeveloped nations will learn to practice adequate birth control during the next century," is a matter of faith or unstated assumptions which leads only to confusion, not to understanding.

Contrasting Views of Man's Future

Burnham Beckwith's optimistic opinion of mankind's ability to overcome the problems of the coming decades differs sharply from Dennis Meadows' more gloomy views.

The following summary has been prepared by the editor to suggest the general tenor of dispute. The summary does not do justice to either viewpoint, but hopefully is equally unjust to both.

What will happen in the next few decades?
Meadows: There will likely be a marked decline in standards of living. The world's population may experience a "dieback" to more supportable levels, as a consequence of starvation, pollution, and other factors.

Beckwith: Despite the critical problems posed by population growth and pollution, there will be continued gradual economic progress.

What does history show?
Meadows: Famine, plague, and resource depletion have been evident in the fall of many empires. We should not assume that some as-yet-undiscovered

factor will release our society from the life cycle which has characterized all societies in the past.

Beckwith: History shows us 10,000 years of social progress. This progress may be expected to continue.

Will the developed countries suffer more than the undeveloped, if there is a traumatic population crisis?

Meadows: Yes, partly because the undeveloped countries use much less scarce natural resources per capita, and partly because the developed countries have highly organized, integrated, and specialized economies that are highly vulnerable to disruption.

Beckwith: No, because the organization, integration, and specialization of the advanced countries will enable them in the future—as in the past—to solve their economic and social problems. Furthermore, their relatively high per capita resource use will permit them to reduce such use sharply without any famine or serious hardship.

How useful are computer simulations?

Beckwith: A computer can only trace out the implications of the assumptions that are fed into it. "Garbage in, garbage out."

Meadows: The computer's ability to trace out the implications of the assumptions fed into it is a big advantage, for it forces scientists to be very precise about the assumptions upon which their statements are based. If the computer is given correct assumptions, it can trace out their implications—a feat that may be difficult or impossible for the human mind.

Will we have enough raw materials in the years ahead?

Meadows: No, because more and more of the world's irreplaceable resources are being used up and population is rising steeply.

Beckwith: Yes, because:

1. The steady advance of technology enables man to use ever poorer deposits. (For this reason, material costs have not increased even though the richest material deposits have been used up.)

2. There is no good reason to assume that technological progress will fail to develop new and cheaper substitutes for nearly all scarce natural materials.

3. Where necessary, we can radically reduce demand for most scarce minerals by redesigning consumers' goods and changing social habits.

Will we have enough food?

Meadows: No, because population growth will eventually outstrip man's ability to grow sufficient food.

Beckwith: Yes, because scientific research in food production will continue. Within a generation or two, it may yield methods of producing cheap synthetic foods which will solve man's basic food problem for all time.